Housing the Workers, 1850—1914

HOUSING THE WORKERS, 1850—1914

A Comparative Perspective

Edited by
M.J. Daunton

Leicester University Press
a division of Pinter Publishers
London and New York

363,5
H8421

First published in Great Britain in 1990 by Leicester University Press
(a division of Pinter Publishers Ltd)

Editorial offices
Fielding Johnson Building, University of Leicester, University Road,
Leicester LE1 7RH, England

Trade and other enquiries
25 Floral Street, London, WC2E 9DS, England

British Library Cataloguing in Publication Data

A CIP catalogue record for this book
is available from the British Library.
ISBN 0-7185-1315-0

Library of Congress Cataloging-in-Publication Data

Housing the workers, 1850–1914 : a comparative perspective /
  edited by M.J. Daunton.
      p.   cm.
   Includes bibliographical references (p.   ).
   ISBN 0–7185–1315–0
   1. Poor – Housing – History. 2. Working class – Housing – History.
I. Daunton, M.J. (Martin J.)
HD7287.95.H68   1990
363.5'9623 – dc20   90 – 5737
                                                           CIP

MB

Typeset by Mayhew Typesetting, Bristol, England
Printed and bound in Great Britain by Biddles Ltd.

Contents

List of contributors

M.J. Daunton is currently professor of modern history at University College London, and has written extensively on British housing. He is now engaged on a general economic and social history of Britain, 1700–1914 and a history of the City of London.

Ann-Louise Shapiro ia associate professor of history at Wesleyan University where she teaches Modern European Social History and in the Women Studies program. She is the author of *Housing the Poor of Paris, 1850–1902* (1985) and is currently at work on a book on the meanings of female criminality in *fin de siècle* Paris.

Patricia Van den Eeckhout obtained a doctorate from the Free University of Brussels for a study of the social and economic conditions of the city in the nineteenth century, and has published sources on wages and rents in Brussels. She is currently researching at the Free University on social history and leisure.

Renate Banik-Schweitzer was trained as an architect before obtaining her doctorate from the University of Technology in Vienna for a study of social housing in Austria up to the Second World War. She is currently working at the City Archives of Vienna, and has research interests in comparative urban history, planning history and housing.

Gábor Gyáni was an archivist with the Budapest Capital Archives before moving to the Institute of History of the Hungarian Academy of Sciences in Budapest, where he is a research fellow. He has published a study of family and household in Budapest, and has books forthcoming on workers' housing in Budapest and public space in the metropolis.

Nicholas Bullock read architecture at Cambridge, where he is now a Fellow of King's College. He lectures on architectural history at Cambridge and the Architectural Association in London. He has previously published a study of housing reform in Germany, and is now engaged on a book on housing and reconstruction in London, 1940–51.

1 Introduction

M.J. Daunton

The initial inspiration of this collection of essays on the comparative history of housing came from the massive survey of wages, the cost of living, and rents in the major cities of Britain which was undertaken by the Board of Trade in 1905 and published in 1908; in the next few years it went on to repeat the same approach in the major industrial cities of France, Germany, the United States and Belgium.[1] The motivation for this pioneering exercise in comparative, statistical analysis of the standard of living was clear: there was increased concern about Britain's competitiveness with the rise of German and American industry, and a debate about the calibre of the 'imperial race' in the aftermath of the Boer War and in the face of a falling birth rate. Social reform was on the political agenda, and the government had also, in 1905, appointed a Royal Commission to consider the future of the Poor Law which had provided the basis of social policy in England since 1834. The forbiddingly large volumes which were published by the Board of Trade between 1908 and 1911 provided a mass of detail on individual towns in five countries. The implications were not immediately obvious to contemporaries, and there is little sign that the statistics which were so painstakingly collected were in fact utilised in the debate over the social reforms which were introduced in Britain between 1906 and the First World War.[2] They do, however, provide the historian with material which poses a number of problems concerning urban society before the First World War.

I

The material on Britain has certainly been a valuable source for historians interested in the housing market before the First World War. The primary focus has been upon the wide discrepancy between housing costs across the country, which was not compensated by a parallel variation in the level of wages. The real cost of housing before the First World War, as the figures in Table 1.1 make clear, differed substantially between cities. The provincial towns with the highest level of rents were the naval town of Plymouth (which formed a somewhat anomalous and unusual case), followed by the cities of Scotland and the North-East of

Table 1.1 Rents, wages and housing standards, Britain, 1905

	Rent	Wage*	Ratio of wage:rent	Percentage of dwellings with 3 rooms or less[†]
England and Wales				
London	100	100	1.0	54.1
Plymouth	81	80	1.0	56.6
Newcastle u Tyne	76	90	1.2	58.3
Bradford	59	83	1.4	43.2
Blackburn	50	87	1.7	5.3
Leicester	48	94	2.0	6.1
Scotland				
Edinburgh	81	88	1.1	62.8
Glasgow	76	91	1.2	85.2

Source: PP 1908 CVII, *Report of an enquiry by the Board of Trade into working-class rents, housing and retail prices*, table E, pp. l–li; *Census of England and Wales, 1911, Vol. VIII, Tenements in Administrative Counties and Urban and Rural Districts*, table 4; *Census of Scotland, 1911, Vol. II*, table xxxix
* The wage is that of a skilled builder
[†] 1911

England such as Edinburgh, Glasgow and Newcastle-upon-Tyne. These northern cities were marked by an unfavourable relationship between rents and wages, and by architectural forms which were unlike the dominant English pattern of self-contained terraced houses. In Edinburgh and Glasgow, dense tenement development dominated (Figures 1.1 and 1.2); in Newcastle, the typical property was the Tyneside flat with separate, self-contained units on the ground and first floors of a terraced cottage, each with its own front and back entry and yard. The Tyneside flats were, unlike tenements, completely self-contained and in this way they had more similarity with the English housing pattern (Figure 1.3). Similarly, the back-to-back house which was the typical architectural style in the West Riding of Yorkshire (for example, Bradford) divided the terraced cottage vertically rather than horizontally so that there were two distinct units (Figure 1.4). Elsewhere in England and Wales, the through terraced house was the overwhelming form of working-class accommodation, varying in size from the simple 'two up, two down' of Lancashire, to the larger properties in the Midlands and the South which had back extensions on one or two floors (Figure 1.5). These variations in house rents, architectural forms, and housing standards have provided British historians with a series of questions which have been refined rather than satisfactorily answered.[3]

The attempt to explain the variation in the real cost of housing, and its style and standard, has concentrated upon the broad distinction between the tenements of Scotland and the terraces of England.[4] The

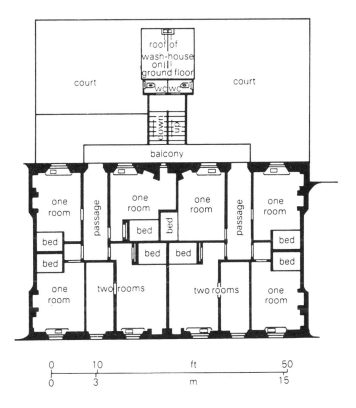

Figure 1.1 Plan of Glasgow tenement, 21 Middleton Place (reproduced with permission from R. Rodger, 'The Victorian building industry and the housing of the Scottish working class', in M. Doughty (ed.), *Building the Industrial City*, Leicester University Press, 1985, p. 159).

figures of the Board of Trade inquiry provide the starting point: the relationship between rents and wages was more unfavourable in Scotland than in England, and had been considerably less favourable in the past, before Scottish wage levels had increased in the second half of the nineteenth century under the impetus of industrialisation. The architectural form had its roots in a relationship between rents and wages more unfavourable than indicated in 1905, but as the relationship became more favourable there were various barriers to change. The building regulations which were imposed by the Dean of Guild Courts tended to be much stricter than in the case of England, which increased costs, and also made a change towards small, self-contained houses difficult. This discrepancy in building costs was intensified by the small scale of firms in the Scottish building industry which tended to drive up costs, and the builders in any case lacked expertise in constructing other architectural

Figure 1.2 Glasgow tenement, Orwell Street, Dalry
(courtesy of Nicholas Morgan).

forms. Most attention has, however, been paid to the land market,
particularly the divergence between Scottish and English land law.

In Scotland, the owner (or 'superior') granted land to a 'vassal' in
return for an annual payment or 'feu duty'; the vassal might in turn
subfeu the site for an increased duty. The feu duty was paid in
perpetuity, and could not be renegotiated at a higher rate, and the
superior had no reversionary right. This, it has been argued, was
fundamentally unlike either freehold or leasehold development in English
cities. Where freehold was the dominant tenure, the original owner
parted with land in return for a capital sum which could be invested;
where the land was leased, the land and the building erected upon it
reverted to the ground owner at the end of the term, and he received
both an annual ground rent and the prospect of capital appreciation. The
Scottish superior was in a different position: there was no capital sum to

(a)

(b)

Figure 1.3 Tyneside flats. The rear of Aline Street in
Benwell, Newcastle upon Tyne, photographed in 1964, shows
the external stairs leading from the upper flat to the separate
back yard (Newcastle City Library). The front view of Tower
Street (Gateshead) shows the two separate front doors leading
to the ground and first floor flats (author's collection).

Figure 1.4 Back-to-back houses. The end of
Mackintosh Street in Halifax shows windows for
two separate houses which were divided vertically
(photographed by Nicholas Morgan, 1980).

invest and no prospect of reversion. The consequence, so it was claimed,
was that 'the superior's natural endeavour is to fix his original conditions
of feuing . . . so as to get as large a return as possible, once and for all',
which meant:

the erection of tenements in order to make it profitable to develop the land
subject to these payments. The high price of land and the erection of tenement
housing react upon one another, that is to say, the high price of land requires
the erection of tenements in order to make the maximum use of it and to spread
the burden of the feu duty over as many payers as possible, and conversely the
power to erect tenements and to impose upon the land a very considerable
property maintains the high value of the land.[5]

The argument was that the feu duty helped to create tenements, and
once tenements existed they made high land prices possible and so

Figure 1.5 Terraced housing, Ethel Street, Cardiff, which indicates the typical layout of bye-law housing in England and Wales from the 1870s to the First World War. The main variation was at the rear of the property, where there might be a one- or two-storey addition (author's collection).

perpetuated their construction rather than low-rise property. It was a vicious circle which was difficult to escape, especially when the building regulations, the expertise of the building industry, and the cultural norms of the residents had all become conditioned by the tenement.[6]

There is, however, a danger that too much weight might be attached to features which are peculiar to Britain in explaining a much wider phenomenon. Tenements were, as the Board of Trade inquiries made clear, not peculiar to Scottish cities; neither were self-contained terraced houses confined to England and Wales.

The 'self-contained cottage is', remarked the Board of Trade, 'the predominant form of working-class housing in Belgium as it is in England and Wales'. There were generally fewer rooms than in England: in Brussels in 1910, 34.2 per cent of households had one room, 22.5 per cent two and 13.0 per cent three, a total of 69.7 per cent. Households were also smaller, so that the Board of Trade felt that there was no great discrepancy in terms of the amount of accommodation. It is, however, important not to confuse the architectural form of a self-contained house with the reality of working-class residence. The degree of 'privatised' space was in fact less than might be assumed, in part because the houses were less likely to have their own water supply and sanitation, and in part because of the high degree of sharing of property. In 1910, in communes with a population in excess of 50,000, 72.8 per cent of households occupied part of a house; in Brussels, the proportion was 85.8 per cent.[7]

'The classes of dwellings in the occupation of the working classes in the United States', commented the Board of Trade, 'are . . . considerably more composite than in England and Wales'.[8] At one end of the spectrum were Baltimore and Philadelphia with self-contained terraced houses with six rooms, and Memphis and Atlanta with detached or semi-detached single storey dwellings. At the other end of the spectrum was New York, which was as much a city of tenements as Berlin or Glasgow. Between the two extremes were cities such as Milwaukee, Boston, St Louis and Chicago where most working-class families lived in two- or three-storey blocks of flats. The percentage of families living in single-family buildings in 1900 ranged from 84.5 per cent in Philadelphia to 17.5 per cent in New York, with 29.0 per cent in Chicago and 32.2 per cent in Boston. However, the individual dwellings within these buildings were generally self-contained and 'privatised', with a relatively high level of facilities. By the First World War, many dwellings had bathrooms and central heating as well as a basic water-supply and sanitation, with few facilities being used in common. Although there was, as the Board of Trade commented, 'a great diversity of type' in American housing, there was also a common theme: the existence of a relatively 'privatised' residential pattern.[9]

In France, there was also a spectrum of architectural form. The large tenement block dominated Paris, where in 1901 there was an average of 13.2 flats per tenement, and also Lyons and Marseilles. At the other extreme was the small house, whether terraced or detached, with one or two floors, which was sometimes divided into two separate units. This pattern applied to Bordeaux and Amiens. Other towns, such as Lille, were divided between the two house forms. There were, however, some common features. The level of facilities and 'privatisation' of space was considerably less than in England and America, and the dwellings were smaller. In Paris in 1911, 24.8 per cent of households had one room, 29.0 per cent two and 22.5 per cent three, a total of 76.3 per cent.[10]

In the case of Germany, there was much greater uniformity of housing in the major cities. The only large town in which single-family houses were typical was Bremen. Elsewhere, the typical pattern was a tenement block with six or seven flats, which usually had three rooms but sometimes two. Single room units were rare, and only in Leipzig were four or five rooms at all frequent. In Berlin in 1900, 8.0 per cent of dwellings had a single room, 37.2 per cent two rooms, and 30.6 per cent three rooms. The level of 'privatised' space was low, with less than a quarter of dwellings in Berlin in 1900 having separate sanitation. Dwellings were, in the years before the First World War, becoming smaller as the proportion of two-roomed units increased, and taking a greater share of income.[11]

It is not enough simply to say that in some cities tenements were dominant and in others self-contained houses were the norm, for there could be considerable variations in the nature of the urban fabric within each generic type. The self-contained houses which were built in the late nineteenth century in English and American cities usually followed a grid-iron layout in which the urban fabric was open, and a clear line drawn between the private space of the house and the public space of the street. However, it was possible for self-contained houses to be associated with a more cellular lay-out, in which there was less distinction between public and private space. This had been true of housing built in some English cities in the early and mid-nineteenth century, such as Liverpool, and it remained the case in some European cities into the later nineteenth century. In Lille, for example, houses were built around courts or *cités* which were entered by a narrow passage and contained from three to forty houses. In Belgian cities, dead-end alleys or *impasses* remained a feature which was viewed with alarm by the authorities in Brussels as a challenge to the decorum of the city.[12] Similarly, there was a difference between tenement cities. In New York, the dumb-bell tenements of the late nineteenth century had a single entry from the street, and were built on virtually the full width and entire depth of a long, narrow plot of 25 by 100 feet. In Berlin, on the one hand, the individual plots were much larger and many of the working-class dwellings were hidden away from public view in courtyards at the rear of the plot. In 1900, 52.3 per cent of dwellings in Berlin faced the streets, and the remaining 47.7 per cent were inferior 'back' dwellings in courtyards which were often dark and airless.[13] The texture of the urban fabric might therefore vary widely among tenemented cities, as well as between them and cities of self-contained houses.

How, then, are these variations between and within countries to be explained? It cannot be suggested that there is anything like a definitive answer. Clearly, there was a variation in the level of rents which did not necessarily move in line with the divergence in wages. At the most general level, the variation in national aggregates shows that the market situation was most favourable in the United States, followed by England, Belgium, France and Germany (Table 1.2).

Table 1.2 Wages and rent levels in five countries, c.1910

	Weekly Money Wage	Net Rent (ex. tax)	Ratio of Wage to Net Rent
England and Wales	100	100	1.0
USA	230	207	1.1
Belgium	63	74	0.9
France	75	98	0.8
Germany	83	123	0.7

Source: Daunton, *House and Home*, Table 4.5

Of course, there were wide variations within each country, as there was

Table 1.3 Rents and wages in Belgium, Germany and France

	Rent	Wage (skilled builder)	Ratio
Belgium, 1908			
Brussels	100	100	1.0
Antwerp	99	92	1.0
Liège	88	84	1.0
Germany, 1905			
Berlin	100	100	1.0
Stuttgart	97	75	0.8
Leipzig	51	88	1.7
France, 1905			
Paris	100	100	1.0
Lyons	77	74	1.0
Bourdeaux	71	67	0.9
Lille	52	65	1.3

Source: BOT, Belgium, xxxix; *BOT, France*, lii; *BOT, Germany*, lv

within Britain. In Germany, for example, there was a divergence between the unfavourable wage:rent ratio of Stuttgart and the favourable ratio of Leipzig which does seem to provide a basis for the explanation of the larger dwellings of Leipzig. However, the figures are not so helpful in France, where the self-contained houses of Bordeaux were associated with a less favourable ratio than Paris (Table 1.3). There is clearly scope for a detailed analysis of the divergence in the housing markets within each country covered by the Board of Trade, and any comments upon the international discrepancies must be very tentative. The broad difference between the housing market of different countries which is shown in Table 1.2 does begin to explain the international variation in the form and standard of housing, as did the figures for rents and wages within Britain.

What remains to be explained is why, on the supply side, rents varied between cities. A common explanation for tenements and for poor housing conditions is that rents were inflated by the actions of property speculators. Caution is, however, needed: in virtually all cities, the same argument was made, and it clearly connects with the political case against a particular social group.[14] Certainly, the precise form of the argument relating to the land market which has been used in Britain cannot be applied, for there was nothing akin to the Scottish feu system. Freehold development was in fact common in most European cities. The argument that high land prices caused tenements could indeed be reversed. The existence of a tradition of living in flats, possibly caused when town walls constricted the area for housing, might lead to a cultural acceptance of tenements; when suburban land did become available, the toleration of residence in flats meant that land could bear a higher price which made it the subject for speculation.[15]

Whatever the direction of causation, there is, unfortunately, a dearth of solid information on the price of land in different cities. There is a suggestion that land prices might differ considerably even between tenement cities, and that speculation might not necessarily be a feature. Berlin and Vienna had radically divergent experiences. Land accounted for 40 per cent of the total development costs in Berlin, yet only 20 per cent in Vienna. This discrepancy in land prices was reflected in the absence of land companies in Vienna (except for a short period before the crash of 1873), whereas the *Terraingesellschaften* were an important feature in Berlin. On the other hand, Vienna had a much higher level of rent tax, amounting to 40 per cent of gross rents, which limited profits and forced builders and landlords to reduce costs. The result might be that tenements and poor housing conditions in Berlin are to be explained by the land market, and in Vienna by the uniquely high level of rent tax which was introduced in 1820.[16]

Another factor might be the cost and availability of capital. Working-class housing in most cities was a favoured investment for members of the lower middle class, who treated it as a sort of pension fund to provide for old age, widows and children, although in Paris wealthy rentiers became more dominant over the second half of the nineteenth century.[17] The owners of working-class housing usually borrowed in order to finance their purchases, and the sources which were available to them varied between cities. In Britain and the United States there was an active local market in funds provided by solicitors and building societies or building and loan associations which mobilised small savings. The conclusion which has tended to emerge from recent work on Britain is that the capital market for housing did not have strong connections with other markets, but appealed to a particular type of savings: the result was that building was rarely choked off by capital shortages. Rather, builders tended to over-supply housing, which led to a glut and a collapse of construction, so that demand for capital fell. The building cycle determined the demand for capital rather than the supply of funds acting as the major influence upon the level of building.[18] This was not necessarily the case in other countries. In Budapest and Vienna, for example, it is argued that the supply of capital did determine the building cycle. The housing sector might need to compete for funds with other outlets, in economies where there was less capital available. There might also be a greater role for mortgage banks, savings banks, and life insurance companies. The mortgage banks in Berlin, for example, raised their funds by the sale of debentures which meant that housing finance was much more integrated with other sectors of the capital market, and it is suggested that when there was an upturn in building it proved difficult to meet the demand for mortgages. Even when there were similar institutions to the building societies of England or the building and loan associations of the United States—such as the First Savings Bank of Austria which invested the small savings of the lower middle class and better-off workers in safe outlets—they might be less successful in mobilising funds because of the lower level of wages and a more skewed income distribution than in Britain and the United States. The relative shortage of funds might therefore reduce the supply of housing, and increase costs.[19]

The nature of demand for housing provides the other side of the equation. This is not so simple as the figures provided by the Board of Trade might suggest. The emphasis was upon wage rates for particular occupations, such as building workers, which varied widely between and within countries. This is clearly a significant and interesting phenomenon which needs to be explained,[20] but it does obscure a number of important features which might be of considerable importance for the housing market. There is an in-built assumption in the Board of Trade figures that the crucial determinant of demand was the income of the male head of household, and that house property was an item of consumption, which ideally accommodated a single family. These are normative judgements which are all open to question, not least from the information provided by the Board of Trade reports.

There was a divergence, in the first place, in the size of the household which the male wage supported. This was indicated by figures provided by the Board of Trade. At a weekly family income of 30–35s, there were 5.2 members per household in Britain, 4.5 in Germany and 3.9 in France, so that the mean German household was 87 per cent of the British, and the French 75 per cent. The wage of a skilled fitter in Germany was 85 per cent and in France 76 per cent of the British level, so that the discrepancy in favour of the British worker was eroded. In any case, the male wage was in many cases not the entire household income. Although French male wages were lower than in Britain and Germany, there were fewer children, which allowed the wife to contribute to the family budget. And despite the fact that there were fewer children in French households than in German, they made a greater contribution to the family income because they could work full-time from the age of 14 whereas in Germany they had to attend continuation schools to the age of 16. The Board of Trade indicated that, at a weekly family income of 30–35s, the husband contributed 91.2 per cent in Germany and 79.5 per cent in France; the wife 6.1 per cent in Germany and 13.8 per cent in France; and the children 2.7 per cent in Germany and 6.7 per cent in France. A comparison between male wage rates might therefore be misleading. Although male industrial wages were lower in France than in Germany or Britain, the greater contribution of wives and children to family income meant that the proportion of families with an income of 40s and above was higher in France (35 per cent) than in Britain (31 per cent) or Germany (15 per cent).[21]

Of course, these figures are themselves open to dispute, for it must be wondered how realistic it is to compare broad national aggregates. There were, after all, major differences within each country. The contribution of the male income was, for example, likely to be far greater in a mining or heavy industrial area than in a textile community. The availability of jobs for women in the textile areas acted to delay the age of marriage which, together with the loss of income as a result of pregnancies, acted to reduce the number of children in textile districts. Further, there might be a different structure to the poverty cycle: miners tended to reach their maximum earnings in their early 20s, before marriage; in textile districts, men were promoted to well-paid jobs in the spinning mills at a later age, often after marriage.[22]

A proper understanding of the demand for housing therefore involves analysis of the structure of the household economy in each town—a task which is not attempted in the essays in this volume, but which is clearly a major requirement in future research. Further, it would be incorrect to view housing simply as an item of consumption by working-class families or households: the property might itself form a source of income and even of production. This was most strikingly the case in those American cities such as Detroit where 'self-build' was common. A working-man might, with the help of family and friends, erect a timber-frame house on a cheap plot of suburban land, investing what has been termed 'sweat equity'. The result was the accumulation of a modest capital asset which would mean that, when land and materials had been paid for, the family would not have to pay for its accommodation. This would lead to a higher net income in middle and old age, when the earnings of unskilled workers tended to fall. The result was to modify the shape of the poverty cycle of the family. Where owner-occupation was achieved by purchase rather than self-build, the benefits of a higher net income later in life might be offset by the drain of loan finance in young adulthood, possibly coinciding with the highest level of outgoings on children. The accumulation of property might in this case be to the detriment of the education and career prospects of children who might be forced into the labour market.[23]

Whether the accommodation was owner-occupied or rented, it could still produce income. Of course, many large cities were, and long remained, centres of workshop production in which there was no clear divide between the place of residence and work, or between family and apprentices and journeymen. In the late nineteenth century, there was, as in the case of Vienna, a trend towards 'spatially coherent dwellings that would permit a group of blood-relatives to live an autonomous private life'.[24] This should, however, not be exaggerated for there might still be a tension between architectural form and the reality of working-class life. Lodgers and sub-tenants undermined the 'autonomous private life' of the working-class family which remained 'permeable' to outsiders, with a lack of clear separation between family and strangers. In Budapest, for example, between a quarter and a third of industrial workers were lodgers in 1911, of whom perhaps half merely rented space in a bed, often in dwellings which had only one or two rooms. In all, 13.7 per cent of the population in 1890 was lodging; the figure in Vienna was 14 per cent in 1890, of whom half were bed lodgers.[25] Clearly, there was little opportunity for privacy and functional specialisation of space in such circumstances.

Such patterns offended against middle-class ideals of the private, self-contained family unit. Criticism was often based upon a misunderstanding of motives, a belief that it represented moral decay and dissolution. In fact, it might represent, as more perceptive commentators on the American city realised, a step towards the acceptance of 'privatised' values by allowing the accumulation of enough money to move to the suburbs.[26] Certainly, taking in lodgers or sub-letting was related to the life-cycle: it was common for young men when moving to the city to become lodgers, and for married couples to take in lodgers when their family income was most strained. It entailed the wife's providing a paid service in the house, which is not captured in the census figures of occupations, or in the calculations of the gross national product.[27]

It is easier to describe differences in the form of housing than to provide an explanation. The history of architecture cannot be understood simply as a process internal to the architectural profession. The physical form of the city might, as in the case of Brussels, be the expression of a political programme and social norms.[28] The internal lay-out of the individual dwelling might, as in the case of Vienna, develop from a pre-existing artisan workshop and residence which rested upon a particular form of domestic production.[29] The scale of the tenement block and its lay-out might depend upon the precise way in which the plot was subdivided, and the nature of building regulations. The existence of land companies, and the availability of sources of capital, also had their impact upon the form of the property. And, once the property was erected, it interacted with the social life of the residents, which demands an appreciation of the structure of the household economy. The architectural form of working-class housing therefore relates to the entire history of the city: its economy, society and politics.

II

The history of architectural form is more than a matter of describing and explaining the physical nature of tenements or houses. It is also necessary to inquire into the social influences of the particular housing form, by asking how it was experienced by residents. A theme which has come to the forefront in the recent literature on Britain and North America relates to the social use of space. The origins of this interest lay in the history of the middle-class house and family, where there was a trend in the nineteenth century towards a much more differentiated use of space between adults and children, male and female, family and servants, and a drive towards privacy so that the public areas of the house into which visitors were invited were isolated from the private sphere which was reserved for the family. These trends were apparent both within the individual house and within the city as a whole owing to the trend towards suburban residence.[30] What this amounts to is an attempt to link the history of the physical form of the house and the social history of the family. Many housing reformers shared this concern, for they saw a connection, in a very crude and deterministic way, between particular house forms and desirable social behaviour. House form was part of the political and moral discourse.[31]

The social use of space varied between cities at a number of different levels. In the first place, the segregation between social groups within the city took different forms. It is easy to assume, following the model of the Chicago school, that by the second half of the nineteenth century a greater degree of homogeneity of areas had emerged in British and American cities, with the middle class in the suburbs, the working class nearer the centre, and the poorest residents clustered on the fringes of the business district. There might, however, be some differences between the two sides of the Atlantic. Suburbanisation has been stressed as a key theme in the social history of America, and it is usually seen as a flight of the middle class from the disorder and threat of the inner city.[32] This might, in fact, be more true of England, for in American it was possible for members of the working class to join in the process as a result of the easy availability of cheap land and the possibility of self-build.[33] Yet, whatever the differences within the English and American patterns of suburbanisation, they should both be set apart from the experience in many European cities.

In Paris, the working class was driven from the centre of the city to the periphery so that, as a contemporary remarked, 'The poor are like an immense rope hemming in the comfortable classes'. The suburbs were more akin to a shanty town, a form of self-build which did not have the American connotations of social mobility and sharing in the middle class experience.[34] In Brussels, the city authorities pursued a deliberate strategy of driving out the poor to the fringe, and attracting the elite to the centre, in imitation of the pattern in Paris.[35] Similarly, in Vienna and Budapest the inner city was bourgeois and the suburbs working class.[36] The process of social segregation took different forms in most cities of continental Europe from the cities of North America and England.

The social use of space might differ at a second level, within the individual building. In the case of British and American cities, it was unusual for residents of a single building to come from widely divergent social backgrounds except, of course, for domestic servants. There might, it is true, be poor families living in back streets or specific blocks within the well-to-do areas, who would provide services such as laundry or gardening or cleaning.[37] In European cities, however, it was possible for the occupants of a single building to be drawn from a broad social spectrum. A common pattern in the middle of the nineteenth century was for the highest status accommodation to be in apartments on the first floor, with each successive floor declining in social status until members of the unskilled working class were found in the attics. In the case of Paris, this arrangement of space within the buildings was overturned in the second half of the nineteenth century, so that buildings became, like quarters of the city, more homogeneous. In 1883, a report on housing conditions in Paris inferred that this was regrettable, and urged that mixed housing should be reintroduced in order to promote social harmony.[38] In other cities, mixed housing did persist. Although there were large areas of solidly working-class accommodation in the suburbs of Budapest, there was also a working-class presence in the inner city where the middle class resided. Even the so-called rent palaces continued to be mixed in their social composition: the better accommodation was on the lower levels and at the front of the building, with status declining at the rear and on the higher levels. Families of differing social status shared a single stairway, and lived in close proximity to one another.[39]

Finally, the use of space within the individual dwelling took different forms. There are two issues: were the dwellings self-contained, or did they use facilities in common; and was there any separation of function within the dwelling? These points amount to asking to what extent the accommodation was 'privatised'. In the tenements of Scotland, differentiation of space could not be well-developed, for in many cases the flats had only one or two rooms which were used for a variety of functions. The kitchen, for example, usually had a 'bed recess' and was used for sleeping as well as for cooking and for the everyday life of the family. Neither was there a clear line drawn between the private sphere of the family and the public areas, for many facilities within the tenements were used in common, whether the staircases, the privies or the laundries and drying areas.[40] In the tenements of New York, attempts were made to reduce the degree to which facilities were shared;[41] in the tenements of European cities, the degree of privatisation was slight. Working-class flats in Vienna, for example, had no internal facilities; they opened onto a corridor where there were toilets and a water supply which were used in common; and in the basement there was a laundry which was available to the tenants in rotation. There was a lack of clear separation between public and private space within the tenement blocks, and close contact with neighbours was a fact of life. Within the flats there was a low level of privacy and of differentiation of function. The majority of units in Vienna had only two rooms, and in Budapest many were single rooms.[42] In English cities, the separation between private and public space was usually achieved. The Tyneside flats, for example, were completely self-contained with no facilities used in common: they had separate front and back doors, with their own back-yards and sanitary facilities. In the back-to-backs of Yorkshire, separation was less easily achieved for there could be no back-yards, and at first common facilities were provided at the end of each block. However, by the end of the nineteenth century a high degree of 'privatisation' was achieved by providing facilities in the basement of each cottage. The use of space within the increasingly self-contained housing stock varied. In the back extension properties, a relatively differentiated use of space was possible. Cooking could be separated from the living room, and a separate room at the front of the house—the parlour—could be assigned for receiving visitors and special occasions from funerals to courtships. Bedrooms were distinct from living rooms, and located on the first floor. In the smaller houses of Lancashire, and in the Tyneside flats and back-to-backs, the use of space was less precisely articulated. Cooking might not be separated from the living room, and it might prove difficult to allocate a room for public presentation.[43]

Buildings and areas of the city should therefore be read as social documents: the physical fabric is too important to be left to historians of architecture and town planning. The form of the city and individual buildings might be part of a conscious attempt to reshape society, which might collide with the expectations of working-class residents.[44] However, even when there was no intent, the physical form of the property and of the wider city might have social consequences for the interaction of residents of different classes, and for the nature of the family. Different forms of housing allowed varying degrees of privacy within the family and between family and outsiders. The interplay between physical form and the social life it contained deserves more attention from urban historians than it has hitherto received.

III

The interest in the architectural style of working-class property does not stop with the social use of space and its impact upon family relationships, for in the comparison between Scottish tenements and English terraces, it has become clear that the former were associated with a considerable degree of social tension and political conflict, whereas in the case of the latter this was not true to anything like the same extent.

There is little doubt that tenements were likely to lead to greater problems of management than self-contained houses. The continuance of communal space in the Scottish tenements created greater problems of management, providing opportunities for tension between tenants and confrontation with the owners, and involving public bodies in the imposition of controls. By contrast, the management of self-contained property was likely to be less problematic for the owner. Although some of the larger terraced houses might be shared by two families, one family was always considered to be the tenant with responsibility for payment of the rent, so that a large part of the burden of management was passed to the working-class family.[45] Tenements also meant that the size of each unit of ownership was larger. Architectural form might therefore affect patterns of ownership and management: it was more likely that some intermediary was required for the tenements than for the self-contained terraced houses. In the case of the tenements of Scotland, the 'factors' stood between the owners and tenants in most cases, a class of non-resident professional managers with responsibility for the collection of rents, the maintenance of the property, the imposition of regulations over common spaces, the payment of insurance and local taxation. The larger scale of capital required to erect tenements might also require a greater number of tiers of ownership, which would create the possibility of tension. In English cities, personal management by the owner was more common.[46]

It is, however, important to guard against the dangers of architectural determinism. The need for controls over the common spaces of the tenements and the interrelationships between tenants did not lead to a single outcome, as the comments of the Board of Trade made clear. In the case of Glasgow, it was very unusual for there to be a resident caretaker or agent to manage and control the tenement block. Instead, there was a reliance upon public regulations and 'factors' or non-resident agents. The public supervision of the common space of the tenements became increasingly tight, and even draconian. The Burgh Police (Scotland) Act 1892 laid down the responsibilities of occupiers to clean stairs, landings and passages to the satisfaction of sanitary inspectors. The owners were inclined to argue for the extension of these public controls so that the local authorities could impose cleanliness within the individual flat as well as in the common areas. The owners for their part relied upon the use of a factor or professional manager of property, who sent salaried clerks to collect rents and to ensure that any repairs were undertaken. The use of resident caretakers was rare: Robert M'Callum who factored 4,000 tenement flats employed only one caretaker.[47]

The system in other tenement cities was different. In New York, the janitor was the key figure, who undertook small repairs, kept the common areas clean, and ensured that city ordinances on matters such as refuse disposal were complied with. The janitor did not collect rents.[48] In Paris, the concierge acted as the doorkeeper who admitted visitors, unlike her counterpart in New York: she also let flats and collected the rents, enforced regulations, cleaned common areas, and collected mail. In return, she had rent-free accommodation as well as a small salary from the owner and gratuities from the tenants. Prospective tenants paid 'key money' (*denier à Dieu*), and a common complaint was that the concierge offered tenancies to those who paid most, and had a vested interest in a high turnover in order to increase her income.[49] In Vienna, the owner resided in about half the properties in 1910; non-residents, or those who did not wish to manage their property, used agents (*Hausverwalter*) who might be either part-timers, supplementing their income as, for example, civil servants, or full-time. They were paid a commission. In addition, there was a resident caretaker, regardless of whether there was a resident owner or an agent, who had rent-free accommodation. The usual pattern was for the husband to take another job, and to leave the work to the wife. The caretaker enforced house rules (*Hausordnung*) which, for example, regulated the hours for the beating of carpets in corridors and the cleaning of common areas. The role of the caretaker was formalised in 1910 in the official regulations of *Hausbesorgerordnung*. The caretaker did not collect rent, and was more like the janitors of New York.[50] In Berlin, the owner might reside in the property and manage it in person. Otherwise, a resident agent (*Verwalter*) who had another occupation, collected rents and controlled tenancies, usually in return for a reduction in rent. The rent usually contained a surcharge for the cleaning of common spaces, lighting and so on; the landlord usually employed a woman resident in the tenement block to undertake these tasks. Refuse was collected by a company formed by the landlords of the city.[51] In Budapest, a housemaster lived in the block, collecting the rents and managing the collective space, in return for rent-free accommodation and a commission from tenants. The housemaster selected tenants, and received a payment from them which, as in Paris, generated a high level of turnover.[52] There was, then, no single solution to the problems of management of tenemented property, and the Scottish system of non-resident management was not the usual pattern.

The architectural form of the tenement might pose problems to which a range of solutions might be found, with varying consequences for the social relationships which arose from the management of property. Architecture did not determine the precise pattern of management, and it might be that the nature of the legal system, independently of architectural form, provided the source of tension in landlord–tenant relations. The problem with the comparison between Scotland and England is that the distinctive Scottish legal system contributed to a severe problem in landlord–tenant relations which can be all too easily laid at the door of the architectural form. The two need to be held separate. The issue which stood at the heart of the problem of landlord–tenant relations in Glasgow was not, in fact, the tenement *per se* so much as the way in which it was let.[53]

The Scottish system was a source of tension largely because of the inflexibility of the contract between landlord and tenant. The vast majority of working-class property in Glasgow was held on annual tenancies, all of which expired on a single removal date in the year: 28 May. Only the smallest property at the bottom of the market was held on monthly tenancies. Further, the decision to take a property was made about four months before the removal date, when the landlord or his agent sent out a 'missive' asking whether the tenant wished to remain or to move. Rents were paid in arrears, usually at quarterly intervals, which meant that the owners were providing accommodation on credit. The landlords had some security through the law of 'hypothec', which gave them power to seize tenants' possessions to the value of the rent for the whole term of the tenancy, even if it was not yet due for payment. This draconian law was in fact little used in the long-let property inhabited by families above the level of unskilled workers, and the crucial point of tension between landlords and tenants of long-let tenements was rather the 'missive' question. There was a tension between short contracts of employment and the long periods of tenancies, and it was this issue which politicised landlord–tenant relations in Glasgow before the First World War.

The campaign for short lets succeeded with the passing of an Act in 1911 which allowed tenancies to expire on the twenty-eighth day of any month, provided that notice of 40 days was given for lets of more than 40 days. The landlords required some compensation, for they argued that the more rapid turnover of tenants would raise the costs of management. This compensation was at the expense of the tenants of monthly property. The landlords had power to evict defaulting tenants, which

was overwhelmingly used against the monthly tenants, and the relationship between landlord and tenant in this class of property was one of
continual litigation. The tenants for their part were aware that the law
could be used against the landlords by lodging an objection to the petition for eviction, which could delay the whole procedure. Landlords
were critical of the law of eviction, which seemed to them to be slow
and expensive, and in 1911 they were given a more speedy means of
ridding themselves of unsatisfactory tenants. Relationships at the bottom
of the housing market were therefore very strained, with frequent
recourse to the courts.

In English cities, the relationships between landlord and tenant were
less problematical, not only because of the different architectural form,
but also because of the divergences in the legal system. In working-class
housing in English towns, tenancies were weekly, continuing from week
to week on payment of rent. The tenancy could be ended by either side
on one week's notice. This gave tenants considerable flexibility, unlike
their counterparts in Scotland, although at the cost of an absence of
security of tenure. In practice, this was not a major issue. Landlords in
English towns were not likely to end the tenancy when rent was paid
regularly, and it was indeed not unusual to retain good tenants by allowing them to fall into arrears during periods of trade depression or of
family crisis, which could then be paid off in instalments when
prosperity returned. The concern of landlords was how to remove
defaulting tenants who had no intention of paying, and here they had
two means of legal redress—distress and summary eviction. The law of
distress permitted the landlord, having given the tenant a warrant for the
rent due, to enter the house between sunrise and sunset on a week-day,
without using force, in order to seize goods. An inventory of goods was
to be made, which would be appraised after five days and sold six days
later at a public auction if the rent was not paid. These powers were
restricted in 1888 when goods up to the value of £5 were exempted, and
the bailiffs who levied distress were required to obtain a certificate from
a county court judge. Of course, landlords had a greater interest in
securing repossession than in seizing goods of little value. In English
cities, the power of repossession was provided by the Small Tenements
Recovery Act of 1838. When rent was due, the landlord could give a
week's notice to quit; the landlord would then apply for a warrant of
ejectment, and possession was ordered in 21 days. The landlord merely
needed to prove that the tenancy had been terminated, which it was on
the expiry of a week's notice. The magistrate then had no option but to
evict the tenant.

This seemed to give the landlord great power, reducing the legal
process to a formality which did not protect the tenant. However, this
should not be exaggerated, for the power of summary eviction was used
much less than in Scotland. English landlords also complained about the
limits set to their power of eviction: it took at least 28 days to remove
a tenant, during which period rent might well be lost. English landlords
were unable to obtain redress for this grievance, whereas their Scottish

counterparts did secure a more speedy process of eviction in 1911. Before 1911, Scottish landlords were obliged to give notice for one-third of the period of the monthly let, and the tenant was usually permitted to remain until the end of the month; by lodging an objection, the tenant would normally win a reprieve of ten or eleven days. The changes of 1911 meant that a tenant who was seven days in arrears would be given 48 hours' notice, and if the rent was not paid a warrant could be obtained requiring the tenant to leave within 48 hours. English landlords had nothing equivalent to this.

Landlord–tenant relations in Scotland were therefore politicised before the First World War, and the Act of 1911 did not solve the problem. Landlords of the erstwhile long-let property complained, with some justice, that their costs were increased. Their grounds for complaint were increased when they became responsible for collecting rates on behalf of the council at a commission which did not compensate them for the additional work. Interest rates were also rising. There was a glut in the property market in Glasgow before the First World War, which made it difficult to pass on the additional burdens to the tenants, with the result that profits were eroded. This provided the background to the explosion of 1915 when the landlords took the opportunity during the war to increase rents, which they attempted to enforce by using the powers of summary eviction which had previously been limited to the bottom end of the market. The result was the outbreak of rent strikes on Clydeside, which contributed to the introduction of rent controls which had a major impact upon the future of the housing market in Britain.[54]

Rent strikes and the politicisation of landlord–tenant relations were features of a number of cities before the First World War. The explanation was not, however, necessarily the same as in the case of Scotland. Long and inflexible annual tenancies were not such an issue in other cities. In Vienna, for example, 41 per cent of lets were quarterly, and 47 per cent (mostly working-class) were monthly; rent was paid one month in advance with automatic renewal.[55] A similar pattern applied in Berlin,[56] while in Brussels tenancies and payment of rent were usually monthly.[57] The Parisian system seemed to pose more problems: rents were paid on the four quarter days, and might be required three or even six months in advance.[58] Generally speaking, however, the nature of the tenancy was not the point of tension so much as the increasing level of rents and shortage of accommodation which placed an intolerable strain upon working-class budgets. The pressure on rent levels which provided the spark for rent strikes could arise from a number of specific issues. In New York, the impact of the new building regulations of 1901 which checked construction at a time of large-scale clearances and immigration caused serious problems.[59] The problem might be intensified, as it was in New York and Budapest, by the so-called 'house lease' system by which the owner of tenement property leased it *en bloc* to a middleman or 'house renter' who could then make his profit by charging the individual tenant what he pleased. This was more likely to lead to tension than the Scottish system of reliance upon house factors who took

a commission. There was, however, nothing inevitable about the outbreak of rent strikes: the cost of accommodation mounted in Berlin
where the 'house lease' system existed, yet there was nothing equivalent
to the events of Budapest and Vienna.[60]

The campaigns against high rents could have an impact upon the
formulation of housing policy. In Paris, a socialist-led Congress on the
Question of Rents was formed in 1883 which was at least in part responsible for the renewed concern of public bodies about the housing question.[61] Similarly, in Vienna a 20 per cent rent increase led to rent strikes
in 1911 and the creation of a Tenants' Association under the leadership
of the Social Democratic Party which saw an opportunity in exploiting
the housing issue.[62] In Budapest, a boycott movement started in 1907,
by which tenants who were evicted for non-payment of rent urged
others not to take flats in the property. This issue was taken up by the
Social Democrats from 1908, and when rents were subsequently
increased a general strike was threatened. The strikes and boycotts which
took place in individual tenements were at least partially successful. This
was the result not only of the organisation of the tenants, but also
because the landlords had lost the power of distress and had instead to
take tenants to court, which was costly and time-consuming. The
providers of mortgages were also alarmed about the security of their
loans, and urged settlement. One outcome in Budapest was the introduction in some properties of collective contracts between the landlord and
a representative of the tenants, the so-called 'steward man', which had
the backing of the SDP and the mayor. The municipality also restricted
evictions to one in any annual let, and controlled rents for that period;
it further introduced council housing which was intended to remove the
tightness in the housing market. This might be interpreted as a victory
for the tenants, leading to an improvement in their housing conditions.
However, the provision of public housing could equally be seen as a
means of strengthening the hand of the landlords. The increase in supply
of low-cost housing would make it easier for landlords to evict tenants,
and they were consequently not hostile to the provision of council housing which would ease the serious tension.[63]

Tenements might, therefore, create greater problems of management
than self-contained houses, but there was no single method by which
they were handled and the varying styles of management might lead to
a greater or lesser degree of tension. Similarly, the legal system which
determined the length of tenancies or the power of eviction formed
another variable which was independent of the architectural form. The
divergences in the nature of landlord–tenant relations which arose from
the interplay of architectural form, management strategies, and legal
codes should provide a major theme in the social history of cities,
deserving consideration alongside relationships between workers and
employers which have been the subject of more research. The precise
nature of landlord–tenant relations might also affect the development of
housing policy.

IV

The development of housing policy has often been interpreted simply as an internal administrative process. The intervention of the British government in order to supplement the private market in housing has been explained in terms of a response to the problem of slums, which pushed councils from clearance to responsibility for replacement and additional housing between the Cross Act of 1875 and the Addison Act of 1919. The main line of the argument has been that in the 1860s a strategy developed of defining 'plague spots' within cities, composed of bad housing and poor sanitary conditions which could be surgically removed by public initiative. This was not seen as a criticism of the existing structure of society and its distribution of income, but was rather perceived as the product of past mistakes. The owners of the slums could therefore be compensated at full market rates and, once the 'plague spots' were removed, there was no need for the mistakes to be repeated. It was believed that private enterprise or semi-philanthropic bodies such as the Peabody Trust would step in to rebuild. It was the tensions within this strategy which, in the opinion of many historians, led to public involvement in rebuilding: the costs of clearance precluded an adequate level of rebuilding at commercial rents, and the local authorities were willy-nilly dragged in to provide replacement housing. From this, a further step was taken in some local authorities to a new, suburban solution from a realisation that 'plague spots' could not be so precisely defined as distinct areas apart from the existing economic and social structure of the city.[64]

Such an analysis has an element of truth as applied to London or Glasgow, yet it is too introverted. It neglects the dynamics within the housing market, and fails to explain why other cities adopted alternative approaches. Birmingham, for example, explicitly rejected the provision of additional housing[65] and, as we shall see, in other countries the housing problem was not necessarily approached in terms of slum clearance leading to a dynamic towards local authority intervention. Explanations in terms of administrative responses are not the full picture; an important factor in the development of housing policy was the nature of the social and political relationships which arose from the housing market, as has already been suggested in the case of rent strikes and the politicisation of landlord–tenant relations which took place in some cities.

A house was not only a place of residence: it was also a source of taxation for local government, and of revenue for the owner. These competing claims upon the house could come into conflict. In the case of Britain, it has been argued that a crisis in local taxation placed an increasing burden upon private landlords, squeezing their profits and leading to an erosion of capital values before the First World War, and to a threat to the survival of the housing market as it had previously existed. The tension in landlord–tenant relations, especially on Clydeside, contributed to the introduction of rent controls, which produced a further reduction in profitability.[66] The decision to opt for council housing as the solution to the problems at the end of the war was a continuation of the prewar erosion of the position of the private landlords, and it should be asked why they were not protected against these threats from high taxation and rent controls.

Housing policy in a number of other countries rested upon the use of money from social insurance funds or savings banks in order to provide cheap loans for working-class housing. A Belgian law of 1889, for example, established local *comités de patronage* appointed by the provincial and central government which were charged with encouraging the construction of working-class houses; the national savings and superannuation funds could invest part of their capital in housing, through societies which were approved by the *comités de patronage*.[67] A similar strategy of cheap loans from insurance funds, savings banks or taxation, was pursued in Paris, Vienna, and Berlin. It was also to an extent followed in Britain, where the Industrial and Provident Societies Act, 1893, allowed a housing company which registered as a public utility company and limited its divided to 5 per cent to borrow half (and from 1909 two-thirds) of its capital from the Public Works Loan Board.[68] The strategy was, however, to die out in Britain whereas it developed in many European countries. By 1913, 20 per cent of the houses being built in Vienna were drawing upon the cheap loans made available by the government, and this approach was to form the basis of the postwar system in both Paris and Berlin. It is worth asking why this divergence took place between the reliance upon council housing in Britain and the encouragement of cooperative housing in Berlin.

In Germany, non-profit, cooperative building societies were permitted to borrow money on favourable terms from the insurance funds which were created by the Invalidity and Old Age Insurance Act of 1890. In Berlin, about 11,000 dwellings were provided by 1914. This contrasts with the Housing of the Working Classes Act which was passed in Britain in 1890, which codified and extended the powers of local authorities to build both replacement and additional housing. Although many reformers and local authorities remained sceptical, preferring co-partnership schemes or public utility companies on garden-city lines, the basis was laid for a marked divergence between Britain and Germany after the war. It was, indeed, already obvious in the capital cities before the war, for the London County Council had built its housing estates at Tooting and White Hart Lane in Tottenham.[69] Why was this the case?

One factor was the lack of political power of small property owners within the British political system, both at the local and national level. There was in Britain nothing equivalent to the three-class voting system of the Prussian state and municipal government which gave more weight to property owners. Consequently, even support of non-profit cooperative housing faced considerable opposition in Germany from those who saw it as a threat to the private sector; the prospect of opposition would be even greater in the case of a large-scale programme of municipal building. Problems at the local level might lead reformers to turn to the federal government for national legislation, which would raise another political consideration: the sensitivity of the states to the power of the Reich. A measure such as the Housing of the Working Classes Act of 1890 was therefore likely to be frustrated in Germany.[70]

The owners of house property had difficulties in making their voice heard within the British political system. This was in part because of the dominance in the political debate before the First World War of the land question, which left house-owners in an ambiguous position. The Liberal case was that the housing problem arose from the parasitical landowners who should be taxed out of existence in order to realise the enterprise of the house-owners; but this seemed dubious to many house-owners, not least because they might also own the land upon which the houses were built. They could decide that their interests were in fact like those of the landowners, to be defended in a united property front; but the problem was that the Conservatives who defended the landowners were in practice not eager to come to the defence of urban house-owners who might be politically unpopular. The nature of the lower-middle-class ideology in any case left the owners of small house property ill-prepared. The prevalent attitude of lower-middle-class groups was formed in the early nineteenth century by the hostility to privileged monopolies supported by the state. These property owners associations which existed in the late nineteenth and early twentieth centuries were opposed to municipalisation and were allied with individualist groups, when perhaps what was needed was state involvement in the housing market to give them a positive role. The German petty bourgeoisie, on the other hand, had a greater continuity with the pre-industrial guild tradition which made collective organisation more acceptable, most particularly when the rise of large-scale businesses posed a threat.[71]

The political system in the two countries therefore weighted the choice against municipal provision in Germany, whereas in Britain it was possible for both options to be considered. The problem in Britain is explaining why the cooperative or public utility company option was rejected. A major explanation is that the groups which might have taken the lead in sponsoring such organisations were content to rely upon the local state. This partly arose from the fact that the municipality was less constrained by the influence of property owners. It was also an expression of the attitudes of the Labour Party and trade unions to the state, which was not seen as a class interest aiming to coerce and contain the working class. When the ideology of the Labour Party moved towards an acceptance that the state was the most efficient provider of services, then the way was open for mass council housing.

The German path was to develop autonomous trade union or political organisations in order to build and own houses which, although they might accept cheap loans from the state, nevertheless retained a large measure of independence in the selection of tenants and the management of the property. There was a sense that the state was biased, a class interest which was hostile to the unions and Social Democrats. In Britain, despite the exclusion of many of the poorest members of the working class from the franchise before 1918, the parliamentary system was not perceived as being distorted in the same way as the system of election to the Prussian Chamber of Deputies with its loading of power according to the amount of tax paid. Social Democrats felt alienated by a system which was manifestly biased against them, so that they refused to participate in 'bourgeois' governments. In Britain, by contrast, there was a greater confidence in the 'fairness' of the state, and an acceptance that Parliament was representative and a proper focus for working-class aspirations. The outcome might be to confine the working class to institutions devised by politicians drawn from higher social classes, but it should be stressed that the politicians were themselves constrained. Once politics had been placed on the basis of a contract, coercion became a risky option. There had to be a measure of sensitivity to charges of class bias in the actions of the government, and a punitive approach would infringe the basis of the stability of the state. The consequence was that the state did not intervene actively in labour relations on the side of capital, but rather guaranteed the corporate rights of unions. Thus Bismarckian social reform was the carrot designed to complement the stick of anti-socialist laws, while the Liberal government in Britain secured union support for national insurance by legalising trade union financial support for the Labour Party. British politics in the later nineteenth and early twentieth centuries, argues Ross McKibbin, were based upon the notion of a class-neutral state in which no class should govern against the working class. This made it easier for the Labour party to turn to the state, rather than to develop its own agencies. The cooperative solution to housing withered.[72]

Of course, the United States opted for neither the British nor the German housing policy; rather, it moved towards the encouragement of owner-occupation. Here an important consideration was the nature of the financial institutions in the housing market. In Britain, the building societies which provided mortgages increasingly became the territory of the middle class, more akin to savings banks than the characteristic institutions of the working class. Building societies and savings banks did not offer sociability and the paraphernalia of status which were supplied by trade unions and friendly societies. Neither were they run by members of the working class, for they tended to be bureaucratic and anonymous. Above all, a strategy of accumulating small sums of money did not make sense for working-class families living close to the margin of poverty: it was much more realistic to opt for insurance against various contingencies, so that money would be available as and when it was needed. Saving and the desire to possess property only made sense higher up the social scale. When the Liberal governments moved into the provision of welfare benefits before the First World War, they wished to avoid state bureaucracies and were able to use the friendly societies and trade unions which supplied insurance against the contingencies of sickness and unemployment; but they were not able to turn to any similar working-class body which supplied housing. The building societies were external to the working-class economy, and it made no more sense to turn to them as agents for the resolution of the housing crisis than to use the municipalities.[73] In this respect, there was a difference from the United States. There, working men were more likely to accumulate small sums in the building and loan associations (BLAs) than to opt for contingency insurance, and the state was willing to consider subsidising the associations as a solution to the housing crisis.[74]

In the United States, the local authorities did not seem so desirable as agents for the provision of housing. American cities were creatures of the states, which conferred their charters and hence determined their legitimate functions. By the time many American cities had obtained the freedom to write their own charters, the progressive impulse was already flagging. British towns and cities were in this sense freer agents: they could obtain private acts from Parliament which were usually followed by general permissive acts which could be drawn upon as the local authorities desired. American city government was also much more influenced by machine politics than in Britain. Contracts to build houses would provide yet another source of kick-backs, and the selection of tenants a further avenue for patronage. Housing reformers favoured the BLAs because they were seen as an antidote to the problems of machine politics, providing, so it was believed, a constituency in favour of economical government, and a counter to monopolies and syndicates. In America, city government was seen as part of the problem rather than as a solution. British cities had had a much longer involvement in municipal trading such as tramways, gas, electricity and water, so that there was less animosity to a change in the boundary between public and private enterprise. The nature of the housing problem also differed between Britain and America. In America, the problem which obsessed the reformers was the tenement, and legislation before the First World War was designed to control the construction of the 'unAmerican' architectural form. The BLAs were seen as a means of spreading the self-contained family home. There was no sense of a general crisis in the housing market before the First World War as there was in Britain: profitability had not collapsed, and owner-occupation was still increasing its share of the housing stock in most cities.[75]

The development of housing policy was, therefore, far from being a narrow administrative response. A full appreciation of the particular course of policy in any country depends upon the political position of lower-middle-class property owners, and the acceptance by the state of working-class bodies and the perception of the state by these organisations. It requires an analysis of the existing institutions within the housing market, and the extent to which they may be utilised by the state. It involves an understanding of the tensions between landlord and tenant, rates and rents, which may cause a crisis within the housing market. The debate over housing policy should, if it is placed in its full context, provide a means of appreciating some of the fundamental features of the social and political structure of cities.

V

The aim of this introduction has been to suggest some of the themes which need to be considered in the analysis of housing in the cities of Europe and America before the First World War. There was no single way of housing the worker, for there were wide variations in the development process, in the quality of the property, in its architectural form, in its method of management, in the legal system which regulated relations between owner and occupier, in the political position of the various parties, and in the character of policy. A concentration upon one city or country makes it difficult to appreciate the complexity of divergences, and it is often only by asking comparative questions that some sense can be made of the housing system in a single area. The historian of Vienna might ask why land companies were unsuccessful there but not in Berlin; the historian of Budapest might ponder what allowed council housing to flourish there yet not in Brussels; the historian of Baltimore or Leicester might inquire why self-contained terraced houses were the norm there, but not in New York or Glasgow; the historian of Philadelphia might puzzle over the exact circumstances which led to building and loan associations there yet not in Birmingham; the historian of Glasgow might consider why property was managed by non-resident factors whereas in Paris *concierges* were the rule. This collection of essays might be more productive of questions than answers, but its ambition will largely be achieved if it allows the discussion over housing markets and policies to escape from the limits of single countries considered in isolation.

Notes

1. PP 1909 XCI, *Report of an enquiry by the Board of Trade into working-class rents, housing and retail prices together with the rates of wages in certain occupations in the principal industrial towns of France*; PP 1908 CVIII, *Report of an enquiry by the Board of Trade into working-class rents, housing and retail prices, together with the rates of wages in certain occupations in the principal industrial towns of the German Empire*; PP 1910 XCV, *Report on an enquiry by the Board of Trade into working-class rents, housing and retail prices, together with the rates of wages in certain occupations in the principal industrial towns of Belgium*; PP 1911 LXXXVIII, *Report of an enquiry by the Board of Trade into working-class rents, housing and retail prices, together with the rates of wages in certain occupations in the principal industrial towns of the USA*.
2. The background of the Board of Trade inquiries is explained in E.P. Hennock, 'The measurement of poverty: from the metropolis to the nation, 1880–1920', *Economic History Review* 2nd ser., XL (1987), 216–19.
3. These variations have been discussed in M.J. Daunton, *House and Home in the Victorian City: Working-Class Housing, 1850–1914* (London, 1983), chapter 3.
4. The following comments on the explanation of the tenements of Scotland is

based upon the work of R.G. Rodger, 'The invisible hand: market forces, housing and the urban form in Victorian cities', in D. Fraser and A. Sutcliffe (eds), *The Pursuit of Urban History* (London, 1983), 190–211; 'The Victorian building industry and the housing of the Scottish working class', in M. Doughty (ed.), *Building the Industrial City* (Leicester, 1986), 152–206; 'Speculative builders and the structure of the Scottish building industry, 1860–1914', *Business History*, XXI (1979), 226–46; and 'The law and urban change: some nineteenth-century Scottish evidence', *Urban History Year-book* (1979), 77–91.

5. *Scottish Land: The Report of the Scottish Land Enquiry Committee* (London, 1914), 292–3.

6. A. Sutcliffe, 'Introduction', 8–9, in Sutcliffe (ed.), *Multi-Storey Living: The British Working-Class Experience* (London, 1974).

7. *Board of Trade, Belgium*, ix, xxv–xxvi; *Statistique de la Belgique. Population. Recensement Général du 31 Décembre 1910, Tome IV, Neuvième Partie, Recensement Spécial des Logements, Section A.*

8. *Board of Trade, USA*, lix.

9. Ibid., xx, xxiv, lxii, 25–32, 56–8, 80–1, 108–10, 144–6, 250–1, 266–7, 326–9, 376–7; *Census of the United States, 1900, Vol. II, Population, Part II*, table 102.

10. *BOT, France*, x–xi, xxxi–xxxii, 16–22, 37–40, 59–60, 170–1, 195–7, 213–5; *République Française, Ministre du Travail et de la Prévoyance Sociale, Statistique Générale de la France, Statistique des Familles et des Habitations en 1911*, tableau XII.

11. *BOT, Germany*, x, xii, 18, 22, 29, 96.

12. On England, see Daunton, *House and Home*, chapter 2 and for Liverpool in particular, A. Errazurez, 'Some types of housing in Liverpool, 1785–1890', *Town Planning Review*, XIX (1943–7), 59–68; *BOT, France*, 171; *BOT, Belgium*, 14–15; Van den Eeckhout, below, 82–3, 85.

13. On Berlin, see *BOT, Germany*, 16, 21–2 and Bullock, below, 189 and Table 6.4; on New York, Daunton, below, 254–5. Plots were also large in Budapest: Gyáni, below, 153–5.

14. For the political importance of the debate on land, see A. Offer, *Property and Politics, 1870–1914: Landownership, Law, Ideology and Urban Development in England* (Cambridge, 1981). The key text was Henry George's *Progress and Poverty*.

15. Sutcliffe, 'Introduction', 9.

16. See Banik-Schweitzer, below, 116, 136; on Berlin, Bullock, below, 192–8. W.H. Dawson, *Municipal Life and Government in Germany* (London, 1914) 165–7 complained of the role of land companies in Berlin.

17. Van den Eeckhout, below, 78–80; Banik-Schweitzer, below, 135; Bullock, below, 203; Shapiro, below, 40.

18. For example, S.B. Saul, 'House-building in England, 1890–1914', *Economic History Review*, 2nd ser., XV (1962–3).

19. Bullock, below, 205–6; Banik-Schweitzer, below, 119; Gyáni, below, 161.

20. On Britain, see E.H. Hunt, *Regional Wage Variations in Britain, 1850–1914* (Oxford, 1973); and for a comparison between Birmingham (England) and Pittsburgh, see P.R. Shergold, *Working-Class Life: The "American Standard" in Comparative Perspective, 1898–1913* (Pittsburgh, 1982).

21. *BOT, France*, xxxv–xxxvi.

22. R.I. Woods and C.W. Smith, 'The decline of marital fertility in the late nineteenth century: the case of England and Wales', *Population Studies* 37

(1983); R.I. Woods and P.R.A. Hinde, 'Nuptuality and age of marriage in nineteenth-century England', *Journal of Family History* X (1985); M.R. Haines, 'Fertility, nuptuality and occupation: a study of coal mining populations and regions in England and Wales in the mid-nineteenth century', *Journal of Interdisciplinary History* VIII (1977); J. Jewkes and E.M. Gray, *Wages and Labour in the Lancashire Cotton Spinning Industry* (Manchester, 1935); J.W.F. Rowe, *Wages in the Coal Industry* (London, 1923), 61–2, 72–3.

23. Daunton, below, 262–4.
24. See Banik-Schweitzer, below, 125.
25. Ibid., 130 and Gyáni, below, 170–1. See also Bullock, below, 223–6.
26. Daunton, below, 256.
27. L. Davidoff, 'The separation of home and work? Landladies and lodgers in nineteenth- and twentieth-century England', in S. Burman (ed.), *Fit Work for Women* (London, 1979).
28. This ideological and social role of architecture is, for example, clear in C. Schorske, *Fin de Siècle Vienna: Politics and Culture* (Cambridge, 1961), chapter 2.
29. Banik-Schweitzer, below, 123–9.
30. D. Olsen, *The City as a Work of Art: London, Paris, Vienna* (New Haven and London, 1986); L. Davidoff, *The Best Circles: Society, Etiquette and the Season* (London, 1973), 24, 74; M. Girouard, *Life in the English Country House: A Social and Architectural History* (London, 1978); J. Franklin, *The Gentleman's Country House and Its Plan, 1835–1914* (London, 1981); R. Sennett, *Families Against the City: Middle-Class Homes of Industrial Chicago, 1872–90* (Cambridge, Mass., 1970); C.E. Clark jr., 'Domestic architecture as an index to social history: the romantic revival and the cult of domesticity in American, 1840–70' *Journal of Interdisciplinary History* 7 (1976).
31. Daunton, below, 256–7; Van den Eeckhout, below, 67–9.
32. Sennett, *Families Against the City*; K.T. Jackson, *Crabgrass Frontier: The Suburbanization of the United States* (New York, 1985).
33. R. Harris, 'American suburbs: sketch of a new interpretation', *Journal of Urban History* 15 (1988).
34. Shapiro, below, 37, 39.
35. Van den Eeckhout, below, 85–8.
36. Banik-Schweitzer, below, 107–9 and Gyáni, below, 165–8, 174.
37. For example, P. Malcolmson, 'Getting a living in the slums of Victorian Kensington', *London Journal* I (1975).
38. Shapiro, below, 52.
39. Gyáni, below, 168.
40. *BOT, Britain*, 509, 534.
41. F.D. Case, 'Hidden social agendas and housing standards', *Housing and Society*, 8 (1981).
42. Banik-Schweitzer, below, 129; Gyáni, below, 171.
43. Daunton, *House and Home*, chapter 2.
44. On the use of design as a political weapon, see M. Swenarton, *Homes Fit For Heroes: the Politics and Architecture of Early State Housing in Britain* (London, 1981).
45. See comment by M. Pember Reeves, *Round About a Pound a Week* (London, 1913), 37–8.
46. D. Englander, *Landlord and Tenant in Urban Britain, 1838–1918* (Oxford,

1983) and Daunton, *House and Home*, chapters 6–7, discuss management and landlord–tenant relations.

47. N.J. Morgan and M.J. Daunton, 'Landlords in Glasgow: a study of 1900', *Business History* XXV (1983), 274–81; Daunton, *House and Home*, 34, 168–73.

48. *BOT, USA*, 39–40, Daunton, below, 278.

49. *BOT, France*, 23–4; Shapiro, below, 49.

50. Banik-Schweitzer, below, 137–8.

51. *BOT, Germany*, 29–30.

52. Gyáni, below, 173.

53. The following comparison between England and Scotland is drawn from Englander, *Landlord and Tenant* and Daunton, *House and Home*, chapters 6 and 7.

54. J. Melling, *Rent Strikes: Peoples' Struggle for Housing in West Scotland, 1890–1916* (Edinburgh, 1983); Englander, *Landlord and Tenant*, chapters 9 and 10.

55. Banik-Schweitzer, below, 138.

56. *BOT, Germany*, 30.

57. *BOT, Belgium*, 17.

58. Shapiro, below, 48–9; *BOT, France*, 23.

59. R. Lawson, 'The rent strike in New York City, 1904–80: the evolution of a social movement strategy', *Journal of Urban History* 10 (1984).

60. Gyáni, below 161, 172–3; Daunton, below, 278; Dawson, *Municipal Life and Government in Germany*, 165–7.

61. Shapiro, below, 51.

62. Banik-Schweitzer, below, 140.

63. Gyáni, below, 175–8.

64. J.A. Yelling, *Slums and Slum Clearance in Victorian London* (London, 1986); A.S. Wohl, *The Eternal Slum: Housing and Social Policy in Victorian London* (London, 1977); C.M.Allen, 'The genesis of British urban redevelopment with special reference to Glasgow', *Economic History Review*, 2nd ser. XVIII (1965).

65. See J.S. Nettlefold, *A Housing Policy* (Birmingham, 1905) and *Practical Housing* (Letchworth, 1908).

66. Offer, *Property and Politics*, Parts III and IV.

67. *BOT, Belgium*, 12–13; Van den Eeckhout, below, 92.

68. Swenarton, *Homes Fit for Heroes*, 11.

69. Wohl, *Eternal Slum*, chapter 10.

70. N. Bullock and J. Read, *The Movement for Housing Reform in Germany and France, 1840–1914* (Cambridge, 1985), 258–76.

71. Englander, *Landlord and Tenant*, chapter 4; Offer, *Property and Politics*, chapter 10; G.J. Crossick, 'The emergence of the lower middle class in Britain: a discussion', in Crossick (ed.), *The Lower Middle Class in Britain, 1870–1914* (London, 1977), 41–8.

72. H.C.G. Matthew, R.I. McKibbin and J.A. Kay, 'The franchise factor in the rise of the Labour Party', *English Historical Review*, 91 (1976), 723–30; R.I. McKibbin, 'Why was there no Marxism in Great Britain?', *English Historical Review*, 99 (1984), 197–31; P. Thane, 'The working class and state "welfare" in Britain, 1880-1914', *Historical Journal* 27 (1984), 877–900; A.E.P. Duffy, 'New unionism in Britain, 1889–90: a reappraisal', *Economic History Review*, 2nd ser., xiv (1961–2), 306–19; H.C.G. Matthew, 'Disraeli, Gladstone and the politics of mid-Victorian budgets', *Historical Journal*, 22

(1979), 615–43; E.P. Hennock, *British Social Reform and German Precedents: The Case of Social Insurance, 1880–1914* (Oxford, 1987), 109; N. Stone, *Europe Transformed, 1878–1919* (Glasgow, 1983), 168.

73. P. Johnson, *Saving and Spending: The Working-Class Economy in Britain, 1870–1939* (Oxford, 1985), 116–24. The Liberals, by extending the status of 'approved society' in the insurance schemes to commercial insurance companies in fact undermined the friendly societies so that the welfare system became *less* self-governing than in Germany: Hennock, *British Social Reform*, 193–6.

74. Daunton, below, 259.

75. C.N. Glaab and A.T. Brown, *A History of Urban America* (2nd ed., New York, 1976); E.E. Wood, *The Housing of the Unskilled Wage Earner: America's Next Problem* (New York, 1919), 268; J.T. Patterson, *America's Struggle Against Poverty, 1900–80* (Cambridge, Mass., 1981), 33; Daunton, below, 265; M.E. Falkus, 'The development of municipal trading in the nineteenth century', *Business History* 19 (1977).

2 Paris

Ann-Louise Shapiro

Mid-nineteenth century Paris was in many ways still a medieval city, striking for its filth, stench and congestion. Narrow, winding streets turned to dust or mud depending upon the weather; wastes flowed above ground in gutter streams; epidemic disease was chronic, spread by intense crowding and a contaminated water supply. Swelled by unprecedented in-migration, the population of Paris doubled between 1801 and 1851 within an essentially static and necessarily overstrained physical cadre. Not surprisingly, as Louis Chevalier has shown, contemporaries viewed the Paris of 1850 as 'suddenly darker and unhealthier, crushed by its mass, stifled by its own respiration, transpiration and excreta'.[1] And, perhaps most important, the evident physical deterioration of the urban environment seemed to anxious observers but the surface reflection of a profound and ultimately more disturbing shift in the character of the city, as the working classes came, by mid-century, to outnumber the middle and upper classes by a ratio of three to one. Contemporary accounts referred to 'unknown populations', 'urban nomads', 'veritable cave-dwellers who awaken as if by enchantment and cover our squares and our cross-roads'.[2] For the more comfortable classes, it seemed that the city had been invaded by an alien breed who had penetrated and, even more, contaminated public spaces.

Investigations of the urban working classes in the 1840s underlined in lurid detail the apparent close connection between physical and moral degradation. Frégier's well-known study, *Des classes dangereuses de la population dans les grandes villes et des moyens de les rendre meilleures*, identifies his subject, for example, as 'the vicious and poor classes who swarm in the city of Paris'.[3] In a similar vein, Buret wrote in *De la misère des classes laborieuses en Angleterre et en France* that 'in the very heart of the busiest centres of industry and trade, you see thousands of human beings reduced to a state of barbarism by vice and destitution . . . The governments are rightly apprehensive. They fear lest formidable dangers may some day burst forth from amid these degraded and corrupted people'.[4] In social and political terms, commentators perceived the urban milieu as pathological, producing a population with withered bodies and corrupted *moeurs*—the human debris of a deteriorating environment. But such vivid apocalyptic images gained a hold on popular perceptions specifically because immediate events moved them from the realm of metaphor into the world of lived experience. The nearly simultaneous outbreaks of revolution in 1848 and cholera in 1849 endowed these fears with a specific content that linked disorder and disease in contemporary minds and provided the framework for a half-century of urban reform activities. Within this context, urban workers who emerged daily from their infested hovels seemed to pose a menace that was, at once, biological, moral and political, placing the whole of society at risk. Hence, for disparate groups of reformers, the improvement of working-class housing became the linchpin in a campaign to disinfect and pacify the working classes so as to preserve the social and political order.

With the advent of the Second Empire in 1850, Napoleon and his Prefect of the Seine, Baron Georges Haussmann, determined to transform Paris, particularly the centre of the city, into an imposing capital befitting their imperial pretensions. Applying the surgical method on an unprecedented scale as treatment for a sick city, they demolished slums and drove broad boulevards though congested areas of the centre, opening up corridors of light and air. With a three-phase plan of street development, they improved circulation and simplified access both to the central markets and to the railway terminals on the outskirts. They added a major system of collector sewers and an enlarged supply of spring water, ·enhancing public health and reducing the incidence of cholera. They embellished the city with public parks, landscaped squares, and grandiose monuments. Invoking the accepted remedy of the times, Napoleon and Haussmann used public works to eliminate some of the most highly visible afflictions of the urban environment.

But the redevelopment of Paris was neither the panacea for urban ills that its promòters promised nor the remedy for inadequate working-class housing. Although some of the worst slums were cleared away, broad boulevards and open spaces created an illusion that belied the reality. The demolition of groups of houses, in fact, produced increasing crowding in remaining buildings as residential areas were converted into streets and open squares. In order to benefit from the heightened demand for the remaining inexpensive apartments, proprietors typically broke up old apartments into smaller units, and further, because there were no controls on the height of interior floors, the size of individual rooms, or the quality of construction materials, tried to squeeze an additional floor into the allotted building space for new constructions, creating apartments in which an adult could not stand upright and interior rooms without access to light or air.[5] The added elegance of the centre produced, then, a smaller stock of inexpensive rentals, a new genre of partitioned space for the poor, and an accelerated geographic polarisation of the classes as the poor migrated to the northern, southern and eastern periphery and the middle and upper classes moved westward. The increased property values generated by the government's public works projects had definitively undermined the pattern of mixed housing (Figure 2.1) in the city centre which had characterised the first half of the century in which bourgeois tenants occupied the larger lower-

Figure 2.1 Cross-section of an apartment house, showing the mixture of social classes in the first half of the nineteenth century, from M. Gaillard, *Paris au XIXe siècle* (Paris, 1981).

floor apartments while working-class tenants lodged in the progressively smaller apartments of the storeys above. This coexistence of poverty and comfort did not survive the urban renewal of the Second Empire which rendered both entire *quartiers* and individual buildings more homogeneous than they had previously been (Figure 2.2). As workers continued to turn over the upper floors of buildings in the centre to the

Figure 2.2 Typical Parisian apartment house erected during the Second Empire, from *The Builder* XVI (1858).

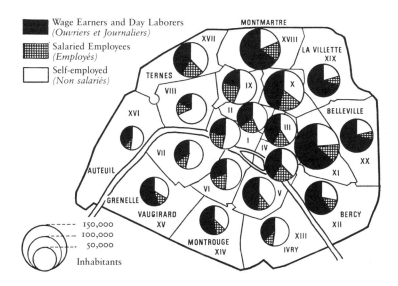

Figure 2.3 The social composition of the population, 1872, from F. Braudel and E. Laborousse (eds), *Histoire économique et sociale de la France, Volume 3, L'avènement de l'ère industrielle, 1789–1880* (Paris, 1976), 799.

domestics of the bourgeois tenants below, and to move to the make-shift constructions of the periphery, an anxious critic noted that 'the transformation of Paris has pushed back the labouring population from the centre to the extremities. They have made the capital into two cities, one rich, one poor; the latter surrounds the other. The poor are like an immense rope hemming in the comfortable classes'.[6] (Figure 2.3)

The rapid increase in the value of land promoted a new conception of the use of urban space. Courtyards, originally intended for ventilation, came to be seen as too valuable to be left unproductive. Proprietors consequently covered over courtyards at the first floor level, converting them into commercial space and, in effect, transforming them into virtual airshafts on a four-square-metre base, repositories for putrefying organic matter strewn from above. As the facades on the new boulevards improved, interior areas were gradually closing in upon themselves, becoming darker, more congested, and increasingly foul. Even as the city centre was rendered more elegant, and even as broad boulevards created a more expansive ambiance, the areas where the working class could afford to live became denser and the apartments smaller as narrow, neglected streets off the main arteries persisted, described by one observer as 'hell at the gates of paradise'. By the end of the century, a uniquely Parisian pattern had evolved in which as much as one third of the population constituted single-person households, 71 per cent of whom lived in one room.[7]

Cheaper prices and lower densities drew workers to the outlying districts which gradually came to reproduce the grim conditions of the

Figure 2.4 Shanties on Boulevard Masséna, arrondissement XIII, in 1910, from the collection of the Bibliothèque de la ville de Paris.

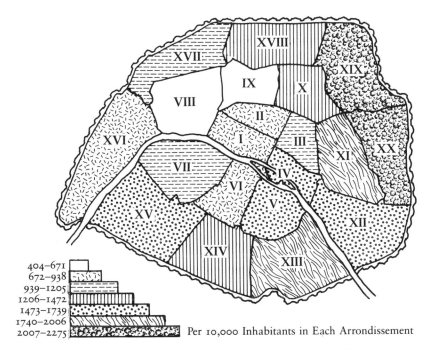

404–671	
672–938	
939–1205	
1206–1472	
1473–1739	
1740–2006	
2007–2275	Per 10,000 Inhabitants in Each Arrondissement

Figure 2.5 Number of persons living in overcrowded conditions (more than two per room) in 1891, from J. Bertillon, *Essai de statistique comparée du surpeuplement des habitations à Paris et dans les grandes capitales européennes* (Paris, 1894), 8.

centre. Many of the new constructions in the peripheral *arrondissements* were plaster and tarpaper shanties hastily erected in the open fields and hence immune from even the minimal regulations which set standards for housing aligning public thoroughfares. The hygienist Du Mesnil described the *terrains vagues* on which clusters of irregular housing were erected as veritable sewers in the open air (Figure 2.4). Private roadways became foul swamps in which decaying matter festered in ruts and potholes, while privies without covers overflowed into courtyards and open gutters intersected public walkways. 'One can say', claimed Du Mesnil, 'that here one breathes death'.[8] Napoleon's incorporation of the suburban communes into the city proper in 1860 had added a working-class population of approximately 350,000 and a territory largely deprived of urban services.[9] These areas were not, moreover, recipients of official bounties. Haussmann's three-phase network of street development did not include the suburban communes, which, once annexed, remained without adequate water, pavement, gas, and sanitation services.[10] At bottom, Haussmann saw himself as the mayor of a modernised capital and scarcely noticed the pattern of haphazard and incomplete development in the outlying areas of New Paris. The growing congestion and deprivation of the periphery (Figure 2.5) seemed to highlight an official blindspot, causing one observer to comment that 'in cleaning up the poor quarters of Old Paris, misery was not suppressed . . . It was, rather, placed out of our sight and unhappily, perhaps, also beyond our preoccupations'.[11]

Official policies and changes in the construction industry combined to exacerbate the shortage of workers' housing. Haussmann's extensive demolitions for street improvements and the increased value of new constructions in the centre produced an upheaval in patterns of ownership as well as in rent scales. As the population of Paris increased by 261,549 between 1851 and 1856, the number of houses actually decreased (from 30,770 to 30,175).[12] Although the number of low rentals increased, it lagged behind the number of workers, a population perennially inflated by those tens of thousands drawn to the city by the promise of work in the building trades.[13] Moreover, before 1860, speculators had tended to invest in foreign railways, leaving the property market to individual entrepreneurs who were often connected with the building industry and bought and developed land essentially for their own use. This pattern reversed itself after Haussmann's first wave of transformations when building societies (that is, private, commercial construction companies) and large-scale investors increasingly gained a greater share of the market and bought up major parcels of land on which to erect expensive housing. As Adeline Daumard has shown, houses in central Paris during the Second Empire became progressively 'more important, more luxurious, and more homogeneous' than in the past.[14] By the end of the Second Empire, the mixed social composition of Parisian proprietors had been replaced by a more homogeneous class of wealthy *rentiers*. Ownership of land in the interior of the city became virtually inaccessible to small merchants, artisans, and members of the lower middle class. The importance of the building society and the large-scale entrepreneur in the city centre was sustained by the fact that the municipality offered communal land for sale in large blocks, while the short-term leases and the chronic demand for inexpensive rentals which characterised the property market in the outlying districts meant that shoddy constructions would remain profitable for the small-scale individual speculator.

Throughout the Second Empire, Napoleon III and Haussmann remained, nevertheless, at least formally committed to the improvement of working-class housing, which they understood as the best means to normalise the working classes—to render them 'inaccessible to the seduction of politics'.[15] Hence, in 1852, the government earmarked Fr. 10 million for ameliorating conditions of working-class life. Of this sum, Fr. 2 million were used for the construction of seventeen houses for workers on the boulevard Mazas,[16] and Fr. 2,130,000 (representing one-third of the anticipated cost) were offered as incentives to builders who would construct working-class housing under government supervision.[17] In spite of the prospect of low rents, tenants appeared only reluctantly. Workers dubbed the Cité Napoléon, a complex built with public subsidies, 'la baraque', the shanty,[18] and rejected uniformly and emphatically the concept of dwellings set aside exclusively for workers—seeing these so-called 'barracks' as a type of poorhouse for small households. They complained that philanthropists and building societies were beginning to relegate the labouring population to special quarters as in the Middle Ages, and urged instead that the government tax vacant apartments to force down the rental price and make available a greater number of lodgings in the mixed housing of the city centre.[19] In testimony to this stalemate, one disgruntled philanthropist complained that the Parisian worker, 'exhibiting a hateful defiance toward the propertied classes, flaunts the defects of his habitation' and refuses to install himself in newer, healthier quarters.[20]

But entrepreneurs and many public officials shared, albeit for different reasons, the reservations of the workers about large communal dwellings, imagining the potential dangers of bringing together so many of the lower orders without appropriate supervision by men of property. According to bourgeois analysis, mixed housing served as 'a permanent school in the benefits of sober economic life',[21] providing a 'bridle' on the worker's conduct and 'positive contacts' between worker and bourgeois that generated 'a sort of human respect which imprinted a character of regularity on the habits of working-class families'.[22] Even Villermé, whose descriptions of the conditions of working-class life had stimulated housing reform, recoiled before the prospect of large communal lodgings. He feared that separating workers from society in general would reinforce their jealousies toward the rich, to whom they already attributed 'so many imaginary wrongs', and worried that those workers whose 'natural vice' led them to perpetual misery could not always be excluded from large common buildings.[23] In his view, common lodgings excited 'socialist follies' and reinforced immoral predispositions.

To defuse these dangers, the owners of the workers' housing complexes that did exist tended to exercise firm control over admissions and behaviour. Frégier, head of a bureau at the Prefecture of Police, suggested that admission be limited to married workers holding a certificate of morality signed by their employers and the mayor of the commune, a recommendation echoed, not surprisingly, by Villermé.[24] Housing such as the Cité Napoléon might have as many as a hundred regulations, while in those units built with government subsidies, the resident concierge was typically supplemented by a manager who made daily inspections.[25] This offence to honour and autonomy was, perhaps, even less palatable than the implied ghettoisation and, by the 1880s, for example, the Cité Napoléon housed only bourgeois tenants.[26]

In the end, then, the official interventions of the Second Empire proved ineffective as both workers and the propertied classes rejected the first experiments in high-rise workers' housing. Napoleon and Haussmann had seized upon public subsidies as a strategy that could accommodate the tension between their fundamental commitment to laissez-faire economics and private enterprise on the one hand, and a search for popular support that required conspicuous public philanthropic action on the other. At

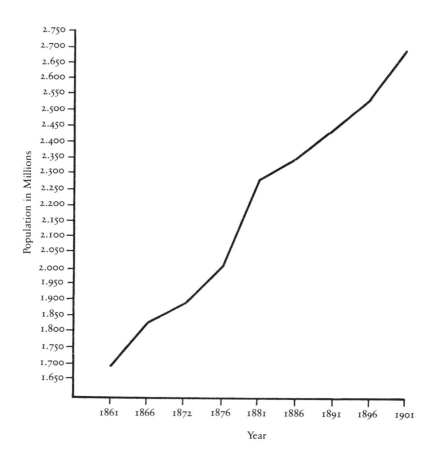

Figure 2.6 Population of Paris, 1861–1901, from *Annuaire statistique de la ville de Paris et du département de la Seine.*

bottom, they remained committed to street improvements as the primary instrument of urban policy, hoping to sidestep the problem of working-class housing by stimulating a building boom that would cause workers to 'level-up' into the housing of their social superiors. While the absence of a genuine reform strategy remained somewhat obscured by the aggrandisement of the capital during the Second Empire, housing problems became, nevertheless, more acute as the number of inexpensive lodgings in the centre declined and the shanty-towns of the periphery mushroomed.

Reversing the demographic patterns of the first half of the century which had produced high densities in the commercial centre, the new pattern of extraordinary growth in the peripheral *arrondissements* continued into the Third Republic. Between 1861 and 1896, the population of the city as a whole increased by 840,693, or 49.6 per cent (Figure

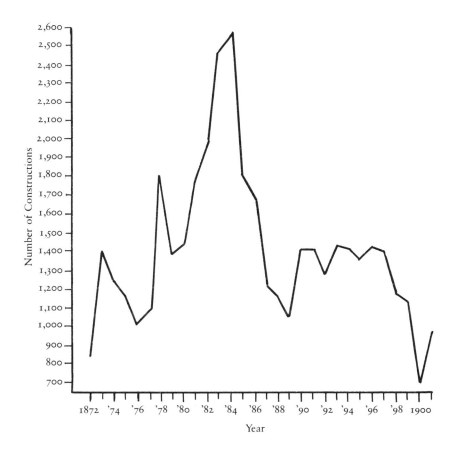

Figure 2.7 Number of constructions in Paris, 1872–1900, from *Le livre foncier de Paris, pt. 1, Valeur locative des propriétés bâties en 1900.*

2.6). But while the population of the central *arrondissements* grew by only 7.1 per cent during this period, the outer districts experienced a rate of growth of 103 per cent.[27] In the largest growth spurt of the period, between 1876 and 1881, which added 280,000 inhabitants to the city, 78 per cent (218,009) settled in the ten outer *arrondissements*. This surge of growth did not, however, stimulate a construction boom to serve the needs of the working-class population (Figure 2.7). Analysts of construction patterns generally conclude that standard theories ascribing building booms to low interest rates and low building costs cannot sufficiently account for building cycles in Paris in the final third of the nineteenth century.[28] Gérard Jacquemet argues, rather, that construction was triggered by the needs of the most solvent sector of the population.[29] Increasingly, entrepreneurs and building societies essentially abandoned the construction of modest and middle-range dwellings in favour of more costly properties. This preference, evident during the boom years of 1878–84, became even more pronounced during the periods of slump and stabilisation in the 1890s.

In Belleville (*arrondissement* XX), for example, in 1888, older lodgings on the rue des Mûriers with modest rents of about Fr. 200 for one or two rooms were occupied by working-class tenants: a painter in the building industry, a seamstress, a laundress, two shoemakers, two day labourers, two workers (undifferentiated), and a single salaried employee. There were few merchants or artisans except for those small businesses which serviced the district—i.e., wine-sellers, rag-pickers, secondhand dealers. By contrast, the new constructions erected in the 1890s along the avenue Gambetta and near the Parc des Buttes-Chaumont attracted tenants, new to the district, who were a socio-economic step above their neighbours. Inhabitants of a new building on the avenue Gambetta included ten salaried employees, three merchants, three proprietors, two students, and only six workers.[30] Thus, although most new building in the final decades of the century did occur in the outer *arrondissements* because, of course, it was there that large tracts of undeveloped land were available, the majority of these constructions tended to be targeted for the better-off segments of the population and to be located most often in the wealthier *quartiers*.[31]

Rising construction costs and the high price of land in the city seemed to preclude investment in workers' housing. In the first place, the financial burden of increasingly stringent construction regulations for buildings aligning public roadways had to be borne by the individual proprietor. The prominent architect Emile Cacheux wrote in 1885 that:

the City of Paris distinguishes itself by its lack of encouragement to builders of working-class housing. . . Thus, in the most deserted quarters, they build grand boulevards; the streets are laid without care for the embankments and excavations required by the bordering properties . . . The City only accepts streets of 12 metres width, paved, with sidewalks, gas-lighted, and provided with sewers. Such a street costs, at a minimum, 300 francs per linear metre, and it is the landowners of contiguous property who shoulder the initial outlays. As a consequence, it is impossible to build lodgings for a family along these streets at a price which workers can afford.[32]

In addition, the average price per square metre of undeveloped land doubled in the 1860s, with substantially higher rates of increase in selected areas,[33] while the 1890s witnessed a further surge of prices.[34] The experience of the Paris Municipal Council is instructive. In an effort to stimulate the construction of low-cost housing in 1890, the Council entertained a proposal that mixed housing (with both middle- and working-class tenants) be constructed with funds and land reserved from public expropriations. The Council insisted on the necessity of building mixed rather than exclusively working-class lodgings because the expropriated parcel in the fifth *arrondissement* was valuable land, worth Fr. 300–400 per metre. After eight months of discussion, the Council concluded that the plan was not feasible, as the actual value of the land had risen, during the preceding six months, to Fr. 600 per metre, and the project was quickly abandoned.[35]

Given the large initial expenditures and high rates of interest, both individual entrepreneurs and building societies would not build working-class housing without the prospect of substantial profits, and these were not forthcoming. In 1852, contractors who had received subsidies from Napoleon III to build low-rent housing realised gains of less than 5 per cent, while later efforts produced even more discouraging results. In the 1880s, the *Société coopérative immobilière des ouvriers de Paris* earned only 3 per cent on its investments and ultimately went out of business.[36] The experience of the *Société philanthropique de Paris* was similar. With the aid of a gift of Fr. 750,000 donated by Michel Heine in 1888, it constructed four buildings containing apartments of two or three rooms, provided with a privy, gas, and direct plumbing, commanding rentals of Fr. 150–300. By 1897–98, the revenue from these buildings yielded a rate of return of a mere 2.21 per cent.[37] Comparable public efforts were equally frustrating. In 1884, the Municipal Council sought to encourage private contractors by creating a model of working-class housing that others could follow. It selected four different building sites in *arrondissements* XII, XIII, XIV, and XV and chose four different architects to submit proposals. In the end, these proposals projected an average estimated rate of return of 3.75 per cent, below the legal rate of interest, and hardly likely to provide the incentive that the Council had desired. In assessing such attempts, one reformer concluded that 'those who undertake this work, which is certainly meritorious and worthy of encouragement, must recognise that if they wish to come to the aid not only of the elite workers, but of the poor, they must resign themselves to expect an extremely small remuneration from their money'.[38] Not surprisingly, the appeal to social conscience had a narrow audience.

Speculators found it both more profitable and less troublesome to build for the middle classes—a predilection made practical by the emergence of a new social stratum in the final decades of the century which created a reliable constituency for middle-range housing.[39] Employees in the tertiary sector of the economy (e.g. commerce, banking, transportation, and service) enjoyed the prospect of relatively stable employment and opportunities for advancement—'les nouveaux locataires solvables'— even when starting salaries were inferior to those of some working-class trades. Proprietors need not depend upon the financially insecure and morally objectionable elements of the working class to fill their rental units. The economist and publicist Paul Leroy-Beaulieu summarised the arguments of the entrepreneur:

Capitalists love their tranquility and their leisure; that is not a crime. If they have 500,000 francs to spend, they would prefer to build a house which will have four or five tenants bound by leases of six, nine, or twelve years, than to construct three or four buildings inhabited by 30, 40, or 50 households with tenancies of three months. In the first situation, they find peace of mind; it is a more agreeable proposition and, if we can use the word, more appropriate. They are not disturbed every instant by demands; they are dealing only with men of their own world; it is rarely necessary for them to evict their tenants or confiscate their property. In houses divided into small lodgings, in contrast, what difficulty! What care and what effort to manage in the midst of these tenants who do not always pay on time! What disagreements if they do not pay at all! A sensitive man does not like to throw his tenants into the street. However, if he is unwilling to do it at one time or another, he engages not in investments, but in ruinous philanthropy. If he does do it, besides the scruples of his conscience, he runs the risk of being spoken of poorly, of being held up to public obloquy as an inhuman proprietor.[40]

Without financial incentives, entrepreneurs had little reason to bear the risks of constructing low-cost housing; profits were not great enough to make such enterprises attractive in and of themselves and could not compensate for the discouraging prospects of unpaid rents, periodic evictions, and unanticipated legal expenses.

Ironically, even as the shortage of working-class housing intensified in the 1880s, the construction industry produced a surplus of luxury dwellings, so that the numbers of vacancies in the city increased as the housing stock available to workers declined.[41] The inevitable consequence of this sustained pressure on supply was a pattern of spiralling rents. As early as 1855, an investigation conducted by the Chamber of Commerce found that wages had not, in general, risen enough to offset the rise in the cost of living that had been inflated especially by rent increases of from 25 to 60 per cent. An anonymous pamphlet of the same period compared the worker's fate to that of Jeremiah in Babylon, who found palaces but no shelter. The modern Jeremiah, 'Haussmannised', cried out that although the city glittered, its people could not afford to live there:

Babylon, Babylon! You are a superb city and your enemies themselves proclaim you queen of the world and fall in admiration before your magnificence, although your own sons rest, exhausted, at the borders of your crossroads asking where they shall sleep the night.[42]

Rents increased dramatically again in the period 1880–89, provoking an investigation by the Prefecture of Police which documented typical increases of 25 to 50 per cent in working-class districts. Discussions of low-cost housing in the 1880s confirm almost without exception that most workers could not pay more that Fr. 300–350 annual rent for an apartment which typically included one or two rooms and a kitchen. In 1887, for example, the economist Arthur Raffalovich estimated that only the elite (or 10 per cent) of the Parisian working class (e.g. jewellers, stone-setters of precious gems, engravers, and mapmakers) who earned Fr. 20–30 per day and a small fraction of skilled labourers (joiners, carpenters, stoneworkers) who earned Fr. 8 per day could afford rents above Fr. 300.[43] But during this decade, while the total number of lodgings increased by 104,836, the number of rentals below Fr. 300 declined by 69,093.[44]

Rent increases in relation to the value of the building were actually greater in working-class districts than in better-off quarters, as proprietors sought to compensate themselves in advance for problems of nonpayment and inconveniences resulting from the alleged irresponsibility of working-

Figure 2.8 'How can this be, Madam? . . . I take the liberty of absenting myself from my building for a few months and this is the state I find you in when I return . . . I'm giving you twenty-four hours notice . . . I'm not even sure I don't have the right to ask your husband to pay damages!', from Honoré Daumier, *Locataires et propietaires*

class tenants. The prototypical avaricious landlord, Monsieur Vautour (the Vulture), became the focus of abuse in pamphlets, caricatures and ballads. With his finger ever on the popular pulse, Daumier captured the new antagonisms of the city in a series of satirical lithographs published in 1854 entitled 'Tenants and Landlords'. In one parody of Haussmann's urban renewal, for example, a proprietor witnessing a demolition exclaims: 'Good! They are tearing down another house. I will raise each of my tenants 200 francs!' A play from the same period displayed a sign offering lodging on the river, between Pont Neuf and Pont des Arts, 'in the Chinese fashion', while the refrain of the popular song urged that 'if you want to be happy, hang your landlord'.[45] Critics described proprietors as 'greedy, pityless, cynical, insolent, and vain', idle parasites reaping huge profits without investing any productive labour, at the expense, always, of the working population.[46]

The refusal of landlords to rent to families with children increasingly became a focus of attack. In his investigations of slum conditions in *arrondissements* XIX and XX, Du Mesnil drew public attention to the plight of families who continued to live in miserable hovels because proprietors of better dwellings had refused to take children.[47] Other accounts reported that, even after the rent had already been paid, expulsions were ordered owing to the birth of a child (see Figure 2.8), causing Georges Piart to write in 1882 of the 'interminable martyrdom of tenants' created by practices which constituted, in effect, 'an encouragement to infanticide'.[48] Summarising popular anger, Piart recounted the following cautionary tale that had appeared in *La Lanterne*:

Proprietor: 'Are you a father, sir?'
Tenant: 'Not yet.'
Proprietor: 'Do you intend to become one?'
[Here the tenant smiles.]
Proprietor: 'Because if I see a child in my building, I will throw it out of the window.'
At these words, instantly overcome by a legitimate exasperation, and finding himself precisely in front of an open window, the tenant seized the proprietor by the leg and threw him into the void!

The story concludes with an ominous warning from Piart: 'Remember this, gentlemen and proprietors—the tenant was acquitted by the jury!'.[49]

In fact, proprietors' rights were so extensive that ordinary practice, even without abuses, generated antagonism. The right of the landlord to his tenants' property superseded that of all other creditors. Consequently, to protect against nonpayment of rents, the standard lease required as its first stipulation that the tenant furnish his lodgings with possessions of sufficient value to cover the amount of the rent.[50] The day after the landlord demanded payment of the rent, he was entitled to confiscate the tenants' furnishings without a judicial order. At this point, the judge assigned a value to the confiscated property, and if the tenant did not pay within the succeeding eight days, his effects were sold. The rights of the landlord-creditor extended further to those possessions which the tenant might attempt to hide with a friend, so that if the landlord could discover the deception within fifteen days, he was permitted to attach possessions held by a third party.[51] Fuelling workers' grievances, *La Bataille* reported an incident between a prospective tenant and the proprietor of a building on the rue des Martyrs in which the landlord refused to accept the tenant because his furnishings were not sufficiently valuable, even though the tenant had offered full payment in advance.[52] Similarly, Piart complained that a proprietor of a dormitory for women factory workers refused to allow beds because the bed was not legally subject to confiscation. Instead, the proprietor insisted upon a divan on which a mattress could be laid so as to afford the landlord the necessary insurance against nonpayment which was his due.[53]

Landlords typically demanded the payment of two terms rent in advance (6 months), seeking to recoup in this way losses on legal fees incurred through earlier evictions. Denis Poulot's chronicle of Parisian working-class life described rent day as 'the sword of Damocles' for which the worker prostitutes himself, the married woman deceives her husband, the mother dishonours herself, and the husband sinks into vice.[54] The eighth of January, April, July, and October witnessed the familiar spectacle of evicted workers, possessions in tow, searching for new lodgings. It is clear, however, that workers sought to redress the balance of power in their own way. According to one observer, tenants did not miss the opportunity to profit from the landlord's difficulties. A typical anecdote of the period described, for example, the way in which a landlord could be held to ransom by his defaulting tenants. The tenant states: 'You spend 60 francs for our expulsion; give us 10, you save 50, and we will depart voluntarily'.[55] But in the end, increasing pressure on a limited supply of inexpensive housing gave landlords a decisive upper hand. Because proprietors paid no taxes on unoccupied lodgings, property remained unrented at no expense to the owners who often held lodgings vacant until they could command higher rents, further exacerbating the mounting belligerency between landlords and tenants. Writing in *L'Economiste français* in 1879, Arthur Mangin deplored the increased arrogance of the landlord:

. . . formerly, the worker often had difficulty in paying his term; today he has difficulty merely in finding lodging; especially because proprietors are no longer content to require an enormous price for the least hovel; beyond that, they impose on their tenants the most intolerable regulations: it is forbidden to have a dog, a cat, birds; it is forbidden even to have children; it is forbidden to bring up water after a certain hour; it is forbidden to hang laundry from the window; in certain houses, the tenant is admitted only on the condition that he not remain home during the day and receive no one. Is this to be at home?—to have to submit to such tyranny under the penalty of expulsion?[56]

Tenants felt equally victimised by the power exercised by the concierges. In most cases, the owner of the building depended upon the concierge to act for him in rentals and evictions. It was accepted practice for the concierge to receive a gratuity (*denier à Dieu*), usually 5 or 6 francs, from the prospective tenant as a sign that an agreement had been reached (Figure 2.9). Tenants complained, however, that the concierge regularly broke the rental agreement when offered a larger sum, so that, in effect, the concierge was in a position to auction lodgings to the highest bidder. They noted that it was in the interest of the concierge to maintain a steady turnover of clientele in order to regularise the flow of gratuities, hence the problem of random, unprovoked evictions.[57]

To cope with their disadvantaged position, workers began to form associations that provided assistance to households escaping at night with their furnishings (*déménagements à la cloche de bois*). Although this activity could hardly provide a general strategy for countering landlords' rights and practices, rumours of organised banditry circulated widely and alarmed municipal officials in the volatile early years of the Third Republic. In March 1881, the municipal chief of police reported that 'revolutionary committees' were organising a new kind of strike by tenants against their landlords. In a dramatic representation of their plight, tenants were to force their own expulsion by refusing to pay

Figure 2.9 'Twenty sous as a gratuity — that skinflint! . . . They'll see how fast I'll give them notice to go to blazes!', from Honoré Daumier, *Locataires et propriétaires*.

rents, whereupon they would descend into the streets with their children and possessions in sufficient numbers to embarrass the government.[58] According to *Le Temps*, on 15 July, 1883, 'the proposition, so often formulated in revolutionary meetings, of not paying landlords in order to resolve the crisis in rents has just received its first application. A proprietor named C . . . was not able to prevent the removal of one of his tenants, named Couchot, who, aided by his comrades, carried away his furniture without paying his rent to the cry of "Long Live the Commune"'.[59] The same story was repeated on 20 July in *Le Figaro* and in *La Patrie* which added that the eight people who participated in the evacuation were part of a roving band operating against landlords.

The fears of public officials were heightened by the presence of returned Communards, granted amnesty in 1879, in the score of newly formed socialist organisations that had begun to address the housing problem in terms of the specific conditions of the early 1880s. The prospect of increased traffic and windfall gains presented by the International Exposition of 1878 in Paris had set in motion a precipitous rise in rents. Until the beginning of 1879, workers apparently endured the new charges with the expectation that rents would shortly return to more normal levels, but when this failed to happen, worker discontent became more vocal and better organised. In the summer of 1882, Paul Lafargue, Marx's son-in-law and an important activist in Paris, urged the formation of a league of tenants to orchestrate resistance.[60] The Marxist leader Jules Guesde claimed that he had collected 4,000 signatures on a petition demanding rent reductions and a tax on rents—a petition that would inevitably be rejected by the government, but which would provide 'a good pretext for revolutionary agitation', one that would expose public authorities as mere agents of the property-owning classes and serve as a 'veritable factory to forge socialists and revolutionaries'.[61] One year later, a Congress on the Question of Rents began to meet throughout the city, representing a broad array of socialist and working-class groups.[62] Because these groups could neither coordinate their activities nor sustain interest among a core of committed activists, they were ultimately less threatening to the political order than they appeared. But they did generate a set of proposals designed to ease the pressure on low-cost housing that were considerably more radical than those offered by middle-class reformers. Their demands included: the allocation of funds for the construction of municipal housing; a progressive tax on rents; an end to the private sale of communal lands; limits on the profits of housing speculators; and even the immediate confiscation of all property within the city for public use.

It was, then, the more fragile political equilibrium of the early years of the Third Republic that endowed housing issues, once again, with a serious claim on public attention. The coincidence of socialist agitation and industrial recession in the early 1880s triggered efforts by both the national and municipal governments to undertake a careful review of reform strategies so as to undercut the radical schemes circulating among workers. In fact, the fragmentation of the socialist challenge defused its impact, but the barrage of propaganda disseminated in public meetings and the persistent threat of strikes and demonstrations combined to suggest that the socialist menace was indeed quite real. This was particularly true because 1883 and 1884 were years of economic slowdown characterised by extensive unemployment and an acute recession in the building industry. Hence, although housing issues had disappeared from the public agenda in the decade following the Commune, they re-emerged with compelling urgency in the 1880s; by 1884, the Paris Municipal Council was meeting regularly to consider schemes to improve housing conditions.

The growing number of individual proposals submitted to the Council prompted a summary report by a special commission that was presented in February 1883.[63] While refusing to endorse any particular project, the report did identify the construction of mixed housing, with bourgeois occupants on the lower floors and working-class tenants above, as the ultimate objective of municipal housing policies. This commitment to an older pattern of usage which had begun to disappear during the Second Empire suggested a means to lessen class antagonism and to promote social solidarity. To further this end, official discussions gradually adopted the phrase 'low-rent housing' rather than 'working-class housing' in symbolic denial of class divisions. Workers and bourgeois were to be reconciled through the experience of structured proximity. But this policy direction was pragmatic as well as socially reassuring. The report explicitly acknowledged that the pattern of single-family units in the suburbs which had become characteristic of London could not be transferred to Paris where the working day was longer, the continuity of employment uncertain, and the transportation system deficient. For decades, it had been a well-understood axiom that the Parisian worker rented his district even more than his individual lodging; this wisdom could not be ignored.

The report remained vague as to how to generate an enlarged stock of mixed housing, but it rejected, unequivocally, direct construction by the city. It argued that municipal constructions would be more costly, that they would involve the city, in its capacity as an ordinary landlord, in a morass of administrative difficulties, and that they would inevitably encourage the stream of migrants who pressed on the available housing supply. At the most fundamental level, councillors insisted that they could not justify such a special use of public funds. In a statement urging municipal restraint, for example, one administrator noted that the use of 'the money of all' to provide for those who had nothing constituted charity and lay outside of legitimate municipal functions.[64] He concluded that any scheme to improve housing conditions had to ensure that the city's finances would not be overcommitted and that both the 'independence of the worker and the freedom of the proprietor' would be respected. It is evident that the Council was more comfortable offering guidelines than defining precise solutions.

The activity of the Municipal Council coincided with a parallel investigation undertaken by a blue-ribbon administrative commission, appointed by the Prefect of the Seine in January 1883, with a mandate to study hygiene problems, to survey municipal lands and assess their suitability for low-cost constructions, and to explore financial schemes to promote new building. These discussions were brought into sharp focus by a government proposition to make money available to contractors through the cooperation of the government, the city administration, and the *Crédit foncier*, a private bank controlled by a small group of oligarchs with official connections who did not normally lend money to entrepreneurs of undeveloped land. This proposal, linking national and municipal housing reform efforts, quickly overshadowed all other projects, especially because it seemed to reaffirm the objectives outlined by the Paris Council. In its most important provisions, it stipulated that the *Crédit foncier* lend 65 per cent of the funds for the construction of buildings in which at least half of the inhabitable space was reserved for lodgings of Fr. 150–300 annual rent. The total loan of Fr. 50 million was to be guaranteed by the city and was reimbursable over a seventy-five-year period. Under its terms, the government agreed to exempt the new constructions from transfer fees, window and door taxes, and property taxes, while the city would grant exemptions from roadway assessments and duties on construction materials coming into the city. By easing credit and the burdens of taxation, this financial package sought to tilt the balance back in favour of mixed housing, appealing to entrepreneurs who had discovered that it was easier and more profitable to build for the better-off classes.

Supporters argued that this proposal promised relief on a number of fronts—in one step stimulating the building industry, curbing unemployment, easing class tensions, and lowering rents—and, most importantly, represented the only viable compromise between allowing full responsibility for the housing shortage to rest either with the municipality or with private enterprise. But critics remained unconvinced. To economic liberals, the government's project propelled the city too precipitously away from its long-standing policies of non-intervention—a departure that would allegedly launch the administration on an irreversible path to state socialism. From this perspective, tampering with taxes challenged the inviolability of the free market, while the introduction of 'artificial' exemptions pitted new proprietors against old, generating 'iniquitous and disloyal competition' which constituted, in effect, discriminatory favouritism. State and municipal participation was understood here as inevitably expropriatory and naively utopian. According to one commentator, a policy of tax incentives produced 'the first blow to property, which was but the prelude to an uninterrupted succession of attacks'. He warned:

Former confidence in real property will be sharply restricted, capital will become wary and will avoid investing in construction. The public will cease building, . . . private industry will be paralysed, and, on the day when the state's subsidies are exhausted, the building industry will be dead in Paris.[65]

This general reluctance to manipulate the market was reinforced by specific fiscal concerns. Critics maintained that, by guaranteeing the proposed loan, the city's finances became too vulnerable, while its administrative responsibilities would be costly and time-consuming. But the greatest resistance arose from an entrenched and well-founded reluctance to implicate the city's budgets, even indirectly, in an obligation to the *Crédit foncier*—a reluctance that was both the inevitable product of the financial irregularities by which Haussmann had funded his schemes, greatly overextending municipal indebtedness,[66] and the manifestation of a broad-based hostility toward large enterprises (including financial societies) that were easing smaller concerns out of the market, which was also a legacy of the Second Empire.[67] These antagonisms generated a surprising consensus among opponents of the Left and the Right. The conservative Levraud argued, for example, that the natural process whereby a glut of luxury buildings turned speculators to more modest enterprises had been interrupted by the unfortunate appearance of the government's project. Instead of activating construction, he claimed, the proposal allegedly had halted all building while entrepreneurs awaited the announced tax exemptions.[68] One of his colleagues reported further that, as discussions ensued, societies were forming to buy up undeveloped land, 'hovering like vultures around these projects'.[69] From the other end of the political spectrum, the socialist Joffrin complained that the proposal had diverted attention from the issue of exorbitant rents, the crux of the housing problem, while setting up a scheme which, far from being 'state socialism', constituted 'state protectionism for the *Crédit foncier*' as well as *l'art de faire des rentiers*—a ploy to benefit speculators, landowners, and financiers.[70] He cited the support of *Le Figaro* as evidence that the proposal derived, at bottom, from a desire to close a good business deal for the bank.[71]

Not surprisingly, then, the Municipal Council rejected the government's proposal; the scheme could not finally muster enough support to counter the varied sources of opposition. The issue of subsidies and special exemptions had provoked a re-examination of the relationship between private industry and public sponsorship, raising the fearful spectre of state socialism and forcing an official retreat. It appears that public officials had, in effect, understood their responsibility for housing in the framework of the crisis in the building industry as much as in terms of the social and health problems produced by overcrowding and high rents. These dual priorities emerge quite explicitly in a report by the Director of Public Works which urged the municipality to act as an economic regulator—to initiate public works projects and to expand sources of credit during slump periods, and to withdraw from the scene when private industry prospered.[72] The end of the building recession seemed to argue for a return to a more passive public role. On the other hand, housing reform required a clarification of the joint jurisdictions and responsibilities of state and municipal officials in Paris. Municipal authorities were anxious to preserve their independence from the national government in housing as well as in the related issues of urban and suburban transportation, and were not sorry to see the complicated joint venture disappear from public agendas. And finally, the proposal had triggered latent but virulent hostilities toward the financial establishment, producing a surprisingly unified opposition among representatives of the working and middle classes, while workers sought, at any rate, more direct and immediate relief from high rents than that offered by the proposal at hand.

As the industrial recession subsided and immigration to Paris returned to more normal levels, the motivation to devise a comprehensive urban housing policy faded as well; the momentum that promoted a search for innovative strategies had been expended and a new lethargy set in.

Municipal councillor Jobbé-Duval spoke for a substantial group of his colleagues in 1883 when he wrote that:

... there are insoluble questions, and this is one of them. In preoccupying yourselves with this issue, you will have succeeded in demonstrating to the working class your concern on its behalf; but this is all that you can do. Now, is this demonstration useful? Any reasonable man will see that we depart from the municipal domain and instead of occupying ourselves with the city's business, we lose time in deluding the working class with hopeless dreams.[73]

In succeeding years, the Council attempted, more modestly, to sponsor the construction of model houses as an incentive to private entrepreneurs, but these projects were abandoned, without exception, due both to administrative inertia and technical snags.[74] In the early 1890s, the municipal administration again rather listlessly entertained the possibility of offering official encouragement: by requiring that portions of land taken in public expropriations be reserved for the construction of low-cost housing; by earmarking for workers half of the constructions on land sold by the city in working-class districts; and even by rehousing those displaced by expropriations in buildings or on land acquired by the city. But none of these half-hearted schemes came to fruition.[75] By this time, the perception of urban housing as an issue for which public authorities could legitimately assume responsibility had slipped away. Much of the political urgency surrounding workers' housing had dissipated with the failed threat of revolutionary socialism. And, by the 1890s, the political complexion of the Municipal Council had begun to shift to the Right as workers continued their exodus from the city proper. Although Radicals still dominated municipal politics, their goals were restricted ones. According to R.D. Anderson, Radicalism represented above all the state of mind of the petty bourgeoisie:

The problem for the Radicals was that while it was desirable to offer reforms in order to retain the working-class vote, the larger part of their support came from peasants, shopkeepers, and middle-class people who were content with things as they were, suspicious of the State, and devoted to the values of individualism. Why risk losing their essential votes by trying to put ambitious programmes into practice?[76]

The Municipal Council had effectively lost its mandate and its will for housing reform. By the end of the century, it washed its hands of the housing problem, thrusting it, with considerable relief, back to the private sector.[77]

There was, in fact, throughout this period, a sizeable group of social reformers in the private sector who had mobilised around the question of working-class housing to pursue a reformist programme which was grounded in a conservative social ideology and laissez-faire economics. Following the lead of the social scientist Frédéric Le Play, they identified the inadequacy of the worker's *foyer* as the source of all modern ills. Jules Siegfried asked rhetorically:

Do you want to create, at the same time, contented men who are true conservatives; do you want simultaneously to combat misery and socialist errors; do you want to increase the guarantees of order, of morality, of political and social moderation? Then let us create workers' housing![78]

Through the 1880s and 1890s, then, followers of Le Play vigorously reinvoked the dream of the worker-proprietor who had first appeared during the Second Empire. Writing in the principal organ of the movement, *La Réforme sociale*, Edmond Demolins elaborated the articles of faith of his colleagues:

The possession of his home creates in [the worker] a complete transformation . . . With his own small home and garden, one makes of the worker the head of his family worthy of this name, one who is moral and provident, aware of his roots, and able to exercise authority over his family. He soon forgets the cabaret, whose principal appeal has been to remove him from his miserable hovel. The day when he possesses a pleasant healthful home, the home in which he is King, *his own* home which he loves, where the landlord cannot pursue him . . . his life takes on a peacefulness, a serenity, a dignity characteristic of Oriental men which is nearly unknown among the nomads of our large cities . . . It is therefore of immense social importance for the worker to possess his own home. Soon it is his home which possesses him; it gives him morals, it establishes him, it transforms him.[79]

Because shared lodgings did not seem to hold the moralising potential of a separate dwelling, it followed that the establishment of a stable family life required the privacy of an individual home, without which the worker remained a drifter, a pariah of the established society. The community of workers' housing built at Mulhouse in 1853 by industrialist Jean Dollfus—*the cité ouvrière*—became the dominant model for these reformers: single-family dwellings financed by private enterprise, grouped in units of four, each dwelling with its own garden, in which each tenant could become the owner of his lodgings after fifteen years of mortgage payments. According to bourgeois analysis, if the worker could focus his aspirations on a long-term goal that would make his day-to-day existence more orderly, he might then pull himself out from his debased condition. Contemporaries did not need to be reminded of the moral benefits conveyed by property. The litany was familiar—sobriety, stability, respectability, and thrift. In place of sinister images of physical and moral depravity, reformers substituted the pastoral vision of the responsible worker, surrounded by wife and children, tilling his garden in his spare time and conscientiously saving for the future—able, at last, to appreciate 'this instinct of property that Providence has placed in all of us'.[80] It seemed apparent that, removed from the environment where they became 'envious, greedy, revolutionary, sceptical, and eventually communist',[81] in a single step, workers could be placed in healthful surroundings, tied to the political order, and separated from the unregenerate and criminal elements who populated congested areas of the city. Through home ownership, the worker re-entered the mainstream of social life, transformed from an uprooted nomad into a settled petty proprietor. In the most single-minded way, bourgeois reformers thus sought to remake society in their own image.

Promoters of the *cité ouvrière* presented these constructions as a smart business venture which also served a social purpose. They campaigned so as to assure economists and entrepreneurs that these enterprises were viable on their own terms and were not, in any way, acts of charity. Nevertheless, most projects failed, either because they remained relatively unprofitable for investors or because they were too expensive for all but a tiny elite segment of the working class. One of the models that drew the most attention was the development built by the *Société des habitations ouvrières de Passy-Auteuil*, dubbed the El Dorado of its kind.[82] It consisted of small houses of four or five rooms with a garden in front and a courtyard at the back, each selling at a cost of Fr. 6,000. The rent was set at Fr. 240 per year, to which Fr. 240 for mortgage payments was added, totalling an annual expenditure of Fr. 480, a payment scheme that would give the tenant possession after eighteen years. It is clear that this rent scale exceeded the budgets of Parisian workers.[83] Moreover, such suburban constructions ignored the lack of adequate transportation services to the city centre, while the protracted amortisation schemes assumed a continuity of employment for workers that simply did not exist.

In spite of its practical difficulties, the concept, and perhaps the fantasy, of the *cité ouvrière* continued to dominate bourgeois reform activities through the closing decades of the century. These efforts culminated in 1894 in the Siegfried law on *habitations à bon marché* (low-cost housing) which sought to encourage entrepreneurs by offering financial incentives. Judicial funds raised through court procedures, savings banks, and charities could lend money to construction companies formed specifically to build working-class housing. In Siegfried's analysis, workers were prevented from becoming home-owners because of two factors: French investors preferred government bonds and railroad stocks to real estate, and the civil law required that, with the death of the father, the inheritance be shared.[84] To reverse these patterns, the 1894 legislation made credit available to construction societies, favoured low-cost housing with tax exemptions, and promoted the integral transfer of property to an heir on the death of the primary owner. Local committees were to be set up in each department to facilitate the application of the law. In practice, the law made little impact. In the first place, the creation of local committees was left optional, a fatal loophole that was not closed until new legislation emerged in 1906. Neither were the tax incentives large enough to make an appreciable difference. But most important in the end was the basic reluctance of the French to invest in working-class housing. The transfer of funds from charitable and savings societies to the building industry as provided for in the law simply did not occur in spite of considerable official encouragement. Ironically, the voluminous literature on the *cité ouvrière* obscures the essential failure of this reform strategy. The established classes had produced a solution that offered greater ideological than material satisfaction, and, by the end of the century, even Le Play's followers seemed to accept inadequate workers' housing as an intractable fact of urban existence. They urged their peers instead to reinvent a kind of updated paternalism, buffering class antagonisms by the enactment of selected, limited reforms that would neither compromise private enterprise nor significantly increase state responsibilities for the poor.[85] Dismissing heroic remedies, they hoped, once again, to vindicate private initiative informed by enlightened philanthropy.

More concrete proposals emerged from a newly professionalised group of hygienists who sought to reshape housing reform in terms of their own priorities, focusing especially on overcrowding and the prevention of unsanitary conditions. Abandoning the intransigent problems related to the supply and cost of workers' housing, hygienists directed attention to the creation and enforcement of sanitary codes and the establishment of effective public hygiene institutions staffed by professionals. By link- ing inadequate housing to national security concerns, and by exploiting their new scientific stature conveyed by growing acceptance of germ theories of disease, hygienists were able to present the hovels of the poor as 'microbe factories' manufacturing disease—a clear threat to national strength, but one that could be managed by technical expertise. Insisting that there was 'scientific confirmation' that justified specific cleaning-up activities, they argued that resistance to their intervention flew in the face of science, rationality, progress, and social peace. The explicit promise was that, with the proper sanitary regulations, all contagious illness could be made to disappear.[86] The goal of public hygiene became, then, the destruction of germs and the maintenance of an environment inhospitable to their propagation. The improvement of working-class housing was central to this campaign.

The Melun law of 1850 provided the basis for the pivotal role assumed by hygienists in housing reform. Following the political upheaval of 1848 and the cholera epidemic of 1849—a period that had symbolically linked infection and sedition—the government responded to a growing con- sensus which favoured some kind of public regulation of workers' hous- ing. To this end, it enacted legislation that opened the doors of the poor to public scrutiny for the first time. The new law provided for the crea- tion of Commissions on Unhealthful Dwellings, advisory bodies that were charged with investigating reports of insalubrity in buildings occupied by tenants and with recommending remedial measures. By the 1880s, this innovative, but cautious legislation had become, for hygienists, dangerously obsolete. Because it left the initiative for its application to local governing bodies, the Melun law remained largely a dead letter in France, (except for Paris and Lille), and where commissions did function, their activities were carefully circumscribed. Reformers in the 1880s demanded, in contrast, that there be routine inspection of all lodgings, (including those inhabited only by the proprietor), that there be mandatory disinfections when necessary, that tighter building codes be drawn and enforced, and, especially, that full-time professional hygienists armed with executive authority supervise all of these activities. From 1881 until 1902 when a new public health law finally emerged,

hygiene organisations aggressively lobbied the government with a variety
of proposals to strengthen the 1850 legislation.

Their campaign served to refocus perceptions of the housing problem,
redefining it primarily as a public health issue. This was strategically an
important shift, as public officials were increasingly expressing their
anxieties about national strength in the biological metaphors of organic
degeneration.[87] Hygienists' claims to be able to provide more effective
control of common diseases intersected, then, a growing identification of
the size and health of the population as guarantors of France's place in
the international arena. Lobbyists told the legislature that 'germs were
more lethal to the army than the bullets of the enemy', and, rubbing salt
in an old wound, noted that during the Franco–Prussian war, the German
army lost fewer than 400 soldiers to smallpox while the French army,
with 23,000 deaths, had been decimated by disease.[88] The hygienist
Paul Brouardel argued that recruits from rural areas with poor sanitary
conditions and little regulation could infect entire units, a problem
exacerbated by the billeting of battalions in private homes rather than in
barracks.[89] Not only was it possible to draw the connection between
military strength and housing in this way, but demographic patterns
could be brought to bear to reinforce the sense of urgency promoted by
hygienists. The decline of the birthrate and continued high urban rates
of infant mortality seemed to point ominously to national decadence.
Hygienists and statisticians identified high mortality rates in working-
class districts in Paris as the direct consequence of deteriorating housing
conditions, as the most danger diseases (including smallpox, diphtheria,
whooping cough, measles, typhoid fever, and especially tuberculosis)
increasingly became localised in the eastern half of the city, and even in
a relatively small percentage of the houses.[90] The sanitary census
indicated, for example, that, between 1893 and 1904, 38 per cent of the
deaths of the city came from 5,363 houses, or less than 7 per cent of the
houses. Concentrations of tuberculosis could be similarly pinpointed.[91]
The images of disease-carrying micro-organisms affixed to the workers'
walls, ceilings, furniture and even clothing provided a powerful rationale
for a new direction of housing reform activity.

Legislators, and especially those in the more conservative Senate, were
reluctant, nevertheless, either to expand the authority of hygiene professionals or to create new institutions that might become annoying or
intrusive. One Senator warned that:

. . . by the law of hygiene that you consider today, you will have armed the
representatives of the central power with the right to penetrate when they wish,
on an order from Paris, day or night, into the interior of our homes; to bring . . .
into the interior of our homes their war on microbes, and under the pretext of
the search for a germ or the execution of a disinfection, to open our most
intimate possessions and our most secret drawers.[92]

Responding to cries of approval that followed these remarks, another
Senator predicted the end of romance in France: 'Adieu to intimate
expressions! At the very moment when two spouses converse more or

less tenderly, the sanitary inspector will burst into their home to make a report'.[93] Although a Senator from the Left sought to reassure his colleagues that 'love does not exclude hygiene', powerful opposition to expanding the jurisdiction and authority of hygienists remained.

Rather than enlarge the role of sanitary commissions, legislators chose instead to close some of the most obvious loopholes of the 1850 legislation by strengthening the hand of mayors who were given, in the law of 1902, a broader mandate to protect the health of the commune: they gained jurisdiction over all houses; they could order that improvements be executed at the landlord's expense; they could act even in the absence of a direct complaint. The law further codified and updated regulations for the control of contagious disease and established bureaus of hygiene under the authority of the mayor in every commune of at least 2,000 inhabitants. But it eliminated key provisions as well, most importantly those calling for the creation of an inspection service and for the transfer of final authority in health matters from politicians to health professionals.[94] Disappointed hygienists argued that the excessive caution of legislators had emasculated the new law—that by leaving the final word with elected local officials, bound inevitably to their propertied constituencies, the law had, in effect, preserved the freedom not to act.

By the end of the century, then, it seems that the government had identified the health of the population with its national security concerns and was consequently willing to entertain some active involvement in sanitary regulation. Nevertheless, this involvement stopped short of dealing with the pressing problem of clearing out large pockets of slum dwellings. The law of 1902 sidestepped this crucial issue completely in its failure to revise the outdated compensation procedures established by the law of 3 May, 1841, for expropriated buildings in irremediable condition. Because the law set no limits on the amount of compensation, juries (populated largely by the *haute bourgeoisie*) tended to award inflated indemnities that made large-scale removal financially impractical, while proprietors postponed making improvements in the hope of reaping larger profits through expropriation. In 1904, Jules Siegfried brought in a bill modelled after an English law of 1890 which essentially granted compensation for site value only.[95] The bill reached the Senate in 1910, but by the outbreak of the First World War no action had been taken. Similarly, a bill introduced in 1911 to facilitate the acquisition of whole areas without requiring the irremediable sanitary condition of each individual building had to await action until after the war.

In sum, none of the various groups of reformers who had addressed housing problems in the second half of the nineteenth century were able to devise viable strategies for increasing the supply of working-class lodgings. An examination of their reform efforts reveals above all the conceptual and structural constraints which inhibited their actions and narrowed their options. Bourgeois reformers, determined to protect private enterprise and to limit the growth of state responsibilities, were stymied when the free market did not provide an adequate supply of workers' housing. The fairly conservative fiscal incentives that they were prepared to offer failed to make low-rent constructions attractive to entrepreneurs who could realise greater gains in building for the comfortable classes; but more direct public participation in construction, as well as limits on profits and rents, remained unacceptable. The *cité ouvrière* had captured the imagination of so many precisely because it allowed reformers to cling to normative standards of social and economic life. But it did not resolve municipal housing problems. Only the hygienists' programme achieved some measure of success, and this because they had set more circumscribed goals. In the end, tighter regulation of the sanitary condition of individual lodgings could not guarantee better housing for the poor. With no alternative housing for tenants evicted from insalubrious buildings nor subsidies for large-scale improvements, both rents and overcrowding would continue to increase. Echoing the resignation which characterised housing reformers at the close of the century, the architect Cacheux wrote that repressive laws would be effective only when there were enough suitable lodgings for all workers. In most cases, he concluded, 'public authority is impotent in the presence of men who have nothing'.[96] After more than a half-century in which housing the poor had figured prominently on reform agendas, it seemed to reformers that the solution to urban housing problems had exceeded their reach. Parisian workers, for whom lodgings within the city itself remained largely inacessible, continued to migrate to the outskirts, forming a ring of working-class enclaves that fulfilled, in the end, Corbon's mid-century anxiety that the poor might become 'an immense rope hemming in the comfortable classes'.

Notes

1. Louis Chevalier, *Laboring Classes and Dangerous Classes in Paris during the First Half of the Nineteenth Century*, trans. Frank Jellinek (New York, 1973), 152.
2. *Revue générale de l'architecture*, 6 (1845–46), 153.
3. Frégier wrote in response to a competition on the following topic: 'Research according to positive observations on the elements which compose in Paris or in any other large city that part of the population which forms a dangerous class because of its vices, its ignorance, and its misery; indicate the means which the administration, rich and affluent men, and intellectual and hard-working workers might use to improve this dangerous and depraved class.' Ann F. La Berge, 'Public Health in France and the French Public Health Movement, 1815–1848' (Ph.D. diss., University of Tennessee, 1974), 105.
4. Chevalier, *Laboring Classes and Dangerous Classes*, 139.
5. The only building regulations in force applied to the height of buildings with frontage on the public roadway, fixing the allowed height in proportion to the width of the street. This absence of control prompted a contemporary critic to note that 'too many defective, inconvenient, and unhealthy buildings have been erected owing to the owner's greed and the builder's inventive genius'.
6. A. Corbon, *Le Secret du peuple de Paris* (Paris, 1863), 200.

7. Jacques Bertillon, *Huitième Congrès international d'hygiène et de démographie: Comptes-rendus et mémoires, Budapest, 1–9 septembre 1894* (Budapest, 1896), 423.

8. Octave Du Mesnil, *L'Habitation du pauvre* (Paris, 1890), 14–24.

9. Georges Duveau refers to this demographic shift as 'the proletarianisation of Paris'. See especially, Duveau, *La Vie ouvrière en France sous la Second Empire* (Paris, 1946), 202–18.

10. Jules Simon, *Paris aux Parisiens* (Paris, 1869); Maxime Du Camp, *Paris: Ses organes, ses fonctions, et sa vie dans la seconde moitié du XIXe siècle*, 5 (Paris, 1883), 6.

11. Comte d'Haussonville, *Misère et remèdes* (Paris, 1886), 36.

12. *Résultats statistiques du dénombrement de 1896 de la Ville de Paris* (Paris, 1896), xx.

13. The number of workers rose from 416,000 in 1860 to 442,000 in 1866 with up to 70,000 more seasonal workers at a given period. Pierre Lavedan, *Histoire de l'urbanisme: Epoque contemporaine* (Paris, 1952), 93.

14. Adeline Daumard, *Maisons de Paris et propriétaires parisiens au XIXe siècle, 1809–1880* (Paris, 1965), 203.

15. Paul Taillefer, *Des cités ouvrières et de leur nécessité comme hygiène et tranquillité publiques* (Paris, 1852), 12. Taillefer recounted an incident during the coup d'état of 2 December, 1852, in which a crowd appeared at a workers' housing complex, the Cité Napoléon, to pull the emperor's name off the signpost and entrance gates and to call upon the residents to raise barricades. The working-class tenants of this government-subsidised housing allegedly refused to join the opposition.

16. V. Du Claux, 'Petits logements parisiens', *Annales d'hygiène publique et de médecine légale*, 3rd ser., 9 (1883), 475.

17. Emile Muller and Emile Cacheux, *Les Habitations ouvrières en tous pays* (Paris, 1879), 64–5.

18. Duveau, *La vie ouvrière*, 359.

19. Henry Fougère, *Les Délégations ouvrières aux Expositions universelles sous le Second Empire* (Montluçon, 1905), 20–1.

20. Duveau, *La vie ouvrière*, 348.

21. Louis Lazare, *Les Quartiers pauvres de Paris* (Paris, 1869), 82.

22. Chambre de Commerce de Paris, *Rapport adressé à Messieurs les membres de la Chambre de Commerce de Paris sur la question relative aux salaires des ouvriers et à l'augmentation de loyers et des denrées alimentaires*, par Horace Say (15 June 1855).

23. Louis René Villermé, *Cités ouvrières* (Paris, 1850).

24. Roger H. Guerrand, *Les Origines du logement social en France* (Paris, 1967), 75; Villermé, *Cités ouvrières*.

25. Muller and Cacheux, *Les Habitations ouvrières*.

26. Blanqui noted in 1850 that, in contrast to the situation in London where housing for the poor required that inhabitants wash their hands daily, French workers would never consent to such controls. August Blanqui, 'Des cités ouvrières', *Séances et travaux de l'Académie des sciences morales et politiques* 17 (1850), 240. See also, Archives Nationales, F12 6824, *Règlement à l'usage des locataires. Cités de Marcq-en-Baroeul*.

27. *Résultats statistiques du dénombrement de 1896 pour la Ville de Paris et le département de la Seine*.

28. See especially Lucien Flaus, 'Les Fluctuations de la construction d'habitations urbaines', *Journal de la Société de statistique de Paris*, nos. 5–6 (May–June

1949), 194, 214; Gérard Jacquemet, 'Belleville aux XIXe et XXe siècles: Une méthode d'analyse de la croissance urbaine à Paris', *Annales: Economies, sociétés, civilisations* (July–August 1975), 824–31.

29. Jacquemet, 'Belleville'.
30. Ibid., 829–31.
31. For example, in both *arrondissements* XVII and XVIII where two of the quarters were comfortable and two were more exclusively working-class, more constructions were planned for the wealthier districts. In 1891, contractors filed requests to build 381 floors in the two bourgeois quarters of the seventeenth *arrondissement* in contrast to 211 floors in the poorer sections. Similarly, in the eighteenth *arrondissement*, builders sought to add 280 floors in the more comfortable quarters and only 52 floors in the working-class districts. The largest total number of applications for building permits was filed in the wealthy sixteenth *arrondissement. Annuaire statistique de la ville de Paris et du département de la Seine*, 1881.
32. Emile Cacheux, *L'Economiste pratique* (Paris, 1885), 59.
33. Françoise Marnata, *Les Loyers des bourgeois de Paris 1860–1958* (Paris, 1961). Marnata gives the following figures on the average selling price of a square metre of undeveloped land, calculated with the 1913 value of 100 francs as the basis:

1860	26.0	1865	46.8
1861	31.2	1866	49.1
1862	32.9	1867	53.1
1863	39.3	1868	50.2
1864	43.3	1869	54.3

34. According to the same scale, Marnata found that the price of land per square metre rose from approximately 60.6 in 1890 to 81.5 in 1899. Marnata, *Les Loyers*, 28.
35. Ville de Paris, Monographies municipales, *Les Logements à bon marché: Recueil annoté des discussions, délibérations, et rapports du Conseil Municipal de Paris*, By Lucien Lambeau (Paris, 1897), 1214. (Hereinafter cited as Lambeau.)
36. Cacheux, *L'Economiste pratique*, 8–12.
37. R. Laborderie, *Les Habitations à bon marché en France* (Bordeaux, 1902), 130.
38. D'Haussonville, *Misère et remèdes*, 80.
39. The number of employees in transportation grew from 130,000 in 1870 to 360,000 in 1910 for the country as a whole, and the number of those employed in banking and commerce increased by 50 per cent during the same period of time.
40. Paul Leroy-Beaulieu as quoted in Benoît Malon, *Le Socialisme intégral, 2e partie: Des réformes possibles et des moyens pratiques* (Paris, 1894), 374.
41. Préfecture du Département de la Seine, *Documents statistiques recueillés et coordinés par le service de la Commission des contributions directes de la ville de Paris, 1884* (Paris, 1884), graph 6. There were 3,732 vacancies in 1880, 4,530 in 1881, 4,753 in 1882, 6,498 in 1883, and 10,099 in 1884.
42. *Paris désert: Lamentations d'un Jérémie Haussmannisé*, n.d.
43. Arthur Raffalovich, *Le Logement de l'ouvrier et du pauvre* (Paris, 1887), 278–9.
44. *Le Livre foncier de Paris, pt. 1, Valeur locative des propriétés bâties en 1900* (Paris, 1900).

45. Guerrand, *Les Origines du logement social*, 84.
46. J.J. Danduran, *Les Propriétaires en 1863: Etudes physiologiques* (Paris, 1863). See also *Pourquoi des propriétaires à Paris: Dédié aux locataires* (Paris, 1857); Louis Veuillot, *Les Odeurs de Paris* (Paris, 1867); Alexandre Weill, *Qu'est-ce que le propriétaire d'une maison à Paris: Suite de Paris inhabitable* (Paris, 1860).
47. Du Mesnil, *L'Habitation du pauvre*, 159.
48. Georges Piart, *Locataires et propriétaires: Etude sociale sur les abus de la propriété à l'égard de la location* (Paris, 1882), 9–10. See also Victor Emion and Charles Bardies, *Dictionnaire des usages et règlements de Paris et du département de la Seine en matière de locations, constructions, voirie, etc.* (Paris, 1893), 172.
49. Piart, *Locataires et propriétaires*, 16.
50. Emion and Bardies, *Dictionnaire des usages*, 229; Louis Pabon, *Manual pratique des propriétaires* (Paris, 1906).
51. Emion and Bardies, *Dictionnaire des usages*, 231.
52. Piart, *Locataires et propriétaires*, 39.
53. Ibid.
54. Denis Poulot, *Question sociale: Le Sublime ou le travailleur comme il est en 1870 et ce qu'il peut être* (Paris, 1872), 47.
55. Cacheux, *L'Economiste pratique*, 78.
56. *L'Economiste français*, 24 May, 1879.
57. Piart, *Locataires et propriétaires*, 21; Emion and Bardies, *Dictionnaire des usages*, 174.
58. See reports in Archives de la Préfecture de Police, BA 486: Enquête sur les loyers à Paris, 1871–91.
59. *Le Temps*, 15 July, 1883.
60. Archives, PP, BA 486, report of 22 August, 1883.
61. Jules Guesde, *Ça et là* (Paris, 1914), 229; *Le Citoyen*, 19 June, 1882.
62. Archives PP, BA 486: Congrès sur les loyers.
63. Report no. 8 of 1883, Lambeau, *Les Logements à bon marché*, 54–76.
64. Ibid., 106–7.
65. A. Fougerousse, 'Pour la construction des petits logements', *La Réforme sociale* 1 (1883), 401–7.
66. Haussmann left a debt of Fr 1.7 billion. In 1879, the Municipal Council agreed to repay Fr 283 million of back debts to the *Crédit foncier*, but the full amount was not finally reimbursed until 1928. Jean Bastié, *La Croissance de la banlieu parisienne* (Paris, 1964), 196; Anthony Sutcliffe, *The Autumn of Central Paris: The Defeat of Town Planning, 1850–1970* (London, 1970), 56–8.
67. See, for example, a report from a meeting of the Société d'économie politique, 'De l'intervention de l'état et des municipalités dans la question des loyers', *Journal des économistes* 25 (1884), 452.
68. Lambeau, *Les Habitations à bon marché*, 814–19.
69. Ibid.
70. Ibid., 574–7; 870–2.
71. Ibid., 575.
72. Ibid., 277–9.
73. Ibid., 625.
74. Ibid., 1005–8; 1016–18; 1034–7; 1041–4.
75. Ibid., 1190, 1221, 1223–5.
76. R.D. Anderson, *France, 1870–1914: Politics and Society* (London, 1977), 99.

77. In his study of urban France in the nineteenth century, Marcel Roncayolo notes that this type of stalemate—whereby the lack of municipal funds inhibited public initiatives and produced, instead, endless polemical debates—was characteristic of French cities in general. The absence of the incentive to speculation provided by the public works of Haussmann's tenure contributed to the sluggishness of the construction industry in the final decades of the century, while what new constructions were undertaken were designed for the better-off classes. Marcel Roncayolo, 'La Production de la ville', in *Histoire de la France urbaine: La Ville de l'âge industriel*, tome 4, ed. Maurice Agulhon et al. (Paris, 1983), 87.

78. Jules Siegfried, *Quelques Mots sur la misère: son histoire, ses causes, ses remèdes* (Havre, 1877), 214.

79. Edmond Demolins, 'Les Habitations ouvrières', *La Réforme sociale* 1 (1881), 301–6.

80. Emile Trélat, 'Cités ouvrières, maisons ouvrières', *Exposition universelle internationale de 1878 à Paris: Comptes-rendus sténographiques. Congrès international d'hygiène tenu à Paris 1–10 août 1878* (Paris, 1880), 542. A worker could rent lodgings at Mulhouse (including two rooms, a kitchen, a garret, a cellar, and a garden) on the condition that the worker cultivate the garden himself, send his children to school, make a deposit each week at a savings bank, and pay 15 centimes to the fund for health insurance.

81. Paul Leroy-Beaulieu, *La Question ouvrière au XIXe siècle* (Paris, 1899), 335.

82. Anthony Roulliet, *Les Habitations ouvrières à l'Exposition universelle de 1889 à Paris* (Nancy, 1889).

83. A similar community was built outside Paris at Issy in 1883. The first buildings sold for Fr. 7,000 and later constructions were more expensive. None were bought by workers. In the working-class districts of *arrondissement* XIX, the Société des constructions ouvrières de France did build modest housing, but, again, the protracted amortisation schedules made this project equally impractical.

84. Jules Siegfried, 'Les Habitations à bon marché', in *Les Applications sociales de la solidarité: Leçons professées à l'Ecole des hautes études sociales*, by P. Budin et al. (Paris, 1904), 221, 232.

85. Reformers might encourage, for example, the development of food and construction cooperatives, savings and mutual-aid societies, and retirement plans. Georges Picot, *La Lutte contre le socialisme révolutionnaire* (Paris, 1896), 38, 41, 56; and by the same author, 'Les Moyens d'améliorer la condition de l'ouvrier', *La Réforme sociale* 21 (1891), 45.

86. *Rapport général de la Commission des logements insalubres*, 1884–89.

87. Robert A. Nye, *Crime, Madness, and Politics in Modern France: The Medical Concept of National Decline* (Princeton, 1984).

88. *Journal officiel: Débats parlementaires, Sénat*, 12 February, 1897; Henri Monod, 'La Législation sanitaire en France', in *Les Applications sociales de la solidarité*, 140. In 1901, there were 1,031 smallpox deaths from a population of 14,109,520 living in cities of more than 5,000. By contrast, in a British population of 32,261,003 living in cities of comparable size, only 85 smallpox deaths occurred, while in the entire German Empire in 1897 there were only 5 deaths from smallpox.

89. *Journal officiel: Débats parlementaires, Sénat*, 9 February, 1897.

90. Jacques Bertillon, *De la fréquence des principales maladies à Paris pendant la période 1865–1891* (Paris, 1894), 135, 320–1; also by Bertillon, 'Mouvements de population et causes de décès selon le degré d'aisance à

Paris, Berlin, Vienne', *Deùxième Congrès international d'hygiène et de démographie à Paris en 1900: Compte-rendus* (Paris, 1901), 961; Henri Turot and Henri Bellamy, *Le Surpeuplement et les habitations à bon marché* (Paris, 1907), 9.

91. Turot and Bellamy, *Le Surpeuplement*, 9.
92. *Journal officiel, Débats parlementaires, Sénat*, 12 February, 1897.
93. Ibid.
94. In Paris, building plans were subject to prior approval under an 1852 decree, but there was no inspection procedure.
95. The indemnity was to be calculated on the basis of the building's revenue; however, excess rents beyond the normal capacity of the building, as well as the costs of repairing the property, would be subtracted from the final payment. Siegfried, 'Les Habitations à bon marché', 223–4.
96. Cacheux, *L'Economiste pratique*, 52.

3 Brussels

Patricia Van den Eeckhout

I

'We have not, as have the Parisians and other Latin peoples, a taste for great barracks, divided into apartments, which give so monotonous a character to the boulevards and streets of Paris. We are of Dante's opinion . . . We like to go up our own staircase. Like the Anglo-Saxon, whose cousins we are, we love our home, the family fireside.'[1] This statement of Charles Buls, mayor of Brussels from 1881 to 1899 and author of *L'esthétique des villes* is characteristic of the way in which housing in Brussels, and Belgium in general, is typified by contemporaries and historians. In the Belgian capital, as in London but unlike Paris, it was the single-family dwelling and not the tenement that is supposed to have set the tone. The head of the Brussels *Bureau d'hygiène*, E. Janssens, noted with reference to the 1866 population census: 'In the principal towns of our country, every family wants to live in a separate house, however modest it may be.'[2] Sutcliffe has pointed out that Brussels and other Belgian cities formed part of the girdle of north-western European cities where the majority of people lived in self-contained houses, even in the most densely populated areas. Housing in the towns of Britain (Scotland excepted), Holland, northern France, and north-western Germany shared these characteristics. In the more eastern and southern parts of Europe the multiple-family dwelling predominated.[3]

The image of Belgium as a country of terraced houses (Figure 3.1) is confirmed by a consideration of working-class housing. The Board of Trade inquiry that looked into the housing conditions of the Belgian urban working class stated in 1910: 'The small house occupied by one or two families is the predominant type, whilst tenement houses play only a very small part, and even where they exist, are rarely of large size.'[4] In the chapter on the capital we learn that Brussels working-class housing was no exception to the rule.

The seemingly trivial statement that people were lodged in houses in some areas and lived in tenements in other parts, hides a complex reality which is not easily disentangled. It is often very difficult to find out which were the decisive factors in the 'choice' of a specific housing style. Physical constraints, the existence of city walls, population pressure on available residential land, the level of land prices, building

Figure 3.1 A row of typical Brussels houses in the commercial fifth town district (1870). Note the irregularity in the lay-out of the front, the height of the houses and the height of the respective storeys. Copyright Bibliotechque royale Albert I, Brussels (Cabinet des estampes). Jean Kämpfe.

regulations, the system of tenancy: what seems to play a decisive role in some towns, appears to be of minor importance in others.[5]

Contemporaries seemed to have less difficulty in explaining the predominance of the self-contained house. They all, without exception, assumed an explanation in terms of cultural characteristics. In 1984 a Brussels town councillor spoke of 'an indisputable fact of which we must be aware and which is fortunately inherent in our national character: every Brussels citizen, every Belgian, wants to own his house and live in it'.[6] The head of the Brussels *Bureau d'hygiene* referred to 'a characteristic feature of our national manners'.[7] Some forty years later an official of the Ministry of Labour spoke of an 'innate preference for the single-family dwelling'.[8] Buls' statement which opened this chapter is itself illustrative of the presumed connection between 'national character' and housing style.

These statements were, however, far from neutral. Some of them were made in reference to a late nineteenth-century town planning debate between the advocates of what, schematically, we might call monumental, large-scale, technocratic town planing and the proponents of 'picturesque', aesthetic town planning. The latter admired the informal beauty which arose from the assymetrical design and variety of the old city. They criticised the dull and monotonous character of new quarters the creators of which seemed to have been obsessed with hygienic and circulation problems.[9] This international debate was fought out with respect to Brussels housing between the supporters of single- and multiple-family dwellings. For Charles Buls, a prominent defender of the 'picturesque' and of the organically-constituted city rooted in the national (especially Flemish) cultural tradition, the single-family dwelling was an important component of an autocthonous architecture. The apartment house was regarded as an imported housing style which was not congenial to Belgian national taste.

The importance of the single-family dwelling in the discourse of the proponents of 'picturesque' town planning makes it necessary to check whether their observations were completely true to reality. Was the single-family dwelling effectively predominant in late nineteenth-century Brussels? Had it been predominant before? Let us not lose sight of the fact that not merely town planning or architectural issues were at stake. Pleas for a specific form of housing were in fact very often political and moral discourses expressing clear opinions on urban society. The 'choice' of a specific form of housing was then no more than advocacy of a specific moral order. The fact that the French (and the Parisians in particular) lived in tenements was supposed to illustrate their rather dissolute way of life. The blessings of a strong family life, as a barrier against the moral decay of the city, seemed to be a privilege of the English (and the Belgians) who, in line with their preference for the single-family house, cultivated 'the love of the home'.[10]

This chapter will not seek to answer the question of which factors determined the form of housing for Brussels. The housing form in fact needs to be thoroughly researched, since it is not at all clear whether the existing image of Brussels housing corresponds to reality, either before or after the large-scale transformations of the second half of the nineteenth century, or with respect to the different social classes and areas of town. These questions provide a starting-point from which to look into the general characteristics and the qualitative development of Brussels housing. In comparison with other capitals, little research has been done on this or on related subjects such as the evolution of the urban building cycle, the structure of the urban housing market and patterns of ownership and investment.

II

The population census of 1846 indicated that Brussels, with its 123,874 inhabitants, was the largest Belgian town. However, the surface area of Brussels was smaller than that of comparable Belgian cities, comprising 450 hectares, of which more than 60 per cent was built on. Compared with other European capitals, Brussels was the size of a provincial town, a fact which was often overlooked by the municipal authorities when outlining their town planning policy. In the period from 1795 to 1830, wars and changes of regime had not been conducive to the city's economic and demographic development.[11] In 1830, however, Brussels became the capital of a newly-independent Belgium, the fulcrum of a centralised state, containing the court, the legislature, the civil service, the aristocracy, high finance and the nerve-centre of the Belgian railway system. Population growth accelerated as a result of increased immigration. From the 1830s, however, the city's demographic expansion was surpassed by the growth of the suburbs. The city walls demarcating the town from the surrounding countryside had been demolished in accordance with the imperial decree of 1810, but these adjacent municipalities have remained independent entities. Housing conditions in these suburbs will not be explicitly dealt with in this article.

By 1846 Brussels was established as an administrative and commercial centre and as a centre of wealth and luxury. It appears from the census of 1846 that the liberal professions, civil servants and clerical workers were more numerous in Brussels than in Antwerp, Ghent and Liège. The number of maids and servants was also significantly higher. Some 60 per cent of the population belonged to the working class (containing craftsmen working for a wage, domestic workers, servants and casual labourers and their families), a percentage that would gradually decrease in the second half of the nineteenth century as Brussels was confirmed in its position as an administrative, commercial and financial centre.[12]

In 1846 it was already clear that Brussels had missed the opportunities that had occurred for the creation of modern industry.[13] The capital contained only small-scale industry with very limited mechanisation, orientated on the one hand towards meeting purely local needs and on the other hand towards the export of luxury and fashion goods and books. The clothing, building, wood, leather and food industries accounted for 68 per cent of Brussels' industrial employment. Since many trades were aimed at meeting the needs of the town itself, many craftsmen, workers and tradesmen needed to live close to their customers. In the second half of the nineteenth century, this need to live nearby was to be intensified. Although major industries were not set up within the municipal boundaries of Brussels, it does appear from the industrial census of 1846 that they were certainly not absent in the Brussels area at large. The suburbs of Anderlecht and Sint-Jans-Molenbeek along the Willebroek-Charleroi canal were becoming new centres of, respectively, the textile industry and the modern engineering and food industries, attracting a proletarian population from the capital and the surrounding countryside.

The Brussels labour market was characterised by a pattern of structural underemployment and high seasonal unemployment. As a result, a very

high percentage of the Brussels population was permanently or occasionally dependent on poor relief.[14] The number of people who figured
on the lists of the poor relief administration rose from some 20 per cent
of the Brussels population in the first decade of the nineteenth century,
to more than 30 per cent in the 1840s, despite the authorities' efforts to
restrict the numbers to the limited funds. As a result of these efforts to
hamper the inscription of the needy on the poor lists, the number of
registered poor was periodically below actual need. The increase in the
number of poor registered by the poor relief administration was
exclusively due to the rise in the number of casual poor. Families who
met the requirements of age, disability or size to receive permanent relief
were a stable minority (some 15 per cent of the population). The
combination in the first half of the nineteenth century of structural
underemployment, seasonal unemployment, stagnating or even declining
wages, and rising food prices and rents led to a marked increase in the
number of casual poor receiving help during the winter, in periods of
sickness, and when work was short. The implications of the deterioration of the living standard were such that in the first half of the nineteenth century nearly every working-class family ran a risk of finding
itself at one time or another on the lists of the poor visitor. In the more
prosperous third quarter of the nineteenth century the number of
registered poor declined. In the 1880s and 1890s, a period of depression,
the number of registered poor who were permanently or casually on
relief rose again to more than 20 per cent, and in the worst years even
30 per cent, of the population.

III

Quetelet's map of 1842 (see p. 106), based on data from the Brussels
population census, shows a pronounced spatial segregation of rich and
poor.[15] The data on the number of poor registered by poor relief
administration show that concentrations of paupers were to be found in
the outlying points of the city limits. The development of spatial segregation has not yet been studied, but observations by the visitors of the poor
allow us to assume that the process had been well under way in the first
half of the nineteenth century. Transformations in the centre of the city
pushed the poor to the outskirts of the first, second, third, fourth and
sixth districts.

In the first half of the nineteenth century the population of the first,
and especially of the second, third and sixth districts which at the end
of the Ancien Régime included large areas of unbuilt land, increased
appreciably. The concentration of the working class in the second
district and adjacent parts of the first district had been a fact for some
centuries before. The proletarian character of the first district was
somewhat broken by the aristocratic *Sablon* neighbourhood where the
bourgeoisie and the nobility had resided since the sixteenth and seventeenth centuries. The presence of a poor population was of more recent

date for a large part of the third district, a lower part of the city through which the River Senne flowed and which still contained many bleaching-fields. The fourth district had a mixed character: the river quays were bordered by rich merchant houses, while the smaller streets lodged the artisans and day-labourers which the harbour had attracted. The sixth district shared this mixed character: pauper concentrations contrasted with the dwellings of *rentiers* and the liberal professions. The commer-cial eighth and fifth districts, where many *rentiers* also lived, contained the most densely-built parts of the city. In the 1840s these two districts had less than 2 per cent of the total gardens and meadows. The seventh and the adjacent part of the first district were called 'le haut de la ville' (upper town) because they were some fifty metres higher than the lower parts where the Senne flowed. Since the fifteenth and sixteenth centuries, the nobility and the bourgeoisie had preferred a residence in the upper town to a house in the damp quarters of the lower parts of Brussels. At the end of the eighteenth and the beginning of the nine-teenth century, the 'character' of the upper town was consolidated by the lay-out of a neo-classically inspired, geometric and monumental ensemble of grand terraces, straight and wide streets, a park and a palace. For the first time in Brussels' town planning history, a drastic large-scale transformation destroyed the existing urban landscape and replaced it with a completely new structure.[16] It is not surprising that the govern-ment, parliament and civil service of independent Belgium chose this part of town in which to reside. This neo-classic ensemble corresponded to the bourgeoisie's image of 'the capital'. According to a statement by the architect Cluysenaar, this could not be said of the mainly medieval structures of the lower parts of Brussels: 'Brussels is a capital in the area surrounding the park and the rue Royale and in its remoter quarters; in the centre it is a third-rate provincial town'[17] In the second half of the nineteenth century, the Brussels city council and King Leopold II were to spare neither cost nor effort in order to give Brussels the appearance of a European capital.

Land registry data also point towards substantial spatial segregation. In the definitive registers, Brussels houses were divided into 55 classes for tax purposes; in the highest classes were real palaces and in the lowest the worst slums. For the year 1833–34, there are data on the distribution of these classes throughout the city.[18] This means that we know how the housing stock of the different districts was composed. On the basis of tax data for 1829, Hannes and Despontin aggregated these 55 classes into somewhat broader wealth categories: families living in houses classed 1 to 32 are accounted wealthy, people living in houses classed 33 to 42 are assumed to be middle-class, and families living in dwellings of the classes 43 to 55 are assumed to have been poor.[19] If this categorisa-tion is applied to the housing stock of the city as a whole and to the different districts in particular, we find that in 1833–34 63.44 per cent of the houses in Brussels belonged to the lowest categories (43–55), 27.23 per cent consisted of middle-class housing (33–42) and 9.31 per cent of the houses were inhabited by the wealthy. In the most proletarian parts

Table 3.1 Distribution of houses by tax classification, 1833/34 and the population registered on the poor list, 1842

	Percentage of houses in each district by tax class								Total
	1	2	3	4	5	6	7	8	
Tax class 1–32	6.0	2.1	3.2	9.1	17.8	8.2	22.1	11.2	9.3
Tax class 33–42	19.2	12.4	14.8	34.6	37.2	20.6	45.1	46.3	27.2
Tax class 43–55	74.8	85.5	82.0	56.3	45.0	71.2	32.8	42.5	63.4
Percentage of families registered on poor list									
	29.9	34.1	35.3	14.0	12.7	19.9	4.2	5.1	22.5

Source: Dictionnaire géographique du Brabant, Ms II 386, XIV, fos. 130–1; A. Quetelet, 'Sur le recensement de la population de Bruxelles en 1842', *Bulletin de la Commission Centrale de Statistique* I (1842), 27–162

of town, namely in the second and third districts, 82 to 85 per cent of the housing stock was made up of houses in the lowest categories (43–55). In the first and sixth districts, which contained some important pauper concentrations as well, the houses of the lowest categories amounted to 71 to 74 per cent. In the somewhat more mixed fourth district, 56 per cent of the housing stock consisted of houses in classes 43–55. In the commercial fifth and eighth districts, 42 to 45 per cent of the houses were in the lowest category, while in the aristocratic seventh district this category amounted to only 33 per cent. In this part of town the residences of the rich totalled 22 per cent of the houses, as opposed to 2 to 3 per cent in the proletarian second and third districts (see Table 3.1).

In order to facilitate the classification of thousands of Brussels houses into 55 tax classes, every class had been accompanied by a description of a house that actually existed. Unfortunately, this information linking the physical characteristics of buildings to the tax classification has never been found for Brussels. It could have been an important source for the reconstruction of the physical characteristics of the houses inhabited by different social classes and at the same time have given us a reliable description of the 'average' Brussels house.

IV

The less differentiated data from the population censuses indicate that the Brussels streets were certainly not dominated by tall houses. It appears from the census of 1846 that single-storey houses represented 8.7 per cent of the total, while houses with two storeys amounted to 43.2 per cent, and houses with three storeys or more 47.9 per cent.[20] The absence of separate categories for houses with more than three storeys is indicative of the fact that they probably represented a small minority. Although building height was relatively limited, the average Brussels house was nevertheless taller than most houses in other Belgian cities.[21]

Table 3.2 Percentage of houses with various numbers of storeys, 1842, by district

| Type of houses | District number | | | | | | | | Total |
	1	2	3	4	5	6	7	8	
Ground floor only	6.2	9.6	20.7	11.9	4.3	7.3	0.8	0.2	8.1
2 storeys	56.5	50.9	51.1	43.0	43.3	49.3	24.3	29.2	44.2
3 storeys and more	37.2	39.4	28.2	45.1	52.4	43.4	74.9	70.6	47.7

Source: Quetelet, 'Sur le recensement'

Table 3.3 Registered poor and housing in the third district, 1842

Percentage of registered poor	0–10	11–49	50–100
percentage of houses with 3 storeys and more	53.9	27.5	6.7
average number of rooms per house	6.4	5.3	3.9
average number of families per house	1.7	2.4	2.7

Source: Quetelet, 'Sur le recensement'

Data from the population census of 1842 add some social differentiation to the general picture and can be used, for instance, to answer the question of whether the working class of Brussels was lodged in tenements, subdivided houses or small alley cottages. In the most proletarian districts, the small house with one or two storeys predominated. Only 28 per cent of the houses of the third district, a proletarian part of the city, possessed three storeys and more; in the aristocratic seventh district, 75 per cent of the housing stock was of this size. Houses with only a ground floor amounted to 20 per cent in the third district, against 0.8 per cent in the seventh district. In the commercial eighth district 70 per cent of the houses had three or more storeys, whereas in the largely proletarian first and second districts this house type represented only 38 per cent of the housing stock. (See Table 3.2.)

In the absence of large tenement blocks, the presence of taller houses was clearly a sign of wealth. This also appears to be the case when we move from district level to street level. In the third district, streets with various levels of registered poor were placed alongside the nature of the housing stock. (See Table 3.3.)

These figures confirm that the poorest strata of the population were to be found in small houses with one or two storeys and with two to four rooms. However, even in streets with no poor or only a small number of poor, the average number of families per house was more than one, which suggests that the better-off families were not as a rule the sole occupants of a house. Although Brussels may have been dominated by houses conceived as single-family dwellings, they were not as a rule occupied as such.

Figure 3.2 The one-roomed dwelling of a Brussels domestic tailor c.1910. Archives de la Ville de Bruxelles, nr. 12,305. Photograph reproduced by La Fonderie.

The limited number of storeys and rooms in houses in the proletarian first, second and third districts meant that 48 to 50 per cent of families had only one room at their disposal (Figure 3.2), while 22 to 27 per cent lived in two rooms. In the better-off seventh and eighth districts, more than 60 per cent of families were lodged in dwellings of three rooms and more. It goes without saying that there was hardly any differentiation in the living space of families living in one or two rooms: eating, sleeping, washing and often the professional occupation of the breadwinner had all to take place within the same four walls. Doctors who visited the poor remarked that by shutting off a part of the room people tried to create an alcove, which was usually badly ventilated, to give the illusion of a separate sleeping place.

If we conclude that the small two- to four-roomed house was the predominant type of accommodation in the fairly homogeneous working-class neighbourhoods, the question remains as to how the working class was lodged in the mixed streets. To what extent did its members inhabit outdated, subdivided houses or the cellars and attics of the houses of better-off families? It is difficult at present to give an exact answer to this question. If we are able to believe a report from the 1840s, this form of mixing with the wealthier strata of the population occurred less frequently in Brussels than in, for instance, Paris or Lyons: 'in Brussels the working class is in a sense shunted aside'.[22] According to the reporters, the greater part of the working class was concentrated in the alleys of the first, second, third and fourth districts. According to contemporaries, these alleys formed small self-contained little worlds: 'a labyrinth in which you get lost, a hamlet, a borough in the middle of the big city'.[23] Victor Besme, who was to be involved with all the important Brussels town planning projects of the second half of the nineteenth century, noticed that subdivided middle-class houses often offered better, but also more expensive, working-class accommodation. The principal tenant tried to get a maximum income from subletting the rooms. As a result, most of the working-class families could afford the rent for only one room. The consequent overcrowding eventually led to a deterioration of initially better housing conditions.[24] Other contemporaries stated plainly that the worst working-class lodgings were to be found in the streets with a mixed population.[25] They were advocates of separate working-class quarters where the houses were claimed to be of a better quality as a result of the fact that capital returns were higher when landlords were able to build a row of cottages instead of an isolated house in a mixed street.

The fact that working-class dwellings in the relatively homogeneous working-class districts were relatively small in comparison with other Brussels houses was partly the result of their siting amidst existing buildings. As a result of increasing population pressure and the rising surplus value of building land in the town centre, the enclosed gardens and courts of existing houses were gradually used to provide housing for the poorest strata of the population.[26] It is evident that such restricted building space limited the possibilities for building multi-storey houses. This was certainly the case in the alleys which were laid out in the middle of the nineteenth century, but in the old city centre, where land prices were highest, these same conditions had not prevented the construction of alley houses with three storeys.

In his description of Belgian housing conditions, Eberstadt drew attention to a typical feature of the Brussels *impasse* or passage leading to a dead end:[27] very often the *impasse* was used only to gain access to the houses in the garden or court behind (see Figure 3.3). The passage itself contained no houses and served no housing function. According to Eberstadt, all the variants in Brussels *impasses* could be reduced to this basic pattern. In Antwerp, for example, the lay-out of the alleys was more diverse, often fulfilling a housing function as well. In Brussels the entrance to the *impasse* would very often be hardly noticed amidst the surrounding houses. The *impasse* was frequently an overbuilt tunnel-like passage, closed by a front door and leading through the ground floor of the house fronting the street. In many cases, the width of the built-up court or garden was determined by the width of the front house. Where the built-up court was square rather than long, it was called a *bataillon carré* (infantry square). One may assume that speculative considerations led to the use of this lay-out in those parts of the city where the relation between built-up surface and open space would have permitted other building methods.

IMPASSE DU MUGUET

Figure 3.3 Photograph of a typical Brussels alley, *Impasse du Muguet*, and ground-plan of the same *impasse*. The alley is situated in the Rue Haute which forms the border between the largely proletarian first and the second town districts. Comité de patronage des habitations ouvrières et des institutions de prévoyance, *Enquête sur les habitations ouvrières en 1903, 1904 et 1905*, (Brussels, 1905), I. Photographed by La Fonderie

V

The identity of the owners of these Brussels working-class houses has not yet been the object of research. Neither has this been the case with patterns of ownership in general, or with capital invested in housing and its return. P.C. Popp's cross-section of property real-estate taxation in 1866[28] does provide a starting point, in respect of the ownership patterns of the first district. This part of the city had a considerable number of poor (29.9 per cent), and contained courts and alleys, but it also included representatives of the middle class and the aristocracy. These registers tell us who the owners of the houses of the first district were and to which tax classes their properties belonged. The restriction of this research to one district, owing to its time-consuming character, of course means that we learn only what these people owned in this one district, and we know nothing about their properties in other districts of the town or elsewhere. The indication of the owner's profession provides some idea of social status. It goes without saying that this indication is imperfect. It is in part outdated since the land registry did not need to be notified of a change of profession. It is also incomplete: within most professional categories there is a hierarchy which can only be reconstructed by means of additional source material. The category of *rentiers*, for instance, is a very heterogeneous group, including not only the large land owner but also the modest proprietor. In the category of artisans and traders, only information about their professional income can provide the necessary social differentiation. The ownership of the 2,108 houses of the first district in 1866 is shown in Table 3.4.

Most *rentiers*, traders and artisans possessed only one house in the first district (which does not imply that they lived in it), between a quarter and a third owned 2 to 5 houses and only a minority possessed more than 6 houses (see Table 3.5). Next, the houses of the most important categories of owners have been aggregated to the tax classes 1–55 mentioned above (class 1: annual taxable value of 8,571 francs, class 55: annual taxable value of 24 francs). The category of houses of the classes 43–55, whose occupants may assumed to have been poor, is subdivided into two groups (see Table 3.6).

The *rentiers*, followed by artisans and traders, were the most important category of owners of houses in the lowest tax classes. Within the group of artisans owning houses of the lowest category, the importance of the food sector, with many butchers, bakers and pastry-cooks is striking. Artisans in the wood, building and luxury and precision industries were also important owners of cheap housing. The composition of the property of these groups indicates that 68.09 per cent of the houses owned by *rentiers* consisted of dwellings in the classes 43–55; for traders and artisans the share of this category of houses amounted to respectively 75.34 per cent and 76.13 per cent. Among the house-owners, two clearly delimited groups can be distinguished: those possessing only a substantial town-house and/or a middle-class house (class 1–42) and those

Table 3.4 Ownership of houses in the First district, by occupation, 1866

		Percentage of houses			
rentiers	30.9	manufacturers	2.2	profession not mentioned	6.2
liberal professions	7.0	hauliers	0.7	institutions	1.3
clerks	7.3	farmers	0.3		
traders	20.6	servants	0.2		
artisans	23.1	labourers	0.2		

Source: Tableau indicatif primitif ou liste alphabétique des propriétaires avec relevés de leurs propriétés foncières non-bâties et bâties. Ville de Bruxelles

Table 3.5 Distribution of ownership by occupational groups, First district, 1866

number of houses in ownership:	1	2 to 5	6 to 9	10 and more
		Percentage of owners		
rentiers	66.2	26.7	4.1	3.0
traders	59.6	32.4	5.3	2.7
artisans	66.0	28.6	4.6	0.8

Source: Tableau indicatif primitif ou liste alphabétique des propriétaires avec relevés de leurs propriétés foncières non-bâties et bâties. Ville de Bruxelles

Table 3.6 Ownership of houses in the First district by occupation of owner and tax class, 1866

		Percentage of houses		
tax class:	1–32	33–42	43–49	50–55
rentiers	42.9	32.2	26.6	33.0
liberal professions	19.0	10.3	6.0	3.9
clerks	9.5	10.3	5.3	7.2
traders	15.1	16.2	22.4	21.7
artisans	8.7	20.5	28.1	22.0
others	4.8	10.5	11.6	12.2
	100.0	100.0	100.0	100.0

Source: Tableau indicatif primitif ou liste alphabétique des propriétaires avec relevés de leurs propriétés foncières non-bâties et bâties. Ville de Bruxelles

possessing only houses in the lowest category (classes 43–55). Relatively few proprietors owned houses in both categories (Table 3.7).

Relatively few of the well-to-do seem to have invested in houses of the lowest classes. The owners of these houses formed a relatively homogeneous group with modest fortunes. If we leave the owners of high- and middle-class housing out of consideration and if we focus on those who had at least one house in the classes 43–55, we find that those who had

Table 3.7 Percentage of members of various occupational groups owning houses in tax categories, First district, 1866

	rentiers per cent	traders per cent	artisans per cent
ownership in class 1 to 42	40.9	25.0	24.7
ownership in class 43 to 55	48.6	59.0	62.5
ownership in both categories	10.5	13.8	10.8
unknown class	–	2.1	1.9

Source: Tableau indicatif primitif ou liste alphabétique des propriétaires avec relevés de leurs propriétés foncières non-bâties et bâties. Ville de Bruxelles

no houses in any other class represented the overwhelming majority: 82.28 per cent of the *rentiers* who possessed a house in classes 43–55 owned only houses in this category. In the group of traders this amounted to 81.02 per cent, and in the group of artisans to 85.26 per cent.

These figures confirm a statement by the Mayor of Brussels in 1910 concerning the identity of the owners of working-class housing: 'They are not for the greatest part bourgeois. Among them I have found former labourers with some savings, some petty traders having gathered a modest sum. It is in these social strata that investments of this nature are made.'[29] Victor Besme expressed himself in the same way: 'Property is exploited by proprietors of the inferior class who derive a usurious income from it.'[30] However, not many labourers appear to have been house-owners. A report of 1888 remarked: 'Not one [labourer] is the owner of his house, or, at least, if there are any labourers owning the dwelling they live in, their number is so limited that we can hardly take this into account.'[31]

Where housing is concerned, it is important to note that Brussels was dependent upon freehold tenure, and anyone wanting to build a house had to purchase the building plot. The land and housing markets of Brussels were characterised by fragmented ownership. It appears from the land-registry data that in the 1830s the 450 hectares of the surface area of Brussels (built on or not) were in the hands of almost 7,000 owners. In 1866 this number had doubled. Despite the fact that this number is somewhat exaggerated because owners with properties in several town districts were counted more than once, Brussels was nevertheless a town where ownership was not very concentrated.

The fragmented character of ownership and the modest means of those who were interested in building and buying low-class dwellings as an investment, prevented large-scale exploitation of working-class housing. A piece of land, very often a garden or court next to one's own house, could be enough to 'start a career' as a landlord. Until the 1840s the absence of any regulation allowed the erection of dwellings on nearly any spot and of the cheapest kind, and were even then very limited, precisely to allow the lower middle-class owners to maintain their investments in working-class housing. Apparently, they were the only population group interested in investments of this kind. The structure of the building industry was not conducive to the development of large-scale investments in working-class housing. The Brussels building industry was dominated by the small master working with four men at most but very often with only one or two. The few larger companies appearing in Brussels at the end of the nineteenth century were not involved in house building but in the execution of public works. All sources agree, however, that these modest house-owners charged rack rents. Both in the middle and at the end of the nineteenth century, contemporaries declared that, proportionally speaking, the working class paid one-and-a-half to two times more than the well-off citizens for housing.[32] At a conference in 1894 it was said that working-class housing produced returns of 5, 6 and even 7 per cent.[33] A report to a conference in 1913 stated that owners of houses situated in commercial streets had yields of 5 to 5.5 per cent; in the mixed neighbourhoods where traders, artisans and labourers lived, the return rose to 6 to 6.5 per cent; subdivided houses in the working-class districts, let by the *quartier* (a one or two-room unit) and by the month, yielded their owners 7 to 8 per cent; the owners of *impasse* houses let by the *quartier* and by the week received a return of 9 per cent. Costs for the provision of water and losses on unpaid rents may well have brought this 7 to 9 per cent return down to nearer 6 per cent.[34] It is, however, very difficult to tell how dependable these percentages are. In the middle of the nineteenth century a report on the condition of the working class declared that Brussels landlords obtained a return of 15 to 20 per cent, and a doctor visiting the poor stated that while decent houses rarely produced a return of more than 12 per cent, the owners of slums could receive more than 20 per cent.[35] In 1910 a socialist councillor remarked that the houses of the boulevards had yields of 7 to 8 per cent while the owners of the worst slums received 18 to 22 per cent.[36]

In Brussels (and Belgium in general) hardly any research has been done on the various aspects of landlord–tenant relations. The traditional sources used in historical research on housing offer very little detail on this relationship. This is not a coincidence, for where the letting of houses or land was concerned it was local customs and not the law which mattered. Compendiums synthesising the laws and regulations on house-letting even just before the First World War often refer to the local usages and customs, and the fact that these customs were seldom written down, does not lighten the task of the historian. Judicial archives might certainly shed some light on different aspects of the landlord–tenant relationship, but so far these archives have not been explored.

It is difficult, for instance, to establish the term of the lets of working-class housing in Brussels.[37] Where high and middle-class houses are concerned, there is no problem: they were usually let by the year, rent was paid quarterly, and the period of notice required for the reletting of property was three months. The term of the lets of tenements with three rooms or more, which were usually not occupied by a working-class family, are not known, but it is known that rent was paid monthly or quarterly, and that the period of notice was respectively a month or six weeks. Where the one- and two-roomed dwellings are concerned, the available information on typical accommodation of the Brussels working-class suggests that they were let and paid by the month or the week with a trend towards the longer period in the second half of the nineteenth century. The impression is that weekly lets were limited to the worst and the most shabby dwellings, for instance in the alleys. Wages were usually paid by the week, so that the payment of a monthly rent could create problems. For working-class property let by the month, the period of notice required for reletting was fifteen days and for weekly lets eight days.

Although the landlord's means of legal redress against the tenant can be established,[38] it is less easy to state how and to what extent they were utilised. When the tenant was late with payment of rent, the law permitted the seizure of goods to the value of the outstanding rent. The tenant was supposed to equip his room with furniture adequate enough to guarantee the landlord some compensation for possible non-payment of the rent. The seizure of goods could take place without a judge's approval, one day after the tenant had been requested to pay. It could even be done at once, without a demand, but then the approval of a judge was needed. If the tenant had fled and moved elsewhere, the goods could be seized up to fifteen days after his departure. The furniture could be sequestrated even if rent was not yet due and the tenant had fled before payment day. Landlords complained that when the tenant foresaw the possible sequestration or seizure of his goods, he quickly sold them or took them to the pawnshop.

When the tenant did not pay his rent or when he did not leave when the term of the let had expired, the landlord could apply to a magistrate for an expulsion order. The law of 9 August 1887 regulated the procedure of eviction where low-rented houses or flats were concerned. The objective of the law was to facilitate evictions by reducing the cost of the whole process. Contemporaries commented that many owners of *bataillons carrés* and working-class housing in general had in fact never been bothered by the cost of legal procedure, because they had other means of forcing the tenants to leave, such as obstructing the chimney from outside, by burning sulphur in it, or removing doors and windows.[39]

VI

It has already been remarked that until the 1840s the owners of *impasses* and *bataillon carrés* were not controlled in any way by building regulations. The Mayor of Brussels noted in 1865 that 'Almost all the *impasses* existing in Brussels have been built without any control by the authorities whatsoever'.[40] Since many of these slums were built in what were technically gardens, they were considered private property and were not subject to regulation. Even for houses fronting the public road, building regulations were very limited. The mayor did have the power to condemn insanitary dwellings, but he rarely exercised it.

The law of 1 February 1844 made these alleys on private property part of the public road. On 31 October 1846, building regulations were issued in Brussels which laid down rules on the height of houses, the width of streets, and the height of rooms.[41] According to a statement in 1846, the council had not bothered to regulate the height of houses in the previous period: 'Until now the height of houses has not been determined by very strict rules. In fact, our houses generally are not over-tall. Nevertheless they have a tendency to become taller in the most populated quarters and the busiest streets.'[42] From 1846 onwards, a street had to be at least 10 metres, and an alley 8 metres, wide. Houses built in streets less than 4 metres wide were allowed a maximum height of 8 metres. The greatest height of house was linked to a street width of 16 metres and more. Ducpétiaux[43] pleaded for a restriction of the height of houses in small streets, and referred to England where it was not permitted for the houses to be higher than the streets were wide. He met resistance from other councillors, who did not want to run counter to the proprietors' interests and were worried about depreciation of the properties in the inner town. As for the height of the rooms it was stipulated that a room on a mezzanine level had to measure at least 2.2 metres, while a room in an upper storey had to be at least 2.6 metres high.

The building regulations of 1846 were not applicable to the streets, passages and alleys which were part of, or led to, constructions designated as *bataillons carrés*. The municipality would simply judge individual requests from the owners or builders. It appears from the discussions in the town council that most councillors did not want to bother the proprietors too much.[44] This does not alter the fact that suggestions for changes in the initial plans were frequently made. The few councillors who pleaded for the introduction of more drastic improvements met resistance from the majority of councillors, who were of the opinion that proprietors would not be inclined to invest in working-class housing if too many demands were made on them, for they could not be expected to invest in an undertaking that would produce a lower return than other investments. Under the motto of 'If we ask too much, we'll end up with nothing at all', the necessary flexibility was displayed.

The alarming reports of the 1840s on the sanitary condition of the city and especially of its housing appear to have generated only very limited building regulations, which were not to be changed fundamentally in the second half of the nineteenth century. The building regulations themselves prove that the town council was more worried about decorum than about the actual housing situation. Building permits were delivered on the basis of a sketch of the front elevation, cross-section and ground-plan of the facade. The size of the rooms and the allocation of space within the building were not considered. The stipulations concerning the height of the front probably prevented the construction of tall houses in small streets, but since they did not take the depth of the premises into account they permitted the construction of disproportionately tall houses on small plots.[45]

Changes in the building regulations later led to an increase in the permitted building height, except in the narrowest streets. The regulations of 14 February 1857[46] raised the maximum height of the facade in streets of 9 metres and more by one metre; the tallest house in the widest street could reach a maximum of 19 metres. The building regulations of 8 January 1883[47] increased the permitted building height once more: in streets of 8 metres' width the maximum height rose by 1 metre, as it did for street widths above 11 metres; in streets that were 13 or more metres wide, the maximum height was increased by 2 metres; in streets of more than 15 metres wide, a 21-metre facade was allowed.

The building regulations of 1883 were more stringent with regard to the height of rooms: ground floor rooms had to be at least 3 metres high while a room on the upper floors, mezzanine or attic had to be respectively at least 2.8 and 2.6 metres high. From 1906 onwards the rooms on the upper floors had to measure at least 3 metres. The regulations of 1883 required an inner court for every newly-built house, but it was not until the regulations of 1906[48] that its minimum surface-area was fixed at one-eighth of the premises' total.

As far as sanitation was concerned, connection to the city's public sewer system had been required by the building regulations of 1846. From that year on, every newly-built house had to be provided with a privy unless the municipal authorities allowed the installation of collective ones for several houses. The regulations of 1883 retained the possibility of collective sanitary facilities, but imposed a minimum of one water closet for every 25 occupants. It was not until the building regulations of 1906 that a separate lavatory for every house was absolutely required. The same regulations were the first to insist on an adequate water supply for every inhabited building. Until then, the water supply of the *impasse* had often been limited to a single tap, from which the water was rationed by the landlord. This did not prevent his charging for it separately. The public thoroughfares regulations of 1865[49] had already stipulated that every alley had to be provided with 'sufficient' drinking-water, but it was to be expected that the vagueness of this requirement would not induce many landlords to make the necessary provisions.

Besides these regulations concerning newly-built or rebuilt houses, it was stated explicitly on 2 October 1848[50] that the council was empowered to condemn insanitary dwellings if the landlord had neglected to make the improvements suggested by the city's local medical commission. In 1865 this stipulation was added to the city's public thoroughfares regulations.[51] From 1874 on, sanitary inquiries were carried out by the newly established *Bureau d'hygiène* (Office of Public Health and Hygiene). It appears that houses were seldom condemned: landlords seem to have willingly complied with the Bureau's sanitation requirements.[52] This raises the question of whether these measures were strictly applied, for there is more than a suspicion that the city authorities displayed the same flexibility towards landlords in this as in other matters.

VII

The limited building and sanitary regulations may have reassured the Brussels bourgeoisie, frightened by alarming public health reports which had been underlined by the cholera epidemic of 1849, but they were clearly unable to generate short-term and radical changes in the city's general appearance. This was, however, one of the major aspirations both of the local bourgeoisie and of King Leopold II, who had already given it some thought before he was crowned. 'I am not pleading for exaggerated luxury but I want Brussels to keep up the position which it is entitled to pursue', he declared, adding, 'One has to embellish the centre of government, increasing its air of elegance and pleasure'.[53]

The property tax data for 1833–34 show that this ideal was far from being reached. More than 60 per cent of the Brussels housing stock consisted of dwellings in the lowest tax classes. The fact that in the following decades population growth was particularly marked in the most proletarian districts would certainly not have decreased the proportion of low-class housing. It is evident that the picture of a heavily polluted, regularly overflowing Senne, bordered by shabby dwellings, winding streets and hidden alleys and courts, did not exactly correspond to the image of 'the capital' cherished by the bourgeoisie.

In the middle of the nineteenth century the city council was confronted by the fact that more and more wealthy citizens were leaving the centre, especially the lower part, to settle outside the city limits. In the period from 1856 to 1866, the population growth of Brussels slowed down perceptibly.[54] This meant a serious loss in tax revenue. The authorities complained of property depreciation in the old city districts and feared an exponential fall in property values as the better-off left town.[55] A petition by worried Brussels citizens stated in 1856, probably exaggeratedly, 'That the value of properties in the lower part of Brussels has diminished by more than 40 million (francs) in only a few years'.[56] The suburban boroughs that welcomed the wealthy citizens of Brussels were reproached for taking advantage of the metropolitan facilities without having to bear the cost. One possible solution which was tried was the annexation of parts of the suburban area to the city itself. The Quartier Léopold was created in this way in 1853, encompassing an area of 194 hectares that had attracted well-to-do residents. In 1864 the attractive quarters of the Avenue Louise and the Bois de la Cambre were brought within the city's boundaries. However, more ambitious schemes failed[57] and it became evident that the appearance of the old city centre itself had to change.

A start was made on this in the second half of the nineteenth century.[58] For fifty years, the capital was the scene of large-scale demolition and improvement works which, according to both their defenders and critics, systematically reduced the number of areas providing working-class accommodation. The self-contained worlds of streets, alleys and courts were torn apart. Their relative isolation from the outside world, which contemporaries considered to have encouraged a promiscuous form of cohabitation, was opened up. Wide public spaces, squares and broad connecting roads were created. This town planning policy obviously involved massive expropriation. Legal and financial vagueness in this respect were largely cleared up by the compulsory purchase law of 1 July 1858, which was strongly influenced by the recent French expropriation law.[59] The law of 1858 provided for expropriation on sanitary grounds of working-class areas and created the possibility of compulsorily purchasing premises situated alongside projected new roads or streets. The law specified that proprietors would be compensated according to the value of their property before improvements were carried out. The surplus value resulting from urban improvement was to be recovered by the council from the re-sale of property. Lobbying by the city was behind the terms of the new law, as a result of experience with the first major renovation scheme in the latter half of the century. When the rue Blaes was driven through the proletarian quartier des Marolles between 1853 and 1860, the owners involved had succeeded in gaining compensation that gave them a substantial slice of the surplus value generated by the scheme.[60] It was consequently in the capital that the law of 1858 was most intensely used as an instrument of town-planning policy. The law of 15 November 1867 broadened the scope of the earlier law's application to permit expropriation of complete zones for which an urban improvement scheme or development plan had been approved. Whole districts or parts of districts could be improved or redesigned. Public hygiene was no longer the only accepted justification for a compulsory purchase order: any proposals for improvement or embellishment would be taken into account.

The Mayor of Brussels (1863–79), Jules Anspach, was strongly influenced by Haussmann's transformation of Paris, and started the improvement works to the River Senne in 1867 (the second, third, fourth, fifth and eighth districts). The associated clearance scheme demolished some 1,100 houses, most of which were inhabited by small traders, artisans and workers. The Senne, which flowed through the lower part of the city, was canalised and built over. The winding pattern of streets that had followed the old course of the river was replaced by straight, broad boulevards which connected the northern and southern rail terminals to the city centre. These boulevards were bordered by handsome four- or five-storey houses, whose ground floors were taken up by commercial premises. In order to ensure the grandeur of the buildings along the central boulevards, the municipality awarded prizes for houses with special architectural value. A number of the plots were conceded to a Parisian builder who was to erect houses in 'Parisian' style. The keystones of the scheme, however, were the new Stock

Exchange and the central covered market.

The slums which detracted from the surroundings of the rue Royale and obstructed the view of the monumental Colonne de Congrès were the next to disappear in a slum clearance scheme in the Quartier Notre-Dame-aux-Neiges in the sixth city district. Here too, winding streets were replaced by straight ones and uniform middle-class housing, while just under 700 existing houses were demolished. In the same period, expropriations for the building of a new Palais de Justice were started in the surroundings of the proletarian rue Haute (first district). At the same time, the transformation of the Quartier Vierge Noir (third and fourth districts) in the lower part of the city was being planned. The period in which the municipality took the initiative for large-scale transformations came to an end with Anspach's death in 1879 and the crisis in the Brussels property market. The city's precarious financial situation, and his own town planning theories, inspired Anspach's successor Charles Buls (1881–99) to follow a more prudent policy. The city's role was, however, taken over by King Leopold II and the Belgian government: the era of large-scale demolitions was not yet over. In order to improve communications between the lower and the upper part of town, the Quartier Sint-Roch (seventh district) was swept away in 1897–98. A few years later, compulsory purchase orders were served on the inhabitants of the quartiers of Putterie, Ter Arken and Isabelle (second and seventh districts) in order to open up a rail link between the existing northern and southern terminals.

The Brussels City Council defended the demolition of large parts of the old city with classic arguments: modernisation, traffic flow, public health and embellishment. The health argument was generally more successful than that of embellishment because its interest for the rest of the urban community was more clearly evident. It goes without saying that all these factors did play a part in the vast transformations of the city, yet it should not be assumed that they were the transformers' final goal. They were instruments and products, as were the works undertaken in their name, of a strategy of attracting the wealthy and commercial classes back to the city centre in order to prevent the relative depreciation of the metropolitan area. These aspects were usually less extensively commented upon than the technical, hygienic and aesthetic problems. Only sporadically, when some councillors criticised the social consequences of the city's planning policy, were statements made such as, 'It is not a question of providing the inhabitants of the area with new housing in the same place, but of attracting wealthier layers of the population',[61] or, 'We find ourselves in the absolute necessity, in spite of our sincere wish that it should be otherwise, of having as many tax-payers as possible contributing to the city's treasury, instead of augmenting the number of inhabitants who cost without bringing money in'.[62]

The demolition of the old quarters was intended to provoke the exodus of the poorer sections of the population. The vacant space was confiscated and rearranged by means of infrastructural and improvement schemes in order to encourage the establishment of the aristocracy and the commercial class. The desire to turn Brussels effectively into the prime commercial, financial, political and administrative centre of the country cannot be separated from the ambition to model urban space after the bourgeoisie's own idea of a 'real capital'. Brussels had to become a capital on a European level, a cosmopolitan city that foreigners would no longer consider a mere stop-over between the northern and southern rail terminals.

The ideas involved in the actual working-out of this town planning project were strongly rooted in the neo-classical image of the ideal city, with broad, symmetrical streets which reconciled aesthetic and health considerations. The luxurious houses, *maisons de rapport*, and commercial premises which bordered the boulevards and streets were to alternate with monumental constructions and public buildings accommodating the state's commercial, administrative, cultural, educational and repressive activities, while at the same time transcending the bourgeois values which inspired them.[63] The Brussels Council was very well aware of the fact that sanitation and town planning alone were not enough to attract the bourgeoisie to the city centre. Only the symbiosis of objective functions and image-building could lend the necessary lustre to the metropolitan area, and this could only be represented by the increased property values which the city authorities desired. 'Our territory', they remarked in 1874, 'must have double and treble the value of the suburbs'.[64]

Despite the absence of a general development scheme, each of the specialised functions was allotted its place in the hierarchically structured urban space: in the upper part of the city were the Parliament, the royal palace and the monumental Palais de Justice enthroned above the mercantile and industrious city centre. It was expected that the transformed *quartiers* would mainly be occupied by the aristocracy on the one hand and by shops and the middle class on the other hand. In the less expensive houses some rooms might be occupied by clerks and the best paid among the artisans.[65] In this functional subdivision, working-class housing was not allotted a place. The City Council was aware of the fact that working-class housing was not considered a lucrative investment for the speculative capital to which it appealed to carry out its schemes. The Council itself refused to take any initiatives in this field, expecting and hoping that the reproduction of labour power would take place outside the metropolitan area. It is striking that the advocates of 'picturesque' town planning such as Charles Buls criticised the aesthetic and financial implications of Anspach's large-scale town planning policy, yet completely agreed with the functional reallocation of urban space and the displacement of the working class.

It is difficult, from research so far undertaken, to tell to what extent the City Council achieved its aim. The fact that the sale of plots and houses was more difficult than had been expected, the fact that building along the boulevards progressed slowly and that the companies involved in carrying out the transformations went bankrupt, are all evidence of something other than unqualified success.[66] Critics of Anspach's large-scale redevelopment policy insisted that the architecture of the straight-line, symmetrical street patterns, the cosmopolitan mixture of building styles, and the construction of multiple-family dwellings in the Parisian style, did not appeal to the Brussels citizen. They asserted that the bourgeoisie was not attracted to the new housing, and complaints about building quality were often made. For speculative reasons, the imported Parisian building style was mutilated, sacrificing much light and space.[67] It is clear that the builders were much more concerned with creating a certain image and a stylish decorum than with the effective improvement of housing conditions, even where the wealthier classes were concerned.

VIII

Supporters and critics of the improvement schemes left no doubt that Brussels town planning policy resulted in the reduction of the area providing working-class housing. As early as the 1840s, Ducpétiaux had declared: 'Unceasingly chased by the hammer of the demolisher, they [the people] see a daily reduction in the space they have hitherto occupied'.[68] According to the socialist Councillor, Conrardy, nothing had changed fifty years later: 'Each time a city *quartier* is demolished, working-class dwellings disappear. This results in the gradual abolition of all the streets where working-class dwellings used to be found and these are never rebuilt'.[69] Nobody could contradict him because it appeared that the promises with regard to the provision of alternative working-class accommodation had in most cases never been kept.

The town council had neglected the building of alternative housing, but private investors had not been very active either. Only a few *cités ouvrières*, tenement houses specifically designed for working-class occupation, were built on the capital's territory in the 1860s and 1870s (Figure 3.4). Most of these tenements were five- or six-storey houses consisting of one, two or even four two- to three-roomed apartments on each floor.[70] A distinctive attempt to separate private and public space and to create a functional division within the flat was displayed. In some cases a scullery for cooking and washing was added to the two-roomed dwelling. In other cases the annex was reduced to a lavatory. The facade, imitating the style of middle-class housing, suggested bourgeois respectability. In fact, most of the tenants were 'respectable' members of the working-class: clerks and well-paid artisans who could afford rents which could rise to eighteen francs per month and more.[71] Although the flats at the back and on the fifth and sixth floors were cheaper (thirteen to seventeen francs), it was more than the average Brussels labourer could afford. According to an inquiry in 1890 the average Brussels labourer earned 3.14 francs per day and paid 11.68 francs per month for one room; in other words, he spent some 14 per cent of his income on rent.[72] An inquiry, focusing on the inhabitants of the *impasses* established that rent absorbed not less than about a quarter of the family income.[73] The relatively expensive tenements did not seem to be very

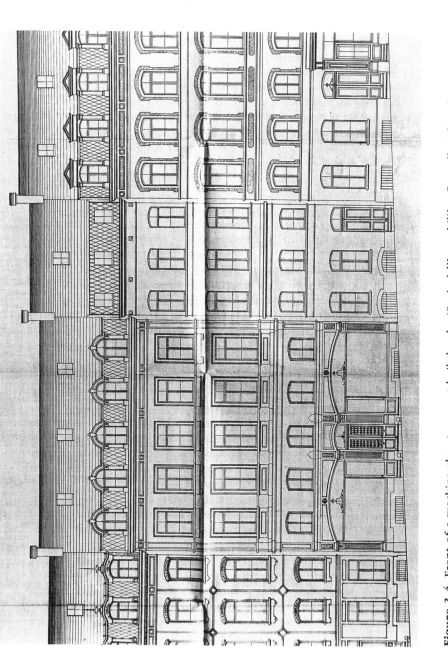

Figure 3.4 Front of a working-class tenement built by the 'Societé l'Immobilière Bruxelloise' in the Rue aux Laines in 1866. Archives de la Ville de Bruxelles, nr. 9875. Photographed by La Fonderie.

popular: contemporaries declared that working-class families disliked occupying the upper floors of multi-storey houses.[74]

Contemporaries were equally convinced that the large-scale clearances had not succeeded in provoking a massive emigration of the lower layers of the population. Several sources confirm that the working-class families did not leave for the suburbs *en masse* but were squeezed into the remaining working-class areas. Whether this was to be permanent will be considered later.

From either viewpoint, the question was gradually considered a major problem by the different factions in the city council, especially during Buls' mayoralty in the last decade of the century, when socialist criticism and proposals somehow forced the liberals to make a stand. The liberal mayors and their faction were of the opinion that the high price of building land in the improved city centre made it unsuitable for working-class housing. As a result, the working class had to emigrate to the suburbs. Cheap transport connecting the suburbs and the centre of the town had to be provided. On a national level this philosophy had already led to the introduction of workmen's cheap railway tickets. The Mayor of Brussels declared that although the fact that the lowest strata had to leave the city should be deplored, nothing could be done about it: it was an international phenomenon which was beyond the city's control. The municipality was by no means to take the initiative with regard to working-class housing, either within the city or in the suburbs. At most, a form of indirect interference might be tolerated, such as the sale of building land at a cheaper price to those who wanted to build working-class dwellings.[75] In 1899 the town council, after having once more rejected a socialist motion, agreed upon a proposal of Mayor Buls. In that very same year the *Société anonyme des habitations à bon marché de l'agglomération bruxelloise* was established. The council was allowed to subscribe for a third of the capital.[76] In the years 1900–12, 197 houses were built in the suburbs.

Not all of the liberal councillors were of the same opinion. Some of them shared the views of Catholic councillors who were in favour of mixing social classes. They warned against the dangers of segregated areas, and they pointed out the advantages (in charity) that the lower classes might enjoy as a result of such class harmony. They also thought that workers ought to be able to live close to their workplace: distance not only cost money but was also time-consuming, which had a negative influence on family life.[77] All such arguments were treated with scorn by Buls, who replied that they were inspired not by a concern for the working class but by the fear 'that in these suburbs a revolutionary agglomeration might be formed, whence hordes of barbarians would move down into the city centre, on the slightest pretext, in order to exterminate the wealthy citizens of the inner city'.[78] The Catholic councillors fought against the non-interventionism of the liberal majority but at the same time they also condemned the 'collectivism' of the socialists. The approach of the Catholic councillors favoured initiatives not by the local authority but by the institutions for relief of the poor.

Socialist councillors declared that the Brussels working class should be enabled to stay in the capital. In order to permit this, they argued that the council should intervene directly and actively in the building of working-class housing.[79] Experience proved, so they believed, that private initiative had been deficient, despite concessions by the authorities. It was equally clear that the law on workmen's dwellings of 9 August 1889, which provided for cheap loans to workers for the building or purchase of a house, had no effect whatsoever in the capital.[80] The law of 1889 was the first important measure dealing with the improvement of working-class housing in Belgium. The National Savings and Superannuation Fund was authorised to invest part of its resources in loans required for the construction or purchase of working-class dwellings. Persons wishing to avail themselves of this provision had to do so through a recognised society established for the purposes contemplated by the law. A loan was granted to such a society on the recommendation of the local housing committee (*comité de patronage*) which was also created by this legislation. The housing committees had to facilitate the construction and renting of healthy working-class dwellings and the sale of such dwellings to working people, and they also had to study the local housing situation. In the city of Brussels, the law of 1889 resulted in a considerable number of inquiries and reports, but did not lead to the construction and renting of working-class housing. In the suburbs of Brussels the situation was different, and there the law effectively resulted in the building of working-class dwellings. The building or purchase of a house in Brussels was beyond the reach of even the wealthiest working-class families. Within the context of the capital, the idea of the labourer owning his house proved to be unrealistic. Another ideal, the building of working-class houses for one or two families, was regarded as similarly unrealistic in the metropolitan context. Apartment blocks of five storeys appeared to be the second-best choice. All the socialist proposals concerning working-class housing were, however, effectively blocked until 1906, when the liberals were obliged to form a coalition with the socialist faction. In that same year a slum clearance scheme was agreed for the proletarian quartier des Marolles, with provision for alternative accommodation for those made homeless. It was not until 1912 that these plans were actually carried out.

The *Cité Hellemans*,[81] as the new scheme's apartment blocks were called, consisted of seven parallel rows of five-storey tenement blocks which formed encapsulated housing units (see Figures 3.5 and 3.6). Within the *cité*, large archways in the centre of each block permitted internal movement and ventilation. There was no passage, however, through the monumental front with its shops on the ground floor. The *cité* with its housing function was strictly separated from the outside world. The architect took great care to reduce the amount of communal space within the *cité*. The staircases were conceived of as a continuation of the street: they were open to the air and finished in the same material as the facade. Each apartment formed a self-contained living unit with all necessary facilities. Sleeping, living, cooking and washing functions were

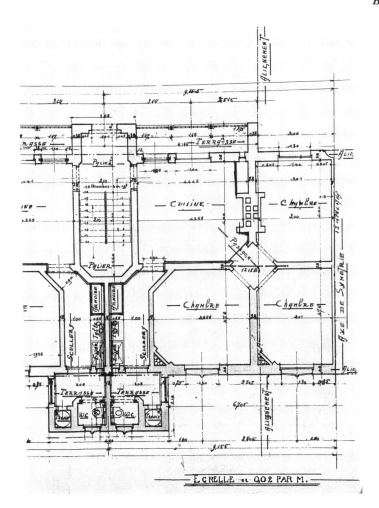

Figure 3.5 The ground-plan of a flat on the second and third floor of block B of the working-class tenements, *Cité Hellemans*, built by the city council (1906–1919) in the Rue Blaes and the Rue Haute. Archives de la Ville de Bruxelles. Photographed by La Fonderie.

separated. A small hall separated the three bedrooms from the kitchen, which was also used as a living room. Cooking and washing facilities were provided not in the living unit but in a separate scullery, through which a small balcony with lavatory and storage space could be reached.

The socialist faction continually emphasised the desirability for Brussels workers to live near their workplace, but the argument was usually not accompanied by actual data on the metropolitan labour market. It appears from the industrial and population census that the proportion of workers who needed to live nearby did indeed increase rather than decrease in the second half of the nineteenth century.[82] The clothing industry, for instance, was of growing importance: in 1896 it

Figure 3.6 The block of flats shown in
Figure 3.5, in 1987. Photographed by P.
Scholliers.

accounted for 34.6 per cent of total industrial employment. Owing to the
seasonal character of this industry, periods of unemployment alternated
with intense activity and extremely long working days. It goes without
saying that such a regime was only tolerable if the workers did not live
too far from the workshop. It should, moreover, be noted that the
restructuring of the Brussels clothing industry led to an ever growing
part of the work being done at home by workers who had to collect and
deliver the work themselves. In the hectic days of the high season, longer
distances meant a loss of time and money. Furthermore, these workers
could not afford high transport costs: their meagre piece-rates were
already eaten into by rent and depreciation of their sewing-machines. In
the leather industry, a similar evolution took place. Other trades needed
to be close to their customers as well: such as large numbers of washerwomen and pressers, hawkers, rag-and-bone men, street and market
traders (whose numbers grew appreciably in the second half of the
century), and all the other trades involved in satisfying the needs of the

town. Of course, this could not prevent the gradual emigration of the working-class families to the suburban communes, resulting in the shrinking of their share in the capital's population. The Board of Trade inquiry[83] at the beginning of the twentieth century stated that the suburban commune of Sint-Jans-Molenbeek had a pronounced industrial character and contained a very large working-class population. In Anderlecht the working classes were estimated to represent about one third of the total population, some of whom lived in the remote semi-rural parts of the commune. The inquiry described Sint-Joost-ten-Noode and Elsene as being inhabited mainly by a well-to-do population. Schaarbeek, on the other hand, was characterised as being mainly lower-middle-class, with a considerable element of the working classes, while for Etterbeek it was found difficult to establish the marked predomination of any particular class.

IX

What was the influence of the transformations of the second half of the nineteenth century on the building style and the housing quality of the Brussels population in general and of the working class in particular? As might be expected, the height of the houses of Brussels increased, as shown in Table 3.8:

Table 3.8 Number of storeys per house in 1846 and 1910 (per cent)

	1846	1910
ground floor	8.7	1.2
2 storeys	43.3	11.6
3 storeys	48.0	51.6
4 storeys	–	27.3
5 storeys	–	6.3
6 storeys	–	1.8
7 storeys	–	0.2
8 storeys	–	–

Source: Ville de Bruxelles, Les recensements de 1910 (Brussels, 1912), 220–1

Unfortunately, the sources for this information provide figures by police divisions and not districts, which masks social differentiation. The first 'division', for example, includes the proletarian first city district together with the aristocratic seventh district. It appears, however, that in the more recently acquired residential areas of the Quartier Léopold, Quartier Nord-Est, avenue Louise and Bois de la Cambre, the three-storey house predominated (70 per cent of houses). In the old (cleared and improved) city centre, three-storey houses represented only about 40 per cent of the total, and four-storey houses about 30 per cent. In the fourth division (the commercial fifth and the sixth district which had been transformed by the Notre-Dame-aux-Neiges clearance scheme) five-storey houses represented as much as 12.5 per cent of the total. In the old city districts, one half to two-thirds of the houses had ground floors occupied by retail businesses, while in the residential districts this figure varied between 10 and 20 per cent.

Data from the Brussels housing inquiry of 1903–9[84] confirm that, as in the 1840s, the alley cottage was smaller than the average Brussels house. The proportion of single or two-storey houses in the alleys was 70.3 per cent, while for the city as a whole this figure was only 12.82 per cent. Houses with four storeys and more, which represented more than a third of the available housing in Brussels, in the alleys made up less than 5 per cent of the total. It is not surprising that houses in the improved city *quartiers* were taller. The increased value of the land in the cleared area, the building regulations which allowed taller houses in the broad boulevards and streets, and the fact that the council itself encouraged monumental building along the most prestigious boulevards, all led to an increase in the height of the Brussels house.

Charles Buls' fear that two- and three-storey houses would be replaced by taller buildings became a reality in the transformed city *quartiers*. Other data from the 1910 census would have caused him even more concern. It appears that very few Brussels families were the sole occupants of their house, even in the wealthier areas where houses were designed to be self-contained single-family dwellings. It is not surprising that in the proletarian first, second and third districts only a minority lived in single-family houses. It should be noted, however, that people living in the alleys were more frequently the sole occupants of their house: it appears from the 1903–9 inquiry that 24 per cent of the families were the sole occupants of their, admittedly small, house. In general, however, living in a single-family dwelling was a privilege of the rich: 68.9 per cent of Brussels families who were sole occupants lived in houses with seven rooms or more. In the commercial fifth and eighth districts and the seventh district, which had always been characterised as aristocratic, it was nevertheless only a minority who appear to have lived in a single-family dwelling. Even in the residential Quartier Léopold (ninth district) and the Quartier Nord-Est (tenth district) fewer than half the houses were occupied by one family. It was only in the very exclusive and outlying avenue Louise and Bois de la Cambre area (eleventh district) that two-thirds of the houses proved to be single-family dwellings (Table 3.9).

How can the relatively low proportion of single-family dwellings in residential areas be explained? On the one hand, it may be supposed that the well-off families who had once chosen to reside in the seventh and ninth districts were gradually moving to even more exclusive areas, such as the eleventh district and other residential neighbourhoods outside the capital. It may be assumed that the houses which they left behind were then occupied by poorer sections of the population, subdividing them in order to be able to pay the rent. Contemporaries declared, however, that relatively recent houses in these and other districts also shared this fate.

Table 3.9 Percentage of families occupying a whole house, by district, 1910

City of Brussels:	13.2				
District 1:	7.5	District 5:	11.5	District 9:	45.1
District 2:	4.8	District 6:	14.3	District 10:	28.7
District 3:	6.1	District 7:	15.9	District 11:	67.2
District 4:	7.0	District 8:	10.0	District 12:	5.7

Source: Ville de Bruxelles, Les recensements de 1910 (Brussels, 1912), 224–47

Confronted by the fact that the houses designed for occupation by one family were not occupied as such, Roupcinsky, a member of the *Comité officiel de patronage des habitations ouvrières de Bruxelles*, asked, 'Are they all occupied by rentiers?'. He gave the answer to his own rhetorical question: 'No, built for one single family, they are let floor by floor and as a result occupied by several families of petty clerks or labourers'. He added, 'The builders have put up buildings destined for one family and there they stand, given over to intense sub-letting.'[85]

It appears that the local authority and private individuals and developers who had built the houses had overestimated the housing requirements of the well-off. Charles Buls admitted this in 1891.[86] Indeed, after the building boom of the 1870s, construction had slowed down and this downward trend was to continue until about 1890. From about 1891 onwards, a new housebuilding boom took place but collapsed again after 1900. Where rentiers or other wealthy people had been expected, there were clerks and manual workers—a rather ironic outcome of the large-scale effort to attract the well-to-do, carefully avoiding the provision of alternative housing for those who were socially undesirable. Meanwhile, Buls had to face up to the fact that in the metropolitan context, building single-family dwellings did not necessarily mean that they would be occupied as such.

The families who moved into the *maisons de rentier* were far from comfortably accommodated, as the houses had been designed and equipped for the needs of only one family. Roupcinsky described them: 'Raised kitchen basements, topped by a "ground" floor with three communicating rooms, of which the rearmost adjoins a smaller "office"; half-way up the stairs a bathroom and lavatory; on each of the two upper storeys two rooms if the front is narrower than 5m.50 or two rooms and an office if the facade reaches 6 metres; under the roof, two garret rooms and an attic'.[87]

The fact that subdivided single-family dwellings appear to have lodged an appreciable number of working-class families raises a number of questions. To what extent did these subdivided houses provide accommodation for working-class families pushed out by improvement and embellishment works? Were the small houses in the *impasses* still the predominant form of working-class housing, and to what extent had they been replaced by other forms of accommodation?

Statements by city councillors suggest that the role of small alley houses was still important: they pointed out that many *impasses* had been pulled down, but they acknowledged at the same time that the resulting homeless were squeezed into the remaining alleys. In the first phase after slum clearance, this was probably true. In a report on working-class housing, Buls stated in 1891 that according to his own inquiry after a slum clearance programme, 76 per cent of the families involved were lodged within a radius of 800 metres of their former home. Only 4 per cent left for the suburbs.[88] Visitors of the poor mentioned that in the remaining alleys even the worst slums, attics and cellars found new tenants. While rents in the renovated quartiers stagnated or even fell, rents in working-class quartiers increased.[89] This certainly ran counter to the image of a modern, healthy and prosperous city. It was undoubtedly with some resentment that Mayor Anspach stated in 1877, 'While on the one hand we take great pains to improve the city, on the other hand ever growing centres of infection are created'.[90]

It may be doubted, however, whether this overcrowding in the remaining alleys could have been maintained throughout subsequent slum clearances. In the 1890s and the first decade of the twentieth century, those involved in the *Comités de patronage des habitations ouvrières* of the suburbs complained increasingly about the fact that the working-class families chased from the Brussels territory added to the already overcrowded situation. When suburban communes such as Molenbeek, Elsene, Sint-Gilles, Schaarbeek and Etterbeek started their own slum clearance projects, the working-class families had to look for lodgings in the remoter rural or semi-rural parts of greater Brussels.[91]

It is true that the number of people living in the alleys of the old city decreased gradually. In 1866 the alleys provided accommodation for 27,273 persons; in 1890 the population of the remaining alleys had fallen to 15,014, while in 1910 only 10,679 persons were left in this sort of accommodation. The census of 1910 showed a decrease in the population of the capital as a whole. In 1920, 7,427 *impasse* inhabitants were counted.[92] If these figures prove that those driven out were not permanently absorbed by the remaining accommodation offered by the *impasses*, they also fail to show to what extent they moved to subdivided houses and tenements.

However this may have been, the presence of the working class outside the *impasses* cannot have been negligible. As has been mentioned, the *impasses* housed 10,679 persons in 1910. The *Recensement spécial des logements* of that same year indicates, however, that one and two-roomed dwellings, the typical housing unit of the Brussels working class, were occupied by not less than 77,525 persons. A large part of those people must have lived outside the alleys and courts.[93] But neither was this type of accommodation inexhaustible. In its comment on the population census of 1910, the local authority noted the gradual disappearance of streets with a mixed population: 'The old Brussels houses with two or three floors occupied by petty traders and a great number of subletters have been completely transformed and even demolished'. In line with the economic function that the city had and

Table 3.10 Percentage of one- and two-roomed dwellings, by district

District	1842								
	1	2	3	4	5	6	7	8	All
1 room	48	50	48	26	25	40	15	21	37
2 rooms	22	27	27	23	25	26	17	17	24
Total:	70	77	75	49	50	66	32	38	61

District	1910												
	1	2	3	4	5	6	7	8	9	10	11	12	All
1 room	43.6	48.3	35.6	38.4	32.7	34.3	30.0	40.0	13.0	10.1	5.4	29.0	34.4
2 rooms	25.8	26.3	27.3	24.2	18.0	20.4	19.6	20.9	14.5	14.5	5.5	32.9	22.4
Total:	69.4	74.6	62.9	62.6	50.7	54.7	49.6	60.9	27.5	24.6	10.9	61.9	56.8

Source: Ville de Bruxelles, Les recensements de 1910 (Brussels, 1912); A. Quetelet, 'Sur le recensement de la population de Bruxelles en 1842', *Bulletin de la Commission centrale de statistique*, I (1842), 27–162

further wished to have, these houses were gradually replaced by buildings whose ground floors were occupied by ever larger business premises.[94]

In the second half of the nineteenth century, many *impasses* and *bataillons carrés* were wiped from the Brussels map. It is not easy to check whether such clearances led to an improvement in housing quality. Some improvements, such as broader streets, laying pavements in the existing alleys and the spread of gas, water and sewer connections, are difficult to measure. Certain data are indicative, however, of the housing situation after the large-scale transformations. One of the most frequently made complaints in the nineteenth century was that whole families were packed into one or two rooms. In 1842, 37 per cent of Brussels families were lodged in one room and 24 per cent lived in two rooms. In 1846, the figures were respectively 44.9 per cent and 22.3 per cent. In 1910 the number of families in only one room had fallen to 34.4 per cent, with a further 22.4 per cent in two-roomed dwellings. As a whole, therefore, the proportion of one- and two-roomed dwellings fell overall from 67.2 to 56.8 per cent. In view of the scale of the transformations, this may be considered a very meagre result. Data on the importance of one- and two-room dwellings per district even indicate that such general figures give too optimistic a picture of what was happening in the eight districts of the old city (Table 3.10).

There was no reduction of one- and two-roomed dwellings within the old city limits. On the contrary, in the eight districts of the original city, the proportion of one-roomed dwellings rose from 37 per cent in 1842 to 39.5 per cent in 1910, while the proportion of two-roomed dwellings remained constant at 24.2 per cent. Only the third and sixth districts, where improvement works had been most radical, show a decrease in this type of accommodation. But this was largely 'compensated' by substantial increases in the fourth, seventh and eighth districts. The fourth and eighth districts had been relatively spared during the transformations. The seventh district had suffered severely in the most recent demolitions. It needs to be said, though, that 54.6 per cent of these one-roomed dwellings were occupied by one person or a couple.

It must be stressed that housing conditions in Brussels were not that much worse than in the suburban communes with a substantial working-class population. In the eight districts of the old city, 63.7 per cent of the dwellings consisted of one- and two-roomed units. In Sint-Jans-Molenbeek the proportion of this kind of accommodation was 56.1 per cent, while in Anderlecht it was 53.2 per cent. Even in the suburban communes where the elite and the middle class were better represented, one- and two-room dwellings accounted for nearly 40 to as much as 50 per cent of the available accommodation.[95]

It is not easy to check whether the specific evolution of working-class housing is similar. There are the findings from inquiries into working-class housing at the turn of the century, but for the middle of the nineteenth century, there is only data on whole town districts. These do, however, provide some useful indications. It appears from the census of 1842 that in the most proletarian districts (the first, second and third districts), 48 to 50 per cent of families lived in one room and 27 per cent of the families were housed in two rooms. Thus, in the most proletarian areas, 75 to 77 per cent of the families were occupying one- or two-roomed dwellings. These figures probably give a too rosy impression of the situation since they provide information on a given district and not on a particular social class. Statements by contemporaries suggest that with regard to working-class housing, one-roomed dwellings were probably more widespread than these figures indicate. Even if this is discounted, we have to conclude that there was little or no improvement in the condition of working-class housing. It appears from the inquiry of 1890 that 90.3 per cent of the 19,284 Brussels working-class families were housed in one- and two-room units.[96] According to the inquiry of 1903–9, which covered 6,756 working-class families, this type of accommodation was occupied by 83.6 per cent of the families.[97] Any apparent improvement has more to do with the methodological differences between the two inquiries than with actual betterment. The inquiry of 1903–9 concentrated on working-class housing in the *impasses*. Although other forms of working-class housing were not excluded, they were under-represented. The focus on alley and court housing took more account of families who occupied an admittedly small but self-contained house with more rooms: it appears from the inquiry of 1903–9 that 24 per cent of the families living in alleys and courts occupied a whole house, against 8.3 per cent of the families living in mixed streets. The proportion of one- and two-roomed dwellings was 87.7 per cent in the dispersed working-class dwellings and 81.8 per cent in the alley cottages.

The fact that the inquiry of 1903–9 concentrated on dwellings in the alleys and courts and neglected lodgings in mixed neighbourhoods had an influence on the Board of Trade inquiry of the same period. The paragraphs on the Brussels housing situation were largely inspired by the already published volumes of the 1903–9 inquiry, and the Board of Trade inquiry consequently reproduced a somewhat biased image of Brussels working-class housing, stating that 'four-roomed houses occupied by two families are common in Brussels', and so neglecting the important proportion of working-class housing outside the *impasses*.[98]

The working-class families of the suburban communes were not much better off although the predominance of single-room dwellings was not as strong as in the capital. In Sint-Jans-Molenbeek 79 per cent of working-class families lived in one- and two-roomed units; in Sint-Gilles this type of accommodation accounted for 81.6 per cent of the working-class housing, in Schaarbeek for 77 per cent, and in Elsene for 75.4 per cent. In Anderlecht the portion of working-class families lodged in one- and two-roomed tenements was only 55 per cent. The fact that a considerable portion of its working-class population was living in separate houses (very often converted farms and stables) in the remoter semi-rural parts of the commune could explain why 45 per cent of the working-class families had the use of three rooms or more.[99]

X

In 1842 the first, second and third districts contained 74 per cent of the city's registered poor. In the sixth district lived another 10 per cent. It appears from the 1910 census that the city's policy, which consisted of getting rid of those 'who cost without bringing money in', succeeded only in the sixth district. In 1910 the first, second and third districts still contained about three-quarters of the city's *impasse* inhabitants. In 1829 and 1846, these three proletarian areas together comprised respectively 47.7 per cent and 48.6 per cent of the city's population. Despite the clearances and the loss of inhabitants these produced, these districts' share of the old city's population rose to 60 per cent in 1910. The sixth district's proportion, on the contrary, decreased from 13.8 per cent in 1846 to 9 per cent in 1910. Although the capital certainly succeeded in getting rid of a substantial part of the working class (the share of the working class in the city's population decreased from approximately 60 per cent in 1846 to 40 per cent in 1910),[100] it is obvious that the nineteenth-century town planners had not succeeded in wiping the working-class areas off the Brussels map. The commercial fifth and eighth districts and the adjacent parts of the seventh district did not resist so well: their share in the old city's population decreased from 28.9 per cent in 1846 to 20.6 per cent in 1910. While the proletarian districts largely succeeded in maintaining their housing character, the better-off and commercial areas of the city saw many inhabitants leave. In their place came, as the council stated in 1910: 'Modern multi-storey buildings whose ground floors are occupied by spacious shops. Sometimes, a whole row of old houses disappear for the construction of a department store or they are absorbed by neighbouring firms. A great number of buildings, particularly in the upper parts of the city, gave way to banks and financial companies.' They concluded: 'The houses of the centre of Brussels are less and less lived in'.[101]

Notes

The author is indebted to F. Winter for correction of the translation.

B.C.B. = Bulletin communal de la ville de Bruxelles
 1. Ch. Buls, *City Aesthetics* (Brussels, 1981 reprint of 1899), 9.
 2. E. Janssens, *Topographie médicale et statistique démographique de Brux-elles* (Brussels, 1868), 34.
 3. A. Sutcliffe, 'La victoire de l'immeuble de rapport: un problème de l'histoire des grandes villes européennes au dix-neuvième siècle', *Histoire sociale. Social history, 13,* (1980), 215-16.
 4. PP 1910 XCV, *Cost of living in Belgian towns. Report of an inquiry by the Board of Trade into working-class rents, housing and retail prices together with the rates of wages in certain occupations in the principal industrial towns of Belgium,* viii.
 5. Sutcliffe, 'La victoire de l'immeuble de rapport', 218-24; A. Sutcliffe (ed.), *Multi-storey Living: The British Working-class Experience* (London, 1974), 1-18; M.J. Daunton, *House and Home in the Victorian City. Working-class Housing, 1850-1914* (London, 1983), 60-88.
 6. *B.C.B.,* 1874, I, 210.
 7. Janssens, *Topographie médicale,* 34.
 8. E. Ver Hees, 'Die Wohnungsfrage in Belgien' in *Neue Untersuchungen über die Wohnungsfrage in Deutschland und im Ausland,* ed. Verein für Sozialpolitik (1901), 189-90.
 9. A. Lees, *Cities Perceived: Urban Society in European and American Thought, 1820-1940* (Manchester, 1985), 180-3; W. Krings, *Innenstädte in Belgien, Gestalt, Veränderung, Erhaltung: 1860-1978* (Bonn, 1984), 78-81, 105-10; M. Smets, *L'avènement de la cité-jardin en Belgique: Histoire de l'habitat social en Belgique de 1830 à 1930* (Brussels, 1977), 63-7.
10. D.J. Olsen, *The City as a Work of Art: London, Paris, Vienna* (New Haven and London, 1986), 89-94; S. Muthesius, *The English Terraced House* (New Haven and London, 1982), 39-43.
11. P. Van den Eeckhout, 'Determinanten van het negentiende-eeuws sociaal-economisch leven te Brussel. Hun betekenis voor de laagste bevolkingsklassen' (Ph.D. thesis, Vrije Universiteit Brussel, 3 vols, 1980), II, 122-41.
12. J. De Belder, 'Socio-professionele structuren' in *Brussel: Groei van een hoofdstad* (Antwerp, 1979), 227-34.
13. Van den Eeckhout, 'Determinanten', I, 41-88; P. Lebrun, *Essai sur la révolution industrielle en Belgique, 1770-1847* (Brussels, 1979), 479-91; M.-R. Thielemans, 'De aanzet van de industrie in het Brusselse voor 1830', *Gemeentekrediet van België. Driemaandelijks tijdschrift* 38 (1984), 182-5.
14. Van den Eeckhout, 'Determinanten', II, 144-62.
15. A. Quetelet, 'Sur le recensement de la population de Bruxelles en 1842', *Bulletin de la Commission centrale de statistique, I,* 1842, 27-162; M. De Metsenaere, *Taalmuur: sociale muur? De negentiende-eeuwse taalver-*

houdingen te Brussel als resultaat van geodemografische en sociale processen (Brussels, 1988), 252. In the sample 87 per cent of the labourers lived in socially homogeneous streets.

16. J. Vandenbreeden and A. Hoppenbrouwers, 'Luister van de 19de-eeuwse gevel', in *Brussel, breken, bouwen: Architectuur en stadsverfraaiïng, 1780–1914* (Brussels, 1979), 100–2.
17. Quoted in Vandenbreeden and Hoppenbrouwers, 'Luister', 117.
18. Dictionnaire géographique du Brabant, MS II 386, XIV, fos. 130–1.
19. J. Hannes and M. Despontin, 'Brussel omstreeks 1830. Enkele sociale aspecten', *Taal en sociale integratie*, 4, 1981, 199–218.
20. *Recensement général de la population (15 octobre 1846)* (Brussels, 1849).
21.

	Antwerp	Ghent	Liège
		Percentage	
Ground floor only	27.86	32.25	16.20
2 storeys	50.54	56.83	45.26
3 storeys and more	21.59	10.91	38.53

22. Dr. Joly, A. Le Hardy de Beaulieu, 'Quartiers et habitations insalubres de Bruxelles', *Conseil central de salubrité publique*, 5, s.d., 1–3.
23. Archives O.C.M.W.–C.P.A.S., C 664 2 bis. See also *Enquête sur la condition des classes ouvrières et sur le travail des enfants* (3 vols, Brussels, 1846), III, 630–4.
24. V. Besme, *Plan d'ensemble pour l'extension et l'embellissement de l'agglomération bruxelloise* (Brussels, 1866), 52–3.
25. *B.C.B.*, I, 101.
26. L. Verniers, 'Les impasses bruxellois', *Folklore brabançon*, 80 (1934), 50–63; R. Eberstadt, *Neue Studien über Städtebau und Wohnungswesen Band III. Die Kleinwohnungen und das Städtebauliche System in Brüssel und Antwerpen* (Jena, 1919), 8–33.
27. Eberstadt, *Neue Studien*, 21, 29. For a detailed description of a Brussels blind alley and its inhabitants: P. Scholliers, 'Proletarische wooncultuur in de 19de eeuw:de Schoenengang in de Brusselse Marollenwijk', *Tijdschrift voor geschiedenis van techniek en industriële cultuur*, 24 (1988), 8–18.
28. *Tableau indicatif primitif ou liste alphabétique des propriétaires, avec relevés de leurs propriétés foncières non-bâties et bâties, Ville de Bruxelles* (n.d.). The 'tableau' is not dated, the accompanying plans are dated 1866. This source is presented in: J. Hannes, 'Atlas cadastral parcellaire de la Belgique de P. C. Popp', *Bulletin trimestriel du Crédit communal de Belgique*, 101 (1968), 137–46.
29. *B.C.B.*, 1910, II, 1556.
30. Besme, *Plan d'ensemble*, 55.
31. Conseil supérieur d'hygiène publique, *Habitations ouvrières* (Brussels, 1888), 110–11.
32. *La Santé d'hygiène publique et privée*, 1854–55, 121. Ch. Lagasse and Ch. De Queker, *Enquête sur les habitations ouvrières en 1890* (Brussels, 1890), 9.
33. *Congrès national des habitations ouvrières et des institutions de prévoyance. Anvers 1894* (Brussels, 1895), 7.
34. *Congrès national des habitations ouvrières et des institutions de prévoyance. Gand 1913. Rapports et compte rendu des séances* (Brussels, 1913), 96–7.
35. Lagasse and De Queker, *Enquête sur la condition*, op. cit., III, 634; Archives O.C.M.W.–C.P.A.S., C 664 2 bis.

36. *B.C.B.*, 1910, II, 1556.
37. J.H. Baton, *Coutume de Bruxelles et usages des lieux en matière de louage des maisons, magasins, quartiers et chambres* (Brussels, 1864).
38. D. Gougnard, *Le bail à loyer et à ferme ou les droits et obligations des bailleurs et locataires en matière de louage des maisons, appartements et biens ruraux* (Brussels, 1911)
39. *Pasinomie*, 1887, nr. 274.
40. *B.C.B.*, 1865, II, 88.
41. *B.C.B.*, 1846, 350–60.
42. *B.C.B.*, 1846, 37.
43. *B.C.B.*, 1846, 350–3. E. Ducpétiaux was the Inspector-General of the Belgian prisons and poor-relief institutions. He wrote on working-class housing, poor-relief, charity, poverty, working-class budgets, education, criminology etc. As a progressive liberal he was a member of the Brussels town council in the years 1845–48.
44. A few examples: *B.C.B.*, 1850, 97–101; 1858, 115–7, 182–3.
45. M. Smets, 'De doorbraak van de Blaesstraat te Brussel, 1853–1860', *Wonen TABK* (1985), 21.
46. *B.C.B.*, 1857, I, 149–50.
47. *B.C.B.*, 1883, I, 99, 104, 108.
48. *B.C.B.*, 1906, I, 575–6, 583, 594, 597.
49. *B.C.B.*, 1865, II, 340.
50. *B.C.B.*, 1848, II, 120–1.
51. *B.C.B.*, 1865, II, 340.
52. *B.C.B.*, 1865, II, 85; A.-J. Martin, 'Le Bureau d'hygiene de Bruxelles, 1874–1889', *Revue d'hygiene*, (1890).
53. E. Descamps, 'Le Duc de Brabant au Sénat de Belgique', *Académie royale de Belgique. Bulletin de la classe des lettres et de sciences morales et politiques et de la classe des beaux-arts* (1903), 290; L. Ranieri, *Léopold II urbaniste* (Brussels, 1973).
54. Population 1842: 113, 207; 1846: 123, 874; 1856: 150, 244; 1866: 157, 905.
55. *B.C.B.*, 1856, I, 165, 179; *B.C.B.*, 1874, I, 228–30; Y. Leblicq, 'Evolutie van het uitzicht van Brussel in de 19de eeuw' in *Brussel, breken, bouwen: Architectuur en stadsverfraaiing, 1780–1914* (Brussels, 1979), 51.
56. *B.C.B.*, 1856, I, 110.
57. Except for the annexation of a part of Laken and Sint-Jans-Molenbeek in 1897; extensive warehouse accommodation for the planned outer port was provided. The quartier Léopold became the ninth cadastral district of the city. The other parts of the annexed area were gradually built upon after the 1870s. The area became known as the Quartier Nord-Est and it formed the city's tenth district. The avenue Louise/Bois de la Cambre formed the eleventh and the harbour installations the twelfth cadastral district.
58. Leblicq, 'Evolutie', 41–91; Y. Leblicq, 'L'urbanisation de Bruxelles aux XIXe et XXe siècles (1830–1952), in *Villes en mutation XIXe–XXe siècles* (Brussels, 1982), 335–425.
59. Ph. Godding, 'L'évolution de la législation en matière d'urbanisme en Belgique au XIXe siècle in *Villes en mutation*, 11–35.
60. Smets, 'De doorbraak van de Blaesstraat', 19–20.
61. *B.C.B.*, 1891, II, 668.
62. *B.C.B.*, 1899, I, 268.
63. P. Loze, 'Historicisme en monumentaalbouw', *Poelaert en zijn tijd* (Brussels, 1980), 112–6.

64. *B.C.B.*, 1874, I, 230.
65. *B.C.B.*, 1874, I, 231.
66. Leblicq, 'Evolutie', 51, 58, 66.
67. Ver Hees, 'Die Wohnungsfrage', 218; A. Brauman, *L'immeuble et la parcelle. Les immeubles à appartements comme éléments constitutifs du tissu urbain. Le cas de Bruxelles 1870–1980* (Brussels, 1982); Leblicq, 'L'urbanisation de Bruxelles', 391.
68. E. Ducpétiaux, op. cit., 62.
69. *B.C.B.*, 1896, I, 39.
70. B. De Meulder, 'Gallerijwoningen te Brussel: proeve van een historisch-typologische analyse van de sociale meergezinswoningbouw in de Brusselse agglomeratie 1870–1914' (Thesis, K.U.L., 1983).
71. *B.C.B.*, 1891, II, 661–3.
72. Lagasse and De Queker, *Enquête sur les habitations*.
73. Comité de patronage des habitations ouvrières et des institutions de prévoyance, *Enquête sur les habitations ouvrières en 1903, 1904 et 1905* (Brussels, 1905); ibid., *de 1903 à 1909* (Brussels, 1910).
74. *B.C.B.*, 1899, I, 599.
75. *B.C.B.*, 1899, I, 255–342.
76. *B.C.B.*, 1899, I, 612; II, 1139.
77. *B.C.B.*, 1874, I, 208–12; 243–7; 1875, I, 118; *B.C.B.*, 1874, I, 218, 251; *B.C.B.*, 1874, I, 223, 263; *B.C.B.*, 1896, I, 751–3.
78. *B.C.B.*, 1899, I, 261–8.
79. *B.C.B.*, 1886, II, 959; 1896, I, 39, 239, 255, 420; 1897, II, 1, 111–18; 1899, I, 343–66, 501–6; 1902, I, 92–101.
80. B. De Meulder, 'Zum belgischen Arbeiterwohnungsgesetz vom 9 August 1889. Kleinwohnungsbau und Städtebau in Brüssel 1889–1914', in J. Rodriguez-Lores and G. Fehl (eds), *Die Kleinwohnungsfrage: Zu den Ursprungen des sozialen Wohnungsbaus in Europa* (Hamburg, 1988), 341–62. The Brussels *Comité officiel de patronage des habitations ouvrières*, established as a result of the law of 9 August 1889, was very active and published inquiries, reports and plans concerning working-class housing. Two of these inquiries are used in this article (see note 32 and 73).
81. De Meulder, 'Gullerijwoningen te Brussel'; B. De Meulder, 'De Cité Hellemans, 1906–1915', *Wonen TABK* (1985), 27–36. The design of the tenements was inspired by the labourers' dwellings of the Hornby Street area in Liverpool.
82. Van den Eeckhout, 'Determinanten', I, 112–83.
83. *BOT, Belgium*, 13–14.
84. Comité de patronage, *Enquête sur les habitations ouvrières*.
85. *Congrès 1913*, op. cit., 94; J.-S. Roupcinsky, *Plus-value immobilière, petite bourgeoisie, logements ouvriers* (Brussels, 1907), 11–13.
86. *B.C.B.*, 1891, 2, 668–9. From the 1880s on, the rent index published is partly based on the rents paid by the tenants of apartments along the new boulevards and streets. Rents appeared to stagnate in the period 1880–1905; P. Van den Eeckhout and P. Scholliers, *De Brusselse huishuren, 1800–1940* (Brussels, 1979).
87. *Congròs, 1913*, 94.
88. *B.C.B.*, 1891, 654–6.
89. Van den Eeckhout, 'Determinanten', II, 221–2.
90. *B.C.B.*, 1877, II, 45.
91. *Moniteur des comités de patronage*, 27 July 1899, 10 October 1899;

Congrès, 1913, 76; *Association pour l'améloriation des logements ouvriers. Rapport annuel*, 1900, 1901, 1907; Van den Eeckhout, 'Determinanten', II, 225.

92. Verniers, 'Les impasses bruxellois'; Ville de Bruxelles, *Les recensements de 1910* (Brussels, 1912); Ville de Bruxelles. MS. Liste des impasses 1867–1890. Population: 1866: 157, 905; 1880: 162, 498; 1890: 176, 138; 1900: 183, 686; 1910: 177, 078.

93. Ville de Bruxelles, *Les recensements de 1910*, op. cit.

94. Ibid.

95. *Recensement général de la population du 31 décembre 1910* (Brussels, 1912–13), Sint-Joost-ten-Noode: 51.5 per cent; Schaarbeek: 41.4 per cent; Sint-Gillis: 43.9 per cent; Elsene: 37.4 per cent; Etterbeek: 38.6 per cent.

96. Lagasse and De Queker, *Enquête sur les habitations ouvrières*.

97. Comité de patronage, *Enquête sur les habitations ouvrières*.

98. *BOT, Belgium*, viii. The results of the inquiry of 1903–1909 and especially the difference between dwellings and inhabitants of subdivided houses and alley cottages are the subject of: P. Van den Eeckhout, 'Enquête sur l'habitat ouvrier à Bruxelles au début du 20e siècle', *Les Cahiers de la Fonderie: Revue d'histoire sociale et industrielle de la région bruxelloise* (1989), 26–33.

99. *BOT, Belgium*, 13.

100. De Belder, 'Socio-professionele structuren', 233.

101. Ville de Bruxelles, *Les recensements de 1910*, 27.

Map of Brussels showing percentage of families, registered on the poor list, 1842.

Source: A. Quetelet, 'Sur le recensement de la population de Bruxelles en 1842', *Bulletin de la Commission centrale de statistique*, I, 1842, 27–162.

1. Streets without inscriptions on the poor list.
2. Streets with less than 10% of the families registered on the poor list.
3. Streets with 10 to 50% of the families registered on the poor list.
4. Streets with more than 50% of the families registered on the poor list.

4 Vienna

Renate Banik-Schweitzer

I

At the end of the eighteenth century, Vienna was a typical *Residenzstadt*: the seat of the imperial court of an European great power, the residence of the central government of an absolutist state, and a manufacturing centre for both luxury goods for export, especially silk fabrics, fancy goods and furniture, and consumer goods for the already large local market of about 250,000 inhabitants in the city and the suburbs. In the traditional trades, production was organised in a system of guilds, that is highly skilled artisans, small masters and their apprentices, producing on direct commission for customers. But the export trades were more and more organised by wholesalers who increasingly used sweated labour of unskilled or semi-skilled workers outside the guilds. The growth of the city was to a considerable extent due to migration of apprentices, most of them from Southern-German countries. In the first half of the nineteenth century Vienna was mainly a textile town: 20 per cent of all employees in the manufacturing sector were occupied in the textile trade.

The urban fabric of Vienna had a very simple pattern at the end of the eighteenth century: a core, the inner city, surrounded by two rings of suburbs. The core, until 1850 identical with the City of Vienna, was surrounded by fortifications and was further separated from the inner ring of suburbs by a glacis extending 300–350 metres which was to become Ringstrasse-zone after the demolition of the fortifications in 1857. The old city of Vienna was later called the inner city and became the first district of Greater Vienna. The inner ring of suburbs, the so-called *Vorstädte*, was incorporated into the city of Vienna in 1850. The inner suburbs were thereafter called the inner districts and numbered 2–9 and 20. The outer ring of suburbs—the *Vororte*—was separated from the inner ring by another rampart and fosse, the so-called *Linienwall*. Formerly it was an outer defence line, but later on it functioned as a border where taxes were raised on consumer goods brought into the city. The outer suburbs were incorporated in 1890, thus creating Greater Vienna. They became the districts 11–19, and were called the outer districts (the tenth district, Favoriten, had been created by separating it from the fourth district in 1874 (see Figure 4.1). Floridsdorf on the left

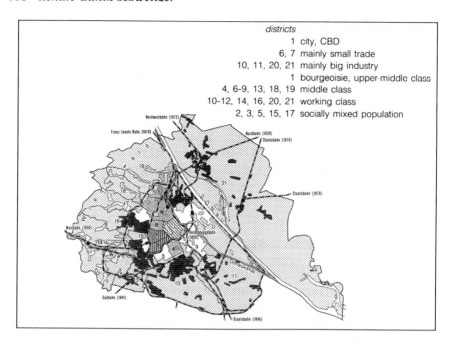

districts

1	city, CBD
6, 7	mainly small trade
10, 11, 20, 21	mainly big industry
1	bourgeoisie, upper-middle class
4, 6-9, 13, 18, 19	middle class
10-12, 14, 16, 20, 21	working class
2, 3, 5, 15, 17	socially mixed population

Figure 4.1 Map of Vienna in 1910, showing the social and economic character of districts.

bank of the Danube was incorporated in 1904, becoming the twenty-first district. Though the two rings of suburbs were far from being homogeneous in themselves, as a whole they differed distinctly from each other as well as from the city centre. The inner city had always been, and remained, the residence of the imperial court, aristocracy, high clergy and bureaucracy. But in former times a numerous population belonging to the so-called 'old' middle class (*alter Mittelstand*) also lived there—artisans, shopkeepers, lower ranks of civil servants. During the industrial revolution which took place in Vienna roughly between 1840 and 1870, the inner city began to develop into the central business district. In the course of this process the middle-class population was forced out of the centre by department stores, banks, insurance companies and the press. These businesses occupied the main traffic arteries: department stores chose Kärntnerstrasse, Stephansplatz and Rotenturmstrasse, banks gathered around Freyung and the press settled in Wollzeile. During this process old houses were demolished and streets broadened, though the network itself mostly stayed untouched. But behind the rows of new and higher buildings remained 'isles' of very old low-rent houses which more and more became the shelter of people forced to accept any unskilled service job such as journeymen, porters, carmen, road transport workers, street-sellers, waiters and waitresses in restaurants and night clubs, washerwomen and charwomen. The old middle class which was forced out moved to the inner suburbs which had already developed into manufacturing districts after they had been destroyed during the second siege of Vienna by the Turks in 1683. The centres of trade were in the sixth district (Gumpendorf) and the seventh district (Neubau) on the left bank of the Wien River because many trades needed water for production. These were the places where most of the skilled artisans lived, but there also were the roots of manufacturing and the sweat-shop system.

From about 1850 sweated labour was not only used in the textile trade but also in clothing and furniture-making, and the growing number of unskilled or semi-skilled workers had to move to the outer suburbs in the Wien valley, to Fünfhaus, Sechshaus, Gaudenzdorf and Meidling, where the cost of living was lower outside the Linienwall. Heavy industry came to Vienna in the late 1830s together with railway construction. In 1838 the first Austrian railway line was opened, the Northern Railway, which was to supply Vienna with coal from the mines of Morava Ostrava (now in Czechoslovakia) and to connect the capital with Cracov. Next came the Southern Railway, opened in 1841, which connected Vienna with Trieste, the main port of the Habsburg Monarchy. The first factories producing railway equipment were established in Vienna. In 1840 the machine building factory of the Southern Railway Company was opened next to the rail terminal just outside the Linienwall and the built-up area, in the later tenth district of Favoriten. This factory was organised and operated by the British engineer John Haswell. About the same time, the Northern Railway Company had its workshops constructed near its terminal in the second district of Leopoldstadt. The pattern of industrial location in Vienna thereafter began to change, especially after both railway lines were connected in 1859. Whereas the valley of the Wien River, following a west–eastern direction, had been the 'spine' of production during the first half of the century, now the main railway lines, running from north to south, became the dominant industrial axis of Vienna. Most of the machine-building factories, and later on the plants of the electrical industry, settled on both sides of these lines. Meanwhile, during the process of mechanisation, the textile industry migrated from Vienna to cheaper locations in northern Bohemia (the new textile centre was Reichenberg, now Liberec, in Czechoslovakia). The abandoned locations in the Wien valley were re-occupied by the expanding clothing trade which was to become, in terms of number of employees, the most important branch of production in the second half of the century. Located nearby were the small workshops of the furniture makers and the producers of fancy goods (pipes, buttons, combs, bags etc.).[1] In all these trades, sweated labour was widely used which forced upon the employees living conditions which were much worse than those of the less numerous industrial workers.

In 1837 about 20 per cent of all Viennese employees in the production sector were engaged in the textile industry, about the same percentage in clothing, and 8 per cent in metal working. By 1869 the proportion of textile workers had fallen to 11 per cent, those of clothing workers had risen to 36 per cent, and metal workers to 11 per cent. Another 11 per cent were employed in furniture making and 5 per cent in the production of paper and leather goods. By 1910 the proportion of textile workers had fallen to 5 per cent of all Viennese employees in the production sector; clothing workers, though their absolute number was 130,000, had fallen to 27 per cent; furniture makers were 10 per cent; producers of paper and leather goods stood at slightly below 5 per cent; and only the proportion of metal workers had risen to 13 per cent in connection with the development of engineering. Compared with Berlin, where textile production, clothing and furniture making had a similarly important position, it must be said that in Vienna the number of employees in these traditional trades was considerably higher—at the expense of modern, technologically advanced industries.[2]

In 1850 about 431,000 people lived in the city centre and the inner suburbs, and about 67,000 in the urbanised area of the outer suburbs. At the end of the industrial revolution in 1869, about 64,000 people lived in the inner city, about 544,000 in the inner suburbs, and 221,000 in the urbanised outer suburbs.[3] The bourgeois revolution of 1848 had given everybody the right to move freely within the Habsburg Empire and almost immediately the stream of migrants to Vienna had multiplied. But now the newcomers were farm hands and semi- or unskilled workers from Bohemia and Moravia, many of whom spoke only Czech and did not understand German; and poor Jewish street-sellers and artisans from Galicia. In 1910 every fourth Viennese of a total population of about two million was Czech or of Czech origin, and every tenth Viennese was a Jew. The unskilled or semi-skilled Czech immigrants went—in the case of women—into domestic service, or were engaged in traditional trades like clothing, furniture or metal working. Many of them obtained only casual jobs.

Vienna was in no way prepared to house these masses of poor immigrants. On the contrary, the industrial revolution was exactly the period when the aristocracy and ascending bourgeoisie celebrated their new alliance with the construction of the Ringstrasse. In a time of extreme capital shortage caused by the demand of railway construction and government bonds, the few remaining funds were used for building upper-middle-class housing and not the desperately needed lodgings for immigrant workers. During the economic upswing following the 1848 revolution, industrial shares paid 8 per cent and more whereas the return on mortgage loans was limited to 5 per cent.[4] In the 1860s, one sixth to one fourth of the houses constructed annually were built in the Ringstrasse zone. However, only 10 per cent of dwellings in Vienna in 1900 were as large as those in the typical Ringstrasse houses.[5] It was a period of reckless waste of human capital. The arriving migrants had to find shelter within the existing structures and this led to an enormous rise in housing density. In 1827 38 persons had lived on average in each Viennese house; by 1857 this number had risen to 50. In 1827 a house-hold (i.e., persons per dwelling) consisted of an average of 4.5 persons, 5.3 in 1857. Living conditions were especially bad in large parts of the second district (Leopoldstadt) where most of the poor immigrants arrived at the Northern Railway terminal. The average number of persons per house in Leopoldstadt was 35 in 1827 but 49 in 1857, and the average number of persons per dwelling was 4.9 in 1827 but 5.9 in 1857.[6] By 1869 the average number of persons per dwelling in Vienna had fallen to 4.7 and by 1910 to 4.6.[7] Together with high rents and low wages this caused a sharp decline in living standards. During the industrial revolution the increase in rents was considerably higher than in the preceding period. Whereas the rent per house between 1830 and 1850 rose by an average of 87 crowns each year, the annual average growth between 1850 and 1870 was 292 crowns.[8]

The beginning of the manufacturing period (1780–1840) had offered artisans and skilled workers rather good chances for raising a family. Before 1780 the annual marriage rate was about 7 per cent of the total population. Between 1780 and 1820 the annual rate went up to 11–12 per cent and the proportion of illegitimate children was about 30 per cent of the newborn. Between 1820 and 1860 the marriage rate fell to 8–9 per cent and the proportion of illegitimate children went up to 40–50 per cent, a percentage never reached again.[9] But this period of declining traditional trade and developing industry was also marked by the beginning of the demographic change from high birth and death rates typical for a preindustrial society, to still high but constantly falling death rates found in industrial societies. This process, which indicates a gradual improvement in living conditions, seems to have started in Vienna in 1855.[10]

In the early 1870s the first large-scale infrastructural measures, like the regulation of the Danube between 1870 and 1875, and the first high quality water supply in 1873, laid the basis for modern development. In the 1880s big industry definitely became the strongest factor in the economy and the small trades underwent a crisis of survival. The leading branches of modern industry in Vienna were capital goods, such as engineering and the electrical industry. But the latter especially was not a distinctly Viennese development, like that of Berlin, for instance. The electrical industry in Vienna depended almost entirely on foreign capital in the form of direct investments by transnational corporations, such as Siemens, AEG, Westinghouse, Brown-Boveri and Ericsson, which limited the growth of their subsidiary companies in Vienna to the supply of the Austrian domestic market. In 1910 10 per cent of all Viennese employees in the production sector were occupied in engineering and in the electrical industry. In Greater Berlin the same rate in 1907 was 13 per cent, although the German electrical industry was to a much lesser extent concentrated in Berlin than the Austrian industry was in Vienna: 25 per cent of all German employees in the electrical industry worked in Greater Berlin but 44 per cent of all comparable Austrian employees were in Vienna.[11] Nevertheless, their modern business organisation contributed to the increase in the numbers of industrial workers, especially of white-collar workers and the highest skilled blue-collar workers, who at the turn of the century became the core of the so-called 'new' middle class (*Neuer Mittelstand*). The dependence on foreign capital of modern industries in Vienna left room for traditional trades, which additionally were supported by the restrengthened conservative forces of the aristocracy and the clergy. The weakening liberal camp was pressed by mass movements of Left and Right which were institutionalised by about 1890 by the foundation of the Social Democratic Party, the only true representative of the working class, and the petty bourgeois Christian Social Party. In 1895 the Liberal Party finally lost power in the City Council to the Christian Socials who ruled the city until 1918.

The 1890s formed the second period of large-scale infrastructural operations which were to lay the basis for the development of Vienna to a city of four million inhabitants. Among those operations, which were mainly financed by central government, were a metropolitan railway, the completion of the system of sewers by the construction of big collective sewers, and a second high quality water supply. But welfare matters were widely neglected. The petty bourgeois majority in the City Council was not willing to compensate for the consequences of capitalism on the labour force when capitalism destroyed the basis of petty bourgeois existence.

The decisive years in the formation of the socio-spatial pattern of Vienna were those from 1870 to 1890. This was the period when all the outer suburbs were urbanised. Between 1869 and 1890 the population of the inner city had, thanks to the Ringstrasse construction, grown slightly to 67,000 inhabitants, that of the inner districts to 743,000 inhabitants, while the population of the outer suburbs had more than doubled to reach 599,000.[12] In this period the inner districts became more and more bourgeois and the outer suburbs proletarian, though there were isles of the opposite social class in both suburban rings. Among the inner districts, parts of the second district (Leopoldstadt) and the third district (Landstrasse) and the twentieth district (Brigittenau) as a whole became proletarianised because the main railway lines which attracted industry ran through them. Among the outer suburbs the future thirteenth district (Hietzing), the eighteenth district (Währing) and the nineteenth district (Döbling) turned bourgeois because they were the only districts of Vienna where the detached house was established.

Until the First World War the Viennese population grew continuously but not as fast as in the two decades before. By 1910 the population of the inner city had fallen to 53,000 inhabitants, that of the inner districts had grown to 890,000 inhabitants, and that of the outer to 1,060,000 inhabitants, including the 77,000 inhabitants of the twenty-first district (Floridsdorf) which was incorporated in 1904.[13] The socio-spatial pattern did not change between 1890 and 1910 but was consolidated. The official census data in 1910 classified 56 per cent of all gainfully employed persons in Vienna as workers. In the inner city there were only 25 per cent which was by far the lowest proportion of all districts, in the inner districts 47 per cent, and in the outer districts 67 per cent. In typical working-class districts, like Favoriten, Ottakring, Brigittenau and Floridsdorf, this proportion went up to 73–77 per cent, indicating a rather homogeneous class structure there.[14]

II

Until the bourgeois revolution in 1848, ground landlords planned the extension of the city by developing their own estates. They were not only the owners of large properties but also judges in minor juridical matters and they had the right to levy taxes upon their property as well as the duty to construct and maintain the infrastructure, mainly streets and sewers, on their domains. The greatest ground landlords in the Vienna region were the City Council in the built-up areas and the Roman Catholic Church represented by monasteries of the Augustine (Kloster-neuburg) and Benedictine (Schotten) order in the development areas. Large areas, like the fortifications, glacis and the military drill and parade grounds, were under state rule and exempted from taxes. If a ground landlord wanted to develop a part of his property, he generally chose a large tract of land adjacent to areas already built-up. He had the street network, generally a rectangular grid pattern, laid out and connected with the existing streets. The new streets and sewers were constructed at his expense. He had the building blocks divided into lots, and they were distributed by lot and sold either to artisans who wanted to build a self-contained house, or to small builders. Artisans then commissioned their house from a builder or a speculative builder constructed three or four houses. One of the greatest advantages of this procedure was that building did not start at the same time everywhere in the development areas but concentrated on a few tracts of land that were built-up in a short time.

The system of financial development at this time has not yet been thoroughly analysed, but loans from private investors always played a considerable part in the construction business. From 1819 private investors were joined by the First Austrian Savings Bank which started to provide mortgages not only for rural but also for urban land. The owners of the new lots and buildings could rent, sell or bequeath their property; their only obligation to the ground landlord was the payment of taxes. The revolution of 1848 deprived the ground landlords of most of their privileges. They remained landowners but lost control of urban develop-ment, that is their planning function, their right to levy taxes, and their obligation to build the infrastructure. As simple landowners they now had to face the competition from other greater owners in the property market. One of the most important among them was Richard Drasche, the heir of a large brickworks to the south of Vienna. After the brickworks had been sold to Wienerberger Brick and Building Company (Wienerberger Ziegelfabriks- und Baugesellschaft) in 1869 Drasche kept the exhausted clay fields and made them the basis of his large-scale property trading business.

The former planning and developing functions of the ground landlords were transferred to the newly formed territorial communities, one of them being the City of Vienna. To exercise its planning function the community was given the right to issue legally binding building-line plans (Baulinienpläne) which consisted mainly of a street network and covered large parts or all of the community's territory. In the 1860s and 1870s, the City of Vienna had some building-line plans designed for the southern development areas (Favoriten) and the area between the regulated Danube and the Danube Canal (Brigittenau) within the city's boundaries. At about the same time nearly all the Lower Austrian communities touching the Viennese border in the west, which represented the western development areas of Vienna, had imposed similar plans on their own territories. All these plans showed rigid grid layouts, occasionally interrupted by triangular or star-shaped plazas of the Haussmann type in Paris. This pattern determined urban development in Vienna until 1914. The fact that building-line plans before the urban design revolution of Camillo Sitte in 1889 were all designed in the same way and lacked any artistic value and individuality meant that the different plans of neighbouring communities fitted together without the guidance of a long-range overall development plan. (See Figure 4.2.)

A former ground landlord or great landowner who now wanted to develop his property had to respect the framework set up by the building-line plan, he had to ask the community's permission for his own subdivision plan, and he had to convey the land needed for street construction according to the building-line plan free of charge to the community which was obliged to construct the necessary infrastructure of streets, sewers and later on water supply. Gas supply for street lighting, and later on for cooking, as well as the electricity supply, were first provided by limited companies (the most important of them being the British Imperial Continental Gas Association) before all these services were municipalised at the turn of the century. Street and sewer construction totally at the expense of the community strained the budget of the City of Vienna during the years of fastest expansion. As a consequence, new streets in working-class districts in particular remained unpaved long after the tenement blocks had been constructed. So the city tried to transfer the costs of infrastructure partly back to landlords and tenants: charges were imposed for the connection of houses to street-sewers and later there was a surtax on rents to finance water supply. But this was not the only problem raised by the separation of previously united planning and developing functions. The city complained that it had some control over urban development but could not initiate or stimulate it. Building-line plans granted the right to build but they did not force landowners to do so within a given time. If a landowner did not want to release his land for building, development could be blocked for years. On the other hand, once a building-line plan was imposed, building could start simultaneously at different points which charged the community with high costs for the infrastructure. As far as landowners were concerned, they sometimes disagreed with building-line plans because they prevented them from making the most profitable use of their land. In such cases the community often had to give in and modify the plan. Modifications had also to be undertaken in the case of building-line plans which covered too large an area. Some of the plans for outer development areas were redesigned twice before a single building had

valid building - line plan

old building - line plan by former property owner, Convent of Klosternenburg neuburg

railway

tramway

green space

house
Figure 4.6

Danube Canal

Figure 4.2 Building line plans of Brigittenau, 1908.

been constructed in the area covered by the plan.

In the second half of the nineteenth century the development and construction process as well as the financial system in Vienna were similar to that in Berlin with one important exception: in Vienna, after the major crash of the Stock Exchange in 1873, there were no limited companies (*Terraingesellschaften*) engaged in land speculation as there were in Berlin reflecting the lack of private capital which could be raised on the Stock Exchange. In Vienna the development process started with a great landowner selling a tract of land, whether to a builder, to a so-called 'building-society' around 1870 or, and this is what generally happened, to a lot trading agent (*Baustellenhändler*). The agent subdivided the land within the framework of the building-line plan into building blocks and the blocks into lots, and conveyed the land for future streets to the city. Then he sold the lots—often in packages covering a whole or half of a building block—to builders who generally did not have enough capital of their own either for buying the lots or for construction. Reliable data about the profits of the lot trading agents have not so far been gathered, but they must have been much smaller than those of *Terraingesellschaften* in Berlin. The builders paid a deposit for the lots and had the far bigger remainder of the purchase price registered in the land register as a debt in favour of the agent. The builder obtained money for construction at rather high interest rates from the same agent, from large suppliers of building materials, or generally from other agents who collected money from small private investors and acted as mediators between their clients and the builders. After construction, the capital value of the building was estimated—and often considerably overestimated in order to force up the sum obtainable for the first mortgage loan to be given by land mortgage or savings banks. With this money the builder paid off the lot trading agent and the greater part of building costs. For the rest he had to raise a second mortgage, generally from a small provincial savings bank or again from small private investors. Then he sold lot and building to a landlord who generally looked for a safe investment for his savings. He paid about 10 per cent of the total cost on account and took over the mortgage loans.

In contrast to Berlin there is not much contemporary literature on Vienna which systematically analyses the land market and the development process, except for a paper by the famous economist and social scientist Emil Lederer who analysed the reasons for rent increases in Berlin and Vienna.[15] Proceeding on the assumption that there were no dramatic differences in rent levels between the two cities, he also found similarities in planning instruments, building regulations, architectural forms, construction costs, ratio of wages to rents and living standards. What really differed were land prices and rent taxes. Land prices seemed to have accounted for 40 per cent of the total cost of tenements in Berlin[16] whereas they might never have exceeded 20 per cent in Vienna.[17] On the other hand, rent taxes amounted to more than 40 per cent of gross rents in Vienna whereas their percentage in Berlin was much lower.[18] These findings led Lederer to the conclusion that high rent taxes must have limited the increase in land prices in Vienna to such an extent that he even denied the existence of land speculation when compared with Berlin.[19] Lederer's argument is supported by two other facts: first the extraordinary political and social position of landlords as the most important tax-payers in Vienna, which will be discussed later; and secondly, the absence of land speculation companies like the Berlin *Terraingesellschaften* in Vienna after 1873. If the enormously high rent taxes in Vienna had not allowed for an increase in the price of land—a given purchasing power of tenants was assumed—the profits in land speculation might not have been high enough to stimulate the participation of limited companies in this business.

During the economic boom between 1867 and 1873, urban development in Vienna speeded up and seemed to become a very profitable business. In this period more than forty so-called 'building societies' (*Baugesellschaften*), which were in fact limited companies, were founded in Vienna the prime aim of which was not building but land speculation. No more than half of them survived the big crash in 1873. Until then, in the few years of their existence, the 'big four' among them—Allgemeine österreichische Baugesellschaft, Union-Baugesellschaft, Wiener Bau-Gesellschaft and Wiener Bau-Verein—had acquired a considerable amount of land of approximately 5 square kilometres in the development areas of Vienna. In 1872 the Allgemeine österreichische Baugesellschaft owned about 2 square kilometres of land and hoped to develop the industrial district of Brigittenau and the so-called 'Cottage' in Währing and Döbling, one of the two early one-family house districts in Vienna (the second was in Hietzing surrounding Schönbrunn palace). In the same year, the Union-Baugesellschaft owned about 0.9 square kilometres of land and Wiener Bau-Gesellschaft another 0.7 square kilometres, mainly in the Wien valley which the company expected to develop by constructing a metropolitan railway.[20] But the crash in 1873 destroyed all of these expectations. Henceforth the 'building societies' withdrew step by step from land speculation by selling their property and concentrating upon building. Their part as property traders and developers was taken over by the lot trading agents. The most important among them seems to have been Julius Frankl who started as a small agent in working-class districts and ended up as a developer of upper-middle-class housing.

Central government was also involved in large-scale land development when it decided to remove military barracks and training grounds from built-up areas to the outskirts of Vienna and to sell the abandoned areas for building purposes. But it acted more in the manner of a great land-owner than as a lot trading agent because it left the business of sub-dividing the building blocks and selling the lots to builders to the City of Vienna. By far the biggest deal was the sale of part of the military drill and parade ground of Schmelz in 1910. It covered a total area of nearly one square kilometre in the working-class district of Fünfhaus in the western part of Vienna. About one third of the total area was divided into 62 building blocks and each of these into about 14–18 lots. The greater part of this area was built-up before and during the First World War.[21]

Though the property market in Vienna was dominated by small land-owners and landlords, in the development areas the great landowners and lot trading agents played the most important part. But there was a significant difference between them. The agent only stayed in business as long as the whole system worked. It is typical that Frankl sold his property in one piece to the City of Vienna shortly after the First World War under unfavourable conditions, after the enormous rise in building costs and when legally fixed rent limitations had left no chance for speculative private building.[22] Great landowners, on the other hand, could sit and wait for more favourable market conditions. It is true that Drasche sold large tracts of his property at the same time as Frankl to the City of Vienna, but this still left a sizeable holding and it was only a few years ago that the last part of 'Drasche land' was sold, again to the city administration. And the Augustine Convent in Klosterneuburg is still today one of the greatest landowners in the north-eastern parts of Vienna.

The building industry in Vienna was organised in both large and small-scale enterprises. The building materials industry, especially brickworks, generally belonged to the first group. Bricks, of which the majority of Viennese buildings are constructed, were mainly produced in Vienna itself, in former times by a handful of brickworks in the outer suburbs, particularly in the south on Wienerberg. Although brick-making did not demand advanced technology, the winning of clay and the burning of bricks needed a considerable amount of capital which increasingly ruled out small producers. So, in the course of time, most of them gave up production or like the Drasche family sold to the one remaining big enterprise, the Wienerberger Company. Founded in 1869 as a limited company, Wienerbergers enlarged its property between 1870 and 1914 from nearly 3 square kilometres to more than 6 square kilometres, most of it in Vienna but also large areas in Lower Austria and Hungary. Until the First World War, the Wienerberger Company was the biggest brick producer under the Habsburg monarchy.[23] The production of building materials was organised on a large scale; the building trade in Vienna was dominated by small enterprises. It was mainly in the hands of small builders, especially in working-class districts. Though the small builder in the course of time had to compete with building companies and co-operative building societies, the share of small enterprises in total housing construction even in 1914 must have been more than 50 per cent. Building was a labour-intensive trade in which only a few technological innovations were accepted and machines were rarely used. But unskilled labour was cheap and easily available, so there was little pressure towards rationalisation. This, on the other hand, guaranteed the survival of the trade's archaic organisation thanks to the 'flexibility' created by the absence of fixed capital costs and the possibility of hiring and firing workers according to business cycles.

The 'building societies' were the large-scale enterprises in the building industry. Though the main purpose of these companies was land speculation and not building, those which survived the crash of 1873 became more and more engaged in the profitable construction of upper-middle-class housing and of public buildings. Wiener Bau-Gesellschaft, for instance, between 1869 and 1902 bought and sold 750 building plots in the city and the inner, largely built-up, districts of Vienna but constructed no more than 127 buildings during this time.[24] Union-Baugesellschaft preferred public buildings. It constructed buildings for the World Fair of 1873, as well as the Academy of Fine Arts, the Palace of Justice, the City Hall, the Houses of Parliament and part of the Imperial Palace, and also gasworks and factory buildings. The company was engaged too in railway construction.[25] But working-class housing was generally left to small builders because it was not profitable enough for limited companies.

The funds necessary for housing construction in Vienna were to a considerable extent raised from small private investors. Their main fields of interest were short-term building loans and second mortgages at rather high interest rates. The secure first mortgage business was taken over in the course of time by land mortgage and savings banks. The most important among them was the First Austrian Savings Bank (Erste Öster-reichische Spar-Casse), founded in Vienna in 1819. This bank primarily collected small savings from middle-class people or better-off workers and was obliged to avoid risky investments. Therefore it took part neither in speculation nor in financing industrial development, but specialised in the first mortgage loan business. Though in the course of time it was joined by other banks, the First Austrian Savings Bank held the leading position until 1914. In 1830, the share of mortgage loans in the capital value (5 per cent capitalisation of the total sum of annual rents) of all houses in the city and the inner suburbs of Vienna was 3 per cent, in 1851 6 per cent, in 1891 24 per cent, and in 1901 no less than 30 per cent.[26] The way of financing housing construction decisively influenced business cycles in the building trade. The waves of annual production in housing followed the ups and downs of the influx of mortgage loans.[27] It was the capital market and not housing demand which steered construction (see Figure 4.3). Since the rate of vacant rooms in Vienna, which is usually taken as a measure of demand, was constantly below a tolerable limit, it cannot explain the considerable variations in building rates. The wave of vacancies resembles those of the production cycle with half a phase interference (see Figure 4.4). Therefore the rate of vacancies can rather be seen as the consequence of the building cycle and not necessarily as its cause.

In the 1850s, investment in railway construction was more profitable than building and therefore building rates were very low.[28] In the early 1860s, building profited from an industrial crisis which had also affected the railway business and gave the First Austrian Savings Bank the opportunity to invest another twelve million florins in mortgage loans[29] after it had spent about fourteen million florins on the same purpose between 1821 and 1851.[30] These sums were mainly spent for the benefit of Ringstrasse construction and not for working-class housing. The boom period of 1867 to 1873 mobilised such a large amount of investment

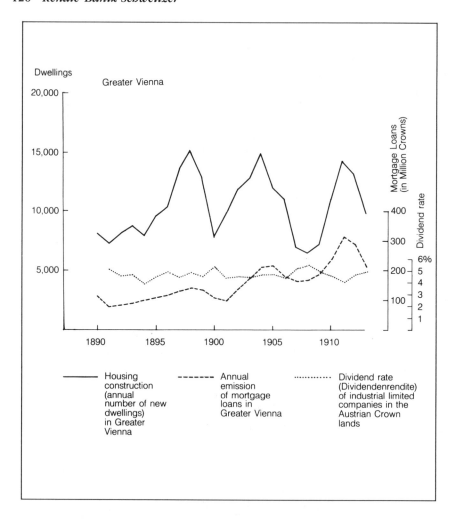

Figure 4.3 Housing construction and issue of mortgage loans in Greater Vienna, and dividend rate of industrial limited companies in the Austrian Crown Lands, 1890–1914, from *Statistiches Jahrbuch von Wien* and Alois Mosser, *Die Industrieaktiengesellschaft in Österreich, 1880–1913* (Vienna, 1980).

capital that even the building industry got a share it had never obtained before. In this period, annual building rates were higher than ever and for the first time a considerable amount of money went into construction of working-class housing, mainly in the districts of Leopoldstadt, Land-strasse and Favoriten.[31] Capital was not only raised by mortgage and savings banks but also by the issue of shares in the newly formed building companies. The crash of 1873 was followed by a long period of falling prices, wages and rents (see Figure 4.5). In the late 1870s annual building

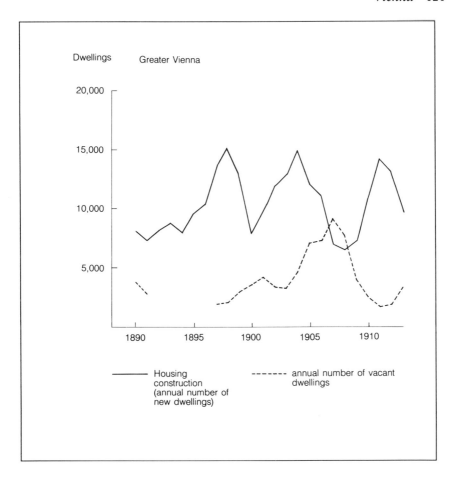

Figure 4.4 Housing construction and vacant dwellings in Greater Vienna, 1890–1914, from *Statistisches Jahrbuch von Wien*.

rates were nearly cut in half. But small investors who had been shocked by the disastrous development of the stock market henceforth looked for safer investment and again engaged in housing. The 1880s put new life into the mortgage loan business, and low wages and prices of building materials encouraged the building industry to take up production again. Interrupted by periodic periods of recession, building rates rose until the First World War. The intensification of the industrialisation process made more capital available even for the building industry. In the last two decades before the war, building was concentrated on the outer districts of Vienna because the central areas were entirely built-up. Besides the middle-class district of Hietzing, working-class districts were now enlarged: Ottakring, Meidling, Favoriten, Simmering, Brigittenau and Floridsdorf. The outer districts of Vienna which had been autonomous Lower Austrian communities until 1890 were the special fields of activity

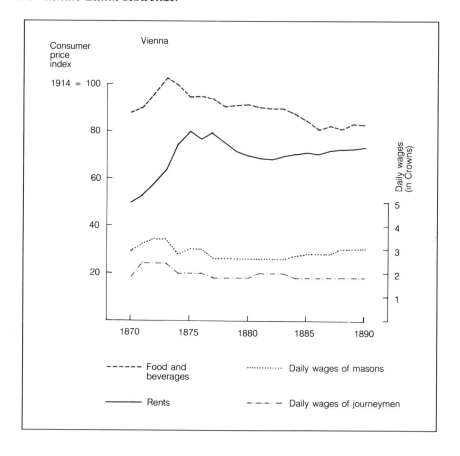

Figure 4.5 Prices, rents and wages in Greater Vienna, 1870–90, from P. Feldbauer, *Stadtwachstum und Wohnungsrot* (Vienna, 1977), and V. Mühlpeck, R. Sandgruber and H. Woitek, 'Index der Verbraucherpreise, 1800–1914', in *Geschichte und Ergebnisse der zentralen amtlichen Statistik in Österreich, 1829–1979* (Beiträge zur österreichischen Statistik 550, Vienna, 1979), 649–88.

for mortgage and savings banks from Lower Austria. In 1914 half of all new mortgage loans in Vienna were raised by these banks.[32]

III

It is well known that Vienna is one of those central European cities which are dominated by the multistoried tenement house. In 1910 only 14 per cent of all houses were single family houses, 8 per cent contained two dwellings, 13 per cent 3–5 dwellings, 16 per cent 6–10, but 49 per cent 11 and more dwellings.[33] At one time there had been a tradition of self-contained housing in Vienna. But within the city it was abandoned when the feudal Habsburg state turned to absolutism, demanding the

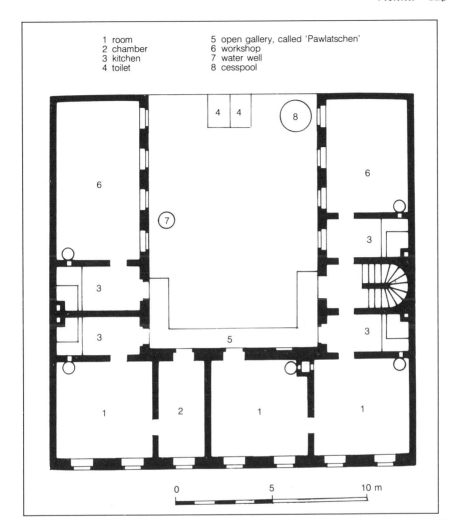

1 room
2 chamber
3 kitchen
4 toilet
5 open gallery, called 'Pawlatschen'
6 workshop
7 water well
8 cesspool

0   5   10 m

Figure 4.6 Artisan's house in Vienna: Gumpendorf, 1807 (first floor).

development of a centralised administration. Within a short period, a considerable housing demand arose from a rather poorly-paid bureaucracy which could not afford a self-contained house in this walled and densely built-up city where the multistoried house already dominated. Taking this into account, the court established a letting system (Hofquartierwesen) which obliged burgher-landlords to let dwellings in their former self-contained houses to members of the state bureaucracy. So in the City of Vienna the tenement system was established rather early. When the inner suburbs were built during the manufacturing period, development of self-contained houses for self-employed artisans was also started. The typical artisan's house in the inner suburbs of Vienna during the first half of the nineteenth century was a U-shaped, one- or two-storied house on a deep plot with a narrow frontage (Figure 4.6). This type of house is said to have been derived from the old wine-grower's house on the outskirts of medieval Vienna.[34] Upper-middle-class houses in the first half of the nineteenth century had distinctly different layouts, not to mention aristocratic palaces which followed the Parisian model of *hôtels* in the city and mini-Versailles at the urban fringe. In the Viennese artisan's house, nearly every room on the ground floor could be entered separately from the inner court and the rooms on the first floor directly from an open gallery (*Laubengang*) called *Pawlatschen*. The interior of the house was not highly differentiated by function. Some of the rooms had hearths with chimneys and were used as kitchens and as living rooms as well. As interior walls were not necessary to secure the stability of the building, they could easily be moved according to any change of use. Rooms of 20–25 square metres were common, chambers (*Kabinette*) of about 15 square metres, and workshops of 50 square metres and more to accommodate the sizeable handlooms of the silk and cotton weavers. When those houses were built they were intended to accommodate the owner's—usually an artisan's—family, his apprentices and his domestic servants. It was a living and working place in one. Therefore even the smaller houses were rather large, with at least six rooms on each floor. The inner court of the house was spacious to allow the necessary outdoor activity in connection with production. The relation between built-up area and court area was about 3:2. In earlier times, the court opened onto a garden at the rear and this, together with the gardens of the other houses, gave the building block a 'green heart'. None of the houses had a water supply or toilets within the building. Water was taken from public wells in the streets or from private ones in the inner courts. Toilets over cesspools were located at the farthest end of the plot according to building regulations which required that unhealthy 'miasmas' should not be let into the house. A public water supply which used filtered water from the Danube was first installed in 1846 in the inner city and the western inner suburbs. Also a system of sewers existed in the same areas, but it was incomplete and inefficient and could not prevent the city from serious cholera epidemics up to the 1870s.

When the use of sweated labour began to spread in the textile trade in the first half of the nineteenth century, this system reduced producers' incomes to such an extent that most of them could no longer afford one of the larger artisan's houses for the sole use of their families. They could do no more than rent rooms in such a house and by doing this the principle of the tenement system was introduced in the suburbs. The sweated labour system also dissolved the traditional family. In domestic textile production, wages were so low that a household could only survive if reproduction costs were reduced to a minimum. Such households often consisted of one or two partial families—a man or a woman with children who did simpler work—and other single men and women who were not relatives but only worked for and with the head of the household and rentpayer. Instead of domestic servants, one of the women, called the 'housekeeper' (*Wirtschafterin*), did the cooking and cleaning for all the others. In households with such an 'open' structure, which were rather temporary working units than communities for life, the desire for domestic intimacy was far from having any chance of realisation. For domestic textile workers, a 'dwelling' was not even a coherent spatial unit. Many of these households occupied two or three rooms scattered about all over the house and members worked, had their meals and slept in the same room.[35]

The change from self-contained to tenement housing in the suburbs started within the existing bulk of buildings. But though the practice of housing supply already showed a tendency towards the tenement system, for new construction there might still have existed an option for the alternative path towards small self-contained houses for low-income groups. But there was another obstacle which can be guessed from the paper of Lederer. Though Lederer denies that land speculation in Berlin and high rent tax in Vienna.forced up rents, he did accept the idea that land speculation in Berlin was based on the tenement system because only multistoried buildings could bear such high land prices. In Vienna, the enormous rent tax played the same role as land speculation in Berlin. It might be assumed that this tax which was imposed first in 1820 was a major factor in establishing the tenement system in Vienna.

When the use of sweated labour was extended in about 1850 to the clothing trade the necessary space for domestic production could be reduced: the sewing-machine needed less room than the handloom and the production units (that is, the households) were little by little restricted to nuclear families. Simultaneously, there was an increase in the number of industrial workers who did not work at home, and who were better paid than homeworkers. This offered them the opportunity to rent a dwelling to live in with their families. This process of social change created a growing demand for small, spatially coherent dwellings that would permit a group of blood-relatives to live an autonomous private life. Such a dwelling had at least to consist of one room and a kitchen. In fact, working-class houses could be found in Vienna from the beginning of the industrial revolution which represented a type of transition from the traditional artisan's house to the later classical tenement house (Figure 4.8). These houses were still U-shaped, now three-storied, but the front part of the house contained two rooms behind each other, one of them a kitchen; the former open gallery had been transformed into an interior corridor. The front room could only be entered when passing through the kitchen which opened on to the corridor and had no direct access to light and air. The side wings of the house stayed the same as in the artisan's house because it was impossible to transfer the new layout to them. But in this forerunner of the classical tenement house the distinct type of prewar Viennese working-class dwelling is already present.

When the building trade started production to satisfy the market, the demand arose for different types of houses with respect to the class composition of future tenants. In Berlin and Budapest, a single type of

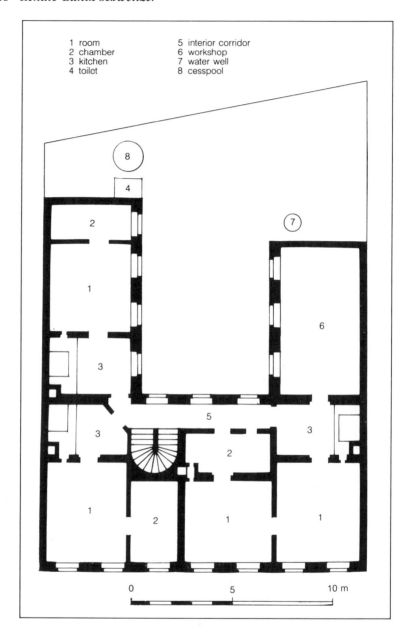

1 room
2 chamber
3 kitchen
4 toilet

5 interior corridor
6 workshop
7 water well
8 cesspool

Figure 4.7 Artisan's and homeworker's house in Vienna: Altlerchenfeld, 1824 (first floor).

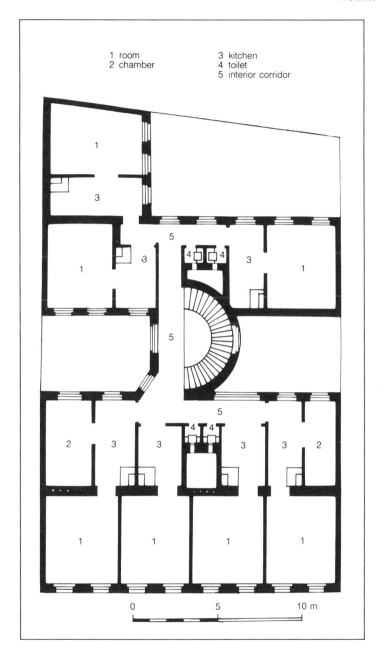

1 room   3 kitchen
2 chamber   4 toilet
                      5 interior corridor

0   5   10 m

Figure 4.8 Workers' tenement house in Vienna: Brigittenau, 1897 (first floor).

multistoried tenement house was developed which could be varied in layout to meet all possible needs.[36] In Vienna the working-class tenement house differed clearly from its middle-class counterpart. This is not apparent from the outside, because the facades of both types were designed in a similar way and decorated with similar stucco ornaments, mostly prefabricated by the Wienerberger Company, and it needs a trained eye to spot the difference. It was the layouts which set the types apart. The only similarity between them was a single staircase, but in the middle-class house no more than four apartments opened directly on to the staircase, whereas a workers' house contained many more dwellings on each floor and these opened on to an interior corridor which ran into the staircase. It is evident that this interior corridor represents the further development of the open gallery of the old artisan's house, but the corridor-scheme was incompatible with the U-form of the old buildings because it demanded windows on both sides of the house. So the typical working-class tenement house of the second half of the nineteenth century had the shape of an I, T or H (Figure 4.8). The greatest disadvantage of this new layout was that the kitchens of the small dwellings which were used as living rooms opened on to the corridor and had no direct access to light and air. Frequently the kitchen was the only room which could be heated and there were no installations within the dwellings. One toilet for two dwellings and one water-outlet for all dwellings on the same floor were situated in the corridor. This water-outlet, the so-called 'bassena', gave the house its common name: in Vienna the classical type of working-class tenement house was called the 'bassena-house'.

Compared with the old artisan's house, this type of house had one advantage: it protected the inhabitants from the direct influence of the weather. But for this improvement workers had to pay dearly with kitchens opening on to the corridor. And the Viennese building industry stuck to the one-staircase-corridor-system because it made construction cheaper. In fact, in 1900 about 60 per cent of all Viennese houses had a single staircase and 20 per cent had none at all because they had only one floor.[37] High building costs were taken to be the main obstacle against improvement of the wretched design of this type of house. For thirty years housing reformers tried to get rid of the bassena-house, only to be told in 1910 by a representative of the building industry: 'If your plot is 12–15 metres wide and you construct small dwellings on a commercial basis you can't provide the kitchens with windows opening up directly to fresh air. Otherwise you have to construct two or more staircases which will force up building costs'.[38] Building regulations permitted 85 per cent of a plot to be built upon. The remaining backyard was characteristically called the 'light-shaft' (*Lichtschacht*) and could not be used for anything. In the cellar of a bassena-house were coal and storage bunkers and the laundry which could be used by each tenant about once a month. The washed clothes had to be carried up to the loft for drying. Ironing had to be done in the kitchens of the dwellings. Rubbish was collected and stored in the dwellings and once a week carried away by the dustman on an open horse-drawn cart.

The one-room-and-kitchen—dwelling became the norm for a worker's family from the 1890s. In 1910 there were about 480,000 dwellings in Vienna and more than 80 per cent of them were built after 1850. The share of the small ones with one or two rooms, kitchen included, had grown from decade to decade until it had reached about 50 per cent in 1900. From then the proportion of bigger dwellings grew slightly but left the working-class districts nearly untouched. In the most important working-class districts of Favoriten and Ottakring, nearly 80 per cent of all dwellings had no more than two rooms, and more than 60 per cent consisted of one room and a kitchen.[39] It frequently happened that 6–8 persons lived in one room and a kitchen. Children often had no bed of their own but had to share one with brothers or sisters. The youngest child normally slept in the parent's bed. Meals were cooked on a hearth built of bricks and fired with coal, which was normally the only heater for the whole dwelling. The ingredients for the meals had to be fresh because there was no storage. Once a week the family bathed in a movable tub in the kitchen. Water had to be heated on the hearth and was used by all family members one after another beginning with father. Family life followed a patriarchal order. Men did no housework, mother served father and sisters served elder brothers if they already went to work. Breadwinners got better food than the other members of the household and their needs were more respected. The dwellings were so small that they forced the inhabitants to develop special techniques which secured them the necessary recreation. After work many men went to pubs with their friends before they went home. When they finally arrived there they expected dinner on the table and their children gathered around it. When father was at home the children had to be quiet and he seldom found time to listen to their daily problems. The children themselves stayed at home as little as they could unless they had to help their parents in domestic production, which was quite common. If possible they tried to play with other children from the neighbourhood in the streets and on empty areas not far from home. Normally they were left to themselves and elder brothers and sisters were expected to care for the younger ones.[40]

In 1900 a working-class family paid about 25 per cent of its income in rent, a lower-middle-class family about 23 per cent, and an upper middle-class family 16–20 per cent.[41] A worker's family that depended on a single breadwinner lived under the constant threat of eviction in times of periodic unemployment. To reduce these risks, workers' families often sublet a bed to a lodger, mostly a single young man, and in this way obtained a substantial contribution to the rent they had to pay. A bed lodger paid more than half of the rent for a one-room dwelling.[42] This particular way of subletting was beneficial for both the letter and the lodger. On one hand, it helped the tenant's family to stay together in the dwelling; on the other hand, in Vienna as in other tenement cities, this became the normal way for a single young unskilled immigrant to start living in the big city. Such a young worker did not earn enough to rent a whole room and he needed somebody to care for him, especially to wash his clothes, because commercial laundries were unknown in Viennese working-class districts.

In 1890 72 per cent of the total population of Vienna lived as family members and blood-relatives in households, 7 per cent as domestic servants, 5 per cent as apprentices, 7 per cent as room-lodgers and another 7 per cent as bed-lodgers (*Bettgeher*). The rest did not live in private households but in institutions. By 1900 the proportion of family members had grown to 76 per cent and that of bed-lodgers had fallen to 4 per cent.[43] Single room-lodgers, many of them students, were typical of middle-class districts and bed-lodgers for working-class districts. At the turn of the century there were 8 per cent room-lodgers · but only 2 per cent bed-lodgers in a middle-class district like the ninth district (Alsergrund) in which the university was located, whereas in a working-class district like Brigittenau 8 per cent were bed-lodgers. Some working-class districts had high proportions of room-lodgers as well but many of them were couples or families which indicated that lodgers in these districts did not earn enough to rent a whole room for one person.[44]

Bed-lodgers had constant contact with non-family members, and the layout of the tenement house meant constant contact with neighbours. Two families used one toilet which they themselves had to clean and all people living on the same floor met when they fetched water from the bassena. Narrative interviews with old Viennese women about how they experienced living in these old tenement houses, compared with the blocks of Red Vienna in the interwar period and with modern social housing, showed the closest and most intensive neighbourhood relations in the bassena-houses:

Solidarity in the bassena-house was much nicer . . . we met in the corridor . . . we danced and chatted at the bassena . . . but now, everybody shuts himself off, like in the superblocks in those days. It was no use stepping out into the corridor, nobody was peeping out . . . and today it is terrible . . . I have not known my neighbours and now, with the elevator—hello and good-bye—not that my neighbour would accept a letter for me, no . . .[45]

In houses where working-class and lower-middle-class tenants were mixed even in the old days contacts were frequently reduced to greeting. The more homogeneous the class-structure of a tenement house was, the more intensive seemed to have been neighbourhood contacts.[46] Children not only played in the streets together but also in neighbouring dwellings where they were given snacks with the children of the 'host'-family. Chatting at the bassena not only provoked quarrels and exercised rigid control over living habits of fellow tenants; it also spread information about minor and major problems of neighbours and established mutual help based on a strong feeling of solidarity. The women borrowed food, pots and pans and did needlework together. If one of them gave birth to a child some of the others helped the midwife and took care of the older children. The deceased were laid out in their dwellings and the house community took part in mourning. But not only

Figure 4.9 Tenants in the interior court of a Viennese tenement house before the First World War, from T. Marzik, *Zimmer, Kuchl, Kabinett: Leben in Wien* (Vienna, 1976).

danger and misery brought them together, it was also happiness when fellow tenants celebrated a marriage or arranged a dancing party in the corridor. Today nothing can show this feeling of solidarity better than old photographs of the whole house community. Being photographed was an expensive adventure then, but it was considered worth while to take a picture of all the inhabitants of a bassena-house in the back yard or in front of the house (Figure 4.9).[47]

Nevertheless, living conditions of workers in tenement houses were a scandal. For a long time the middle class was totally uninterested in how workers lived in bassena-houses. To them, housing reform was only part of a strategy to save the lower-middle class from being proletarianised. So early reform concepts which were really addressed to workers were few and mostly unsuccessful except one modest attempt by the Association for Workers' Houses (*Verein für Arbeiterhäuser*). This Association was founded in 1884 by a philanthropist, Max Steiner, who followed the tradition of the paternalistic workers' colonies in Mulhouse/Alsace which were so much praised by Emil Sax and totally condemned by Friedrich Engels. Like Sax, Steiner wanted to transform the worker from a proletarian to a petty landlord which was the only way for a person without higher education to become a full citizen and taxpayer who would be immune against anarchistic propaganda. Steiner raised the necessary sums for building by issuing shares and getting credit from the City Extension Fund (*Stadterweiterungsfonds*) which had managed the

Figure 4.10 The 'Jubilee Houses' in Vienna: Ottakring, 1898.

Ringstrasse construction and greatly profited from the business. In 1886–87 18 one-family houses were built in the form of terraces in Favoriten. The houses were two-storied and each had a small garden. The smaller ones contained 3 rooms, the bigger ones 4 or 5 rooms, kitchen and toilet. The houses were sold on the hire-purchase system but it soon became clear that an average worker could never afford a house of his own. In fact, the houses were bought by type-setters, mechanics, cabinet-makers and lower civil servants. The whole programme was far from offering a solution to the housing problem of the masses. The Association never started building again and was dissolved in 1894. Its capital was transferred back to the City Extension Fund which was regarded as the only institution qualified for contributing substantially to the improvement of working-class housing. And in a way the Fund met these expectations.[48]

In the 1890s social change began to transform the housing reform philosophy. The industrial bourgeoisie and the liberal high civil servants discovered that in order to maintain production on more organised lines it had become necessary to reconcile the most skilled and best educated workers with the ruling classes. This, among other activities, necessitated

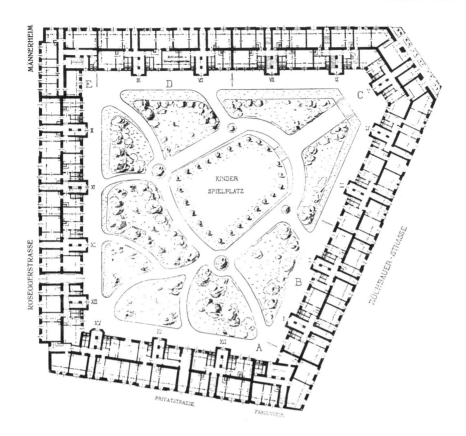

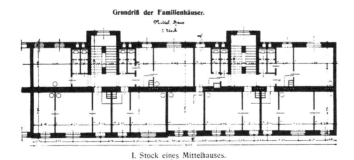

Grundriß der Familienhäuser.

I. Stock eines Mittelhauses.

Figure 4.10 (continued)

the improvement in their housing standard. Now housing reform was addressed to the so-called 'new' middle class consisting of white-collar and the most skilled blue-collar workers. The aim was to create better living conditions for the nuclear family as the basic unit of the state. Insofar as housing was concerned, this meant providing nuclear families with small dwellings which came up to modern health standards. The first step in this direction were the so-called 'Jubilee Houses' (*Jubiläumshäuser*) built in 1898 on the occasion of the fiftieth anniversary of Emperor Franz Josef's accession to the throne (Figure 4.10). These houses represent the transition from paternalistic workers' housing to social housing of the twentieth century. The whole project was developed, carried out and managed by a foundation of industrialists and rich philanthropists. Their fortunes, and credit from the City Extension Fund which again contributed to the solution of working-class housing problems, made building possible. The model function of the project was seen when design and construction were not simply handed over to a master builder as usual. Instead, entries for a design competition were invited. The winners were two prominent architects, Theodor Bach, professor at the University of Technology in Prague, and Leopold Simony. They proposed to build only on the borders of the building block and to leave the interior—about 50 per cent of the block area—free for a garden and for playgrounds. As for the layout of the houses, the greatest progress was achieved by the elimination of the interior corridor typical of the classical tenement house. This meant more staircases but also direct access to light and air for every room. There were more dwellings than usual with two rooms and a kitchen, and every dwelling had its own WC though in general it was still situated outside on the staircase. To stabilise the nuclear family and loosen the bonds of neighbourhood solidarity, subletting of rooms or beds was not permitted. For single persons, two lodging-houses—one for men, the other for women—were constructed. Additionally, the whole complex which covered one and a half building blocks was equipped with baths, steam-operated laundries, shops, a public library, a lecture room and a health and welfare centre.[49] This second attempt to reform working-class housing by change of architectural forms was immediately successful. All the other reform buildings by non-profit building organisations before 1914 followed the example of the 'Jubilee Houses' and they exercised a lasting influence: even the superblocks of Red Vienna in the interwar period were modelled after them.

IV

In Vienna in 1910 only 8 per cent of all residential buildings were one-family houses which were owner-occupied.[50] Most of these houses were situated in the outer middle-class districts so that this pattern of ownership did not occur in working-class districts. In Vienna, more than 90 per cent of housing was rental housing in multistoried buildings. The pattern of ownership was totally dominated by the small landlord who seldom owned more than a single tenement house. In 1910 nearly 70 per cent of all Viennese houses were owned by a single private person and nearly 50 per cent of the houses contained the owner's apartment.[51] Another 20 per cent of the houses were owned by couples or groups of private persons and the remaining 10 per cent was distributed among limited companies, cooperative societies, religious institutions, the City of Vienna and provincial or central government. In working-class districts the proportion of private persons was somewhat higher because institutions preferred more profitable investments in middle-class housing in inner districts. These figures show clearly, as already noted, that neither building companies nor the City of Vienna played an important part in house-owning, though the share of the City had begun to grow a little even before 1914.

Employers who let dwellings to their workers could have been counted among private persons or limited companies but in any case they also played only a marginal role among house-owners. There were some companies, like the railway companies, Wienerberger Company, some breweries and jute factories far from the urbanised area which had to build dwellings for their skilled workers, but altogether these were only some hundred dwellings without any impact upon the working-class housing market. To repeat it, the typical Viennese house-owner was a middle-class private person who owned one tenement house where he or she lived him or herself. And for nearly half of the private owners their house must have been the main source of income. In 1910, 6 per cent of all private house-owners were mainly occupied in agriculture, 24 per cent in industry and trade, 17 per cent in commerce and transport, 8 per cent in professions and civil service, but 45 per cent were persons of private means and among them the majority were women.[52] In Vienna a tenement house was widely regarded as a source of unearned income or a kind of life insurance for middle-class widows, orphans and unmarried daughters. In the opinion of the majority of Viennese house-owners, housing was not a part of the infrastructure which was to secure production and therefore should be cheap and of good quality; rather it was the source of a life annuity offering as high a return as possible. Squeezing the last penny from their tenants was a vital need for most of them, and averting anything that would hinder them in doing so was their paramount political interest.

There were two main factors which reduced their income. One was payment of interest and amortisation of mortgage loans, the other was taxes. It is interesting that the owners seemed not to be primarily interested in influencing the first factor by taking measures to reduce building costs. This was perhaps because such measures might devalue the existing stock of houses, or because as the last link in the chain of producers and distributors of housing they did not have enough influence upon the financing system or building organisation and technology. So tax reduction was their main battlefield and, of course, fighting against any regulations that might give some rights to tenants.

The basis of the rent tax (*Hauszins-und Gebäudesteuer*) was the annual rent of a house. The tax was in theory paid by the landlord but in fact it was shifted to the occupier as part of the rent the occupier had to pay. The question of taxes was so important because taxes on rents were the main revenues of central government and of the City of Vienna alike. Provincial governments and communities like the City of Vienna were authorised to levy their own taxes, so-called surtaxes, in addition to governmental taxes on the same objects of taxation. Additionally the City of Vienna could levy taxes for special purposes, the so-called special surtaxes, for instance for building schools. In Vienna more than 40 per cent of gross rental income was taken by rent taxes, about 60 per cent of them being governmental and provincial taxes and about 40 per cent being municipal taxes (9 per cent special surtaxes included).[53] In Berlin a similar rent tax seems to have skimmed off no more than 20 per cent of the gross rent. High rent taxes were undoubtedly a sign of economic backwardness because they indicated the lack of other sources of tax. The rather slow industrialisation process in Austria–Hungary for a long time offered a too narrow basis for appreciable revenues from income or corporation taxes. And the overall dominant social and political position of the aristocracy made it impossible to raise taxes on land. Moreover, the petty bourgeois Christian Social Party was mainly rooted in Vienna and had only little influence upon provincial and central government politics. So the landlords were powerful in the City Council but not on higher political levels. From 1862 to 1890 all communal rent taxes amounted to 66 per cent of total communal revenues, the proportion falling to 57 per cent between 1891 and 1913.[54] Rent taxes were therefore the largest contributor to communal revenues up to 1914, though their share decreased after 1890, mainly because of the growing importance of profit and income taxes.[55] As far as rent taxes were concerned, Viennese landlords had little influence upon governmental taxation but they could very well act on their behalf in the City Council though the rather numerous group of landladies was excluded because women were not eligible for political bodies before 1918. In 1848 no more than 18 per cent of the elected city councillors were landlords, but this proportion grew rapidly to 48 per cent in 1861 and to 58 per cent in 1879. It then fell to 52 per cent in 1900 and 41 per cent in 1912.[56] This reduction was due to reforms of the electoral law which took into account the growing importance of the 'new' middle class. Nevertheless, the influence of landlords upon decisions of the City Council was great, even though there existed antagonisms within this group. The genuine liberal bourgeois among them who belonged to the power elite were not primarily concerned with the protection of landlords' interests. It was the small landlords coming from the 'old' middle class who with a certain regularity voted against any increase in taxation. When for instance the liberal bourgeois proposed to finance the first high quality water supply system in 1873 partly by increasing taxes, the petty bourgeois fraction voted against another surtax on rents.[57] And in fact the small landlords rejected any further attempts to raise rent taxes until

1914, though it must be admitted that pressure upon them loosened in the course of time when other sources of taxation became more attractive.

After the foundation of the petty bourgeois Christian Social Party by the future mayor Karl Lueger in 1890 the small landlords became their crack troops. And when in 1895 the Lueger party defeated the Liberal Party and won a majority in the city council which it maintained on the basis of an unequal electoral law until 1918, the small landlords had the best position to fight off any attempts to reduce their profits, such as urban planning measures, housing reform laws, new building regulations, an expropriation law, and rent control laws. But the city council was not the only representation of landlords' interests. They had also organised themselves in a Landlords' Association (*Hausbesitzervereinigung*) which published a newsletter (*Hausherren-Zeitung*) and advised members. In case of litigation the court was almost always with the landlord and not with the tenant.[58]

As the main contributors to communal revenues and as typical representatives of the propertied classes the landlords in Vienna held a high social position. It is partly reflected in the first words of an old popular Viennese song: 'My father was a landlord and silk manufacturer . . .'. Their political status weakened in the course of time when other social classes came into power and they never played a decisive role in local politics. The real significance of their social position lay in the near absolute power they exercised over hundreds of thousands of tenants and especially the poorer ones among them.

V

If the landlord was a resident owner he usually managed the house himself. This included letting of dwellings, eviction of tenants, rent collection, filing the annual rent tax return, ordering repairs and having the building whitewashed from time to time. Landlords who were not residents or could and would not manage their houses themselves relied on agents or administrators (*Hausverwalter*), especially in fiscal matters. So it is not surprising that, according to advertisements in *Hausherren-Zeitung*, many of them were civil servants, some retired fiscal officers who took a part-time job fighting the paper war to increase their meagre salaries or pensions. Part-time agents seem to have been paid a lump sum of some hundred crowns per year and not to have had any power over tenants. Full-time agents in particular worked for landlords who were not able to manage their property, especially widows, unmarried daughters and children. Their payment was 2–5 per cent of the total rent collected and they substituted for the landlord in all his functions, including the relationship with the caretaker.

In 1900 70 per cent of all Viennese houses—self-contained houses included—had a caretaker who was generally a resident.[59] Until 1910 when special regulations (*Hausbesorgerordnung*) defining the rights and duties of caretakers were published, a caretaker had the legal position of a domestic servant of the landlord. But it can be taken for granted that the new regulations did not do much more than codify already established rights and duties. It was the caretaker's duty to supervise tenants when using the collective space in the house, so that they followed house rules (*Hausordnung*) along the lines of the following found in a tenement house constructed in 1900:

Tenants are requested to keep the staircase, the corridors, the laundry and the water-outlets clean, to handle the water-taps correctly, not to throw garbage, rags, bones or broken pieces into the toilets, not to store ashes in the loft and not to chop fire-wood or coal in the kitchens. The beating of carpets and the brushing of clothes in the corridors has to be finished by 10 o'clock in the morning. Washing has to be done in the laundry. Unnecessary stays on the staircase and the corridors have to be avoided.

Rules like this clearly show the landlord's intention of educating immigrant farm hands for city life, and the desire to stop unwanted tenants' solidarity by confining them to their dwellings. House rules had not the force of a law but by hidden threat of eviction tenants were expected to follow them and the caretaker had to ensure their observance. It was also the caretaker's duty to light the staircase and the corridors during night time and to clean the collective space in the house as well as the pavement along the street front of the house. He was not obliged to do small repairs by himself but many caretakers did so. And he could take another job if he had a substitute for the work in the house. A caretaker's job was intensely sought after in Vienna because payment included a rent-free two-room dwelling in the house he worked in. As far as it can be deduced from the advertisements in *Hausherren-Zeitung*, the average applicant for a caretaker's job was a couple without children, the man being a construction worker who left most of the work in the house to his wife. It was common in Vienna for the landlord and caretaker to live in the same house, so that the caretaker only partly represented the landlord. Usually the caretaker did not collect rents but there are exceptions and he often acted as an intermediary between landlord and tenants looking for a dwelling.

The legal basis of tenancy in Vienna was not a special law but the Civil Code which to a great extent was based on Roman Law. In 1900, 3 per cent of all Viennese dwellings were let for half a year, 41 per cent quarterly and 47 per cent monthly (the rest was unknown). Generally speaking, the larger and more expensive the dwelling, the longer was the term of the let. In the case of cheap dwellings (annual rent no more than 200 crowns), 78 per cent were let monthly.[60] If the rent was paid on time, the tenancy continued without explicit renewal of the agreement. Rents had to be paid in advance, in tenement blocks generally on the first day of each month. Although the lets were short, they posed serious problems to many workers who were generally paid weekly wages. They were often in arrears and this fact was one of the main reasons for notice and eviction. In the case of monthly lets, landlord and tenant had the right to give two weeks' notice in advance of the next date of rent payment. The dwelling had to be vacated by the tenant by the last day of the month during which he was given notice. If he had not moved in time, the landlord could apply for an order for dispossession which was executed immediately. Against defaulting tenants the landlord had the power to seize goods to the value of the unpaid rent, but not below subsistence level. This was therefore considered a minor threat because most of the defaulters did not have enough possessions to make it worth while. It was the landlord's right of swift eviction and of arbitrary rent increase that gave tenants a highly insecure position and caused serious tension in landlord–tenant relations. A satirical magazine commented on this by having a landlord remark to his friends: 'Gentlemen, it's all very simple, I do it this way: a tenant who does not pay the rent in time will be evicted, a tenant who *does* will pay a higher rent next time'.[61]

There were no institutions to whom tenants could appeal for protection. Medical officers on the payroll of the city administration were inclined to treat landlords with care, as the main taxpayers and as an important pressure group in the City Council. But even law courts and the police who were independent of the City Council in general sided with the landlords. The persistent housing shortage in the market for small dwellings meant that landlords could choose their tenants and their rules were rigid. Unoccupied dwellings were announced on scraps of paper pinned to the entrance door, frequently without any information about how much was to be paid. Every prospective tenant had to present himself as a petitioner to the landlord or to his representative on earth, the caretaker, and after a cross-examination about his living conditions the dwelling was let to him or not. In the first place, large families were not welcomed. In 1911 *Arbeiter-Zeitung*, the newspaper of the Social Democratic Party, reported the following as in no way unique:

On August 15 the landlord Georg Pawlas gave the art metal-worker J. Patzak, 20 district (Brigittenau), Denisgasse 44, notice to quit his dwelling because he had six children. On September 1st Patzak was to move out but he could not find another dwelling in time because of his many children. The following day Patzak was evacuated, his furniture was brought to a storage depot after it had been left for hours on the street and was soaked with rain. He went with his children to the police station where he stayed overnight. Two following nights he stayed in the asylum and workhouse where he was given only 20 crowns to rent a dwelling. Naturally he—with his six children—did not find a suitable one. It was not before four children . . . were given to municipal children asylums that he found a kitchen for himself and the remaining two children.[62]

To find a dwelling was one thing, to keep it was another. As there was absolutely no protection for tenants against unwarranted notice to quit, the slightest incident was sufficient for eviction. An old man, born in Vienna in the family of a Czech tinsmith, remembered: 'The sons of our landlord . . ., two beastly types who always pestered others, once threw my sister down the stairs and she was seriously hurt. When I thrashed the bigger one of them, my family was given notice to quit'.[63] Every year the tenants of about 30 per cent of all Viennese dwellings were given notice—much more in working-class than in middle-class districts.[64] Many old Viennese workers and their wives remember having lived in four or five dwellings one after another when they were children:

My parents moved very often . . . in Kriehubergasse the two children were unwelcome . . . then we lived in Herzgasse where we lost our keys which was enough and we had to move again, this time to Zentagasse . . . in Siebenbrun-nengasse we were given notice because the landlady did not want a tailor [the father] working in her house . . . then we moved to Wiedner Hauptstrasse.[65]

And all these modern nomads, as Werner Sombart called them, lived in perpetual fear of the landlord. His nasty tricks, like turning off water and shutting off toilets, the unforeseen raising of rents, his right to distrain the property of a tenant who could not pay the rent in time, and especially the threat to be given notice led some tenants to commit suicide and others to acts of individual resistance—but these acts did not in the least change the landlords' attitudes.

The rent strike in 1911 was not caused by the system of tenancy, but by the announcement of a rent increase of about 20 per cent at the same time as there was a big increase in food prices (see Figure 4.11). Some houses of especially hated landlords were besieged by some hundred people, windows were smashed by stones, caretakers and landlords were beaten up and abused.[66] But police easily overcame these spontaneous revolts and revolutionary energies were soon channelled into the first Tenants' Association (*Mietervereinigung*) which was founded under the guidance of the Social Democratic Party in the same year.[67] But all this made very little impression on the landlords. It was the legal protection of tenants against eviction and rent increase established in the last year of the First World War which at last broke their power. But fear and hatred against them were so deeply rooted in the working-class popula-tion that it did not disappear at once. Charles Gulick remarked in 1950 that

Whoever had the chance to talk with Viennese workers about their housing conditions before the War recognised how much revengeful hatred had been built up in their hearts against the 'rent vultures' and 'house tyrants'—hatred that arose from great injustice and maybe not to a lesser extent from the little every-day tortures inherent in the whole situation.[68]

When after 1918 the Christian Social Party made attempts to abolish tenants' protection regulations, the hostile image of the landlord—as a fat figure, flat-footed with pot-belly, bald head or bowler hat and thick moustache—was still ready for use by the Social Democratic Party and helped them win elections in the interwar period.[69]

VI

Building regulations shaped housing in Vienna to a considerable extent.

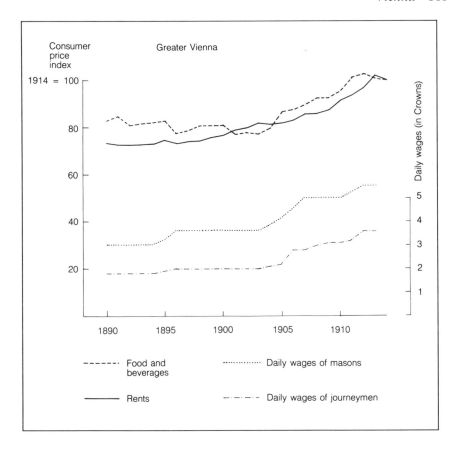

Figure 4.11 Prices, rents and wages in Greater Vienna, 1890–1914, from Feldbauer, *Stadtwachstum* and Miihlpeck, Sandgruber and Woitek, 'Index'.

In the first half of the nineteenth century their function was primarily to maintain order and security. They dealt with the stability of buildings, with protection against fire and contagious diseases. It was the new building regulations of 1859 which completely changed this policy. Building was now liberalised in the same way as other trades at the same time. In 1859 the guild-system was abolished, and building regulations were only to set the frame for free enterprise. But nevertheless there were some regulations which made late nineteenth-century Vienna look as it does today.

First there was the rule that all streets had to be 16 metres wide and as straight as possible. This was the basis of all the checkerboard building-line plans in the outer districts. Then constructors were directly encouraged to build the typical Viennese working-class dwellings: 'The building owner . . . may also plan smaller dwellings consisting of one room and a kitchen or even a single room with a provisional hearth'.[70] Finally, there was the rule that houses were not to be taller than 25 metres—which led to the tendency not to build any houses lower than that—and that each floor had to be at least 3 metres high which limited the number of storeys per house to five. There were, however, no definite regulations indirectly influencing sanitary conditions, for instance about building density, types of houses, number of toilets and ventilation of dwellings. And so the typical tenement house covered acre after acre and building density grew steadily.

In 1883 new building regulations were to stop the worst excesses of unhampered development—interestingly in the same year when restraints on trade were introduced to limit uninhibited competition. In future, no more than 85 per cent of a plot was to be built upon. This was a very high percentage but without this regulation density would have increased further. And there had to be at least one toilet for two dwellings. This was the last word before 1914. Whenever housing reformers tried to abolish the Viennese type of tenement house by modifying building regulations they were rejected by the building industry's and landlords' lobby in the City Council.[71]

Sanitary controls seem hardly to have influenced the main developments in housing. Sanitary controls were first tightened in the 1870s when the disastrous effects of the industrial revolution had become visible and when the first large-scale measures were undertaken to improve the environment: the regulation of the Danube in 1870–75 and the first high quality water supply in 1873. At the same time, serious efforts were undertaken to improve the system of sewers and to force the paving and cleaning of streets. In the early 1870s the sanitary problems in housing were increased by the flooding of the Danube in 1872, and by a cholera epidemic in 1873, the year of the world fair in Vienna, when thousands of foreign workers were attracted to the city in addition to those who were already occupied in water regulation works. Up to 1890 2,000–3,000 dwellings with sanitary defects were inspected annually by the Public Health Service. The complaints concerned damp, badly ventilated and overcrowded dwellings, defective toilets, sewers and cesspools, and polluted wells. And additionally there was about half this number of complaints concerning unhealthy sleeping conditions of apprentices in small workshops, in particular of shoemakers and furniture makers.[72] However, orders to rectify the sanitary defects did not normally lead to thorough repair or even demolition and reconstruction of the house. In most cases the defects were superficially eliminated and did not lead to structural change.

After 1890 controls of housing conditions were no longer reported, probably in part because of the beneficial impact on sanitary conditions by large-scale infrastructural measures and partly because the bulk of modern dwellings built between 1870 and 1890 contributed to the improvement of living conditions.

The latter fact might also have been the reason why slum clearance was not an important tool for influencing working-class housing. 'Slum clearance' in Vienna was piecemeal and a private matter. The usual triggers for slum clearance, like railway construction or construction of thoroughfares, did not work at this time. Vienna needed no Baron Haussmann because there was enough space for modern high quality buildings on the glacis areas which had never been built upon. The railways did not have to cut through built-up areas to the city centre because when they were constructed they only served long-distance transport and not commuting, so that the terminals could be built outside the urbanised area. Thoroughfares from the railway terminals to the city centre, like those built in Paris, were also unnecessary because the existing streets were adequate. And thoroughfares in the centre itself, like Kärntnerstrasse and Rotenturmstrasse, were made by demolishing and rebuilding one house after another according to individual decisions of the owners—a process that took about thirty years and did not create masses of homeless people at one time who could have been regarded as a threat to the public.[73] Demolition and reconstruction in the inner districts also did not happen as a result of slum clearance schemes. Reconstruction took place when the middle-class population which had been forced out of the inner city looked for new homes close to their jobs in the city because there was no efficient public transport to enable them to live in new, distant, suburbs. The necessary building operations were carried out through piecemeal and scattered development. And in the outer districts, to which the workers forced out of the inner districts had moved, slum clearance was unnecessary because the buildings were new.

The land market, as a possible field of political influence and control, was almost entirely left to free enterprise. Around the turn of the century there had been serious attempts to enact a communal expropriation law but the opposition of the building industry and landlords' lobby was so strong that it never came into existence. Zoning may be regarded as an indirect way of achieving a certain degree of control over the land market. In 1893 the City of Vienna published a zoning plan covering the whole urbanised area which became part of building regulations. This plan indicated industrial areas, high density areas for mixed use, high density residential areas, and areas that were reserved to terraces or detached houses. The reason this plan was accepted without opposition was that zoning simply followed the already existing urban pattern. One can say that it prevented the worst but not that it was an instrument for shaping the land market according to specific political intentions.[74]

In the long run, the raising of funds for working-class housing apart from the capital market had the greatest influence upon the improvement of housing conditions. The effects were, however, only marginal before 1914. First there was financing of working-class housing by philanthropists. Successful examples of this way, like Steiner's houses and the Jubilee Houses, were few in Vienna but philanthropists were the first to make miserable housing conditions a matter for discussion and to suggest plans for reform. The next generation of housing reformers at the turn of the century—liberal civil servants in government, university professors, physicians and leading members of the new Social Democratic Party—then promoted financing by government, either by spending money raised by taxation or by using social security funds.

The latter approach was developed by the Workers' Accident Insurance Company of Lower Austria (*Niederösterreichische Arbeiter-Unfallversicherungsanstalt*) which built about 200 workers' dwellings in Floridsdorf between 1900 and 1906.[75] A slightly better result was achieved by the State Railways which constructed about 600 employees' dwellings in Vienna between 1900 and 1910 financed by their pension funds.[76] But the relative backwardness of Austrian industry did not allow social security funds to accumulate enough capital to start building on a larger scale.[77] The City of Vienna spent money from the pension funds of municipal workers (tramway and gasworks) for construction of about 3,000 small dwellings for their employees between 1911 and 1914.[78]

The alternative approach of using taxes emerged from discussions among social-liberal housing reformers in the Centre for Housing Reform in Austria (*Zentralstelle für Wohnungsreform in Österreich* or ZWÖ) formed in 1907. They enquired into what caused the permanent shortage and mean quality of working-class housing in Vienna and concluded that the nature of the capital market was primarily responsible for grievances, especially the difficulty of getting second mortgages on reasonable terms. In 1909 ZWÖ published a 'Proposal to establish a government housing welfare fund endowed with returns from rent taxes'. Housing reformers had not succeeded in the long battle for a reduction of rent taxes, and they now tried instead to divert a part of tax revenues to the advantage of housing reform. In the same year the Ministry of Public Works submitted a bill on 'rent tax reform and the creation of a government housing welfare fund' to parliament where the bill was used as a weapon in the struggle against the increase in food prices. At this time, the Liberal industrial bourgeoisie, together with the Social Democrats, opposed higher food prices which were blamed upon the Hungarian aristocracy. Since the government depended upon the great Hungarian landowners, it was unlikely that the Liberals and Social Democrats would win this campaign for a better working-class standard of living. The conservative forces in Parliament knew they would win the war, but allowed their opponents to win a battle as a face-saving exercise. In 1910 a law was passed concerning the construction of small dwellings (*Kleinwohnungs-fürsorgegesetz*). This law created a government fund (*Kleinwohnungsfür-sorgefonds*) supplied by tax revenues on existing buildings which was to secure second mortgages for construction of small dwellings.[79] Since only non-profit building organisations could appeal to the fund, it immediately stimulated the development of cooperative building associations which mushroomed in Vienna, increasing from seven in 1910 to sixty in 1912.[80] These associations did not have the intention of raising the necessary money for building from the savings of their members. Their only reason for existence was that they could appeal to the fund for security for second mortgages raised on the capital market, provided they could themselves supply 10 per cent of estimated building costs. But even this 10 per cent was too much for most of the workers, so the advantages of the fund were more or less only to the benefit of middle-class associations. Nevertheless, in 1913 the non-profit building organisations—institutions managing pension and welfare funds as well as cooperative building associations—were said to have reached about 20 per cent of annual housing production in Vienna.[81] Although housing still depended to a great extent on the capital market after the scheme of 1910, and the supply of lots was entirely left to market forces, this fund was taken as a model for governmental financing of social housing in Austria in the interwar period.

VII

In the second half of the nineteenth century, Vienna was the relatively modern capital of a relatively backward empire. The dominant social position of Vienna was rooted in the modern elements of society—high skilled blue- and white-collar workers in advanced processing industries —who were much more concentrated in Vienna under the Habsburg monarchy than were their German counterparts in Berlin. Nevertheless, the proportion of modern social groups in Berlin was higher than in Vienna where they owed their existence mainly to capital investment by foreign transnational corporations which limited the growth of their subsidiary companies in Vienna to the supply of the Austrian domestic market. Therefore the representatives of pre-industrial society, especially the 'old' middle class and petty bourgeoisie of artisans, shopkeepers and civil servants, had much more political and social weight in Vienna than in Berlin.

The social and economic backwardness of the Habsburg monarchy is not least indicated by the fact that revenues were mainly raised from urban rent, and not from other sources of taxation. The rather slow process of industrialisation limited revenues from income and corporation taxes, and the dominant social and political position of the aristocracy prevented the imposition of taxes on land. The enormously high Austrian rent taxes seem to have been unique in Middle Europe and were to a great extent responsible for the specific structure of the land and housing market and the pattern of landlord–tenant relations in Vienna. Possibilities for expansion in a walled city were limited, architectural forms checked further development towards small self-contained houses for low-income groups, and low wage-levels as a result of the high amount of sweated labour contributed, but rent taxes seem to have been a major factor in the spread of the tenement system in Vienna by forcing up building density. High rent taxes also limited the 'profits' of all other participants in the development and construction business, which therefore remained small-scale in nearly every respect. Ground rents were limited so that land speculation did not attract limited companies as in Berlin. Builders tried to reduce construction costs and therefore remained loyal to the typical Viennese tenement house with a single staircase and interior corridors. Moreover, there seemed not to have been enough surplus private capital which was attracted by urban development. The financial system depended to a greater extent on money from small private investors than in Berlin. And rather low profits from their property led landlords to look more for secure than for speculative returns.

The fact that they were the main contributors to state and municipal tax revenues gave the landlords in Vienna an extraordinary political and social position. The preferences of state and municipal fiscal policy meant that a petty bourgeois party was the dominant political element in the City Council, when in other German, Austrian and Hungarian cities liberal parties stayed in power. Within the sphere of action of the City Council, the Christian Social Party, representing landlords' interests, blocked every attempt towards reform of working-class housing. Since low wage-levels prevented Viennese workers from self-organised improvement of their housing conditions, the first steps toward systematic reform measures were left to the state government.

Notes

1. Renate Banik-Schweitzer and Gerhard Meissl, 'Industriestadt Wien. Die Durchsetzung der industriellen Marktproduktion in der Habsburgerresidenz', *Forschungen und Beiträge zur Wiener Stadtgeschichte*, vol. 11 (Vienna, 1983).
2. Banik-Schweitzer and Meissl, 'Industriestadt Wien', 57, 58.
3. Renate Banik-Schweitzer and Wolfgang Pircher, 'Zur Wohnsituation der Massen im Wien des Vormärz', in *Wien im Vormärz. Forschungen und Beiträge zur Wiener Stadtgeschichte*, vol. 8 (Vienna, 1980), 133–74; Renate Banik-Schweitzer, 'Zur sozialräumlichen Gliederung Wiens 1869–1934', *Publikationen des Instituts für Stadtforschung*, vol. 63 (Vienna, 1982).
4. Peter Feldbauer, 'Stadtwachstum und Wohnungsnot. Determinanten unzureichender Wohnungsversorgung', in *Wien 1848 bis 1914. Sozial- und wirtschaftshistorische Studien*, vol. 9 (Vienna, 1977), 54, 62.
5. *Statistisches Jahrbuch der Stadt Wien*, 1902.
6. Josef Ehmer, Maps 3.7.1/1 and 3.7.2/1 from Felix Czeike and Renate Banik-Schweitzer (eds), *Historical Atlas of Vienna* (Vienna, 1984).
7. Banik-Schweitzer, 'Zur sozialräumliche Gliederung'.
8. Banik-Schweitzer and Pircher, 'Zur Wohnsituation der Massen', 168.
9. Josef Ehmer, 'Familienstruktur und Arbeitsorganisation im frühindustriellen Wien', *Sozial- und wirtschaftshistorische Studien*, vol. 13 (Vienna, 1980), 40–56.
10. Jürgen Friedrichs (ed.), *Stadtentwicklungen in West- und Osteuropa* (Berlin–New York, 1985), 360.
11. Banik-Schweitzer and Meissl, 'Industriestadt Wien', 57, 58.
12. Banik-Schweitzer, 'Zur sozialräumliche Gliederung'.
13. Ibid.
14. Ibid.
15. Emil Lederer, 'Bodenspekulation und Wohnungsfrage', *Archiv für Sozialwissenschaft und Sozialpolitik*, vol. XXV (Tübingen, 1907), 613–48.
16. Lederer, 'Bodenspekulation', 615.

17. Feldbauer, 'Stadtwachstum', 243.
18. Lederer, 'Bodenspekulation', 618, 621.
19. Ibid.
20. *Jahrbuch der österreichischen Industrie 1903–4*, 22–41.
21. *Amtsblatt der Stadt Wien 1911*, 427.
22. Felix Czeike, 'Liberale, christlichsoziale und sozialdemokratische Kommunalpolitik, 1861–1934', *Dargestellt am Beispiel der Gemeinde Wien* (Vienna, 1962), 85.
23. *Jahrbuch der österreichischen Industrie 1911*, 279.
24. Hans Bobek and Elisabeth Lichtenberger, *Wien: Bauliche Gestalt und Entwicklung seit der Mitte des 19. Jahrhunderts* (Graz-Köln, 1966), 53.
25. *Jahrbuch der österreichischen Industrie 1903–4*, p. 36.
26. Banik-Schweitzer and Pircher, 'Zur Wohnsituation der Massen', 161.
27. Feldbauer, 'Stadtwachstum', 308–14.
28. Ibid., 61.
29. Ibid.
30. Banik-Schweitzer and Pircher, 'Zur Wohnsituation der Massen', 161.
31. Feldbauer, 'Stadtwachstum', 71.
32. Bobek and Lichtenberger, *Wien*, 53.
33. *Österreichische Statistik, N.F.*, vol. 4, part 1, 'Häuseraufnahme 1910' (Vienna, 1914).
34. Bobek and Lichtenberger, *Wien*, 216, fig. 1.
35. Banik-Schweitzer and Pircher, 'Zur Wohnsituation der Massen', 150, 166–7.
36. Renate Banik-Schweitzer, 'Wohnverhältnisse in Berlin, Wien und Budapest um die Wende zum 20. Jahrhundert. Siedlungsforschung', *Archäologie-Geschichte—Geographie* 5 (1987), 177–204.
37. *Statistisches Jahrbuch der Stadt Wien 1902*.
38. Renate Banik-Schweitzer, 'Die Kleinwohnungsfrage in Wien um die Jahrhundertwende', in Juan Rodriguez-Lores and Gerhard Fehl (eds), *Die Kleinwohnungsfrage, Stadt-Planung-Geschichte*, vol. 8 (Hamburg, 1988), 431–50.
39. *Statistisches Jahrbuch der Stadt Wien 1902*.
40. Reinhard Sieder, '"Vata, derf i aufstehn?" Kindheitserfahrungen in Wiener Arbeiterfamilien um 1900, Glücklich ist, wer vergisst . . .?' in Hubert Ch. Ehalt, Gernot Heiss and Hannes Stekl (eds), *Das andere Wien um 1900* (Vienna, 1986), 39–112.
41. *Österreichische Statistik*, vol. LXV, part 1 (Vienna, 1904).
42. Ibid.
43. Banik-Schweitzer, 'Kleinwohnungsfrage', 432.
44. *Statistisches Jahrbuch der Stadt Wien 1902*.
45. Michael John, 'Hausherrenmacht und Mieterelend; Wohnverhältnisse und Wohnerfahrung der Unterschichten in Wien 1890–1923', *Österreichische Texte zur Gesellschaftskritik*, vol. 14 (Vienna, 1982), 110.
46. Ibid., 125–7.
47. Ibid., 73.
48. Wolfgang Hösl, 'Die Anfänge der gemeinnützigen und genossenschaftlichen Bautätigkeit in Wien' (Unpublished PhD thesis, University of Vienna), Vienna, 1979, 61.
49. Ibid., 65–94.
50. *Österreichische Statistik, N.F.*, vol. 4, part 1, 'Häuseraufnahme 1910' (Vienna, 1914).
51. Ibid.

52. Ibid.
53. Maren Seliger and Karl Ucakar, *Wien. Politische Geschichte 1740–1934* (Vienna, 1985), vol. 1, 455.
54. Ibid., vol. II, 802.
55. Ibid.
56. Ibid., vol. I, 604 and vol. II, 965.
57. Renate Banik-Schweitzer, 'Liberale Kommunalpolitik in Bereichen der technischen Infrastruktur Wiens', *Wien in der liberalen Ära: Forschungen und Beiträge zur Wiener Stadtgeschichte*, vol. 1 (Vienna, 1978), 91–119.
58. John, 'Hausherrenmacht und Mieterelend', 58.
59. *Statistisches Jahrbuch der Stadt Wien 1902*.
60. *Österreichische Statistik*, vol. LXV, part 1, Vienna, 1904.
61. John, 'Hausherrenmacht und Mieterelend', 38.
62. Ibid., 30. A crown became the Austrian currency in 1900: two crowns were equivalent to one guilder or florin.
63. Ibid., 29.
64. *Statistisches Jahrbuch der Stadt Wien 1890–1913*.
65. John, 'Hausherrenmacht und Mieterelend', 37.
66. Ibid., 41.
67. Ibid., 43.
68. Charles A. Gulick, *Österreich von Habsburg zu Hitler*, vol. II (Vienna, 1950), 81.
69. Ibid., 144.
70. *Bauordnung für die k.k. Reichshaupt- und Residenzstadt Wien, Reichs-Gesetz-Blatt für das Kaiserthum Österreich. Jg. 1859, LII Stk. vom 29. September 1859*.
71. For this in detail see Banik-Schweitzer, 'Kleinwohnungsfrage'.
72. *Verwaltungs-Bericht der Stadt Wien* (years 1871–1889).
73. Karl Mayreder, 'Stadtentwicklung' in P. Kortz (ed.), *Wien am Anfang des XX. Jahrhunderts* (Vienna, 1905), vol. 1, 49–79.
74. Renate Banik-Schweitzer, 'Der Bauzonenplan von Wien 1893. Ein Instrument der Wohnungsreform?' in Juan Rodriguez-Lores and Gerhard Fehl (eds), *Städtebaureform 1865–1900, Stadt-Planung-Geschichte*, vol. 5/11 (Hamburg, 1985), 389–420.
75. Hösl, 'Die Anfänge der gemeinnützigen', 94–7.
76. Ibid., 100.
77. Banik-Schweitzer, 'Kleinwohnungsfrage', 439.
78. Albert Lichtblau, 'Wiener Wohnungspolitik 1892–1919', *Österreichische Texte zur Gesellschaftskritik*, vol. 19 (Vienna, 1984), 93.
79. Banik-Schweitzer, 'Kleinwohnungsfrage', 441.
80. Hösl, 'Die Anfänge der gemeinnützigen', 162.
81. Banik-Schweitzer, 'Kleinwohnungsfrage', 441.

5 Budapest

Gábor Gyáni

Budapest did not become the true capital of Hungary until as late as the mid-nineteenth-century when, during the War of Independence of 1848–9, Pest was the seat of the first independent Hungarian government and Parliament. The collapse of both the Revolution of 1848 and the War of Independence against the Habsburgs meant that the city ceased to play this role for several decades. In the next two decades of Habsburg absolutist rule up to 1867, Pest—the core of the would-be Hungarian capital—experienced very considerable economic development. By the early 1860s, Pest's grain trade had become a dominating factor in the entire Hungarian economy, and its steam-powered flour mills, the largest in Europe, processed grain from the whole country. Milling and a number of other industries brought prosperity as early as the 1850s. A similarly dynamic population growth occurred at the same time: the combined population of the three towns of Pest, Buda and Óbuda was 134,000 in 1851, and jumped to more than 270,000 by 1869.[1] Budapest thus became the second most populous city of the Austro-Hungarian monarchy in the 1870s, when it was the sixteenth largest city in Europe.

The acceleration of the city's development to become a metropolitan type of urban settlement by the turn of the century was given a strong and sudden impetus from the 1870s. The origins of this development lay with the compromise between Austria (that is, the Habsburg monarchy) and Hungary in 1867, which established the Dual Monarchy. As a result, Hungary regained its independent status, albeit sharing a common emperor and army with the Austrian half of the monarchy. Of course, maintenance of a common military establishment required concerted policies in both finance and foreign affairs.

The re-establishment of the internal political autonomy of the country meant that Budapest again became the governmental and administrative centre of Hungary. The three distinct and closely adjacent towns along the Danube—Pest, Buda and Óbuda—were administratively united in 1873, but the initial steps to transform them into a single city as a physical entity were actually made in 1870. The Hungarian government set up the Board of Public Works (BPW) on the lines of London's Metropolitan Board of Works. It was established, remarked the Prime Minister, 'to develop the capital, Budapest, . . . into a true city . . . with a place among the capitals of the civilised western world, worthy of the

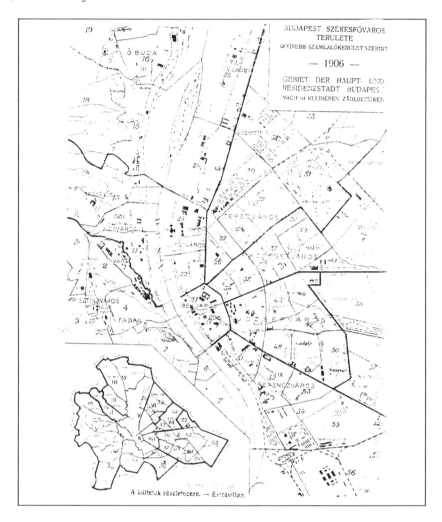

Figure 5.1 Map of Budapest in 1906.

prestige of the Hungarian state and its 15 million inhabitants'. (See Figure 5.1.)

I

The BPW was a state institution, standing above the municipal authorities, and the relationship between the two sides led to tensions and conflicts during the ensuing years. Although half of the members of the Board were delegates from the two towns of Pest and Buda, the other half, as well as the president and vice-president, were appointed by the Ministry of the Interior. Thus, unlike its counterpart in London, the

BPW did not really represent the interests of the local government against those of the central government in power. In the case of a tied vote on the Board, the president was entitled to a casting vote; and when the Board and the city council held divergent views on the same issue, the final decision was taken by the minister himself.

The power given in principle to the Board over the local authorities was demonstrated in practice during the course of preparing the comprehensive building regulations for Budapest in 1886 and 1894, and in numerous other instances of developing the infrastructure. The city council was responsible for the creation of the infrastructure as a whole, but the Board retained the privilege of judging and approving the plans submitted, and controlling their implementation. Beyond that, the BPW was seldom involved in these issues, apart from the case of some of the major thoroughfares, or the embankments and bridges of the Danube. The preparation of land for development, which meant control of the provision of the entire infrastructure, was actually carried out by the Board in the case of Andrássy Avenue when, as a result of the crisis of 1873, the private entrepreneurs reneged on their commitment.

The BPW soon after its foundation prepared a new survey of the capital. In 1871 there had been an international competition for a city development plan, and from the three prize-winning entries—two from Hungary and one from England—the Board drew up and eventually executed its own plan. This created the present layout of Budapest with its wide, long avenues converging on the city centre and its three rings of boulevards leading to bridges (some of which were not built until much later) over the Danube. It is clear that the plan adopted was deeply influenced by the examples of two large continental cities—Vienna and Paris—whose renewal and physical transformation had started somewhat earlier. They embodied the dominant concept of modern city planning, and provided the model which late-comers strove to imitate.

The powers of the BPW encompassed the financing of public buildings, the creation of a large-scale urban infrastructure, and the supervision of all building activities in the city. As far as the latter were concerned, the Board was responsible for the regulation of land use and the standards which house-building had to attain. The Board strictly defined the exact ratio between the number of storeys of houses and the width of the street; prescribed the possible building methods and the materials to be used; and required that the houses should join each other by party walls. These regulations on street width and the height of buildings were, it was claimed, amongst the strictest in Europe at the time. Although landlords and property speculators were both strongly dissatisfied with these regulations, and incessantly fought against them, they had little visible success. However, they were amply compensated by the state in other ways (for example, by tax subsidies and land policy), so that their opposition was easily contained.

More comprehensive building codes were issued in 1886 and again in 1894, when the city was divided into four zones: the high-density city centre; the lower-density suburbs on the Buda-Hill; a mixed area of villas and tenement houses; and the factory districts which were also high density. Standards were adapted to each zone, so that the building codes varied from zone to zone. The construction of houses of more than five storeys was not permitted as it had been under previous regulations, and only three-storey houses were allowed to be built in all locations, regardless of the width of the street. Where a five-storied house was allowed, no more than 80 per cent of the plot could be built upon. Although standards were strict with respect to street widths and the height of buildings, the regulations were highly permissive in the use of individual plots. The consequence was that both the city centre, where land speculation flourished most, and certain outer zones became very densely built. The Board even defined the minimum size of dwellings, which meant that a flat (including a kitchen and room) with merely 161.4 square feet, or a room with only 107.6 square feet, conformed to the official minimum requirement. The regulations at the same time prohibited the creation of basement-dwellings, the number of which was considerable up to the 1890s.[2]

The regulations imposed and the standards set by the BPW fundamentally influenced the quality of housing built in each of the zones, thereby indirectly having an effect on the social composition of these areas of the city. But the zoning ordinances did not lead to extreme segregation in Budapest. The factors which operated against segregation were numerous and manifold, and will be discussed later.

The regulations of 1894 remained in force until the end of the period studied here. Only on the eve of the Great War were new regulations issued which doubled the number of zones to eight. The building code limiting the maximum number of storeys of houses was abandoned at the turn of the century, so that houses of more than five storeys could be built from the early twentieth century onwards.

The existence and the wide scope of activities of the BPW clearly indicate the weight of the role played by the state in the city-building process. State intervention was not confined to the cases so far mentioned. Two further aspects are worth mentioning: the intervention of authorities at times of epidemics, and the way they disposed of the city's land.

When the third wave of the European cholera epidemic of 1863–75 reached the Hungarian capital, it resulted in the death of large numbers of people—2,000 in 1866 and even more in 1873.[3] However, the municipal authorities showed striking indifference towards the whole matter and were reluctant to take any defensive measures against the spread of the epidemic.[4] However, by the time of the following wave of 1881–96, their attitude had changed substantially. First, the long-standing intention of erecting wooden barracks was finally carried out: four barracks each comprising 70 family rooms and six common halls were set up.[5] In addition, the disinfection of private dwellings (including rented flats) was ordered. The number of dwellings actually disinfected within this scheme amounted to 3,200 in 1896; from the mid-1880s on more than 10,000 dwellings a year with sanitary defects were regularly inspected by the public health authorities.[6] Finally, the recurrent threat and reality of ravaging epidemics gave birth to the concept of municipal housing projects. The epidemic experience was undoubtedly closely associated with raising the question of municipal participation in house-building activity, first asserted by Ambrus Neményi at the 1883 session of the General Assembly of the Municipal Board of the capital.[7]

The second issue was the availability (and even temporary ownership) of city land for clearance and new buildings. As early as 1868, before the beginning of any large-scale rebuilding, a law was passed to facilitate expropriation. Any territory in Pest and Buda could be expropriated by public authorities in order to widen or straighten streets and squares, to open new thoroughfares, or to erect public buildings. Furthermore, every inflammable and unhealthy factory which threatened the lives of neighbouring residents could also be removed, and its site expropriated without any difficulty. Another law, enacted in 1881, invested the Minister of Public Works and Transport with the right to make decisions in expropriation cases. The intention of this law was to accelerate the existing procedures. Under the new law, the price of any site that the state, BPW or the city council intended to expropriate was fixed by a jury consisting of representatives of both property owners and the authorities. As a general rule, the prices fixed by the juries were high, so that few of the cases had to be settled by legal action.

The systematic accomplishment of the general renewal schemes was only partially possible, owing to the limited access of the state and the city to urban land. The right of expropriation provided by the new laws was strictly confined to single estates and to cases where public buildings were intended to be erected. The state and municipal authorities were not given a free hand in expropriations, and they did not have the power that Haussmann had possessed in mid-century Paris.

The state (BPW) and the city council had different standings as landowners. While the former could not be considered a permanent landowner, the city itself possessed a very considerable quantity of land, amounting to more than 13,000 acres in 1874. During the following decades, this territory gradually diminished and by 1908 had been reduced to about 10,000 acres. Of the 3,000 acres that were disposed of, more than 40 per cent were yielded at disproportionately low prices to private investors or the state, and were not primarily used for housing construction.[8]

Despite the limits of the legal framework, extensive estates owned either by the municipality or especially by private landowners were obtained by purchase and expropriation. The extensive estates and tracts were regularly parcelled out undivided, which meant that a very special type of tenement house became widespread and even dominant. Along the major thoroughfares, large blocks of three- or five-storey tenement houses were frequently built, without many side-streets around them. These large tenement blocks contained far more dwellings than similar edifices usually had in other central European cities such as Vienna,

Prague or Munich. The reason for this lay in land-speculation. The speculator sought to cram as many apartments as possible into a single building, thereby minimising his costs per unit. And in turn the level of rent-income to be drawn from a tenement house dictated the value of the building site, thereby strengthening land speculation. The land-speculator played a central role in the process of late nineteenth-century urban development in Budapest.

As a contemporary observer noted, the speculator:

... never purchases an expensive plot and very rarely one that is developed for building. On the contrary, he piles up extensive estates lying in the outer areas of the city at a ridiculously low price and waits for the time when the evolution of the city pushes the builders towards the outer districts, especially to his particular speculative holding. The fact that the extensive agricultural territory which had not been utilised so far is transformed into a building site greatly increases the value of the land. And the landholder is eager to increase the price higher and higher. First, he subdivides it into building plots, then yields some portion of it for building purposes at a reduced price, occasionally free of charge, in order to attract building activity. When finally urban development is forced to use his estate, then the land-speculator steps forward in his undisguised role, raising the price of the plot as high as he can.[9]

The land speculator bought an estate from the original landowner and obtained a mortgage for a higher valuation than he paid for it. The land and mortgage were then entered in the register book at the higher value which anticipated the development of the site. In this activity, the speculator was strongly supported by the building codes and zoning, for the landholder within their scope 'always fixes the price of the site at its sale to the builder in accordance with the possible use, taking into account the prospective profitability of the house to be built on it'.[10] Since the minimum size of plots in each of the zones was large enough to build a high and extensive tenement block, the more intensive utilisation of the building site by an increase in the number of storeys necessarily resulted in a rise in the price of plots. The speculator subdivided the estate, and arranged with builder middlemen to erect tenements on the plots. These middlemen were usually 'men of straw' who had insufficient capital, and they obtained funds from the banks with the support of the speculators. This mortgage was also entered in the register book. The property might become overcharged with loans, and the banks often acquired buildings because the middlemen were unable to pay the finance charges.[11]

The remedies that were offered were the same as were widely discussed, and sometimes even implemented, in other European countries. Some endorsed the introduction of the leasehold system which would distance the ownership of land from the ownership of housing. It was possible to point to Ujpest, an industrial suburb of Budapest, where part of an estate owned by the Károlyi family had been made available for building on leasehold.[12] Similar propositions had been advanced during the 1880s and 1890s, when the council also accepted this notion. However, despite the legal framework which was then established, only a few buildings were erected in this way.[13]

Ferenczi, who both as a writer and a council official was one of the leading personalities in the housing reform movement, further widened the agenda. Beside the leasehold system, he proposed the introduction of a number of new taxes. First, he advocated a so-called betterment tax that (following Henry George's analysis) would tax the unearned increment enjoyed by the landholders. Subsequently, he proposed a new kind of purchase tax to curtail the profits gained from frequent sales of the land. Finally, he wished to alter the taxation of land which had not yet been built upon. He suggested a so-called building-site tax which would impose on the land a tax burden according to its real prospective market value. Nevertheless, Ferenczi was sceptical about the efficiency of these measures, and particularly the betterment tax, for he had seen that tax reform had been only partially successful in some of the German cities. In fact, neither the new system of taxation, nor other measures that were so eagerly put forward by housing reformers and supported by some members of the council, were ever put into practice.[14]

The drive to increase profitability operated even in the case of the adoption of the mixed tenement house. Such tenements contained dwelling units for a variety of rent levels: larger and more elegant flats were located on the lower storeys and at the front; gradually moving upwards and backwards, in particular to the rear of the house, were more dwellings which contained only one or two rooms and a kitchen. In tenement houses where the stock of dwellings was so diversified in quality, the open circular gallery alone made it possible to reach the ever-growing number of back-yard flats (Figure 5.2). In sharp contrast to Vienna and any other capital and city in central Europe, the circular gallery became the major architectural solution in Budapest.

Similarly, the endeavour to build quickly and cheaply led to the rejection of the alternative architectural form based upon more than one stairway and a deep gateway. Thus, the tenants of the same block who belonged to very diverse social classes had to share the same stair and the circular gallery. Separate back stairs were maintained primarily for servants, and the lower-class residents were to be found only in inferior parts of the houses, notably in the apartment blocks on the most elegant thoroughfares such as Andrássy Avenue. The distinction between private and public space was much less sharp, and the spatial distance between socially diverse tenants was much less than in Western European cities.[15]

The apparent attachment to the original limits of the plots when they were used for buildings and the special land-use codes of the BPW together account for the exclusive spread of multi-storey tenement houses and the total lack of self-contained houses. Within the confines of the first, second and in a large measure even the fourth zones, the size of building-sites was defined in a way that made profitable the construction only of big tenement blocks, although as early as the beginning of the 1870s it became apparent that there was some public aversion to multi-storey tenement houses (or 'rent barracks' as they were called).[16]

Figure 5.2 Interior of rent barracks showing circular gallery.

These voices did not die away as time passed; parallel with the uncompromising rent-barrack building boom, critical voices became ever louder.

What were the sources of funds for large-scale projects carried out by the public bodies, to acquire land for avenues and boulevards, and to provide the urban infrastructure and public buildings? The BPW's capital was provided by a loan from a French–Austrian consortium in 1870 to the value of 24 million forints. In order to amortise the loan, the state could rely upon, in the first place, the revenue flowing from the sale of previously expropriated lots and those in the possession of the state for a longer time; and in the second place the income drawn from the labour service levy, which in the single year of 1874 amounted to 77,500 forints.[17] These revenues went into the so-called capital fund. It is noteworthy that each financial request the Board submitted had to be approved by Parliament.

The financial provision for house-building was exclusively assumed by private capital up to the first decade of the twentieth century. Before going into more details, however, it is important to delineate the overall building achievement from the mid-nineteenth-century onwards.

II

Since the mid-nineteenth century, and particularly from the 1870s, the role of immigration in the rapid growth of Budapest was considerable. In contrast to several European and North American capitals and major cities, the spectacular increase in the population of Budapest was largely channelled into industry. Budapest was at once both the industrial and the administrative centre of the country, and one crucial, and perhaps dominant, attraction to immigrants was the dynamic progress of its industries.

Table 5.1 Population of Budapest

	Number	Index
1869	270,476	100
1880	360,551	133
1890	492,237	182
1900	717,681	265
1910	880,371	325
1913	930,666	344

Source: Vörös, *Budapest, IV*, 377, 577

During the period from unification up to the First World War, Budapest's population more than trebled and, consequently, neared a million (Table 5.1). No other European metropolis except Berlin matched this rate of growth. As a result, Budapest which in 1870 ranked only sixteenth amongst European cities, had risen to eighth by 1910. The increase was most marked in the 1890s when more than 225,000 inhabitants were added to the city.

Similarly, house-building activity was not an even process, for feverish construction cycles were interrupted by serious recessions. Even prior to unification, the rhythm of building activity had not kept pace with population growth. Between 1857 and 1872, the total population grew by 50 per cent in Pest, while the number of houses only increased by 29

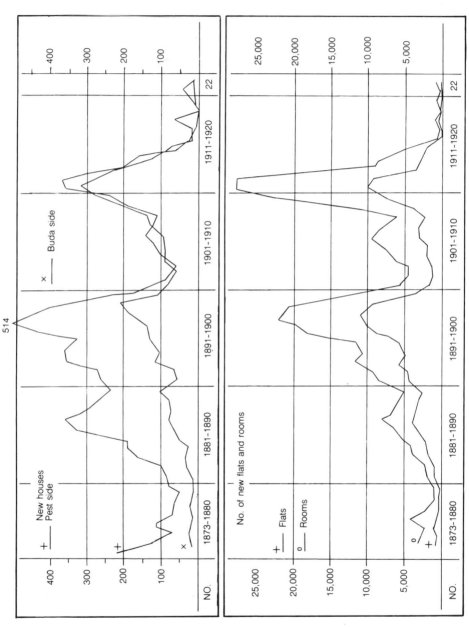

Figure 5.3 Building cycle in Budapest, 1873–1922.

per cent. The situation in Buda was even worse. House-building moved from stagnation in the 1850s, to prosperity which lasted to 1873, interrupted by a short-term slump between 1863 and 1867. The boom ended in 1873, when an economic crisis first shook the burgeoning Hungarian capitalism.[18] (See Figure 5.3.)

In this first phase, the appearance of large numbers of multi-storey tenement houses was a distinctive feature. Since they were mainly intended for, and priced for, middle-class tenants, their growing numbers did not alleviate the depressed housing situation of the poor and the workers. The growing scarcity of workers' housing resulted in the increase of basement flats. In most instances they were established in one- to three-storey houses on the outskirts, whose relatively poor landlords attempted to turn the scarcity of workers' housing to their own advantage.[19]

Who were the investors and the landlords? Those involved in investment in house-building and in the ownership of housing at this time were mostly aristocrats and the wealthy members of the traditional citizenry of Pest, including many Germans and Greeks. A further characteristic component of the landlords was the group of rich merchants and the leading architects who were also successful building entrepreneurs. To be sure, there were differences among these subgroups, but for most of them investment in house property served less as a speculation than a secure source of income. These capital owners were not profit-maximising investors, for they considered house property as an annuity, which also gave them desired prestige in contemporary Hungary.[20] Another benefit of house-building was the fast return of capital, due to the relatively high level of house rents. The importance of housing property in the fortunes of the wealthiest and in the entire economy of the city is suggested by the fact that one quarter of houses in Pest were in the hands of the thousand biggest taxpayers, who also received 40 per cent of the revenues from house rents.[21]

House-building suffered a downturn after 1873 for seven years, at a time when other types of building (public construction and infrastructure) continued to expand. Public buildings (excluding infrastructure) represented half of the total value of construction work between 1875 and 1885, while private building accounted for 15 per cent.[22] The years of protracted stagnation undermined the operation of recently founded building companies. In the wake of the prosperity of the 1860s, the capital of limited companies in the building industry had soared to 5 million forints by 1870, and to more than 8 million by 1873. Moreover, a new giant company was established on the last day before the slump: the Building Society of Pest (Pesti Épitötársaság), which collected 10 million forints as its capital stock. In the ensuing crisis they all went bankrupt. Six of them, with a capital stock of approximately 3 million forints, were totally liquidated, including brick works and building companies.[23]

The conclusion may be drawn that in the upswing of house-building until 1873, the big joint-stock companies played an enormous role. They took the best part of the large-scale public projects and private investments relating to multi-storey tenement blocks, and even monopolised brick production. Small-scale building firms also continued, primarily involved in the far more modest construction of self-contained houses and the one- to two-storey tenement houses in workers' districts.

A new upswing of the building industry and an increase of capital allocation in the housing sector began in the 1880s, and continued up to 1889. After two years of slump, the intensity of capital investment returned to the previous level. The 1890s were the most flourishing period of house-building that Budapest ever saw in its history. The end of the decade saw the end of that last magnificent prosperity. The feverish building surge of the 1880s and 1890s was deeply embedded in a markedly altered social and cultural background. Consequently, the processes of that particular period were accompanied by several new features.

The nature of landlords and the place of housing in total investment were affected by the fact that the economic structure was in a state of profound change (see Table 5.2). It was a period of swift and wide-scale industrialisation. The industries which were expanding were connected with the infrastructure (railway and house construction), the demands of the state apparatus (armaments, public buildings), and the needs of a rapidly modernising agriculture (machines and chemicals). This created a rapidly widening domestic market. As a result, heavy industry, mining and to some extent the food industry, were to lead the way in industrialisation. Budapest, along with its traditional central role in the milling industry, more and more became the principal seat of the engineering and iron industries. The place of Budapest in Hungary's economy as a whole can best be demonstrated by the following figures from the end of the period under review: Budapest provided half of the trade and accounted for one-third of the entire industrial output of the country, and was responsible for 40 per cent of Hungary's entire national wealth.[24]

These processes deeply restructured the whole of the economy, and exerted an influence on the housing sector. First, despite the surge in house-building, this kind of property did not retain its former significance in the 1880s and 1890s. Comparison between the lists of the greatest taxpayers in 1873 and 1888 clearly shows that the proportion of the very rich who relied on housing property as a single source of income declined markedly. It was the position of the old urban bourgeoisie which was most threatened by the new tendencies. By 1888, most of the aristocrats who had previously owned very considerable housing property, and even some other traditional landlord groups, had disappeared from the list. They were partially substituted by those retired merchants who, having left business, started to live exclusively on their housing property. In summary, while in 1873 landlords represented by far the largest group amongst the great taxpayers, 43.4 per cent of the total, they had decreased to 17.7 per cent by 1888.[25]

Secondly, owing to the building boom of the 1870s and 1880s, building entrepreneurs and traders significantly improved their positions, as is indicated by their significantly increased showing in the ranks of the great taxpayers: their presence had nearly doubled to 4.6 per cent by 1888. Within this group, the leading and richest architects were gradually replaced as entrepreneurs by newcomers with very considerable amounts of capital, but without any professional qualifications. This change was due in part to a new law which removed the need for professional qualifications at the highest levels of the building industry.[26]

Building companies (including those involved in the production of building materials) increased their productive capacities. While in the 1880s the number of limited companies decreased to three or four, in the subsequent decade their number regularly exceeded ten, and was usually around 12 to 14. The profitability of the companies also increased considerably: in the 1880s they only paid dividends of 4 to 5 per cent but in the 1880s the average dividend soared to 10 per cent.[27] Despite the ever-growing size of joint-stock companies, the distribution of company size within the building industry remained unchanged for there was also an increase in the number of small firms. According to a survey of 1891, just prior to the great upswing, most building firms were made up of small-scale workshops: 40 per cent of them had no employees, and the average number of employed workers was only 11.[28]

The spectacular increase in private house-building in the 1890s was made possible by the involvement of new sources of funds, both bank loans and from the mortgage loan business. Their availability led to intense building activity, despite the fact that loans were granted under relatively unfavourable conditions: the average interest rate of 4.75 per cent was higher than in western European cities.[29] House-building in Budapest absorbed 16.8 per cent of all the mortgage loans in the country in the mid-1890s. The overwhelming majority were floated by the savings banks, although large loans were primarily provided by the credit banks.[30] It was commonly held by contemporary observers that the supply of capital rather than the demand for housing by the lower classes regulated the rhythm and intensity of house-building activity. The same was true of Vienna and Berlin.[31]

Arising from the expanding role of banks, a wholly new form of financing, the so-called 'house-leasing system', began to evolve from the mid-1890s. A contemporary commentator explained that 'an entrepreneur rents a multi-dwelling house or greater part of a house from the landlord to sublet it as a whole or by single dwellings'. The system was gradually extended to finance an increasing proportion of house-building. The investors and would-be landlords did not have the amount of capital required to complete the construction, and yielded unfinished buildings to a house-renter, who paid both the rent for six months or a year in advance, and the 'caution money'. With this sum, the original investor could complete the building.[32]

House-building was an enterprise which was highly, albeit selectively, subsidised by the state in the form of tax allowances and the granting of immunity from state taxes. The state imposed taxes on property; the municipality by contrast did not tax property to any great extent, and

Table 5.2 Occupational groups in Budapest

| | Percentage of economically active population | | | |
	1880	1890	1900	1910
1. Industry				
self-employed	4.9	7.3	8.1	7.1
clerks, managers	0.1	1.3	2.1	3.0
workers	26.0	28.1	31.5	34.0
2. Transport, commerce				
self-employed	4.0	4.0	4.5	4.3
clerks	1.3	3.1	4.4	5.5
workers	5.6	8.3	9.1	9.4
3. Civil service				
self-employed	1.7	0.9	1.0	1.4
clerks	4.0	3.8	4.6	4.7
assistants	2.3	1.6	2.5	2.8
4. Day labourer	18.9	12.5	5.0	2.3
5. Domestic service	19.0	15.1	14.8	14.2
6. Others (private means, pensioners etc.)	1.9	3.6	3.3	3.2

Source: Census volumes

derived its income from rents from its own property, sales taxes, and a proportion of various state taxes. As early as 1868, a law was passed to establish the immunity of new buildings from state taxes for fifteen years, or for twelve years in the case of rebuilding where clearance preceded the construction. A new law passed in 1871 further widened the scope of immunity from state taxes to include houses which were high enough and located along the Great Boulevard and Andrássy Avenue, the most important thoroughfares. The law also granted them immunity from the communal tax for a fifteen-year term, and some tax relief was also promised for the subsequent fifteen years. In 1875, a new law extended the time limits of previous tax-reliefs. It supported the building of three- or more storey houses within the belt of the Great Boulevard by granting immunity from state taxes for twenty-five years; houses located outside that area could enjoy similar advantages for twenty years. At the same time, tenement houses comprising one- or two-roomed dwellings were also given some tax-relief for ten years in respect of communal taxation. Despite this relief to small properties, and the extension in 1907 of immunity from state taxes to houses rented or purchased by labourers from their factories, the advantages offered by successive tax-relief laws mostly favoured the creation of middle-class dwellings and the more elegant flats, rather than workers' houses. As a contemporary expert pointed out, 'these singular tax-reliefs meant rather a state and municipal gift given to the property owners and the first landlords'.[33] These 'gifts' were highly valuable, for, as data from 1897 showed, the state tax, communal tax and other public costs could together absorb 33 per cent of the income from house rent.[34] The tax relief largely left local finance untouched since most property taxes were levied by the state. The increasing costs of municipal government were in any case largely met by borrowing rather than by internal sources of funds. The city had recourse to foreign loans in 1873, and this accelerated from the turn of the century, reaching a peak just before the First World War when the total debt amounted to 430 million Koronas. The council housing programme of 1909 was financed with foreign loans.[35]

At the beginning of the twentieth century, house-building again suffered a downturn: the capital spent on construction between 1900 and 1904 was exactly half of that during 1895 to 1899. A new upswing started only after 1905, culminating in 1911–12.[36] The tensions arising from the poor housing conditions of the lower classes were becoming most acute in the 1900s. This was the era both of the rapid increase in rents, especially in the years after 1906, and the hectic reactions to that situation in the rent-strike movement of 1909–10. At the end of the spectacular house-building boom based on the mortgage loan business, more and more builders went bankrupt. This led to an increase in the role of the mortgage banks as landlords: a considerable proportion of the new houses were then handed over to the banks which were the actual investors standing behind the builders.

There were innumerable signs of a deep crisis. It was apparent by this time that the market mechanism alone was insufficient to satisfy the pressing needs of poor people for small and inexpensive accommodation. The state was compelled to face the fact that its direct involvement in house-building was essential to eliminate scarcity. With a strong determination to increase the supply of workers' housing, the state started a project in 1908 to construct a large housing estate, which was completed in 1914. It was built just across the border of the city and was named after Wekerle, then Minister of Finance, for the simple reason that the Ministry was the sole investor in and owner of the estate. By 1914, the Wekerle housing estate consisted of 3,657 dwellings with around 20,000 residents. The rent of one- or two-roomed flats in the cottage-style two- or three-storey buildings were much lower than in the private sector.

The city itself decided to implement a similar project when a liberal mayor, István Bárczy, came to power in 1906. After some initial steps in the 1890s and 1900s when single model tenement houses for workers had been built in various parts of the city, the Municipal Council launched its wide-scale house-building programme in 1909. The City Council constructed 6,200 to 6,300 houses for rent by 1914. Most accommodation consisted of one-room dwellings; about a quarter were in tenement blocks, and the remainder in smaller constructions which formed distinct residential districts. These districts, which numbered seventeen, were similar to the Wekerle in attempting to popularise cottage-type building. The rents of council houses were low enough to compete successfully with market prices. While the Wekerle was inhabited exclusively by skilled workers employed by state firms, the tenants of the mostly one-roomed municipal houses represented more diverse categories of the working classes.

The emergence of state and municipal efforts to create workers' houses therefore meant that more than 10,000 new dwelling units were added to the existing stock. The majority—two-thirds—of them were financed and built by the Municipal Council, and most of the houses—four-fifths—were in estates. The significance of the projects can best be demonstrated by the fact that in 1914 10 per cent of the working class, numbering 55,000 people, are estimated to have resided in state-owned or council houses.[37]

Factories also made some efforts to build accommodation for their own employees. The first housing estates of this sort were established in the 1870s and 1880s, but their major development occurred much later, in the 1900s. Generally, the large state firms were the most frequent and ambitious investors, especially those associated with the railway in Budapest, and mines and metallurgy in the countryside. In Budapest, MÁVAG (the railway machinery factory) had an extensive housing estate as early as the 1870s, and built a new one with 3,000 mostly one-roomed dwellings by 1911. The rents here were very reasonable, and the flats were mostly available for skilled workers, many of whom were recruited from abroad. The extent of the contribution of the state or private firms to workers' housing must not, however, be exaggerated.[38]

There is a final question to be answered: did the landlords have a special political status, could they be considered as forming an interest group? There is no clear-cut picture of the group politically, but Vörös has pointed out that there was an unambiguous divide between two fundamental types by the beginning of the twentieth century.[39] Therefore, barely any common interest survived which could be articulated. The wealthiest members of the group, each of whom owned a number of houses in the city centre and who monopolised tenement houses in the area, enjoyed a strong presence on the Municipal Board Committee and also formed the core of the House Owners' Association.[40] The owners of small, single house properties in the outer districts which had been built before the renewal of the city centre, who were the true landlords of the huge masses of proletarian residents in Budapest, were socially and economically separate both from the upper segment of the landlords and from the authorities, including the city authorities. Consequently, conflicts rarely emerged between the organised private landlords and the state or the city, since the authorities always did their best to favour the wealthiest and most influential investors through tax-reliefs which related to the areas of the city where they had property rather than to housing as a whole. The organised landlords were therefore not compelled to fight against the authorities or to pursue a separate policy as a pressure group. Only at one point did they oppose the state and the City Council—in 1908–9, when the state-supported and Council projects were set in motion. However, the opposition which the projects met could not become overheated, for the landlords were also aware that this housing policy actually eased tensions rather than imposing new burdens on the private rental sector. It should be remembered that this was the era of the most vehement rent strikes.

III

The majority of workers, and obviously of other segments of society as well, always lived in rented flats. Precise data are not available on the ratio between owner-occupiers and tenants, but the figure which is known for 1910, that 8.6 per cent of industrial labourers owned a house or part of a house, clearly shows the insignificance of owner-occupation in this sector. Prior to this date, owner-occupation may have been more common, for as the multi-storey tenement house came to be the dominant form of accommodation in Budapest, owner-occupation (especially in self-contained houses) declined amongst the working class. While in the 1870s as many as four-fifths of Budapest houses were one-storied buildings, their proportion dropped to 50 per cent by 1914. Simultaneously, the percentage of four- or five-storey (and even higher constructions) rose to 22 per cent by the close of the period under consideration.[41]

The composition of the housing stock also changed over the decades. In 1870, just before the BPW had been established, the share of one-roomed dwellings in Pest alone was 34.6 per cent, and exactly half of the population resided in them.[42] The percentage of the smallest dwellings gradually increased with the passage of time and reached 45.2 per cent in 1906. However, the increased proportion of such accommodation housed a somewhat smaller part of the population, only 43 per cent in 1906.[43] The trends in housing stock and the division of the population among the various residences clearly show that some improvement actually occurred in housing density.

Areas lying outside the Great Boulevard and in extensive territories in Buda were in fact full of old one-storied buildings as late as the start of the twentieth century (see Figure 5.4). Nevertheless, only a minority of them were used as self-contained family houses; the majority were rented as multiple tenancies. The only exceptions were those in the Buda Hills, where upper-middle-class property-owners maintained villas for residence in summer. An ordinary working-class residential district with traditional tenement houses (rent barracks) was described by a contemporary observer in 1911 as follows:

Most of the buildings are one-storied rent-barracks, but wooden shacks housing people are still frequent here. They usually contain one 'room'. The dwellings in rent-barracks, just as cells in a prison, are aligned closely side by side. The courtyards are regularly full of dirt and mud . . . In one two-storey house 343 persons reside. Similar conditions are also to be found elsewhere. In a one-storied rent-barrack . . . the number of residents is 97. There are only three privies attached to the house . . . Moreover, one of them is maintained for the landlord. The dwellings in that area consist of a room with one window, and a kitchen without any window.[44]

Figure 5.4 The Tabán district on the slope of the Gellért hills on the Buda side of the Danube, c. 1890.

Figure 5.5 Traditional working-class tenement in the inner city on the corner of Duna Street, c. 1895. Such buildings were to be replaced by higher, multi-storey 'rent palaces'.

The next example, from the 1890s, was reconstructed from archival sources. The one-storied rent-barrack was located in an outer section of the Great Boulevard and was soon replaced by a multi-storey apartment house. The original property had eleven occupied units, only one of which (inhabited by the landlord himself) was two-roomed, the rest being one-roomed and, with a few exceptions, looking into the inner courtyard. There were four basement flats in addition, the tenants of these being day-labourers. The social make-up of residents of the other dwelling units represented the most diverse categories of the working and lower classes. The rents of basements were only 30 per cent lower than for apartments facing the courtyard.[45]

As time passed, such low-rent apartment houses were gradually substituted by their multi-storey and somewhat modernised counterpart: the rent-palaces in the city centre and low-income, multi-storey rent-barracks in working-class residential quarters. Despite the great need for the latter, the low level of the purchasing power of the population inhibited the elimination of the housing shortage. The four- or five-storey apartment houses for workers contained at best dwelling units with two rooms, but most frequently the lodgings were only one-roomed. These huge blocks were erected primarily in certain areas of Pest, such as Angyalföld, the outer portion of Józsefváros and Ferencváros. They may be illustrated from a source relating to a rent-barrack from 1902–4. The three-storey houses located in the district called Erzsébetváros contained six shops on the street level, and 27 dwellings. Two-thirds of them consisted of only one room and a kitchen, all facing the courtyard; there were five dwelling units with two rooms, and four with three rooms. The tenants of the three-roomed units belonged to the lower middle classes (shopkeepers, hairdressers, tailors etc.). The one-roomed tenancies, on the contrary, were all occupied by workers (day labourers) or poverty-stricken artisans and tradesmen. In a rent-barrack like this, there were no longer any basement dwellings, and the rents were usually higher than in old-style tenement houses.[46]

As mentioned earlier, not even the rent-palaces entirely excluded lower-class residents. The mixed type of apartment house with very diverse dwellings and residents' social status was preferred in Budapest throughout the period. A four-storey house in a quarter named Terézváros (somewhat outside the Great Boulevard) contained six dwellings with one room, two with two rooms, and twelve with three rooms. Accordingly, lower-middle-class tenants (teachers, clerks, persons of independent means, commercial travellers) dominated the house, although some of the small tenancies were held by skilled workers.[47] Again, at the turn of the century, an elegant rent-palace on the Great Boulevard was occupied by lower-middle-class and working-class tenants in the two-room dwellings facing the courtyard; the landlord, who was a member of parliament, mining entrepreneur and landowner also lived in the property, occupying—as was the rule—the street apartment on the second floor.[48] And the case may be generalised.

The housing available to workers, regardless of location, contained most frequently one room (with one or two windows) and a kitchen without a larder; the rooms usually faced the courtyard, and were located at the rear of the building. They were mostly heated by iron stoves and housed on average five persons. Their two distinguishing features were their smallness and overcrowding, which was associated with the sub-letting system in its two forms, the one when a room and the other when only a bed was rented by a lodger. The official standard for measuring overcrowding was modified from time to time, so that we are not in a position to decide whether the density rate grew worse or improved with the passage of time. In 1870 in Pest, when the measure of overcrowding was defined as four or more residents sharing one room, two-fifths of the population or around 80,000 people were considered to live in such miserable circumstances.[49] In the 1880s, a dwelling was considered to be over-crowded if more than eight persons slept in a room (two children being equal to one adult). On this definition, around 1880 17 per cent of all rooms with a total of 150,000 residents were defined as being overcrowded or 40 per cent of the total population.[50] According to a less extreme calculation, the number of congested houses in 1881 was 4,785 but their number nearly doubled by 1891, soaring to 7,178. That meant that 12.3 per cent of the total population in 1881 and 13.2 per cent in 1891 might be classified as living in overcrowded conditions. Evidently, a majority belonged to the working classes. It is clear that overcrowding was always closely associated with basement locations: both in the 1870s and the 1890s a quarter of the population which was overcrowded rented a basement flat. This particular type of residence was common up to the 1890s. During the 1870s around 10 per cent and still in 1881 8.7 per cent of the population lived in basements. As a consequence of the official ban on the creation of new basement dwellings, the share of these lodgings began to diminish in the 1890s: the proportion of residents living in basements dropped to 5.4 per cent by 1891, with a similar proportion of basements in the housing stock. The trend was uninterrupted and the share of these residences was as low as 1.1 per cent in 1906.[51]

It was the growing importance of assessing overcrowding, and in particular of alleviating the misery engendered by the relatively high housing density, which prompted statisticians to investigate the phenomenon with more precision. A special survey was made in 1893, in which much more refined standards were set. Overcrowding was considered to begin when the quantity of air per person fell below 10 cubic metres. The investigation concluded that the number of crowded dwellings was only 2,749 which housed around 20,000 people. Despite the restriction imposed on the creation of new basement flats, nearly 20 per cent of the residents of crowded dwellings lived in basements. The crowded dwellings contained in all except 5 per cent of cases only one room, and the proportion of children under 16 among their residents was 33 per cent.[52]

The next survey providing data on overcrowding was conducted in 1906. Unfortunately, the methods applied then to measure the

Table 5.3 Number of lodgers

	Number	Percentage of population
1870 (Pest only)	29,159	14.5
1880	50,940	13.7
1890	69,384	13.7
1900	85,846	11.7
1906	110,260	13.9
1910	127,626	14.5

Source: Körosi, *Elöleges Jelentés az 1870,* 7; D. Laky, *Az Albérlök es Ágybérlok Szocialis és Gazdasági Viszonyai Budapesten* (1929), 33.

phenomenon were again altered; the criterion of high density was defined as four or more persons per room. On this definition, 88,000 people, living in more than 10,000 dwellings, were considered as being overcrowded. This relatively high housing density involved 7.7 per cent of the housing stock and 12 per cent of the population.[53]

What lay behind overcrowding; who were the people who constituted the residents of single-roomed dwellings rented primarily by manual labourers? An answer to the question is provided by the evidence of a contemporary sanitary inquiry. The municipal health official concluded that the basement dwellings of a building in Terézváros should be vacated as soon as possible. The reason for this was the overcrowding and unhealthy conditions. The landlord who replied to the charges claimed that:

. . . basement flats in my house do not lie lower and are not darker than those in the neighbouring house . . ., the unhealthy conditions found in them are solely attributable to the residents, who never ventilate the rooms, and who smoke, wash, iron inside; moreover, although the tenants are renting the flats for themselves and their families, having once moved into them they soon take in lodgers in a number that inevitably leads to overcrowding.[54]

It is indisputable that the housing density was not caused primarily by any general pattern of multi-generational co-residence or a high rate of fertility producing a large number of infants and children living with their parents. The explanation is rather the perpetual presence of strangers in family homes.

Most of the lodgers, usually two-thirds of them, were men. Evidently, women tended to become living-in servants which meant that they had a lower demand for sub-letting than men.[55] Another remarkable feature is that half of the lodgers were so-called bed-lodgers.[56] (See Table 5.3.)

The uneven distribution of lodgers in the housing stock further aggravated the density of occupation of the smallest dwelling units. In 1891, one third of lodgers lived in dwellings officially defined as over-crowded. Figures from 1906 show that 36.8 per cent of workers' housing held lodgers. Single-roomed dwellings accounted for 51.9 per cent of all the dwellings with lodgers; the proportion of single rooms with lodgers was 33.6 per cent. A somewhat higher percentage of the two-roomed tenancies (39 per cent) took in lodgers.[57]

The aggregate figures which are cited above do, it is true, also include non-working-class lodgers such as students, but the overwhelming majority of them were recruited from the ranks of manual labourers. The proportion of workers among the lodgers might range from two-thirds to three-fifths and, as a consequence, at least one-quarter and perhaps one-third of industrial workers must have been lodgers in 1911.[58] In one sense or another, nearly every member of the working class was involved in subletting. When workers first migrated to the city, they could only find shelter for themselves as lodgers. After spending some time as sub-tenants, they finally married and could manage to become a tenant. Reaching that higher status, they sublet beds or a room to young, unmarried and recently arrived lodgers whose circumstances were similar to their own previous condition.

Overcrowding meant that there was not sufficient space available for privacy in an average workers' house. Since the overwhelming majority of the working class—four-fifths in 1906—lived in one-roomed dwellings, the private domain had to be shared with numerous persons. In addition, the intimacy of family life was seriously affected by the permanent presence of sub-tenants. Thus, the use of domestic space was dictated solely by necessity, which can be demonstrated by two factors: more than one person shared, as a rule, a single bed; and the functional division and utilisation of different parts of the dwelling were practically impossible. In the 1890s, data relating to overcrowded houses show that only 71 per cent of the residents had the privilege of sleeping in a bed, of whom only 5.2 per cent had the bed to him- or herself; over three-quarters shared the bed with one other person, and a further sixth with two others.[59] The lack of space that could be used privately also manifested itself in the multifunctionality of all parts of the dwelling. It was very common to use even the kitchen for a variety of purposes; it provided the scene during the day for cooking and eating, and fulfilled the function of a living room as well. And as the single room was insufficient to house every resident of the dwelling at night, even the kitchen was converted into a sleeping place. Finally, in the total absence of bathrooms, bathing took place there.

Overcrowding meant a real restraint on the development of any privacy and domesticity within the walls of the home. But in most instances the people living amidst such conditions were not dissatisfied with their domestic arrangements. On the contrary, their attitude towards the congested living space was frequently positive; there was a need for sociability, and they tended to look upon it as a desirable condition. This may be supported by passages from an autobiographical novel dealing with the early twentieth century. The author of the book, Lajos Kassák, an internationally known avant-garde artist and poet, was of working-class origins and had initially supported himself as an industrial worker. He lived together with his mother and sisters in the notorious

Hétház (Seven Houses), a large tenement block of lower-class residents located in a working-class district named Angyalföld. He explained his feelings when he moved with his mother to a bigger flat in the same building:

We just walk up and down in the two-roomed dwelling. It is an unusually big space to us and the silence means emptiness . . . So far [when living together with others] we have not yet perceived how unendurable, uncomfortable it is to live here. Two rooms. Why two rooms for us?[60]

Before long, they took in a sub-tenant to occupy the room 'left empty'. Their attitude is understandable given the fact that so many people shared beds, which had been the case in Kassák's previous home.[61]

IV

The relation between landlord and tenant was based on an almost unlimited contractual freedom. Legal regulations assumed that the contracts, as in the case of employment, were concluded between two equal partners. The legal framework was provided by successive municipal bye-laws, of which the one issued in 1885 provides the starting point.[62] The most important paragraphs of that regulation dealt with the term of the tenancy; when the rent should be paid; and the conditions of notice to quit or eviction. There were no general instructions or recognised practices as to whether or not the contracts should be written agreements. They were also considered to be valid without a deposit, which otherwise could amount to 5 per cent of annual or 20 per cent of monthly rent.

Landlords were given a free hand in determining the duration of tenancies. As the text of the bye-law reads: 'We know of tenures concluded for an indefinite period, and ones valid for a quarter or half a year and even for shorter terms'. It might be supposed that annual lets were more frequent in the case of well-to-do tenants than the poorer residents. The reason for this was the fear of landlords, and especially house-tenants, of their not obtaining the rent. The house-tenants often tended to shorten the term, transforming the annual or somewhat shorter tenancies to monthly or weekly lets.[63] No comprehensive statistical data have survived on the average length of tenancies, but monthly lets were probably the most preferred in working-class districts where weekly lets were also common.[64]

According to the bye-law, tenants were required to pay the rent in advance on the first day of the commencement of every house-rent quarter or new tenancy. A separate sum, the *házbérkrajcár* (house-rent farthing) was fixed and paid by the tenants to the municipal authority as an automatic contribution to the communal tax. This amounted to 3 per cent of the rent from 1873 on, and in aggregate terms was nearly as considerable as the communal tax paid by the house-owners.[65]

The conditions determining the notice to quit may be considered one of the most critical points of tenure contracts. The bye-laws defined the period of notice as three months in annual lets, two weeks in monthly, and two days in weekly lets. During the period of the tenancy, rents could not be increased. Under the house-lease system, this sort of temporary control of rents was not provided, and the managers could freely convert the tenancies to much shorter ones and evict the tenants. This was done quite frequently in cases when the tenants were in arrears with the rent.[66]

The large tenement buildings were managed directly by the caretaker or house-master as he was called, an employee of the landlord who resided on the spot in a one-roomed dwelling on the ground floor in the courtyard. He was responsible for regularly collecting the rents and maintaining both the cleanliness and order of the house. It was not uncommon that a deputy caretaker was also employed, paid by the house-master. The accommodation for the house-master was a payment in kind, and his wage came from the tenants; according to customary law, every one of them usually paid him 2–4 per cent of the rent every month.[67] The caretakers fulfilled a central role in the life of congested tenement buildings by their incessant monitoring of every square foot of public space inside the building. The caretakers in the rent-barracks of a working-class district were 'selected from the most brutal and aggressive elements' and were likely to be corrupt. Since they had the authority to select tenants, and received an extra payment from those seeking a dwelling, they were ready to evict sitting tenants on any pretext whatever.[68]

The state, the city council or their companies, the banks, and the private productive firms, managed their housing property or lease indirectly through the so-called house-warden. The warden acted for the landlords or house-renters, and usually supervised more than one tenement house. Unlike the caretakers, the house-wardens did not reside in the houses they managed and had a higher social standing as members of the middle classes, many of them being lawyers or public and private salaried staff. But, occasionally, even the banks themselves engaged in housing management. The Magyar Kereskedelmi Bank rt (Hungarian Commercial Bank Company) for example, set up a separate department for this purpose and in 1910 was house-warden for 42 tenement houses. Payment was fixed at one per cent of the house rent revenue.[69]

The preponderance of shorter (weekly or monthly) tenancies meant that the continuous raising of rents was easy. The ever-growing burden of rent on the workers' household budget meant that the percentage of expenditure on housing reached at least a fifth, but sometimes a third of the family income.[70] And this was more and more the case as the period came to its close. The reactions of the residents to the financial strain of housing were variegated and might result in sub-letting as a supplementary source of income; or frequent changes in tenancies producing great residential mobility; or the rejection of the increased demands by the mounting of a rent-strike.

Lodgers, including night-lodgers, seemed to be inevitable concomitants of permanent tenancy. Evidence from the mid-1890s shows that at least half of the rent could be covered by the lodgers' contributions.[71] It is no wonder that when the mobile lodgers and bed-tenants left, the tenants could not afford to pay their regular weekly rent and were forced to move.[72]

Sources shedding some light on residential mobility all suggest its vitality. It is impossible to determine the exact percentage of workers in the overall total, but it might be supposed that the overwhelming majority of removals occurred in lower-class tenancies. To assess the approximate extent of working-class mobility, some figures may be quoted. During one month—August 1883—around 14,000 families and 16,400 single persons (presumably lodgers) changed their residence. This amounts to an estimated 56,000 families a year, so quite a large proportion of the population was on the move.[73] According to another calculation, the number of removals was around 50,000 in 1906. As a result, residents changed in a third of the tenancies in the course of that year. The transport companies at the same time estimated the number to be about 26,000, which included only removals within the confines of the city. A further 10,000 cases were assumed to occur to and from the countryside, and another 5,000 removals were effected without the facilities of transport companies.[74] These highly tentative figures demonstrate both the intensity of residential mobility, and the emergence of a new trend around the turn of the century as large numbers (especially of labourers) drifted to the environs of Budapest.

It was also from the turn of the century that suburban settlements around Budapest began to expand more swiftly. And, although the majority of their immigrants came from the country rather than from Budapest, the suburbs attracted residents of the capital too. The number who left the city for these settlements was estimated by statisticians at 50,000 between 1900 and 1906; according to other calculations this figure might have risen to 80–100,000 between 1900 and 1909. And these are not the most generous estimates.[75] A distinguishing feature of the suburbanisation process in Budapest was that manual labourers, the poorer segments of the working classes, rather more than the well-to-do middle classes, provided the bulk of those leaving the city. They, together with their fellows arriving from the countryside, were becoming commuters. They were induced to do so because they could obtain cheaper accommodation only in these settlements, where many of them even managed in time to build self-contained family houses.

Everybody who remained within the borders of the capital, in the course of their wanderings between residences, also had a number of options. Since the average rent level of workers' housing differed greatly from district to district, there were occasions early in the twentieth century when the average rent of one district could be only 20 per cent of the one with the highest average rent.[76] This comparison applies only to one-roomed dwellings.

The minor economic depression that unfolded after 1906 was

associated with a spectacular increase both in rents and food prices. Precise data on the trend in rents are not available, and it is difficult to determine whether the rise in rents was simply a concomitant of the general process of inflation, or showed a distinct trend. The rents of workers' housing rose by around 20 to 30 per cent between 1893 and 1906.[77] The rate of increase thereafter proved to be even higher; the nominal value of rents for one-roomed dwellings soared by 100 per cent between 1906 and 1913, and that for two-roomed tenancies rose by around 34 per cent during the same period.[78]

The fact that the steady rise in rents suddenly turned into a hectic upward move may be explained partly by the operation of the house-lease system. Rent levels were significantly increased by the separation of the landlord and the house-renter. As Ferenczi remarked, 'These entrepreneurs [the house-renters] earned the same and sometimes even higher profits for the landlords as they had enjoyed earlier; and so, they put the burden of increased rents combined with their own high profits onto the tenants'.[79] Obviously, other factors also operated in the same direction.

The tensions which immediately arose in the rental sector, with special regard to mass evictions, led to overt conflicts between landlord and tenants. The opposition on the side of the tenants was first manifested in the form of house boycotts against individual landlords in 1907. Residents who were not able to pay the increased rent and who were therefore evicted, called upon those seeking dwellings to boycott the houses concerned. These calls were publicised in newspapers and posters, and met with much success. As a result of this, and the solidarity of the tenants still living there, many landlords were forced to conclude collective contracts which severely restricted their rights. In the meantime, the Social Democratic Party, which had not hitherto expressed any opinions on housing issues, soon joined the boycotters. The party organisation held 32 mass meetings at district level on 30 April 1908 and declared a struggle against the landlords.[80]

What explanation can be given for the obvious success of the boycott movement? Evictions by court procedure proved to be too costly and lengthy. The costs were actually higher than the amount of loss the landlord suffered by consenting to the rent reduction which the tenants were demanding. As a result of these struggles between landlords or house-renters and tenants, the prices of plots soon declined significantly in the areas concerned, and this threatened the interests of the original investors. 'The banks dealing with mortgage loan businesses follow with close attention the area of the combat and where a "tenant strike" seems likely to emerge, there they press the landlords to come to an agreement with the tenants, because they are fully conscious that in most instances the amortisation is at stake'.[81] The landlords and the house-renters were, for a time, a weak counterforce to the boycotters. The ownership of the rent-barracks in working-class districts was rather diffused. Although some measure of concentration within the ranks of the house-renters was brought about by the formation of consortiums of eight to ten houses, they were heavily dependent on the banks and were restricted in their autonomy.

The collective agreements resulting from the boycotts were concluded between the landlord or house tenant and the representative of the tenants, the so-called 'steward man', with the mediation of the local SDP organisations and the indirect support of the mayor. They regulated the rents, dealt with the employment and dismissal of caretakers, handled the conversion of weekly tenancies to monthly ones, and guaranteed the security of lets for a definite duration; they also defined the responsibility of the landlord for renovation. Their validity was sometimes guaranteed by the local SDP organisation and the courts against the manipulations of the house-renters who, under the pretence of cessation of the house-lease, attempted to abrogate the contract. The steward man, who was designed to replace the caretaker, held the moral responsibility only for guaranteeing the contract.[82] There is only scanty data relating to the people who were elected steward men. They might be, in all probability, the most politically conscious and educated members of the working class who were involved in either a trade union or in the social democratic movement.

New conflicts emerged when the landlords collectively decided to raise rents in February 1909. The boycott movement then turned into a violent rent strike and the tenants on occasion barricaded themselves within the houses (Figure 5.6). The municipal authorities reacted by launching their own building project and issuing a new tenancy law. It allowed only one eviction in each property during the year, and provided rent control for that period. By using the advantages inherent in these new measures, the tenants began to refuse payment of the new rents. In addition, according to the modified civil code enacted at the same time, the landlord was henceforth required to take legal action against tenants in arrears, instead of simply distraining their movable goods as had been done in the past. The time-consuming and expensive legal procedure that replaced the simple administrative one also induced the landlords to arrive at an agreement with the tenants. Ultimately, the SDP threatened the landlords with a general rent-strike timed for the summer of 1910. These efforts and events together led to partial success. In the course of 1910, successful rent-strikes were organised in 223 tenement houses where 11,000 tenants (and further subtenants) lived. The landlords of 180 of these houses arrived at an agreement with their tenants, resulting in collective contracts, and evictions were implemented in only eleven cases.[83]

Nevertheless, as incidents in the Hétház tenement block clearly demonstrated, the landlords retained some of their power. During the boycotts, they attempted to prevent would-be tenants from joining the movement by requiring a deposit and persuading them to sign a declaration against the boycotts.[84] Their endeavour then achieved only partial success. They met with more success, however, in the counter-offensive against the rent-strikers by resorting to the conversion of monthly lets to weekly tenancies, which meant an immediate eviction of the residents;

Figure 5.6 Rent strikers: 'The rent barrack that
is stormed. Tenants' riot in the capital'.

or refusing to give tenancies to those coming from boycotted houses.
Moreover, evictions were backed by the municipal authorities which had
started its council housing project and provided transitional accommodation in wooden barracks for those evicted. The example of the Hétház,
where an intensive rent-strike dominated life for a couple of months,
showed the continued resistance of landlords to the strong solidarity of
the residents. In that particular block, owned by a bank and housing
about 500 workers' families with around 2,000 people, the evicted
tenants did not leave the building. As a contemporary petition vividly
reported, 'due to the ever repeated evictions, more than 25 persons are
living together in single dwellings of the Hétház'.[85]
It may be added that it was not exclusively the proletarian rent-
barracks which suffered from the practice of increasing rents to high
levels. Many tenement houses occupied partially or totally by lower-
middle-class residents also shared these problems and even revolted
against them. When the petty bourgeoisie resided with workers in the
same building, the barriers separating them from each other during times
of peace immediately lost their significance in the common struggle
against the landlord or house-renter. An entire ritual of protest came into
existence which made the everyday life in each of the houses very like
a permanent carnival.

Not only the raising of rents, but also the indifference of the landlords to elementary sanitary standards, the poor quality of workers' housing, and the mass evictions that followed from slum clearances, could increase the discontent of tenants in these years. This can be seen in a petition relating to another tenement block near the Hétház:

The landlord of that tenement block is not willing to put into effect the regulations of municipal authorities; he does not vacate the banned dwelling units . . . and he refuses to make them fit to live in, failing to fulfil the sanitary requirements. Since the residents adhere to the execution of the regulations, the landlord has declared his intention to demolish the flats and evict the residents, because he is sure of the full support of the authorities. If the landlord keeps his promise, 80 families or 700 people will be homeless.[86]

All that the Council was able to do in this particular case was to provide a warrant requiring the maintenance of the flats at least for a couple of months, and implementing the most necessary improvements in sanitary conditions.

As evidence for the indirect intervention of the City Council in disputes such as this, the following passage from the same document is worth quoting:

True, these dwellings are of public danger and their demolition is inevitable. The residents were promised council housing as soon as the small buildings now under construction are finished. But, what will happen to them until that time?[87]

The quotation reveals the highly contradictory role the Council was playing in the dispute. By constructing council housing, municipal authorities indeed contributed to the improvement of workers' housing conditions. But this really meant strong support for the landlords in pacifying the rent-strike movement, for the growing supply of low-rent council housing somewhat weakened the opposition of the remaining tenants who struggled against the landlords in the private rental sector. This already anticipates the future, with the partial or total suspension of the unregulated free market from 1916 onwards and the growing weight of council housing in the entire sector. It is, however, a new chapter in the history of housing in Budapest.

Notes

1. K. Vörös, *Budapest Története, Volume IV* (Budapest, 1978), 187.
2. Ibid., 393–4.
3. R. J. Evans, 'Epidemics and revolutions: cholera in nineteenth-century Europe', *Past and Present* 120 (1988), 125.
4. Vörös, *Budapest, IV*, 208.
5. D. Schuler, *A Hajléktalanság Kerdese a Székesfövárosban* [The Question of Homelessness in the Capital] (Budapest, 1935), 17.
6. Vörös, *Budapest, IV*,411: G. Thirring, *Budapest Székesfőváros Statistiztikai*

Évkönyve, I, 1874–94 [Statistical Yearbook of Budapest Capital, I, 1874–94] (Budapest, 1894), 109.

7. A. Neményi, *A Budapesti Lakáskérdés* [Housing Problem in Budapest] (Budapest, 1883); Budapest Föváros Levéltára [Budapest Capital Archives, hereafter BFL], IV. 1403.a.341/1883.
8. I. Ferenczi, *Községi Lakáspolitika és Lakásügyi Intézmények* [Municipal Housing Policy and Institutions for Housing] (Budapest, 1910), 135.
9. B. Szántó, 'Budapest lakásdrágaságának okai és megszüntetésének mödjai' [The causes of high housing costs in Budapest and the ways to put an end to it], *Huszadik Század*, XXIV (1911), 555.
10. Ibid., 556.
11. Ferenczi, *Községi Lakáspolitika*, 107–8.
12. Ibid., 567–8.
13. Ferenczi, *Községi Lakáspolitika*, 167.
14. Ibid., 130–60.
15. P. Hanák, 'Polgárosodás és urbanizáció: Bécs és Budapest városfejlödése a 19 században' [Embourgoisement and urbanisation: urban development of Vienna and Budapest in the nineteenth century] in idem., *Kert es a Mühely* [Garden and the Workshop] (Budapest, 1988), 39.
16. D. Tasner, *Pesti Lakásreform* [Housing Reform in Pest] (1871).
17. Vörös, *Budapest, IV*, 302.
18. G. Kövér, *1873: Egy krach anatómiája* [1873: Anatomy of a Crash] (Budapest, 1986).
19. Vörös, *Budapest, IV*, 196.
20. Ibid., 198–9.
21. Ibid.; idem., *Budapest legnagyobb adófizetöi, 1873–1917* [The Greatest Taxpayers in Budapest, 1873–1917] (Budapest, 1979), 18.
22. A. Petrik, 'Budapest fejlödése az utolsó 25 év alatt' [Evolution of Budapest during the past 25 years], *Épitö Ipar* 36 (1909), 319.
23. G. Thirring, 'Budapest épitöipara és épitkezései' [The building industry and the construction of Budapest], *Közgazdasági Szemle* XXIV (1900), 443–4.
24. L. Katus, 'Economic growth in Hungary during the age of dualism, 1867–1913: a quantitative analysis', in A. Pamlényi (ed.), *Social-Economic Researches on the History of East-Central Europe* (Budapest, 1970), 57; G. Ránki, 'Budapest szerepe az ország gazdasági fejlödésében' [The role of Budapest in the economic development of the country], *Tanulmányok Budapest Multjából* XX (1974), 54.
25. Vörös, *Budapest legnagyobb adófizetöi*, 68, 78–80.
26. Ibid., 80–1.
27. Thirring, 'Budapest épitöipara', 444 and *Budapest Székesfövàros Statisztikai Évkönyve*, 170.
28. Thirring, 'Budapest épitöipara', 438.
29. Ferenczi, *Községi Lakáspolitika*, 39.
30. Vörös, *Budapest, IV*, 347.
31. See R. Banik-Schweitzer, 'Wohnverhältnisse in Berlin, Wien und Budapest um die Wende zum 20 Jahrhundert', *Siedlungsforschung: Arhäologie-Geschichte-Geographie*, 5 (1987).
32. O, Vermes, 'A budapesti házföbérleti rendszer jogi és gazdasági megvilagitásban' [The house lease system in Budapest in a legal and economic light], *Városi Szemle* 11–12 (1912), 673.
33. Ferenczi, *Községi Lakáspolitika*, 42.
34. Idem., *A munkáslakás-kérdés különös tekintettel Budapestre* [The Question

of Workers' Housing with Special Reference to Budapest] (Budapest, 1906), 150.

35. Vörös, *Budapest, IV*, 471–3, 664–5.
36. Vörös, *Budapest, IV*, 595.
37. G. Gyáni, 'Lakáshelyzet és otthonkultura a munkásság körében a századfordulön' [Housing situation and domestic culture amongst workers at the turn of the century], *Századok* (1989).
38. Ibid.
39. Vörös, *Budapest legnagyobb adófizetöi*, 125–6.
40. S. Szöcs, *Budapest Székesföväros Részvétele az 1905-6 évi Nemzeti Ellenállásban* [Participation of Budapest Capital in the National Opposition of 1905-6] (Budapest, 1977), 15, 19.
41. Thirring, 'Budapest épitöipara', 450; Vörös, *Budapest, IV*, 592.
42. J. Körösi, *Elöleges Jelentés az 1870: évi Januar Elsején törtrènt Pesti Nepszàmlàlàs Eredményeiröl* [Preliminary Report on the Results on a Census Made on 1 January 1870 in Pest] (Budapest, 1871), 335.
43. *Fövàrosi Statisztikai Közlemények* [Statistical Communications of the Capital], Vol. 43, tables 23, 28.
44. G. Alpári, 'Egy számlálóbiztos feljegyzéseiböl' [From notes of a census taker] (1911) in G. Litvàn and L. Szücs (eds), *A Szociológia Elsö Magyar Mühelye* [First Workshop of Hungarian Sociology] (Budapest, 1973), Volume II, 183.
45. BFL IV.1411.b, Mayer Lajos gyámsági ügye [File of Lajos Mayer's guardianship], 1890.
46. BFL IV.1411.b, Blasovits gyámsági ügye, 1885 [File of Blasovits' guardianship].
47. BFL IV.1411.b, Csihál József hagyatéka, 1891 [File of Jozsef Csihal's inheritance].
48. Hanák, 'Polgárosodás és urbanizáció', 34–5; idem, 'Bérház a körúton' [Rent-house on the Boulevard], unpublished manuscript.
49. Körösi, *Elöleges jelentés az 1870*, 7.
50. Neményi, *A budapesti lakáskérdés*, 13.
51. Ferenczi, *Községi Lakáspolitika*, 82; Thirring, *Budapest Székesföváros*, 34–7.
52. Thirring, *Budapest Székesföváros*, 38.
53. *Fövárosi Statisztikai Közlemények, Volume 43*, 42–3.
54. BFL IV.1407.b.565/1883-VI.
55. G. Gyáni, 'A chapter of the social history of women: female domestic servants in the labour market, Budapest 1890-1940', *Acta Historica* 32 (1986).
56. Thirring, *Budapest Székesföváros*, 39.
57. Ibid., 39; Fövárosi Statisztikai Közlemények, Vol. 43, 59, 202–3.
58. Gyáni, 'Lakáshelyzet és otthonkultura'.
59. Thirring, *Budapest Székesföváros*, 38.
60. L. Kassák, *Egy ember elete* [Life of a Man] (Budapest, 1974), 857, 860.
61. Gyáni, 'Lakáshelyzet és otthonkultura'.
62. S. Berényi and K. Graber, *Lakbérleti jog és Eljárás* [Tenure Law and Procedure] (Budapest, 1901).
63. Vermes, 'A budapesti házföbérleti', 685.
64. Z. Szabados, 'A budapesti lakásuzsora és a házboykottok', *Renaissance*, 25 August 1910, 751.
65. J. Varga, 'A lakásügy mint közgazdasági és szociális probléma' [Housing as an economic and social problem] (Budapest, 1918), 7.

66. Vermes, 'A budapesti házföbérleti', 685.
67. M. Pásztor, *Eladósodott Budapest* [Indebted Budapest] (Budapest, 1907), 49.
68. Szabados, 'A budapesti lakásuzsora', 753.
69. Ibid., 754.
70. Gyáni, 'Lakáshelyzet és otthonkultura'.
71. Pàsztor, *Eladósodott Budapest*, 42–3.
72. Ferenczi, *A Munkáslakás-kérdés különös tekintettel Budapestre*, 26.
73. Neményi, *A Budapesti Lakáskérdés*, 11.
74. Ferenczi, *Községi Lakáspolitika*, 326.
75. Ibid., 27.
76. Gyáni, 'Lakáshelvzet és otthonkultura'.
77. Ferenczi, *A Munkáslakás-kérdés különös tekintettel Budapestre*, 19.
78. E. Borsos, *A magyar lakásügy a háboru kezdetétöl, I köt* [Hungarian Housing from the Start of the War, Vol, I] (Budapest, 1930), 26.
79. Ferenczi, *Közsègi Lakáspolitika*, 25.
80. Ibid., 26.
81. Szabados, 'A budapesti lakásuzsora', *Renaissance*, 25 Sept. 1810, 181.
82. Ibid., 178; Vermes 'A budapesti házföbérleti', 686; Ferenczi, 'A lakásügy állása és haladása Magyarországon ás utolsó három évben' [The state of housing and its development in Hungary during the last three years], *Városi Szemle*, 1913, 628–30.
83. Ferenczi, 'A lakásügy állása', 628.
84. Vermes, 'A budapesti házföbérleti', 686.
85. BFL IV.1409.b.6972/1910.
86. BFL IV.1409.b/1910; see also Szabados, *Renaissance*, 25 September 1910, 752.
87. BFL IV.1409.b.6973/1910.

6 Berlin

Nicholas Bullock

In 1901 Berlin faced a housing crisis. The shortage of housing was the
most acute for 30 years[1]: in a city of 1.9 million people there were only
1,761 unoccupied dwellings. With barely 1.5 per cent of the total housing stock classified as 'empty', there was less housing available for those
searching for accommodation than at any time since the boom years of
the early 1870s. People were leaving the city, not because they were
unable to find work, but because there was nowhere to live. In 1901, for
the first time in years, the population of the city actually fell, a situation
attributed by contemporaries to the sheer shortage of housing. Rents rose
sharply, but not enough to encourage investment in new housing. Conditions facing those wishing to build new housing were discouraging:
interest rates were rising as the economy expanded and mortgages were
extremely difficult to obtain, a situation not helped by the failure of
three mortgage banks in 1901.

Barely a decade later the Berlin housing market was yet again in crisis.
The nature of the problem was different: now it was the landlords who
were desperate to find tenants. As interest rates rose and demand
dwindled, some landlords raised rents, some lowered them, but the level
of forced sales and foreclosures rose during 1912 to its highest ever
prewar level. Even the land companies, cushioned against the normal
movements of the market by their links with the large banks, were facing
mounting difficulties and the massive fall in the value of their assets.

Events such as these dramatised both the problems facing the worker
in his search for housing and the difficulties faced by the building
industry and those involved in residential development. To many
contemporaries the ups and downs of over-production and acute housing
shortage seemed a painful, if inevitable, part of the way in which private
enterprise provided housing. Between the late 1880s and 1914 the housing market in Berlin experienced five distinct phases of over- and under-
production. The period begins with a building boom which reached a
peak in 1890. Even before the mid 1890s, as supply exceeded demand,
the boom died away to be followed by a period when the volume of new
house-building was low. This was followed around the turn of the
century by a period of acute housing shortage which slowly encouraged
an increase in production; during the first half of the 1900s production
was again rising. But by 1907, the level of building was once more

slowing as the economy as a whole began to falter and with it the demand for housing. After 1911, the entire system of private enterprise in Berlin was more convulsively shaken than ever before by bankruptcies and liquidations, caught again by over-production and falling occupancy rates.

That Berlin, like many large German cities, faced a 'housing problem' had been recognised as long ago as the late 1850s. Concern on this account may have waned in the years of economic stagnation during the late 1870s and early 1880s, but from the mid 1880s the issue was again at the forefront of anxiety over the 'social question'.[2] The housing question was widely debated by the groups concerned with social and economic progress like *Verein für Sozialpolitik* (VfSP) from 1885 on; it was discussed by sanitarians, the clergy, doctors, architects, even employers' organisations; it was addressed in a host of pamphlets which offered a wide variety of different nostrums for resolving this particularly intractable problem. Yet despite this apparent familiarity with the 'housing problem', the housing difficulties in Berlin at the turn of the century seemed somehow even more difficult to resolve than elsewhere.

To Werner Hegemann, looking back over the development of the city, Berlin was 'die grösste Mietskasernenstadt der Welt'.[3] Despite first-hand knowledge of New York with its notorious tenements, Hegemann still regarded the awfulness of housing conditions in Berlin as exceptional. To others like the members of the VfSP with access to comparative information on the density of housing development and the levels of over-crowding in cities like Vienna, London, Paris or St Petersburg, housing conditions in Berlin seemed especially deficient in both quality and quantity.[4] To economists like Eberstadt, one of the leading writers on housing before 1914, whose *Handbuch des Wohnungswesens*[5] first published in 1909 remained the standard work on housing even after the First World War, housing conditions in Berlin were simply confirmation of the unnatural forces of speculation behind the production of housing in the capital:

. . . from the preparation of raw building land to the occupation of the finished dwelling, the form of the development of our cities and the whole trade in land has been taken over by the process of speculation. The division of land into sites ripe for development is a question of speculation. The form of layout, the form of the building and the production of housing are all determined by the processes of speculation. The ownership of land and property are in the hands of the speculators; they too control the supply of capital for building and the system of registration in the Grundbuch.[6]

Did housing production in Berlin deserve Eberstadt's description as something uniquely inadequate?

I

By the middle of the nineteenth century, the great majority of Berliners,

Figure 6.1 Typical residential developments in Berlin
(a) Mietshaus for the affluent on the Kurfürstdendamm, 1890
(*Source: Berlin und seine Bauten*, Vol IV).

irrespective of class, were living in apartments or tenements. By the 1850s, in contrast to the eighteenth century when many families had lived in individual houses, this form of apartment living had become the norm for all but the most affluent, or those who lived in the suburbs in housing which still survived from an earlier period.[7] To those familiar with English housing, Berlin looked forbiddingly dense; an English doctor described it as 'a tableland of bricks and mortar 72 feet high, cut up by intersecting valleys representing the streets'.[8] Even to Berliners born and bred, the new forms of development were viewed with distress. As early as the 1850s, Beta (a popular Berlin journalist) was attacking the courts in the new housing for having the proportions of a Prussian officer's riding boots.[9]

The size and quality of these apartments might differ widely. The social geography of the city was easily read from its architecture (Figure 6.1). At one end of the scale there were the lavish apartments in the new *Mietshäuser* being built in the south-west where there might be no more than two dwellings to a floor, with elaborate internal planning to ensure an appropriate division between family and servants. At the bottom end of the market there were the tenements of working-class areas, referred

Figure 6.1 (b) Mietskasernen for the working-classes in Wedding Meyershof, Ackerstrasse, just before 1914
(*Source:* Geist and Kuervers, *Berliner Mietshaus*, 65).

to pejoratively as *Mietskasernen*, or 'rent barracks', with 50 to 80 two- or three-room dwellings packed on to a site, offering little more than minimal shelter and a view on to a court the dimensions of which made it little more than a light-well.

But despite these differences, the system of production which created

1853 The maximum height of the building (A) was determined by the street width (12 m minimum to 22 m maximum) measured to the opposing building line; the minimum court dimensions (B) were fixed at 5.60 m × 5.60 m giving a minimum court area of 31.60 m².

1887 The maximum height of the building (A) was determined as before and the number of habitable storeys limited to 5. The roof storey was generally set back at an angle of 45°, but this might be increased to 60° if the resulting increase in overall height was equal to or less than half the height of the roof storey set back at 45°. Court size was set at a minimum of 60 m², although for corner sites a minimum of 40 m² was permitted; the minimum court dimensions (B) were fixed as the height of the building less 6 m.

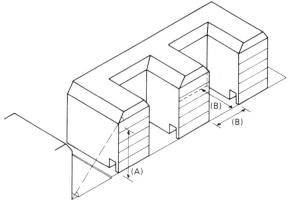

1897 The maximum height of the building (A) was determined as before, but provisions were made to allow a more elaborate treatment of the façade with turrets, balconies, gables and bays. Minimum court area (in building zone 5) was increased to 80 m², but corner sites were still permitted a minimum court size of 40 m². Minimum court dimensions could now take advantage of combining courts on adjacent sites: the minimum dimension for combined courts (B′) was fixed as the minimum court dimension for a single court (B) plus ⅓B to take account of the advantage conferred by the adjacent court.

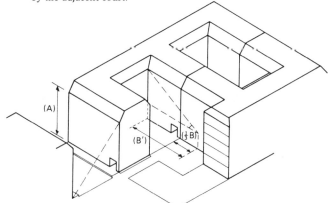

Figure 6.2 Diagrammatic representation of the building bulk controls in the Berlin Building Regulations of 1853, 1887, 1897
(*Source:* Bullock and Read, *Movement for Housing Reform*, 92).

these different types of housing, the mechanisms of development, the role played by the land companies, the method of financing, together with the planning and legislative framework which determined their form, were essentially the same for luxury as for working-class housing. For the developer creating luxury apartments on Kurfürstendamm, quite as much as for the small speculator building working-class tenements in Wedding; the number of dwellings that could be placed on a site was a crucial calculation. This maximum permissible density for a site was determined in large part by the building regulations; it was this form of control that did much to determine the form of housing in Berlin.

For the city of Berlin, developments during the *Gründerjahre*, the boom years of the early 1870s, had been governed by the building regulations drawn up in 1853 (Figure 6.2)[10] These established a relationship between street width and building height, an absolute height limit, together with a minimum court size, said to be determined by the needs of a horse-drawn fire pump. In the suburbs and neighbouring municipalities such as Charlottenburg the building regulations of the authorities bordering the city of Berlin permitted only a more open form of development.[11] But by the 1860s the high density *Mietshaus* form of layout typical of the city was already spreading to the north and east as builders started to develop the newly subdivided land on the outskirts. As Assmann's *Grundrisse der städtische Wohngebäude*[12] demonstrates, a range of 'type' plans was already established by the mid 1860s. During the 1880s and early 1890s, there was a growing standardisation of the form of housing and the pattern of development as the scale of operations of many developers increased and whole streets rather than individual buildings were laid out at a time.

In 1887, after prolonged discussion amongst planners, architects and sanitarians about how best to limit the density of new development, the new building regulations for Berlin were finally published.[13] While the new regulations did something to limit density by increasing the minimum court size (from 31.6 to 60 square metres), the overall effect of the new regulations was to extend for the first time to the suburbs and Charlottenburg the higher density development typical of Berlin. Given that new building was now inevitably concentrated in the suburbs, and given the volume of building during the boom of the late 1880s and early 1890s, the net effect of the new regulations was thus to *increase* rather than to limit density for the city as a whole. From the late 1880s onwards, this increase can be followed in the rising proportion of dwellings on the fourth floor and above.[14]

In 1892 new regulations were again introduced in an attempt to limit the density of development. They reduced the permissible envelope of development by increasing the minimum court size, and did much to increase the apparent size of the court by encouraging the linking of courts on adjacent plots in return for a reduction in the size of the individual court. More important still, these regulations also introduced into Berlin the system of *gestaffelte Bauordnungen*, or graduated building regulations for different areas or zones of a city. First tried in

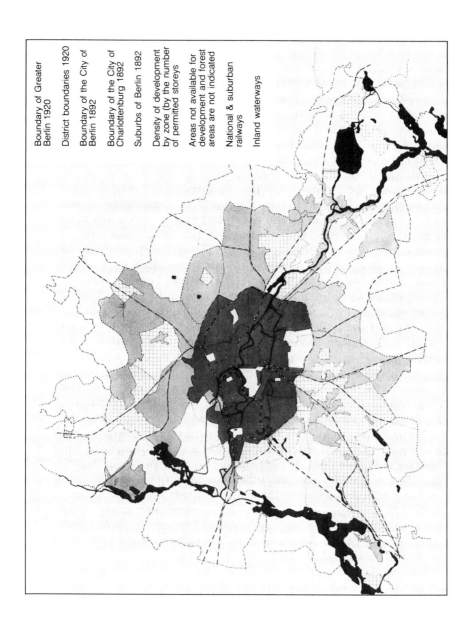

Boundary of Greater
Berlin 1920

District boundaries 1920

Boundary of the City of
Berlin 1892

Boundary of the City of
Charlottenburg 1892

Suburbs of Berlin 1892

Density of development
by zone (by the number
of permitted storeys

Areas not available for
development and forest
areas are not indicated

National & suburban
railways

Inland waterways

Figure 6.3 Density zoning in Berlin after the Regulations of 1892
(*Source: Berlin und seine Bauten*, Vol IV).

Altona and championed by reforming groups such as the *Verein für üffentliche Gesundheitspflege* (VföG), these new regulations made it possible to maintain a high density of building in the centre while allowing an 'open' form of two-storey semi-detached or even 'villa' building in the suburbs.[15] In Berlin, from 1892 existing densities were preserved within the Ringbahn but only low density two-storey development was permitted beyond, and in certain areas such as Grunewald only villa building was permitted (Figure 6.3).[16]

The impression of density in Berlin's housing was not simply a product of the height of the building: many contemporaries commented on the oppressive feeling of enclosure from living in a dwelling looking on to a small court. In more affluent areas where the number of dwellings per floor ensured a view on to the street for all, or where the court was large, this might be no great hardship. But in working-class areas where a high proportion of dwellings was necessarily hidden away from the more open and public life of the street the problem was only too evident. The attractions of living in the 'front building' overlooking the street were reflected in the higher rents, and the higher social standing associated with this kind of dwelling.[17] From the 1870s onwards the proportion of buildings giving on to courts rather than directly on to the street showed a gradual increase. Contemporaries like Goecke and Eberstadt argued that this was mainly due to the larger and deeper plots which resulted from the street layouts in the rapidly expanding suburbs (Figure 6.4).[18] The oppressive feeling of enclosure in these courts may have been offset by the greater width of many plots in these areas, and by the changes introduced by the building regulations of 1892, but the number of courts per plot rose, as did the number of court dwellings.

The character of these inner courts varied greatly: in middle-class areas the court might be planted, genteel in character, and controlled by the porter; in working-class areas the view into the court might be very drab but might serve a variety of very different uses, from a children's play area to a yard for various forms of industry. In Luisenstadt the courts tended to be larger than those in the north or north-west but typically contained a high concentration of small-scale industry: a lumber yard, a printing shop, a builder's yard or small-scale chemical or food manufacturer, all of which would need direct access to the street through the large gateway common to courts in the area. In the north, in areas like Wedding, the courts were predominantly residential and, generally, fully enclosed, with access to the street through the front building.[19]

The building regulations acted as an important set of constraints on the forms of Berlin housing. But to contemporaries the typical Berliner *Miethaus* was above all a product of the way in which housing was produced. For those who attacked the quality of housing in Berlin, it was the high level of expected returns on land which distorted the whole system of housing production, leading to the overvaluation of land, the distortion of the system of housing finance, and high levels of rent.

To contemporaries it would have been natural to begin any discussion of the supply of housing by examining the way in which agricultural land

Figure 6.4 Street layouts in working-class areas of Berlin showing the increase in the depth of plots for the 1870s (a) the 1890s, for (b) opposite (*Source*: Geist and Kuervers, *Berliner Mietsbaus*, pp. 346, 367).

(a)

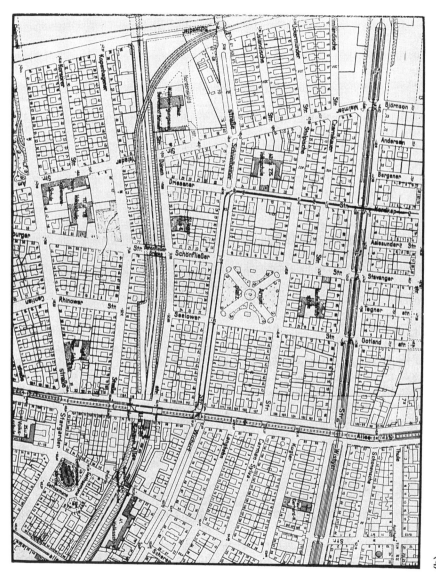

(b)

was prepared for residential development. By the 1890s the pattern of land ownership was varied but most land ready for building was predominantly in freehold ownership and much of it was in private hands.[20] The large royal domains had been broken up in the years after the Napoleonic wars and the large areas of common land that still surrounded the city in the 1830s, such as the Berliner Hufen to the north, and the Koepinicker Feld to the south-east, had been enclosed and sold off to private ownership during the 1830s and the late 1850s respectively. However, a number of government departments were still large landowners in the years before the First World War and were often eager to maximise their income from the sale of land surplus to their needs. These departments might develop smaller parcels of land like any other developer, but it was in the disposal of large tracts of land in the suburbs, such as the Tempelhofer Feld, owned by the Militärfiskus, that their decisions were potentially so important for the development of the city. By the 1890s much of the land being developed for housing was owned by the land companies. They had already acquired land from the original peasant owners sometimes as early as the 1860s, although even after the turn of the century small farmers still owned much of the land in the village centres surrounding the city, such as Schöneberg. As the map of land-ownership by land companies in Schöneberg suggests, the number of companies working in a particular area was often considerable, though even large companies such as the Berliner Boden Gesellschaft preferred to work in a few limited areas where they could use their local knowledge and political contacts to the full (Figure 6.5).

The actual process of development was straightforward enough. During the 1890s most developments were being carried out by *Terraingesellschaften*, or land companies, which were publicly quoted companies, generally larger than the companies involved in land in the 1870s and often enjoying close links with large banking interests.[21] Many had been founded in the boom years of the early 1870s, only to be bought up by the banks in the crash of 1873, and many were still partly owned by banks. According to Carthaus, the starting point was the estimate by the developer of the return to be made on the sale of a building plot by taking into account the probable level of rents and the number of dwellings that might be accommodated within the maximum permissible envelope for a site. Speed and stealth were crucial to the developer in order to pre-empt the possibility of rival 'counter-bids', and to dissuade the farmer from comparing the price for his land, often offered as a 'cash in hand' deal, either with his neighbours, with whom he might form a cartel, or with the value of the land when sold later as a plot 'ripe' for development. Though farmers seem to have been slow to appreciate the value of their land in the 1870s, they seem to have been fully alert to its value by the 1890s, as is evident from the memoires of Georg Haberland, director of one of the largest of the Berlin land companies, the *Berliner Boden Gesellschaft*.[22]

Once in possession of the plot the *Terraingesellschaft* would seek to prepare the plot for development as rapidly as possible. Speed was

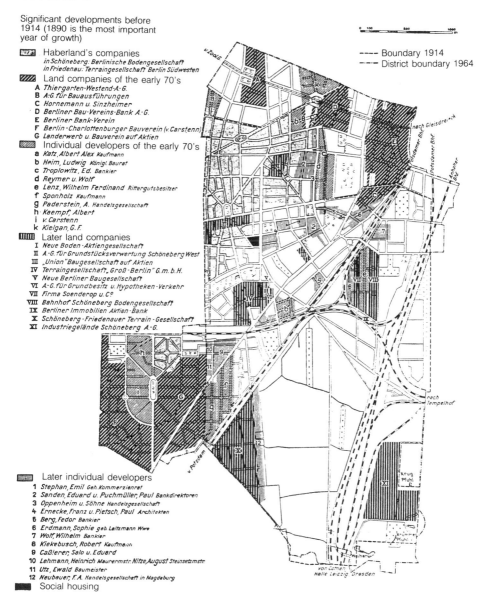

Land companies

Significant developments before
1914 (1890 is the most important
year of growth)

▨ Haberland's companies
  in Schöneberg: Berlinische Bodengesellschaft
  in Friedenau: Terraingesellschaft Berlin Südwesten

▨ Land companies of the early 70's
  A *Thiergarten-Westend-A.-G.*
  B *A.-G. für Bauausführungen*
  C *Hornemann u. Sinzheimer*
  D *Berliner Bau-Vereins-Bank A.-G.*
  E *Berliner Bank-Verein*
  F *Berlin-Charlottenburger Bauverein (v. Carstenn)*
  G *Landerwerb u. Bauverein auf Aktien*

▨ Individual developers of the early 70's
  a *Katz, Albert Alex Kaufmann*
  b *Heim, Ludwig Königl. Baurat*
  c *Troplowitz, Ed. Bankier*
  d *Reymer u. Wolf*
  e *Lenz, Wilhelm Ferdinand Rittergutsbesitzer*
  f *Sponholz Kaufmann*
  g *Paderstein, A. Handelsgesellschaft*
  h *Kaempf, Albert*
  i *v. Carstenn*
  k *Kielgan, G.F.*

▥ Later land companies
  I *Neue Boden-Aktiengesellschaft*
  II *A.-G. für Grundstücksverwertung Schöneberg West*
  III *„Union" Baugesellschaft auf Aktien*
  IV *Terraingesellschaft „Groß-Berlin" G.m.b.H.*
  V *Neue Berliner Baugesellschaft*
  VI *A.-G. für Grundbesitz u. Hypotheken-Verkehr*
  VII *Firma Soenderop u. C°*
  VIII *Bahnhof Schöneberg Bodengesellschaft*
  IX *Berliner Immobilien Aktien-Bank*
  X *Schöneberg-Friedenauer Terrain-Gesellschaft*
  XI *Industriegelände Schöneberg A.-G.*

▥ Later individual developers
  1 *Stephan, Emil Geh. Kommerzienrat*
  2 *Sanden, Eduard u. Puchmüller, Paul Bankdirektoren*
  3 *Oppenheim u. Söhne Handelsgesellschaft*
  4 *Ernecke, Franz u. Pietsch, Paul Architekten*
  5 *Berg, Fedor Bankier*
  6 *Erdmann, Sophie geb. Leitzmann Wwe*
  7 *Wolf, Wilhelm Bankier*
  8 *Kiekebusch, Robert Kaufmann*
  9 *Caßierer, Salo u. Eduard*
  10 *Lehmann, Heinrich Maurermstr. Nitze, August Steinsetzmstr.*
  11 *Utz, Ewald Baumeister*
  12 *Neubauer, F.A. Handelsgesellschaft in Magdeburg*
■ Social housing

---- Boundary 1914
—·— District boundary 1964

Figure 6.5 The activities of the land companies in a section of Schöneberg
(*Source:* Escher, *Berlin*, p. 274).

necessary both to catch the market at the right moment and to limit the amount of time the company would have to bear the costs involved in putting the land on the market as building land. The costs were high. Voigt[23] estimated that the *Kurfürstendamm Gesellschaft* operating in Charlottenburg in the 1880s was paying around 24 marks per square metre, or around half the eventual sale price, in interest and 'improvement' costs to cover paving, sewers and lighting, and this took no account of the cost of land it had 'lost' for roads. Estimates from the 1890s suggest that the costs of preparing land for building might be as high as 25–50 per cent of the selling price.[24] By the turn of the century the cost to a developer of a 10,000 square metre plot bought at 10 marks per square metre might rise to 29.25 marks per square metre after the surrender of land for the streets and the cost of lighting, paving and sewers. Such costs required considerable capital resources and raised the price, though not the profits on land. Those in the property lobby, concerned to rebut the charges of their critics, argued that it was these charges rather than the profits on the sale of land which inflated land prices.[25]

The second stage in the process of preparing land for development was its sale to a builder. By the turn of the century few *Terraingesellschaften* were directly involved in the relatively more risky task of developing their own sites, at least out of choice, and preferred to leave this to a separate developer, often a builder. Generally the *Terraingesellschaft* would seek to sell its land already subdivided into building plots. This sale might take a variety of different forms. At times of high demand, sites might be bought and sold several times by middlemen, the *Baustellenmackler*, in search of a profit on each transaction. These middlemen might have only minimal resources: Schiffmann and Allers, for example, were only one of a number of companies which operated in this way. They owned around forty land companies dealing only in developed land backed by minimal resources of their own until the crisis in property and land forced them into bankruptcy; Schiffmann reportedly fled Berlin for America leaving debts of over 2 million marks.[26]

Sometimes plots might be sold to a subsidiary company specially created for this purpose, sometimes to one of its own shareholders. In boom times this created an extra opportunity for profit, permitting extensive 'insider dealing', and would also make it possible to inflate the value of the company by recording, at least for public consumption, a handsome profit on its books. In troubled times this would have the advantage for the company of shortening its tenure of the land, thus reducing its exposure to the market, secure in the knowledge that the limitation of liability would protect the parent company from any serious loss. In cases where the subsidiary company found itself in trouble, the parent company might buy back the site at a reduced price, to hold the site against an improved future price. In the sharp recession which affected property in general and the land market in particular after 1910, a number of land companies found themselves in great difficulties, for example the *Berliner Terrain- und Bau-Akteingesellschaft* which had to be rescued by a consortium of interests and liquidated with huge losses.[27] But in general, despite huge losses in the quoted value of their shares, the land companies were able to hold on to their land. Backed by the capital behind them, and secure in the belief that the value of urban land would inevitably increase, they felt prepared to wait for an up-turn in the economy to start trading again.

The final stage in preparing the land for development would be the sale of the individual plot to a builder. Generally characterised as a 'man of straw', with little or no capital of his own,[28] the builder would frequently be offered financing as part of the sale. This would leave him in a position in which he could not bargain down the price of the plot. While the maximum price for a site would have to be related to some estimate of the eventual rents from the finished building, the price paid by the builder could be inflated by the land company so that a substantial part of the financing for the whole development would be spent on the purchase price of the site alone. With their ease of access to capital, those selling land were normally in a position to secure the necessary financing to achieve this. For the land companies, or the sellers of the site, the sale and this form of financing, willingly abetted by the banks, were much less fraught with risk than for the builder. Because of the system of registering in order of priority all charges on a property in a *Grundbuch* or register of interests, the land company with its charge registered first would be well protected by the value of the site, while the builder would be very much more exposed. Thus a builder would frequently pay for the purchase of the site with a first mortgage and part of a second mortgage, each secured in the *Grundbuch* and protected by the value of the site.[29] This would leave the financing of the construction, the *Baugeld*, to be covered by a third mortgage with less security and thus only obtainable at much higher rates of interest.

In the analysis of housing reformers like Mangoldt, secretary of the *Verein Reichswohnreform* (VRWG), or Adolf Damaschke, leader of the *Bund deutscher Bodenreformer* (BdB), it was this process of speculation in land, made possible by a system of financing to the advantage of the land companies at the expense of the builder, that lay at the core of the housing problem.[30] This widespread conviction was strengthened by the success of the propaganda campaign mounted by Damaschke and the BdB, and further fuelled by the surge of land prices in the boom of the late 1980s and early 1890s. A few dissenting voices apart, the developer of land was widely presented as an unscrupulous speculator who was able to make vast personal gains with the assistance, and at the expense, of the community as a whole.[31]

A sense of the excitement to be had from successfully speculating in land is to be found in Georg Haberland's autobiographical account of his activities as the director of the *Berliner Boden Gesellschaft* from the 1890s to the 1930s.[32] He made his fortune out of developing middle-class areas such as the Bayrische Viertel where his plans for the Victoria-Luise Platz were even commended by the Kaiser himself. But Haberland was the exception rather than the rule. It was this kind of success that confirmed the image of the *Terraingesellschaften* and their directors as benefiting so conspicuously at the expense of the community in the eyes of contemporary housing and land reformers.

But in contrast to the satanic image of the land companies in the demonology of the BdB, economists emphasised the low returns to be made on land: while the profits of the few during a boom might attract attention, the falling prices and low profits suffered by so many in a recession were hardly the stuff of publicity. A study by Edward Wagon,[33] for example, showed that the return on land in Berlin between 1884 and 1900, a period which included the boom of the late 1880s and early 1890s, was only 1.5 per cent. Emmy Reich argued that, taken over a twenty-year period, the profits of land companies were discouragingly low: by comparison with all forms of publicly quoted companies, the land companies did worse over this period than any others apart from those producing table linen.[34]

Some explanation for these low returns may be found in the structure of the land companies and the shadow side of their operations. The land companies obtained financing direct from the capital market, not from the mortgage sources used for the purchase of residential property, and one way in which large sums could be made in 'land' was to speculate directly with the shares in a *Terraingesellschaft*, rather than to make a profit through the company from the sale of land. This kind of operation was greatly assisted by the form of many of the companies by the end of the 1890s: as the original owners sold out, many of the land companies were being set up as publicly quoted companies on the stock exchange, with different groups of shareholders enjoying very different rights and benefits. One way to secure a profit for the original owners was to sell out the original shares, or even to create a second series of shares at a vastly inflated price.[35] This was a quick way of making money without having to wait for land to increase in value, or for a building to be completed. To carry this off, what mattered was the apparent value of the company at the time of the sale of the shares; this might be stoked up by profits from a few well-advertised sales, or even from sales to subsidiary companies held by the company's 'founder members'. With the company's value inflated in this way, the shares would be sold on the stock exchange to eager, if gullible, investors, leaving a handsome profit for the original owners. Perhaps in these terms we can explain both the persistent and widespread suspicion that those engaged in land development were successful speculators of dubious integrity, and the apparent low profitability of the quoted returns on the land companies' shares. The attempt to encourage investment in the land companies by emphasising the profits to be made in land would have confirmed the prejudices of housing and land reformers, while abetting the purposes of the land companies' founders. Moreover the success of their ploy in persuading investors to buy shares at inflated prices would be only too painfully compatible with the low subsequent rates of return recorded by economists like Reich and Wagon.

However, it is important to shift our focus from the sleazy operations of the land companies, and the scale of the profits they may have made, to examine the effect of land costs on total development costs. Was the price of land as important an issue in determining the price of housing as Eberstadt insisted, and were the rents charged for housing so obviously burdened by the dealings of the land companies as he believed?

While the price of land in Berlin was generally high, as Eberstadt and others asserted, the value of land varied sharply between different areas for different uses, and, contrary to the widely-held contemporary opinion, its value appears to have increased less rapidly than did other components of residential building. Some indication of the proportion of total building costs represented by the cost of land is given by Andreas Voigt in a paper 'Die Bodenbesitzverhältnisse, das Bau- und Wohnungs-wesen in Berlin', read before the VfSP.[36] In contrast to the later studies which based their findings on data drawn from a number of individual cases, Voigt was able to arrive at an assessment of the relative cost of the land by identifying the cost of building construction and subtracting this from the total value of the property. The estimation of building costs he based on the valuation of the *Feuerkasse*, a valuation used for insurance purposes to calculate the replacement cost of a building; the value of the property he derived from the municipal tax or 'common' value as registered in the *Mietssteuerkataster*. Voigt admitted that these assessments might both be subject to error, but he felt justified, never-theless, in using them as the foundation for his calculations. Basing his study on these assumptions, Voigt constructed a general ranking of land costs as a proportion of total building costs for the different districts for the whole of Berlin. From these tables the differences between commer-cial and residential districts emerge clearly. So too do the differences between working-class and other residential districts.

This ranking of land values was naturally reflected in the proportion of building costs due to land (Table 6.1). For the city as a whole, in 1895, land accounted for 62 per cent of the total development costs, but in working-class districts this value was lower: in the Stralauer Viertel it was 45 per cent, in Wedding and Gesundbrunnen 47 per cent, in Luisenstadt (jenseits des Kanals) it was 33 per cent, while in Moabit it was only 28 per cent, a value comparable to the lower estimates of land values provided by those with a property interest: Heinrich Hoepker (29 per cent),[37] Siegfried Ascher (28 per cent)[38] and Georg Haberland (27 per cent).[39]

Voigt's study also reveals something of the changes in the value of land during the economic cycle. Using an extended time series he was able to confirm the general expectations of his contemporaries and to support the general proposition that the value of land moved cyclically with economic activity, rising rapidly during periods of economic expansion and rising only slowly, if at all, during periods of recession. But while Voigt confirmed the conventional wisdom in this respect, the evidence that he assembled on the low relative importance of land costs in overall housing costs challenged widely-held views on the damaging effects of

Table 6.1 Land costs as a percentage of total development costs (A), and cost in Reichsmarks per square metre of land (B), for selected districts of Berlin

	1880		1895	
	A	B	A	B
City of Berlin	49	149	62	261
Va ⎱ Vb ⎰	22	34	33	88
VIIa ⎱ VIIb ⎰	28	54	45	125
Xb	29	31	34	82
XIIIa	18	15	47	27

Va   Luisenstadt jenseits des Kanals (westlich)
Vb   Luisenstadt jenseits des Kanals (östlich)
VIIa   Stralauer Viertel (westlich)
VIIb   Stralauer Viertel (östlich)
Xb   Rosenthaler Vorstadt (nördlich)
XIIIa Gesundbrennen
Source: Voigt, 'Bodenbesitzverhältnisse', 254–60

land prices on housing prices and thus rents.

Despite its shortcomings, Voigt's study attempted to identify systematically, in a way that Eberstadt's impressionistic sampling did not, the importance of land costs as a proportion of overall housing costs for different parts of the city. In areas where land was being prepared for middle-class housing, it might well be possible to find the kind of profits that Eberstadt and his followers were describing; in these areas the operations of the land companies would certainly add considerably to the final costs of housing. But as Voigt's study showed, in working-class areas, where the land costs amounted to between only 25 and 50 per cent of a much lower cost, the effect of the land companies was necessarily less obvious. In these areas the development costs of paving, lighting and sewers would be relatively more important than the profits made by the land companies. For many in reforming circles, carried along by the 'scientific' evidence of Eberstadt or the rhetoric of Damaschke, the way in which land was prepared for building seemed to be the source of the housing problem, but in the working-class areas where the problems of housing were most acute, it was first the cost of development, then the costs of construction and financing, not the profits in land, that seemed to increase the cost of working-class housing from the 1890s onwards.

With the land prepared for development, the next step in the process was to sell the land to somebody who would actually build on it. To contemporaries the contrast between the resources and the sophistication of the land companies stood in sharp contrast to the characteristics of the typical Berlin *Bauloewe* of the time.[40] By comparison with the rapid development in the scale of the land companies and the mortgage banks, house-building remained, even after the turn of the century, a relatively small-scale and primitive branch of industry. Nevertheless there were gradual advances even in this sector of the building industry: between 1890 and 1907 there was an increase in the size of general contracting firms, reflecting in part the greater scale of residential developments in this period. Thus, in Berlin, although there were no building firms employing more than 200 workers in 1890, there were 20 by 1895, and by 1907 the number had risen to 31; by 1907, 25 per cent of all firms in this sector employed more than six workers compared with 1890 when only 15 per cent did so.[41]

With the cost of developing a typical working-class block as high as 250,000 to 300,000 marks, the financial arrangements for building were often both elaborate and precarious. To many contemporaries Eberstadt's examples seemed plausible illustrations of how a typical block might be financed. Thus the first mortgage would be arranged by the land company, perhaps through its parent bank. Having spent much of this first mortgage on the purchase of the site, the builder would then be forced to find the *Baugeld*, or construction money, from a second or even a third mortgage. To increase the maximum amount that he could borrow in this way he would take every opportunity to increase his mortgage limit, using techniques like the overvaluation of the future value of the finished building through fire insurance companies prepared to overlook the niceties of property valuation in return for large insurance premiums.[42]

The security enjoyed by the land company was in marked contrast to the risks taken by the builder during the whole period of development. The builder had to take second place at a time, often a considerable period, when he was very much more exposed to the difficulties of the market. Goldschmidt remarks that a builder could normally only have his name entered as the owner of the site when the basement of the property was complete.[43] To meet the costs of development the builder might have recourse to a number of stratagems. Reich reports that it was common practice in Berlin in the 1890s for the builder to pay off his suppliers and his workforce only when the building was finally sold.[44] There are frequent accounts of plasterers, plumbers, roofers and other small sub-contractors being forced to supply both materials and labour 'on credit' in order to get payment at all. When interest rates were high and *Baugeld* hard to obtain, builders might even accept the purchase of materials 'on commission' through the land companies.[45]

Who were the builders of working-class housing? Generally they were craftsmen, bricklayers, carpenters or others who had the entrepreneurial 'itch' and were prepared to organise labour, financing, and sub-contractors and to take upon themselves the risks, and the possible gains, for doing what they would otherwise be doing for others. The risks were high, as the level of bankruptcies records, and the margin of success was determined more by the luck of the market, or the timing of completion of a building in relation to the economic cycle of boom and recession. Throughout the whole period of construction, and right up to the sale of the building, the builder remained exposed to every fluctuation in interest rates and was faced with almost certain bankruptcy if demand should fail, as it had done in the mid 1870s and again in the 1890s, leaving him with an unsaleable building. But if he caught the market right, the returns on his own investment could be spectacular; in a boom, for example, it was quite common to have rented the building to capacity even before completion.[46]

The quality of much working-class housing was inferior, built to the minimum standards enforced by the *Bauordnungen*. There was nothing to be gained through good rather than cheap building: money was to be made by reducing expenditure on materials and labour to a minimum. It was small wonder that the industry was criticised by many contemporaries for encouraging malpractices of every kind. Reich comments on the attractions to the unscrupulous of the dramatic profits that could be made during a boom,[47] and reviewing the collapse of the Berlin building industry in 1912, Dr Rusch emphasised the danger to labour and building material suppliers from the incompetence and greed of residential developers, many of whom operated without professional training of any kind.[48] Neither formal qualifications nor capital was required for residential building. Working together with a land company, the builder himself needed only to raise sufficient capital for the *Baugeld*, and even the financing of this could be spread over a considerable period. A Berlin builder would have to pay only a third of the costs of building materials on ordering, a third on the commencement of construction, while the final third had only to be produced on the sale of the building.[49] But despite the occasionally huge profits and the very limited resources required, the average gains for residential construction were estimated to be low. The dividends of 10 per cent reported by the very few companies which were publicly quoted and published their accounts were exceptional, as both Reich and Ascher would agree.[50] However high the profits made during the short period of furious building activity between 1902–6, long-term profits were low: certainly during the depression that set in after 1907 large number of builders went bankrupt. Without their sources of the banks to back them, small and medium-sized builders were brutally exposed to the shortage of capital in the Berlin property market after 1910. Even large, well-established firms such as Kurt Berndt, which had links to the Deutsche Bank and the Schaafthausen'scher Bankverein, went into liquidation in 1912. Significantly, the Deutsche Bank as a preferred creditor was able to recover its assets in full; however, the loss to building material suppliers and craftsmen, estimated at over 2 million marks, was not made good.[51]

The primitive and precarious nature of the house-building industry was reflected in two ways in the cost and volume of housing built in the twenty years before the war. First, wages rose rapidly but without an equivalent increase in productivity, thus leading to higher overall production costs. Secondly, given the under-capitalisation of the industry, its financing was critically dependent on the cost of capital and the fluctuating stage of the capital market. Ascher estimates the increase in the overall construction costs of new residential building in Berlin to have been from 180–270 marks per square metre in 1890 to 195–290 marks per square metre in 1900 for the simplest standards of construction and finish.[52] Setting aside the very limited effect of the higher standards demanded by tougher building regulations, the most substantial portion of this increase was caused by the rapid rise in wages in the building industry from 1893 onwards. Examining the wages of a number of trades, Ascher concluded that wages in the industry had generally increased by as much as 60–70 per cent from 1895 to 1910. But this increase in wages can be shown to have been offset by a less rapid increase in the cost of materials and components. This was due in large part to a far greater efficiency in the fabrication and supply of materials: not only were components such as doors and windows now commonly manufactured off-site in greater quantities and, in real terms, more cheaply, but innovations in the production of materials such as bricks also reduced costs. While the price of materials such as bricks, cement and tiles varied with demand, naturally rising at times of peak construction, the general trend in material costs was downwards.

The cost of production must also include the cost of financing the purchase of the site and the period of construction. Although these costs were often no more than 10 per cent of the total construction costs, this, given the way in which residential development was financed, might well be the margin between profit and failure, particularly as these costs varied sharply with the state of the capital market (Table 6.2).[53] The rate for borrowing for first mortgages, generally used to pay off the cost of the site and protected by the security of the Grundbuch, would be low, but the substantial amount involved and the period over which the loan might be required could result in considerable expense. To these costs had to be added the cost of borrowing the *Baugeld*. Because of the system of payment for materials and labour, both the level and the period of the loan would be far less than the full costs of construction. However, because of the high risk involved in this phase of development, interest rates for *Baugeld* were generally 1 per cent, occasionally as much as 2.5 per cent, above the rates for first mortgages. Taking as an example the financing of a development in 1910, Hoepker concluded that the financing costs might account for about 10 per cent of the total production costs, but, in periods of high building activity during a boom when money would be more expensive, these costs could rise to nearer 15 per cent of the total.[54]

Taken together, the different components of the construction costs of housing amounted, according to Andreas Voigt's study, to approximately 40 per cent of the total cost of housing production in 1895 for the whole city. In working-class areas the proportion was substantially higher, nearer 60–70 per cent. Furthermore, these costs tended to increase in line with general economic activity, rising relatively more rapidly than land at a time of economic expansion, thus increasing rents still further.

The ownership and management of property in Berlin during the two decades before the war appears to have been as fraught with the constant

Table 6.2 Interest levels for the different types of capital used in residential development

Year	Reichsbank discount rate	Market discount rate	Interest rate for first mortgages	Interest rate for second mortgages	Rate of interest on debentures of the German Mortgage Bank at the end of each year
1870	4,89	4,50	4,75—6	6 —8	4,35
1871	4,16	3,62	5 —6	6 —8,50	4,50
1872	4,29	3,94	4,50—6	6 —8	4,55
1873	4,95	4,50	4,50—5,75	6 —7	4,59
1874	5,38	3,25	4,50—5,75	5,50—7	4,61
1875	4,70	3,75	4,50—5,75	6 —7	4,62
1876	4,16	3,04	4,50—6	6 —7	4,62
1877	4,42	3,17	4,50—5,50	6 —7	4,61
1878	4,34	3,04	4,50—5	5,50—7	4,61
1879	3,70	2,60	4,50—5	6 —7	4,57
1880	4,24	3,04	4,50—5	5,50—6	4,49
1881	4,42	3,50	4,25—5	6	4,42
1882	4,54	3,89	4,25—4,75	5 —6	4,37
1883	4,05	3,08	4,25—4,75	5 —5,50	4,30
1884	4,00	2,90	4,25—4,75	5 —5,50	4,22
1885	4,12	2,85	4 —4,75	5 —5,50	4,10
1886	3,28	2,16	3,75—4,50	5 —5,50	3,94
1887	3,41	2,30	3,75—4,50	4,50—5	3,91
1888	3,32	2,11	3,75—4,50	4,50—5	3,88
1889	3,68	2,63	3,50—4,50	4,50—5	3,52
1890	4,52	3,78	3,75—4,50	4,50—5	3,81
1891	3,78	3,02	3,75—4,50	4,50—5	3,83
1892	3,20	1,80	3,75—4,50	4,50—5	3,85
1893	4,07	3,10	3,75—4,50	4,50—5	3,85
1894	3,12	1,74	3,50—4,25	4,50—5	3,83
1895	3,14	2,01	3,50—3,88	4,25—4,75	3,74
1896	3,66	3,04	3,50—4,25	4,25—5	3,69
1897	3,81	3,09	3,50—3,75	4,25—4,75	3,66
1898	4,27	3,55	3,75—4,50	4,25—5	3,66
1899	5,04	4,45	3,88—3,75	4,50—5,50	3,67
1900	5,33	4,41	4 —5	4,75—5	3,69
1901	4,10	3,06	3,88—5	5 —6	3,71
1902	3,32	2,19	4 —5	4,50—5	3,72
1903	3,84	3,01	3,75—4	4,75—5,25	3,70
1904	4,22	3,14	3,75—3,38	4,75—5	3,73
1905	3,82	2,85	3,75—4,50	4,50—5,50	3,66
1906	5,15	4,04	3,75—4,50	5 —6,50	3,86
1907	6,03	5,12	4 —5	5 —7	3,76
1908	4,75	3,53	4,25—5	5,50—6,50	3,78
1909	3,92	2,86	4,25—4,50	5 —6	3,99
1910	4,35	3,52	4 —4,75	5 —6	3,80
1911	4,40	3,54	4 —4,75	5 —6	3,83
1912	4,95	4,22	4 —5	5 —6,50	4,75
1913	5,88	4,98	4,25—5	5,50—7	3,99
1914	4,89	2,84	—	—	3,85

Source: Carthaus, *Zur Geschichte*, 222

risk of bankruptcy and forced sales as the construction of housing. Nevertheless, the attraction of investing in residential property was high. Home-ownership was very limited by the 1890s so that demand for rented accommodation was high—indeed 97.7 per cent of all dwellings were rented.[55] Investors, whose funds came predominantly from the mortgage banks, were drawn into the housing market as landlords by the promise of handsome profits to be made either through managing property as a source of regular income, ideal for those seeking a 'steady' return, or, more aggressively, by realising the value of the house as a speculative venture. Though those owning land and property were prepared to unite, in the *Haus- und Grundbesitzer Vereine*, the resources and the interests of those dealing in residential property were very different from those of the land companies. In contrast to the wealth of literary sources on the subject, there is little statistical information on the social and economic characteristics of residential landlords, but data collected by the statistical office of Charlottenburg in 1906 gives some substance to the image of the landlord as the personification of the petty-bourgeoisie.[56] Haberland records that a wide variety of people invested in residential property. They included professionals like doctors, professors and civil servants, respectable widows and a host of petty-bourgeois figures like small businessmen, managing clerks and small shopkeepers, all attracted by the promise of a secure income together with the chance of a golden 'nest egg' on sale.

To these groups the attraction of investing in property is clear from Haberland's account of contemporary expectations[58]: it was customarily assumed that rent would cover mortgage repayments and other costs such as taxes and repairs, together with a 5 per cent profit on the original capital investment and 1–1.5 per cent interest on the total value of the property to cover the cost of administration and rent collection. Larger landlords, owning a number of properties, and those renting higher up the market might employ an agent to collect rents, but in working-class housing, the landlord frequently lived in his own property and collected the rents himself to reduce the costs of administration and control to a minimum. In Haberland's example the landlord purchases a building for 300,000 marks, investing only 30,000 marks and paying only 6,000 marks in fees, legal charges and taxes. According to then current usage, he would have expected to make 5 per cent on his capital and costs (i.e. on the 36,000 marks) as well as a further 1 per cent on the value of the building; together this would yield a return of 4,800 marks, to many a handsome income for so little work and such a small initial investment of the landlord's own capital.

However, despite these attractions in theory, the chances of maintaining this level of income were affected in practice by a number of complicating factors, particularly at the lower end of the market. During a period of economic expansion it might not be difficult to keep flats let, and rents could be raised to meet the extra cost of higher interest rates, although it should be remembered that for every 1 per cent increase in mortgage interest rates, rents had to rise between 10–15 per cent.[59] But in a recession, the landlord might have no such room to manoeuvre. As the proportion of empty dwellings mounted, it would be correspondingly more difficult for the landlord to let his tenements. As Carthaus noted, this might lead landlords either to reduce rents in order to attract tenants, or, paradoxically, to raise rents to maximise profit on the tenants available.[60] As rental income declined it would be increasingly difficult to meet the interest payments on a house which might be as much as 96 per cent mortgaged, even though interest rates might well come down in a recession. As Carthaus's examples show, an extra 1 per cent in interest on the financing costs of housing could spell bankruptcy for those so heavily mortgaged. The difficulties faced by landlords in a depression can be inferred from the level of forced sales:[61] during the recession of the early 1890s they accounted for 20–25 per cent of all property sales. During the crisis of 1911–14 the volume of forced sales rose spectacularly: throughout the period 1900–05 it remained below 500 per year, between 1907–13 it remained at over a thousand per year and in 1912, it reached the record level of 1,609 forced sales per year, or nearly 50 per cent of all sales.

The task of realising a substantial profit on the sale of a property was even more fraught with complications. In the long term, the rise in the value of the land due to the growth of the city was generally sufficient to produce an increase in the value of most properties. Thus it should have been possible to sell any property at the right point in the economic cycle to make enough to pay off the mortgages and still retain a handsome profit. But in practice there were difficulties in managing property over the period necessary to show a real increase in the value, and the chances of making a substantial profit were certainly dependent on the fluctuations of the economic cycle and the changing state of the capital market. The task of selling a property as the market turned down might be very difficult, but with the return from rents falling, and possibly with interest rates rising (a combination of events experienced after 1910) the need to sell might lead to desperate measures. To increase the value of a property, by inflating the apparent returns in rent, some landlords were even prepared to allow tenants to live rent free for one week in three, or to discount a portion of the rent in return for signing rent contracts agreeing a fictitiously high rent.

The difficulties faced by the builder in finding *Baugeld* during a boom, or by the landlord in meeting his mortgage payments during a slump, were only symptoms of the larger problem of securing capital for residential development and for working-class housing in particular. These difficulties sprang essentially from the low profitability of housing when compared with other forms of investment. This is what determined the behaviour of the institutions which provided capital for housing and their operation at different stages in the economic cycle.

Because of the limited capital possessed by most developers and landlords, nearly all the money invested in housing was borrowed on the capital market.[62] The principal source of finance was the mortgage banks. Until the 1890s they were almost the only source, but during the

1900s their share of the total declined, until by 1914 it was just over 40 per cent. As their share of lending contracted, the activities of the savings banks and life insurance companies expanded. However, the operations of the mortgage banks still serve as a typical illustration of the behaviour of these institutions. Unlike the building societies in England, the mortgage banks raised money not from the investment accounts of large numbers of small borrowers, but from the sale of debentures.[63] Money raised in this way was then lent in the form of mortgages to developers or owners of property. In general, mortgages were arranged for a period of ten years and were lent in aggregate at a slightly higher rate than the mortgage debenture rate—the difference was usually less than 1 per cent, but it did occasionally go higher. The rates at which individual mortgages were lent depended not only on the state of the market, but on the type and security for the loan and even on the area of the city in which the loan was to be made. Loans on first mortgages were lent at rates between 1 and 1.5 per cent lower than second mortgages, while the rate for *Baugeld* might be as much as 0.5–1 per cent up on this again. Variations in the rates for different types of loans are given in Table 6.2. Mortgages for working-class and suburban housing were generally 0.5 per cent more expensive than those for the better quality of housing in the west of the city which was favoured by the mortgage banks.[64] Generally the mortgage banks tended to concentrate on the less risky first mortgages, leaving the provision of second mortgages and *Baugeld* to private investors. The balance between the different types of mortgages is suggested by Paul Voigt's studies of lending in Charlottenburg in the 1890s.[65] On old property, first mortgages accounted for 60.5 per cent of the value, second mortgages for 20.25 per cent and other forms for the rest. On new property the balance was 78.5 per cent for first mortgages and 14.4 per cent for second mortgages.

Of great importance were the changes in these mortgage rates over time and the relationship between these rates and the operations of the rest of the money market. An understanding of the operations of the mortgage banks at different points in the economic cycle is of key importance in investigating both the cost of borrowing, and thus the effect of financing on rents, and the volume of capital that was available for residential development at any time. Given the relatively low return on housing, even during periods of expansion when the housing market was strong, the extent to which mortgage rates could rise was limited and this naturally restricted the rise of the debenture rate. Thus the attraction of these debentures and, in consequence, the flow of funds into the mortgage banks did not rise even during a period of economic upturn. By contrast, during a depression, when the housing market was weak and demand for mortgages low, the mortgage banks would attempt to protect the value of their debentures, even buying up debentures when their price fell. The consequence of keeping the price of debentures up in this way was that the interest rate remained relatively stable.

The resultant stability of rates in relation to the economic cycle contrasts clearly with the fluctuation in share prices: the debenture rate resembles much more closely the rates for bonds and state and federal securities. The consequence was a flow of funds into the mortgage banks which lagged behind the economic cycle. When the general interest rates were low, as in periods of recession, the debenture rate was relatively high and money flowed into the mortgage banks; conversely, at times when the economy was buoyant, the debenture rate was relatively low and the mortgage banks found it difficult to attract investment. Thus, when the housing market was strong, the demand for mortgages could not be satisfied.

Occasionally, however, as in the crisis years 1910–14 this anti-cyclic pattern might be broken. What produced the particular severity of the crisis in these years was the painful but less frequent combination of falling demand together with rising interest rates. It was loss of confidence in the inflated value of land, and in the land companies themselves and their paper assets, rather than competition for capital with other forms of investment, which raised interest rates; it was this that created the shortage of capital and led eventually to the collapse of the market.[66]

The conjunction of events during the crisis years of 1910–14 may have been exceptional, but it serves to underline yet again the central importance for all those engaged in the provision of housing of the cycle of economic growth and recession. For the director of the land company, as for the small landlord, the state of the market and the strength of demand for housing were critical. As we move from examining the various agencies engaged in the supply of housing to measuring the demand for housing, the condition of the local economy of the city provides a natural starting point for our discussion.

II

An effective, if crude measure of the aggregate demand for housing is provided by the growth of the city's population. In the period between 1890–1914, the most important component of this growth was already that due to the rate of natural increase which seems to have run at an average of just over nine per thousand between 1890 and 1910. By comparison with the relatively long-term demographic developments, which might shape the rate of natural increase, the increase in population through immigration was much more volatile, reflecting directly the cycle of economic development and the opportunities for employment in the city. In her discussion of the housing market between 1890 and 1914, Reich identifies three separate phases of activity which shaped the volume of immigration.[67] The opening period, after the sharp recession of the early 1890s, was characterised by economic expansion, which was the result of the growth of heavy industries such as metalworking, engineering and electrical engineering. This period of expansion seems to have lasted until late 1898 when the economy began to falter. The second period began with the crisis of 1900 and two further years of economic difficulty. But by 1903, economic recovery was already under

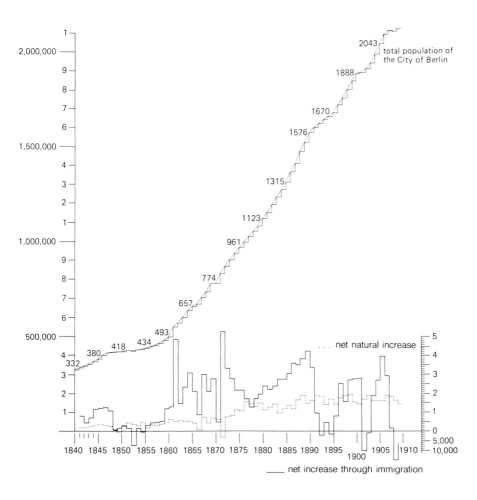

Figure 6.6 Population growth, immigration and natural increase in Berlin 1840–1914
(*Source:* Bullock and Read, *Movement for Housing Reform*, 19).

way, led by foreign trade, much of it with the USA. This phase of growth continued until 1907, the end of our second period. The third period, starting in 1908, was principally a period of deepening recession which continued beyond 1910 to the war. As the variation in migration (Figure 6.6) demonstrates, the cycle of boom and slump affected the demand for housing. In times of prosperity, the increase in migration might still be substantial: in years of peak migration like 1905, 39,564 people might enter the city. Equally, in periods of depression the population might decline: in 1908, a year of declining employment prospects, 20,854 people left the city. Generally, however, the aggregate growth of population, at 13 per cent during the period 1895–1900, was double that of the preceding five years, and only started to fall off after 1907.

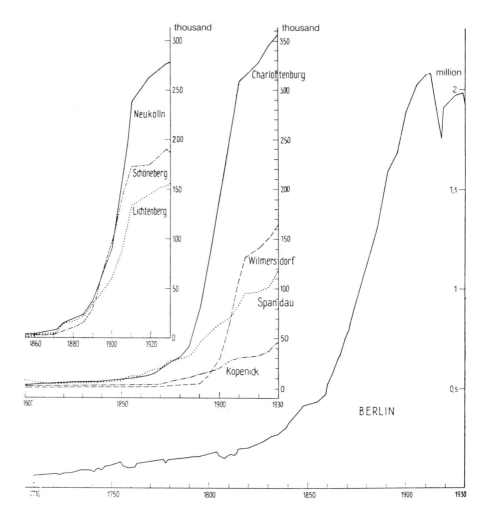

Figure 6.7 Population growth in the suburbs
(*Source:* Leyden, *Gross-Berlin*, 86–87).

But more important for the discussion of the balance between the supply and demand for housing than any aggregate measure of demand was the changing pattern of population distribution within the metropolitan area. Certainly, in the twenty years before the war, the growth of population was very uneven: the most obvious change was the increasingly rapid growth of the suburbs and the outer districts of the city at the expense of the inner areas.[68] On the one hand, non-residential uses forced housing out of the central areas, and on the other, the relocation of industry further out, the so-called *Randwanderung* to the Ringbahn, led to the outer districts becoming more attractive for working-class housing. In 1895, the population of the suburbs formed only 17 per cent of the total population of Greater Berlin, but by 1900 this had risen to 29 per cent, and by 1910 to 45 per cent; by 1919 the population of Berlin and its suburbs was virtually level (Figure 6.7).[69] The basic forces behind this transformation were to be found in the new pattern of accessibility created by the expansion of public transport, and the relocation of industry.

The transformation of the railway system, in particular the completion of the *Ringbahn* in 1877 and the opening of the *Stadtbahn's* east–west link across the city in 1882, had done much to improve accessibility across the system of public transport in Berlin during the 1880s.[70] During the next two decades these improvements and continuing expansion of public transport were to have important consequences for the way in which the city was to develop (Figure 6.8). But the immediate impact of these changes was on the location of industry, not housing.

Seeking larger sites, industries like metalworking, engineering and electrical engineering were drawn beyond the built-up area to sites around the *Ringbahn* which offered cheap land and good access to both waterways and railways.[71] Borsig had closed his works near the Oranienburger Tor in 1878 to move his factory, which already employed over 5,000 men, to a larger site in Moabit that was well served by both rail and water. Siemens and Halske acquired a large site in Charlottenburg in 1883 which, greatly expanded four years later, was to form the basis of their operations in Berlin for the next thirty years. AEG, which had traded from the Schlegelstrasse for over twenty years, moved in 1887 to a new factory in Wedding, and in 1895 to a 90,000 hectare site on the Voltastrasse from which it could secure direct access to the *Ringbahn* on a specially constructed branch line. This outward movement of industry, the first *Randwanderung* (Figure 6.9a), to the *Ringbahn* and areas about 5 kilometres from the centre of the city, increased the attraction for the workforce of areas like Moabit, Wedding, Charlottenburg and other areas where the growth of working-class housing could follow the growth of industry. By the late 1880s and the early 1890s, the population in the outer districts and the suburbs of the city was already growing apace. This process of outward growth during the twenty years before the war was to continue and even to gather pace, creating new concentrations of industry between 15 and 20 kilometres from the city centre, the *zweite Randwanderung* (Figure 6.9b). Again, the example of Borsig illustrates the way in which heavy industry continued to search even further out for more and cheaper land with direct links to water and rail. In 1898 the firm again moved its factory, from Moabit, to a huge 28,003 hectare site on the Tegler See. As a necessary adjunct to this scale of expansion, Borsig built workers' housing, schools, and in effect a complete new settlement to provide for the day-to-day needs of his workforce.[72]

By 1914 the location of manufacturing industry had changed dramatically from the situation in the 1870s. To the north, manufacturers like AEG were following Borsig, developing along the Nordbahn and its branch lines, and seeking access to the system of waterways on that side

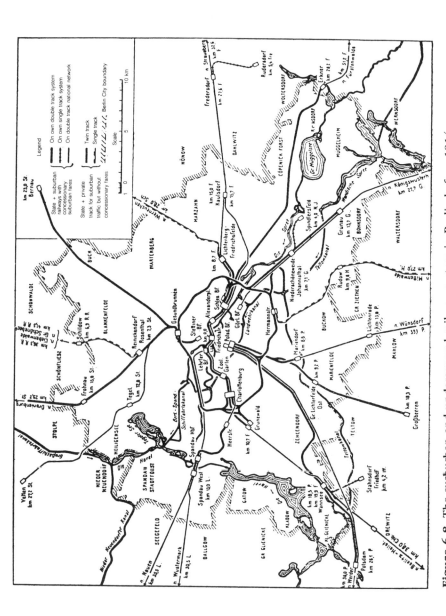

Figure 6.8 The surburban and underground railway system in Berlin before 1914
a) the Ring-, Stadt- und Vorortbahnen
(*Source*: Radicke, 'Personennahverkehrs', 12, 13).

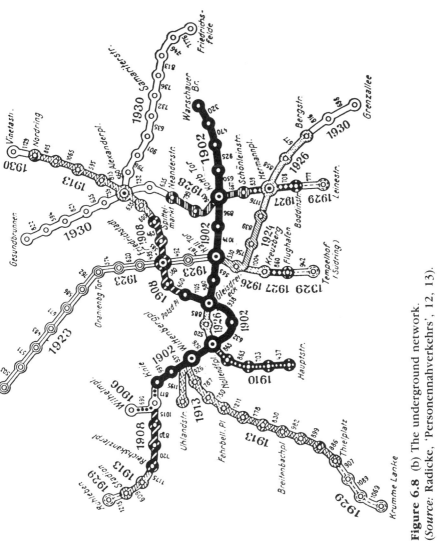

Figure 6.8 (b) The underground network.
(*Source*: Radicke, 'Personennahverkehrs', 12, 13).

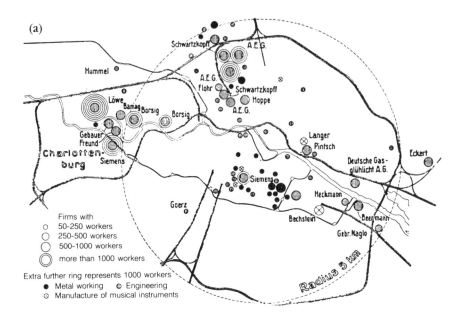

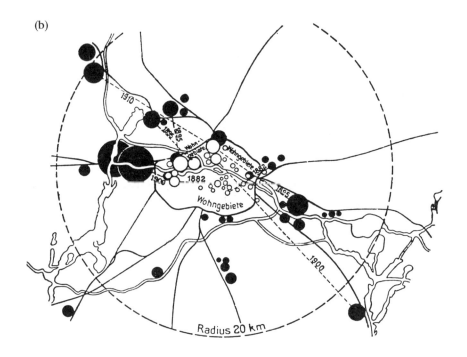

Figure 6.9 The first (a) and second (b) 'Randwanderungen'
(*Source:* Zimm, *Entwicklung*, 66, 89).

of the city. To the south and south-east a new concentration of industries like AEG, Konrad Lorenz and others were expanding between the Frankfurter and Goerlitzer railways out into areas which were well served by waterways such as the Teltow canal, like Mariendorf, Buckow and Lichterfelde. To the west what was later to be Siemenstadt, well connected to the Havel, was already starting to grow along the Hamburger and the Lehrter railways.

This major relocation of employment led to a substantial increase in demand for housing in the outlying districts of the city and in the suburbs. But the expansion of the suburbs was not just a product of new employment opportunities. It was also the dramatic increase in the availability of public transport during the 1890s, which stimulated this centrifugal pattern of growth.[73] The decade witnessed an enormous increase in the overall volume of travel in the city. In the period 1890–95, the volume of trips for all types of transport increased by 35 per cent, and this increase continued more rapidly during the second half of the decade: between 1895–1900 the number of trips rose by a further 68 per cent. In the decade after 1900 the volume of travel continued to increase, but the rate of growth slowed to 50 per cent in 1900–05 and to 30 per cent in 1905–10.[74]

The greater part of this growth was made up of commuter travel, and from 1890–1914 the proportion of travel by different forms of transport remained broadly stable (Figure 6.10). Half of all trips were by tram, a form of transport which, with electrification and a new city-wide structure of administration, became increasingly efficient as a means of travel to work within the city. More important for the growth of the outer districts of the city and the suburbs was the expansion of the services provided by the various suburban rail systems, the *Ring, Stadt and Vorortbahnen*, which maintained their share of the greatly increased volume of travel, emphasising the value of this form of transport both for trips between the outer districts and suburbs, and between the city and these areas.

During the late 1880s and the early 1890s the volume of trains that could be run on the Ring and a number of the radial suburban lines was greatly increased by doubling the number of tracks. To the south-east the same pattern was repeated. Not only did trains run more frequently; they also served more stations, thus extending and consolidating the impact of public transport in opening up these outer areas of the city for housing. Equally important was the effect of the new fares introduced at the beginning of October 1891. In place of the standard state-wide tariff, the authorities now introduced for suburban travel a system of concessionary fares, priced by zones, to complement that already available for travel on the *Ring*. This considerably reduced the cost of suburban rail travel and made it possible for the first time for workers to live in the suburbs and to commute to work by train.

These increases in accessibility and the changes in the pattern of employment during the 1890s had a dramatic effect on the growth of population in the suburbs. In the graphs of population growth plotted by

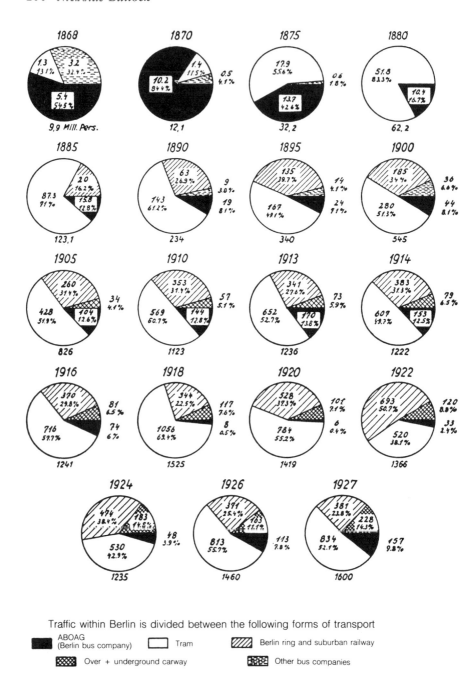

Traffic within Berlin is divided between the following forms of transport

■ ABOAG (Berlin bus company)   □ Tram   ▨ Berlin ring and suburban railway

▓ Over + underground carway   ▦ Other bus companies

Figure 6.10 The proportion of trips by different modes of transport (*Source:* Radicke, 'Personennahverkehrs', 9).

Leyden (Figure 6.7) the impact of these developments can be clearly seen in the surge of growth in the new municipalities like Charlottenburg, Schöneberg, Lichtenberg, Neukölln/Rixdorf, and in the smaller suburban communes like Weisensee or Reinickendorf (Figure 6.10). This rapid expansion in numbers represented a massive increase in the demand for new housing, and, in response, a huge volume of new building: by 1905, for example, average occupancy rates in many of the rapidly growing suburbs were higher than those in the city of Berlin even though dwellings sizes were, if anything, smaller than those in the city.

While the growth of the city's economy encouraged the development of new housing on the outskirts, the same processes of growth were leading by the turn of the century to substantial reductions in population in the old central areas.[75] Leyden shows that between 1880 and 1914 central districts lying within a radius of 1.5 kilometres of the Hausvogteiplatz had experienced a fall in population from 256,000 to just over half that figure, 137,000. With intense competition for central land from uses such as offices, commerce and various forms of government, the numbers of dwellings in the very centre of the city were being reduced by what contemporaries were already calling 'City Building'. But, unlike London, housing in traditionally working-class areas such as Luisenstadt, the Stralauer Viertel or the Rosenthaler Vorstadt seem to have remained largely unaffected by these pressures. While landlords of more expensive housing bemoaned the flight of their tenants to the new suburbs, the occupancy rates in the central working-class areas seem to have remained higher than those further out. For the skilled worker, with regular and comparatively well-paid employment in one of the new expanding industries beyond the *Ringbahn*, the new suburbs may have been a welcome relief from the noise, the congestion and the low quality housing of the inner districts. But to the semi-skilled and the unskilled, access to the variety of employment opportunities in the centre, in trades such as building or clothing, was generally dependent on finding somewhere affordable to live within walking distance, or at most a short tram-ride away from work, even if this meant crowding into older housing in the centre of the city.

III

By 1914 the inability of the system of housing production to react to, let alone anticipate, demand must have been painfully obvious. But if private enterprise could not even respond adequately to the general city-wide demand for housing, how could it hope to provide for the needs of working-class families at the bottom end of the market where the problems of management had always been extreme, and where profit margins were slimmest?

In order to make comparisons between housing conditions in working-class and other areas of the city and its suburbs, a limited number of areas will be considered where the concentration of those with unskilled

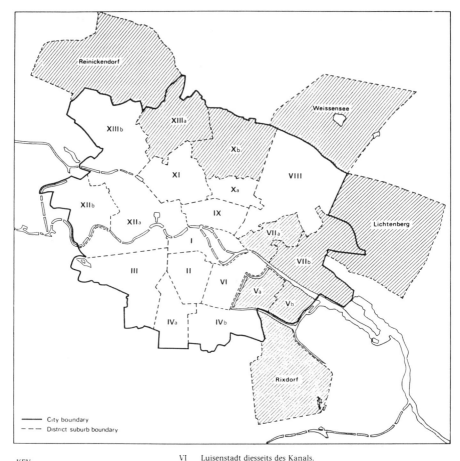

KEY

I	Berlin. Cöln. Friedrichswerder. Dorotheenstadt
II	Friedrichstadt
III	Friedrich und Schöneberger Vorstadt
IVa	Friedrich und Tempelhofer Vorstadt (westlich)
IVb	Tempelhofer Vorstadt (östlich)
Va	Luisenstadt jenseits des Kanals (westlich)
Vb	Luisenstadt jenseits des Kanals (östlich)
VI	Luisenstadt diesseits des Kanals. Neucöln
VIIa	Stralauer Viertel (westlich)
VIIb	Stralauer Viertel (östlich)
VIII	Königsstadt. Königsviertel
IX	Spandauer Viertel
Xa	Rosenthaler Vorstadt (südlich)
Xb	Rosenthaler Vorstadt (nördlich)
XI	Oranienburger Vorstadt
XIIa	Friedrich–Wilhelmstadt. Tiergarten. Moabit (östlich)
XIIb	Moabit (westlich)
XIIIa	Gesundbrunnen
XIIIb	Wedding

Figure 6.11 Diagrammatic map of the boundaries of city districts and selected suburbs just before the First World War: the districts and suburbs referred to in the text are shown shaded
(*Source:* Bullock and Read, *Movement for Housing Reform*, 199).

and semi-skilled occupations was highest (Figure 6.11). The choice of the
districts is based on the occupational structure of the population in each
district recorded in the census of 1910 and the districts selected for
comparison are those where the concentration of unskilled and semi-
skilled workers was greatest.[76] Six city districts and four suburban areas
were chosen as having over 40 per cent of their working population
classed as unskilled or semi-skilled in seven major categories of employment: metalworking, engineering, woodworking, clothing, building and
shopkeeping. Other occupational categories having substantially fewer
employees, were ignored as insignificant in determining the choice of
district.

Two of the city districts, the Rosenthaler Vorstadt, district Xb, and
Gesundbrunnen, district XIIa, are located in the north-west and north
where metalworking and engineering were the predominant forms of
employment. In the former the metalworking industry, with its relatively
high wages had been replaced by the building industry as the largest
employer, but in Gesundbrunnen, one of the new suburbs that expanded
so rapidly during the 1880s and 1890s, metalworking was still the largest
single employer, followed by building and engineering. The remaining
four districts, districts Va and Vb (Luisenstadt jenseits des Kanals,
westlich und östlich), and districts VIIa and VIIb (Stralauer Viertel,
östlich und westlich) are located in the eastern sector of the city, where
employment was more diverse with clothing, woodworking and the
building industry as major employers, but still with about 10 per cent of
all employment in metalworking. In Luisenstadt both districts had similar
types of employment: metalworking and wood-based trades predominated but commerce and building also provided employment for
about 6 per cent of the workforce. In the Stralauer Viertel both districts
shared a similar emphasis on wood-based trades, building, and
commerce, with the latter particularly important in district VIIa.

The suburban areas chosen are Rixdorf, Lichtenberg and Weissensee
which lie to the east and the south-east, and Reinickendorf which lies to
the north of the city.[77] In the first three areas the pattern of employment was broadly similar: in Lichtenberg and neighbouring Weissensee,
'general commerce', clothing, transport and engineering predominated,
in Rixdorf employment was comparable but with a higher proportion of
the workforce in the building industry. In Reinickendorf, however, the
pattern of employment was very different, with engineering far
outreaching all other forms of employment.

One of the most obvious characteristics of housing in working-class
areas was the sheer density of development: even by comparison with
the working-class housing built in the early 1870s, the housing of the
1890s and the 1900s seemed more densely built. This increase in density
was dramatised by the 'Behausungsziffer', an index employed by housing
reformers to measure the population per site (though without taking any
account of the area of the site).[78] According to this index, the overall
density of housing, particularly in working-class districts had increased
(Table 6.3). This impression of density was a product not only of taller

Table 6.3 Residential densities for selected districts and suburbs of Berlin: (a) the percentage of plots with different residential densities, (b) the average number of people per plot or *Behausungsziffer*

	(a) Percentage of plots with different densities expressed in number of inhabitants			(b) Average number of people per plot
	1–100	101–200	207+	
1900				
City of Berlin	74.7	22.2	3.0	77
Va	68.0	28.6	3.3	90
Vb	45.2	43.1	11.5	120
VIIa	75.2	21.2	3.4	83
VIIb	50.7	44.1	5.1	103
Xb	44.3	48.5	7.1	114
XIIIä	66.8	27.2	6.0	84
Reinickendorf	99.7	0.3	0	17
Rixdorf	74.0	24.3	1.5	69
Weissensee	100	0	0	15
Lichtenberg	86.6	11.8	0.8	54
1905				
City of Berlin	74.0	23.0	2.9	77
Va	71.4	26.4	2.1	84.5
Vb	51.7	39.5	8.7	111.2
VIIa	75.0	18.7	2.6	78.2
VIIb	57.1	40.6	2.1	100.8
Xb	46.2	47.8	5.8	111.5
XIIIa	65.7	27.4	6.7	86.3
Reinickendorf	97.8	1.8	0.1	
Rixdorf	71.7	27.1	0.1	
Weissensee	97.0	2.6	0.3	
Lichtenberg	88.0	11.3	0.6	

Va	*Luisenstadt jenseits des Kanals (westlich)
Vb	Luisenstadt jenseits des Kanals (östlich)
VIIa	Stralauer Viertel (westlich)
VIIb	Stralauer Viertel (östlich)
Xb	Rosenthaler Vorstadt (nördlich)
XIIIa	Gesundbrunnen

(*Source:* a) *Stat. J. Berlin*, Vol. 32, 265–67; Vol. 33, 146
b) *Stat. J. Berlin*, Vol. 27, 198–99; Vol. 33, 147)

Table 6.4 Proportion of the dwellings of different types in Berlin, 1890–1900

	1890	1895	1900
Cellar	7.70	5.94	5.12
Ground	15.89	13.43	12.77
1st floor	18.49	16.18	20.76
2	19.85	19.56	20.02
3	20.19	20.72	21.10
4 +	17.26	22.97	19.32
Front dwellings	56.06	53.66	52.66
Rear	43.91	46.31	47.66

(Source: Eberstadt, *Handbuch*, 138)

Table 6.5 The percentage of dwellings (excluding business premises) of different sizes in selected districts and suburbs of Berlin

	Size of dwelling expressed in no. of heatable rooms					% of small dwellings with 0–2 rooms
	0	1	2	3	4 +	
1905						
City of Berlin	1.1	49.3	29.8	10.8	8.8	80.2
Va	1.2	58.4	27.3	8.7	4.4	86.9
Vb	1.1	69.8	20.4	5.8	2.9	91.3
VIIa	1.2	53.0	28.3	10.0	7.5	81.5
VIIb	0.8	54.7	32.8	8.5	3.2	88.3
Xb	0.9	51.4	32.2	11.6	3.9	84.5
XIIIa	0.7	55.1	33.8	7.4	3.0	89.6
Reinickendorf	0.3	43.9	41.7	11.0	2.7	85.9
Rixdorf	0.5	50.5	38.3	7.8	2.7	89.3
Weissensee	0.9	55.0	34.3	7.3	2.2	90.2
Lichtenberg	0.6	54.1	35.7	7.3	2.0	90.4
1910						
City of Berlin	1.7	47.2	32.6	10.2	7.3	81.5
Va	2.0	69.8	20.8	4.9	1.8	90.8
Vb	2.7	58.9	27.0	7.7	3.5	93.3
VIIa	2.7	53.2	28.3	9.5	5.8	84.2
VIIb	1.9	50.9	37.6	7.1	2.3	90.4
Xb	1.9	50.4	38.9	7.1	1.4	91.2
XIIIa	1.9	57.2	33.6	5.4	1.7	92.7
Reinickendorf						
Rixdorf						
Weissensee						
Lichtenberg						

(Source: 1905: *Grundstücks-Aufnahme 1905*, Part 1, 70–78; 1910: *Grundstücks-Aufnahme 1910*, Part 1, Vol. 2, 48–9

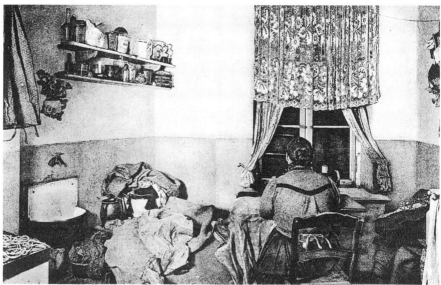

Figure 6.12 (a) Interiors of working-class tenements in Berlin a) Kitchen and living-room in a two-room dwelling in the rear building of a Berlin tenement block in 1904
(*Source:* Geist and Kuervers, *Berliner Mietshaus*, 502).

blocks but also of an increase in the proportion of rooms looking into courts, rather than on to the street, which resulted from the larger sites being developed in the 1890s (Table 6.4).[79]

Not only were working-class areas more densely developed, the

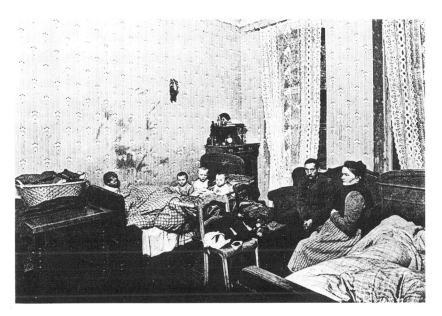

Figure 6.12 (b) Kitchen and living room in a two-room dwelling in the side building of a Berlin tenement block in 1912
(*Source:* Geist and Kuervers, *Berliner Mietshaus*, 504).

dwellings in these districts were also smaller (Table 6.5). If the proportion of dwellings with one and two rooms for the city as a whole is compared with the proportion in the six working-class districts, this difference emerges clearly: four of the six districts and three of the four suburbs had about 10 per cent more of these smaller dwellings than the average for the rest of the city. Moreover in the Stralauer Viertel westlich (district VIIa), where the proportion of small dwellings was lowest, this was balanced by a higher proportion of dwellings which were also used as workshops or for other non-residential uses.[80]

Facilities within these dwellings were minimal (Figure 6.12).[81] In blocks built in the 1860s and 1870s water would generally have been available only in the court; toilets too would have been placed here, shared between 40–50 dwellings. From the 1890s the standard of new accommodation might have improved: kitchens would have running water, waste drainage and a built-in coal-fired stove for heating and cooking; toilets would still be communal and after 1887 were placed against an outside wall for ventilation, either on the common corridors or landings. While new middle-class dwellings might well be equipped with central heating, hot water, electricity and even telephones, most working-class dwellings still lacked hot water and central heating even in the mid–1920s.[82]

Dwellings in working-class areas were not only more densely packed onto the site and smaller, they were also more crowded and more frequently used to take in lodgers than dwellings in other parts of the city. In general terms, there seems to have been a decline in the number of people per dwelling between the 1890s and 1914, a period in which dwelling sizes remained largely stable. Thus in 1890 the number of people per dwelling for the city as a whole was 4.17, while by 1900 (a period of intense housing shortage) it had actually fallen to 3.89, although in some of the suburbs such as Rixdorf the mean number of people per dwelling was higher than in the city with 4.42 people per dwelling.[83]

Despite this general decline, working-class housing was relatively more densely occupied than housing in the city as a whole: in 1910 the six working-class districts had a higher occupancy rate, measured as the average number of people per room, than that of the whole city (Table 6.6). Moreover the dwellings of a given size tended to have a higher number of residents than equivalent dwellings in the city as a whole (Table 6.7).

Overlaid on these levels of occupancy was the additional burden of lodgers. In Berlin there existed a hierarchy of different types of lodgers: at the most genteel end of the spectrum was the *Mieter* (or *Untermieter*) who would probably have the use of a whole room, occasionally a self-contained apartment within a larger dwelling, for a considerable period of time.[84]. On a very similar footing were the *Chambregarnisten*, or those who rented the *Chambre Garnie*, often young men in education, preparing for a profession, or advancing towards public service. Less common by the 1890s, and less genteel, were the dwindling number of lodgers, the apprentices, trainees and others, described in the census as *Burschen, Commis, Lehrlinge, Gesellen und Gehilfe*, who lodged with their employers. They might remain some time in the same house but would frequently share a room, or a corner of the workshop, with

Table 6.6 The percentage of dwellings of different sizes with different numbers of inhabitants

		Inhabitants per dwelling						
		1	2	3	4	5	6	7
City of Berlin rooms								
	1	70	19	5	1	1		
	2	8	27	27	19	9	4	1
	3	3	11	23	22	15	9	4
Va	1	70	2	5				
	2	8	31	28	18	8	3	1
	3	3	15	24	17	8	3	7
Vb	1	64	25	7				
	2	4	23	28	22	12	2	2
	3	2	12	23	24	18	1	4
VIIa	1	67	20	5				
	2	10	32	25	16	7	3	1
	3	3	15	24	22	14	9	4
VIIb	1	65	24	9				
	2	5	22	27	20	11	4	2
	3	2	14	21	20	17	10	5
Xb	1	64	22					
	2	4	25	29	21	11	4	1
	3	1	15	23	23	15	8	4
XIIIb	1	64	21					
	2	6	25	27	20	10	5	2
	3	1	13	20	22	17	10	6

Source: Stat. J. Berlin, Vol. 32, 24–67

others, sometimes even a bed. Finally at the bottom end of the scale were the casual lodgers, the *Schlafgaenger*, who might take a part of a room or a share of a bed for a short period, perhaps only for a night or two before moving on to another family.

The composition of households in Berlin was the subject of exhaustive statistical analysis by the city's statistical office.[85] They identified households by six variables and differentiated between thirty-two different types of household, plotting the results over five time-periods for dwellings classified by the number of heatable and unheatable rooms. As the authors recognised, the sheer wealth of data makes analysis difficult but a number of significant trends do emerge: first, the study revealed the steady growth of families who took in no 'outsiders' at all. Secondly, the analysis suggested a rapid decline in the number of *Schlafgaenger*: in 1890, they accounted for 6.2 per cent of the city's population, but by 1900 this had fallen to 5.4 per cent, and by 1910 it was down to 4.27 per cent. The study also showed a reduction in the number of households taking in *Schlafgaenger* from 15.83 per cent in

Table 6.7 Occupancy levels for dwellings of different sizes in selected districts of Berlin, expressed as the number of people per dwelling

| | | people per dwelling | | |
		1–2	3–4	5–7
City of Berlin		Percentage of dwellings		
	rooms			
	1	89	7	
	2	36.1	46	14
	3	14.6	45.6	28
Va	1	90	5	–
	2	39	46	12
	3	18	41	22
Vb	1	79	7	–
	2	27	50	20
	3	14	47	32
VIIa	1	69	5	–
	2	42	41	11
	3	18	46	27
VIIb	1	84	–	–
	2	27	48	18
	3	16	41	28
Xb	1	64	–	–
	2	29	50	16
	3	16	46	27
XIIIb	1	64	–	–
	2	31	47	17
	3	14	42	33

Source: 1880: *Stat. J. Berlin*, Vol. 10, 8; 1910: *Stat. J. Berlin*, Vol. 32, 960–67

Table 6.8 Household composition for selected districts of Berlin 1910

| | Percentage of dwellings with: | |
	No lodgers	*Schlafleute*
1910		
City of Berlin	82.3	10.2
Va	80.9	13.1
Vb	85.9	11.0
VIIa	79.0	14.0
VIIb	88.1	8.9
Xb	88.4	8.3
XIIIa	86.1	10.8

Source: Stat. J. Berlin, Vol. 32, 268–76

A1 and A2   The average return on a dwelling (for all dwellings and rooms)
is used as a proxy for rent

B   The percentage of empty dwellings

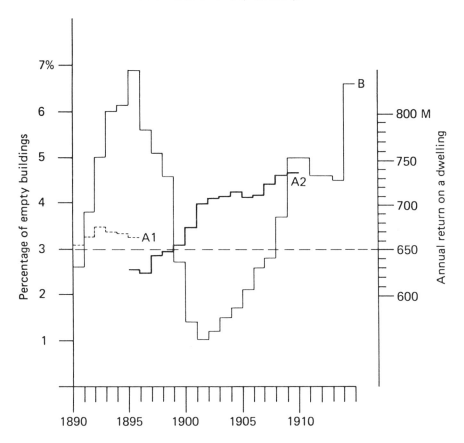

Figure 6.13 The percentage of empty dwellings and the level of rents in
Berlin 1890–1910
(*Source:* Bullock and Read, *Movement for Housing Reform*, 198).

1890 to 13.13 per cent in 1900, a significant decline in view of the real
pressures on housing at the turn of the century. However, against this
overall background, there was generally a higher proportion of
Schlafgänger in working-class areas than in the whole city. (Table 6.8)

The relationship between the 'host' family and its lodgers varied
widely and evades firm classification.[86] The established lodger might
well become 'part of the family'; many lodgers were relatives, eating and
living with the family, contributing to the household as they could and
paying rent when able to do so. But *Schlafgänger* in Berlin, unlike their

Table 6.9 The percentage of empty dwellings for selected districts and suburbs of Berlin

	Percentage of empty dwellings		
	1900	1905	1910
City of Berlin	0.6	1.5	5.0
Va	0.2	0.5	3.8
Vb	0.4	0.5	3.9
VIIa	0.5	1.0	4.9
VIIb	0.4	3.1	5.7
Xb	0.4	1.2	7.9
XIIIa	0.3	2.5	8.9
Reinickendorf	0.5		
Rixdorf	0.5		
Weissensee	2.0		
Lichtenberg	0.3		

(*Sources:* 1900: *Stat. J. Berlin*, Vol. 27, 200; 1905: *Stat. J. Berlin*, Vol. 29, 104; Vol. 33, 144–45; 1910: *Stat. J. Berlin*, Vol. 32, 303)

counterparts in the Rhineland, appear generally to have formed only minimal links with the host family. *Schlafgänger* might be offered a minimal breakfast and then faced the disadvantage of being bundled out on to the streets at the end of each night, thus leaving them without a 'home', or anywhere to cook or rest during the day. To the host family, *Schlafgänger* might be a mixed blessing. Despite the anxieties of the housing reformers, *Schlafgänger* generally provided a welcome supplement to the income of the host family; they were often an economic benefit in hard times, rather than the moral liability which so troubled the housing reformers.

Rents in Berlin reflected the changing balance of supply and demand.[87] In periods of high demand, such as the crisis years of the turn of the century, rents might rise appreciably, reflecting both higher costs to the landlord and, generally, a greater ability on the part of tenants to pay: thus in 1900 as the economy expanded and the number of empty rooms fell, rents rose (Figure 6.13). As demand slowed rents might decline, but, as has been seen, for most small landlords even a small reduction in income would create difficulties. Thus the fall in rents might be slower than the rise during a period of expansion. This was particularly true lower down the market (Table 6.9). If the economy turned down, and the demand for larger and more expensive housing fell back, the demand for smaller and cheaper housing might still 'hold up' as people moved down market to reduce their housing costs. Rents in cheap housing thus tended to be more stable than those in more fashionable areas. Rents in the city as a whole increased only marginally between 1905 and 1910 and, while rents in fashionable Schoeneberg and Tiergarten fell, rents in working-class areas actually rose.

Table 6.10 The average rent levels per dwelling in selected districts and suburbs of Berlin

	Average rent (in Marks) for all dwellings			Average rent for a 2-room dwelling
	1900	1905	1910	1910
City of Berlin	443	465	464	427
Va	(351)*	357	367	428
Vb	(281)	324	334	425
VIIa	(392)	385	394	414
VIIb	(321)	355	363	409
Xb	(280)	340	361	419
XIIIa	(270)	300	321	379
Reinickendorf	201	287		
Rixdorf	256	328		
Weissensee	203	261		
Lichtenberg	231	289		

* The figures in parentheses are calculated by taking the differentials in the annual rental value for each district (from the *Mietssteuerkataster*) and multiplying this by the average rent for the whole city.

(*Sources:* 1900: calculated from *Stat. J. Berlin*, Vol. 27, 200–01; 1905: *Grundstücks-Aufnahme*, 1905, Part 1, 43, 70–78; 1910: *Grundstücks-Aufnahme*, 1910, Part 1, Vol. 2, 48–49)

Even when aggregate figures show an overall balance between demand and supply there might still be very considerable variation between the availability of housing and demand in different working-class areas. During the acute housing shortage at the turn of the century when the proportion of empty dwellings stood at 0.6 per cent for the whole city, the shortage was yet more acute in working-class areas: in Luisenstadt, for example, only 0.2 per cent of all dwellings were empty. Even in the suburbs where the proportion of empty dwellings was slightly higher than in the city as a whole, the shortage in working-class areas was more acute and indeed almost as critical as in the city districts. But changing locational patterns might alter this:[88] in 1908 when, overall, 3.42 per cent of all dwellings were empty, the number of those empty in Luisenstadt was right down to 1.9 per cent. Here, as a result of demand for land for other uses, there had been a net decrease in housing, forcing population to the outer districts and the suburbs, and away from employment. In Gesundbrunnen, however, the number of empty units was as high as 6.8 per cent, reflecting the volume of new building in the suburbs: in Wedding, for example, the number of empty dwellings in 1910 was more than double the 1903 total.

The rent paid for a dwelling at any time also varied according to size and location: even for the same size flat within the same development rents depended on the floor, and whether the flat looked on to the street or a court.[89] Nevertheless, average rents in working-class districts were lower than elsewhere but not markedly so (Table 6.10). In 1910 the rents for both a one-room and a two-room dwelling in Gesundbrunnen, where the number of empty properties was high, was around 12 per cent lower than rents for the whole city. But in other more central working-class areas, like Luisenstadt where demand was higher and the number of empty units lower, rents might be equal to, or even slightly above, the average for the whole city.

Nor were rents for working-class dwellings necessarily lower in the suburbs. Average rents, over all sizes of dwellings, for the suburbs, compared with average rents for Berlin, did tend to suggest a lower level in the suburbs than in the city. But this was not always the case. Data cited by Reich show that the rent in 1905, when there was no shortage of housing, for a single-room dwelling in Rixdorf, one of the larger suburbs, was actually marginally higher than the average rent for an equivalent dwelling in the city.[90]

In 1868, Hermann Schwabe, then director of the Berlin Statistical Office, had formulated the *Schwabe'sches Gesetz* relating income to rent,[91] but the comprehensive data on household income and expenditure necessary to investigate the issue systematically were not available before 1914. However, some information on the subject, though contradictory and not strictly comparable because of differences between 'per capita' and 'household' income, is provided from two sources, first, the information collected for the income tax returns and from average rents and, secondly, a number of surveys of household income and expenditure carried out by the statistical offices of a number of cities and the Reich Statistical Office itself. Most interesting are the two surveys carried out by the Berlin Statistical Office in 1900, both based on samples of semi-skilled households where the head of the household was typically a carpenter, sales assistant or similarly employed.[92] Both groups had a similar 'per capita' income which was below the mean per capita income for the whole city, and both groups spent nearly the same proportion of income on rent. But, significantly, both groups spent a lower proportion (16.35–17.6 per cent) of income on rent than might have been expected from other contemporary studies.

Complementary to these findings are those based on the use of income tax data. Ascher,[93] for example, adopts this latter approach. Using aggregate income tax data for the city he arrives at an average income per inhabitant which he then compares with the average rent for all dwellings. On this rather abstract basis he calculates that in 1900 the average proportion of income spent annually on rent was 19 per cent for an average per capita income of 605 marks, and for 1910 he optimistically estimated that an average expenditure on rent had declined to 17 per cent on a per capita income of 782 marks.

But the relative optimism of Ascher's figures and the data obtained from the family income and expenditure survey were challenged by others. Kuczynski, director of the statistical office in Schoeneberg, produced figures in 1911 to show that in Schöneberg those with annual incomes of 12,000 marks were paying as much as 32.4 per cent of their incomes in rent.[94] To Schwabe's original axiom, 'the lower the income, the higher the proportion spent on rent', he added 'the smaller the dwelling, the higher (proportionally) the rent'.[95] Kuczynski's findings may have been distorted by the particular circumstances in Schöneberg, one of the wealthier suburban municipalities to the south-west of Berlin, but in his concern over the portion of income paid in rent by the poorer families, he echoed the anxieties of the housing reformers generally.

Despite the level of income spent by many of the working class on rent, neither rents, nor the more general relationship between landlord and tenant appear to have become as sharp a focus of conflict between classes in Berlin before 1914 as Englander argues was the case in Britain.[96] This was not for want of provocation. The contractual relationship between landlord and tenant appears to have been as loaded against the tenant in Germany as in Britain, and during the 1890s Flesch and other housing reformers were campaigning for a form of contract which would be less punitive to tenants and would offer speedier redress to landlords.[97] In working-class housing many landlords lived in their own properties and seemed to exercise a prurient interest in the affairs of their tenants as a way of maintaining 'standards' and the conditions of their properties. Landlords were widely attacked as greedy, petty tyrants who seemed quite prepared to evict tenants for the most trivial misdemeanours. Even defenders of property were insistent on the need to differentiate between 'responsible' landlords and the rapacious villains whom they acknowledged to be operating at the bottom end of the market.[98]

Individual tenants and their families might try to adapt in a variety of ways to the inadequacies of the market. Neefe's statistics on housing conditions in Berlin underline the frequency of movement within the city, particularly at the bottom end of the market;[99] perhaps moving offered the prospect of better accommodation or at least a change of landlord. The 'moonlight flit' was one established way of escaping the landlord or his agent on rent-day. But evidence of larger scale protest is not available; the individual rent collector or the individual landlord may have been hated, even assaulted, but there appears to have been little common solidarity amongst tenants in opposing landlords. There was no obvious organised alliance of working-class tenants to resist rent increases and to counter the actions of landlords through some form of direct collective action. During the war, and again during the 1930s, there is firm evidence of rent strikes and protests against landlords in areas like Wedding and Kreuzberg, but nothing similar appears to have been organised before 1914.[100]

It is true that there were various tenants' organisations or *Mietervereine* in cities such as Berlin before 1914. The first of these tenants' organisations was founded in Erfurt during the 1870s, and was followed by the formation of similar organisations in a number of cities during the 1880s; the *Berliner Mieterverein* was founded in 1888.[101]

But these *Mietervereine* were of little use in battling for the rights of individual tenants. They appear to have been content to play a more general role in campaigning for better housing conditions, aiding and abetting middle-class reforming organisations such as the BdB or the VRWG, and concerned primarily to counter the propaganda of property interests which was being presented with growing efficiency from the mid 1870s onwards by the various *Haus- und Grundbesitzervereine*.

By the 1890s the failings of private enterprise were widely recognised. Not only was the existing system of housing seen to be unable to respond to demand, but the housing that it did supply was evidently inferior in quality and insufficient in quantity. That the smallest, most crowded, most densely-built dwellings should be, in addition, the most expensive in relative terms was damning evidence of the inability of private enterprise to provide adequate housing for the working classes in large cities like Berlin. But how was this existing system of housing production to be reformed?

IV

By the early 1890s, concern over the housing problem was no longer confined to a narrow campaigning group of sanitarians and architects, it was widely regarded as one of the most pressing elements of the larger *Sozialfrage*.[102] The question was now taken up by a range of different groups representing a wide spread of opinion, from the broad mainstream of reforming liberalism to associations and organisations representing more specific interests. But despite the level of debate on the subject, and the beginnings of a campaign for national legislation, a *Reichswohngesetz*, to regulate the problems of housing, the ways in which the housing conditions for the working classes might actually be improved were still limited during the 1890s. The range of ideas being discussed by organisations such as the VföG, or the VfSP had yet to be tried in practice.

But by 1900, as the VfSP met to discuss the housing problem for a second time, there had been crucial developments on a number of different fronts.[103] First, the 1890s had seen the initial application in practice of a number of the ideas being championed by the housing reformers: the strengthening of sanitary controls on housing through a system of housing inspection, the introduction of 'stepped' density regulations, or the making of leasehold land available for non-profit housing. These initiatives might still be limited to one or two cities such as Frankfurt or Ulm, but they did indicate what could be done with the necessary political support. Secondly, there had been a substantial increase in the volume of housing being provided, outside the framework of private enterprise, by different forms of non-profit organisation: the limited dividend housing companies, and, above all, by the various kinds of housing cooperatives.

It was crucial for the expansion of the non-profit sector to overcome the shortage of capital which had been recognised as early as the 1860s as the greatest barrier to its growth. Equally important for the growth of the cooperative sector was the need to introduce some form of limitation to the liability of the individual member, the absence of which had hindered any real expansion of the cooperative housing movement.

During the early 1890s both these problems were addressed. The introduction of limited liability for individual members of cooperatives with the legislation of 1 May 1889 made it much easier for cooperatives to borrow capital. The provisions of the Invalidity and Old Age Insurance Act of 1890 established for the first time the possibility of using the funds of the regional insurance boards, set up under the invalid and accident insurance legislation of the 1880s, to provide capital for the building of working-class housing.

These two developments did much to encourage the work of both the limited dividend companies and the housing cooperatives. As the funds of the regional insurance boards became available, the volume of housing built by the non-profit sector grew appreciably. The achievements of this sector before 1890 had been extremely meagre: Jaeger records that although there were only 50 cooperatives in existence in 1879, their number had fallen to 28 by 1888.[104] By 1890 the number of houses built by all forms of non-profit housing organisations was no more than 13,109. But after 1890 the non-profit sector expanded rapidly: in the decade before 1900, a further 10,666 dwellings had been built. The growth of the cooperative movement was particularly strong: by 1900 the cooperatives had already built 9,838 dwellings, and with 202 new societies having been founded in this decade, were in a position to expand production still faster. By 1914, the number of societies had risen to 1,538 and were housing something like 40 per cent of their membership in 21,002 dwellings.

Despite the scale of this achievement, the growth of the non-profit sector remained very uneven. With the active support of the regional insurance boards in areas such as the Rhineland, Westphalia and Hanover, cooperatives flourished, encouraged by the foundation of regional associations to promote the construction of non-profit housing. But in other areas, particularly in Berlin, the non-profit sector was much less successful. At a conference organised by the *Centralstelle für Arbeiterwohlfahrtseinrichtungen* in Berlin in 1892 at which the use of the regional insurance boards' funds for working-class housing was discussed, Dr Freund, speaking for the Berlin board, had urged the case for caution, emphasising the need to balance the flow of money into the fund and the level of claims that the Board might need to meet.[105] By 1914, when most boards had lent up to 50 per cent of their resources, the board in Berlin had lent only 7 per cent of its funds. The limited use of these funds was reflected in the slow expansion of the non-profit sector before 1914.[106]

Berlin had been the birthplace of the non-profit movement in Germany in the 1840s, but progress since these early days had been slow.[107] By 1890, the city could boast only four non-profit societies and of these the

Berliner gemeinnützige Baugesellschaft (BgB) and the *Alexandra Stiftung* had built little since the 1860s. After nearly 50 years the BgB managed only 369 dwellings and the Alexandra Stiftung only 235. Of all four institutions, only the *Berliner Baugenossenschaft* was actively building, and by 1890 it had only built 40 single-family houses.

During the 1890s, the non-profit sector in Berlin had expanded.[108] It is true that neither the BgB, nor the *Alexandra Stiftung* had built more dwellings and the *Verein zur Verbesserung der kleinen Wohnungen*, another large non-profit company, had still not finished its development on the Weissbachstrasse. But the cooperatives had started to build: by 1900 the *Berliner Baugenossensschaft* had built 213 and the *Berliner Spar- und Bauverein* had built 227 dwellings. The acute housing shortage around the turn of the century stimulated the non-profit sector to action. By 1902 two new cooperatives had been established: the *Vaterländischer Bauverein*, launched by trade union and Christian National interests, and the *Berliner Beamtenwohnungsverein*. By the end of 1903 the number of non-profit dwellings was rising: there were 2,531 dwellings of this type in Berlin, and just under half (1,075) had been built by the cooperatives. By the end of 1905 production had risen to 3,754, although a major part (2,610 dwellings) of the housing built by the cooperatives was now built by the new *Beamtenwohnungsverein* (1,128 dwellings) for a more affluent market. This pattern of building did not change significantly before the war. By the end of 1913 the three limited dividend companies had built 1,356 dwellings. By 1914 the ten *Arbeiterbaugenossenschaften* had built between 5,500 and 5,600 dwellings, and to this should be added the construction of a further 290 dwellings and 333 rooms in non-profit lodging houses. The work of these cooperatives was almost matched by the work of the *Beamtenwohnungsvereine* which, starting in Berlin only in 1890, had already built about 3,700 dwellings by 1914 (Figure 6.14).

As a crude estimate of the total volume of non-profit housing built in the Berlin area before 1914, it may be assumed that altogether the different types of organisation, including the *Beamtenwohnungsvereine*, built of the order of 11,000 dwellings. As a proportion of the total stock of housing in the city this achievement lagged far behind that of Frankfurt or the cities in the Rhineland.[109] If the total number of dwellings built before 1914 by the seven principal organisations operating within the city of Berlin (excluding the *Beamtenwohnungsvereine*) was around 7,500 and the total number of dwellings in the city was around 600,000, then the non-profit sector cannot have built more than 1.25 per cent of the total stock, and this is probably a generous estimate. The equivalent figure for the whole of the Berlin area, including the surrounding municipalities and suburbs, was even smaller. But it was probably more typical of the general level of achievement across the country as a whole than that in the Rhineland or a city like Frankfurt.

Defenders of the non-profit sector like Albrecht[110] believed that, despite the limited volume of production, much had been won by 1914: a framework of housing provision had been established which was no

Figure 6.14 City centre non-profit housing, the housing reformer's ideal: Alfred Messel's development on the Proskauerstrasse for the Berliner Spar- und Bauverein, 1897–8
(*Source: Berlin und seine Bauten*, Vol IV).

longer motivated by the profit motive of private enterprise. Perhaps in some areas such as the Rhineland enough housing had been built by the limited dividend housing companies and the cooperatives to suggest what might be achieved by a more widespread expansion of the sector, and even to exercise some beneficial effect on the local housing market. But to others, like Eberstadt, the work of the non-profit sector was little more than a diversion from the real task of improving housing conditions through a restructuring of the way in which private enterprise operated.[111] Above all it was necessary to abolish the *Mietskaserne*, the form of housing which made it possible to sustain the unnatural system of production that had evolved by the turn of the century. To some, reform might be won through a reorganisation of the way in which housing production, and particularly the preparation of land for building, was financed. To the *Bodenreformer*, the taxation of the unearned increment on urban land would transform the forms of urban housing.[112] To yet others, improvement might be secured by more active control by the city of the ownership and use of land within its control either through the market, or by using the planning powers that Prussian cities had enjoyed since 1875. By the turn of the century housing reformers were exploring a wide range of alternative policies many of which touched in one way or another on controlling the use of urban land for housing.

One of the first, and one of the most effective ways to control the use of land was through the kind of 'stepped' building regulations for which the VföG had been campaigning during the 1880s and which were first introduced in a range of cities in the early 1890s.[113] To many housing reformers this was the first effective means of limiting the density of new development; to land reformers this was the first real advance in controlling the exploitation of urban land. At the meeting of VföG at Magdeburg in 1894, speakers had welcomed Eberstadt's support as an economist for what they saw as public health measures. To Eberstadt this system of density zoning offered the opportunity to reduce the density of development, thus limiting the speculator's return, and hence the price of land. Damaschke identified the new 'stepped' system of density controls as 'the most important means to combat the damaging inflation of land prices' yet introduced.[114]

By the mid 1890s, when the system of 'stepped' building regulations had already been successfully adopted by over 50 cities, large and small, including Berlin, arguments about ways to control the use of urban land for housing had shifted. During the years before 1914 debate amongst the different groups concerned with urban land reform, the *Bodenreformer*, housing reformers, the economists, the planners and municipal leaders, was now dominated by two central issues; the demand for a sales, or land transfer tax on the 'unearned' increase in the value of urban land, and the campaign for the cities to develop a municipal land policy. Both issues were of direct relevance to the housing question: both measures offered the possibility of controlling land values, hence housing density and housing form, and housing costs and rents.

The attraction of a new form of taxation on urban land was natural. Land reformers of all convictions were keen to see the community benefit in some way from the increase in the value of land that the community itself had created, rather than allowing this to fall into the hands of the land speculator as untaxed and unearned income. It is hardly surprising that a tax on this 'unearned income' should be an important focus for these differing interests.

In 1893 a number of important reforms to the structure of local taxation in Prussia had been introduced by Johannes Miquel as finance minister.[115] This legislation, known under the portmanteau title of the *Kommunalabgabengesetz*, was intended to help the finances of the communes, the *Gemeinden*, by increasing their income, both by ceding to them a number of sources of taxation formerly used for state taxes and by reassessing existing sources of revenue. It seemed to provide the very opportunity to establish a new basis for taxing property and land; significantly, the law was presented as enabling legislation leaving details of taxation to be worked out to suit the requirements of the individual city.

Since 1861 land was taxed not on its actual yield but on a potential yield assessed at the time when much of the land being developed in urban areas in the 1890s was still in agricultural use; little had been done to revise these early assessments. Buildings were taxed in an equally outmoded way: the taxes were assessed every fifteen years and were levied at the level of 4 per cent on the average return over the preceding ten years, providing only a feeble weapon with which to tax the very rapid growth of areas like the Vororte in Berlin.

The legislation of 1893 provided an opportunity for change, and most cities introduced modifications to the existing method of taxing land and property which differed crucially from the old system in being assessed on the 'common' or sale value. The new method did not necessarily lead to a higher return but its defenders claimed that it did provide a more equitable distribution of the tax load. In particular it had the advantage that land kept off the market was now generally liable for tax, thus removing an anomaly which had long infuriated land reformers. It also provided the means to control the speculators' practice whereby a plot of prime building land might be taxed as nothing more than a cabbage patch, leaving the owner to collect a massive and unearned increment in value when finally sold.

The use made of the provisions of the *Kommunalabgabengesetz* varied from city to city and reflected the local balance of interests, in particular the strength of the property lobby. In Frankfurt where Miquel, architect of the new legislation, had been mayor and where he had been succeeded by Adickes, an important figure in reforming circles like the VföG or the VfSP, the city had eagerly taken advantage of the new provisions to reassess taxes on property and land, used and unused.[116] By comparison in Berlin, a city with a strong property lobby—Baron estimated that 64 per cent of the *Stadtverordneteversammlung* represented some form of property interest—resistance to increases in the level of property taxes was high.[117]

The ability to tax unused land might be hailed as an advance, but for most reformers the prospect of some form of tax on the profits made on the sale of land appeared far more important. Frankfurt, for example, had instituted a form of *Umsatzsteuer*, or conveyancing duty before most Prussian cities were to do so after 1893.[118] Berlin too started to levy a property transfer tax of this kind in 1895 without provoking a vigorous response from property interests. Initially the tax was assessed at the rate of 0.5 per cent on the sale price of building and developed land, undeveloped land was at first assessed at 1 per cent of the sale price, but from the turn of the century the level of assessment rose to 2 per cent of the sale price.[119]

However the tax was most keenly championed by land and housing reformers was the *Wertzuwachssteuer* (WZS) a tax on the 'unearned' growth in the value of property or land between sales. Ever since the early days of the land reform movement this had figured as a key element of the programme, and it remained until the First World War one of the most important planks of the platform of the *Bund deutscher*

Bodenreformer.[120] The first city to introduce the tax in practice was Frankfurt am Main. Adickes, whose contribution to new developments in tax reform, land policy and city management was crucial and who represented a worthy continuation of the tradition that had started with Miquel, won acceptance from the Magistrat for the tax in 1904 and introduced a minimum levy on the sale price against which might be set the cost of improvements, calculated on a sliding scale taking into account the time of the sale and the price of the property.[121]

The introduction of the WZS at Frankfurt was followed by its adoption in broadly similar form in a number of other cities: in 1905 in Cologne and Gelsenkirchen, in 1907 in Dortmund, Bremen and Kiel. By 1911, 650 *Gemeinden* (out of a total of 76,000) had introduced some form of WZS although its adoption in larger cities was less rapid.[122] As the tax became more widespread, a range of local variations grew up: the level of taxation in Breslau was cited by Dawson as being typical of many. Here the first 10 per cent of the increment was free of taxation, an increment of between 10 and 20 per cent was taxed at 6 per cent of the excess of price over that at the previous change of ownership and so on, with a maximum levy of 25 per cent of the increment where this was greater than 100 per cent. Following the successful introduction of the WZS in a number of individual cities, the BdB turned its attention, under Damaschke's orchestration, to agitation for a *Reichswertzuwachssteuer*, and after a furious campaign of agitation, it became law in 1911. Under its provisions half of the tax on the unearned increment might be appropriated by the state, leaving 40 per cent for the local authority and 10 per cent for the Reich, although some provision was also made for those cities who had started to levy the WZS before 1911 to retain their original income.[123]

Assessing the value of these various taxes on the unearned profits made from land and property as a way of achieving the aims of the reformers is fraught with difficulty: certainly contemporaries were divided about their effectiveness. There was general agreement that the new taxes were more equitable than the old arrangements, and it was clear that the community might now derive some benefit from the increase in the value that it conferred on land and property, even if this was very much more limited than the land reformers had hoped. The major increase in income from taxes continued to come from the revised general land and property taxes, not from taxes such as the WZS. Thus the total tax revenue from property and land in cities such as Frankfurt and Cologne rose from 6.8 per cent and 11.3 per cent (of all tax income) respectively in 1893, to 27.4 per cent and 28.3 per cent by 1910.[124] In Berlin the increases were comparable. By contrast, the proportion of income brought in by the *Umsatzsteuer* and the WZS was very small: in Berlin the income from the WZS represented only 3.7 per cent of all tax revenue in 1910, barely one eighth of the income from general property taxes. The limited yield from these taxes might be partially explained away in a city like Berlin by the mounting difficulties facing the markets in land and property, but there were many who remained sceptical of their real value. To housing reformers like Eberstadt both the WZS and the RWZS failed to strike at the core of the problem, the way in which money was used in the financing of land and property. Land reformers might trumpet the success of the WVS but to reformers of all colours, the government's use of the RWZS smacked more strongly of fiscal opportunism than a real desire to implement reform.

But to property interests these taxes, particularly the WZS, appeared as a major blow, and the strength of their reaction suggests these taxes were not without effect. In the Berlin Vororte the tax was vigorously resisted; its timing, introduced in the year when the boom in the property market first started to slow, was particularly unwelcome. The situation in Schöneberg where Georg Haberland's company, the Berliner Boden Gesellschaft, was developing large areas of suburban land, gives some impression of the response of the property lobby.[125] While the introduction of the *Umsatzsteuer* seemed to have passed with little difficulty, the WZS was seen by Haberland as a real threat to property. Closely involved in local politics through his property interests, Haberland was at various times a member of a variety of local councils: he was on the council of Wilmersdorf, and the Kreis Council of Teltow; he was also a *Stadtverordnete* in Berlin. Despite his position and the active assistance of *Haus und Grundbesitzerverein* in Schöneberg and the Bezirksverein der Berliner Ortsteile, the municipality introduced the WZS in Schöneberg in 1907. Haberland seems to have taken it as a personal affront: he resolved to cease working in the district and set about campaigning actively against what he regarded as an unjust imposition on private enterprise.

Despite vigorous resistance from property interests, the law was eventually introduced in the City of Berlin in 1910, after a campaign which enjoyed widespread support, fuelled by popular reaction to the activities of the land companies in the outskirts.[126] The timing of the WZS came as an added blow to property interests which were already facing the beginnings of the crisis that was to last until 1914. The introduction of the RWZS in 1911 added further to the discomfort of property circles where it was argued that the new tax might absorb between 10–30 per cent of the profit to be made on a sale. The rush to beat both the WZS and the RZWS led to a flurry of sales in 1909–10, and to the winding-up of a number of land companies which were unable to continue trading in the increasingly difficult climate created by the erosion of profit margins through the new taxes. Property interests mobilised against them. A new campaigning organisation, the *Deutscher Hausbesitzerbund*, was set up in May 1911 in Berlin with the express purpose of combating the propaganda of the BdB and abolishing the RWZS.[127]

Potentially more successful as a means of overcoming the damaging effects of urban land speculation, and more widely supported, was the growing interest from the 1890s onwards in encouraging the development of a systematic land policy for German cities. If the municipality, in the role of large landowner, could exercise significant pressure on the land market, the reformers held high hopes that it would be able to challenge the way in which other landowners used their supposed 'monopoly' of land. Supporters of a municipal *Bodenpolitik* or land policy argued that a determined programme of municipal land purchase and management would lead more effectively to communal control of the use of land than any other policy.

German cities had long possessed powers to buy land and many already had large holdings of land by the 1890s, both within their city boundaries and outside as a reserve for future use.[128] By the turn of the century many cities were offering this municipally owned land for the building of non-profit housing to break the economic 'stranglehold' of the land speculator. The success of this policy turned on the continued exclusion of the speculator, even after the development of the land for housing: if this type of housing could later be bought and sold on the open market, the benefits of the city's *Bodenpolitik* would be lost. The idea of some form of leasehold system, or some provision to buy back the land once it had been sold was thus an important development of the cities' land policies.

In Germany the old system of leasing had almost died out in urban areas until the growth in land as a marketable commodity led to a revival of interest in the subject: during the 1890s, the BdB strongly supported establishment of a system of leasehold tenure, or *Erbbaurecht*.[129] The first significant translation of these ideas into practice dates from Adickes's introduction in 1900 in Frankfurt of a leasehold contract to make municipal land available for non-profit housing. But initiatives of this type were still limited to a handful of cities before 1914, and the use of leasehold land for housing was further frustrated by the difficulties of securing financing, a problem only resolved in Frankfurt by the creation of a system of financing through a special *Erbbaukasse*.

The frustrations over the introduction of a system of leasehold tenure and the difficulties of establishing a coherent *Bodenpolitik* were in large measure a product of opposition from the property lobby so strongly represented in Prussian state and city government. The strength of these interests is well illustrated by Adickes's attempts to ensure that the protracted task of assembling land for development could not be thwarted by owners who refused to sell in order to force an inflated price for their land.[130] While the *Fluchtliniengesetz* of 1875 provided compulsory purchase powers to acquire the land for roads and streets, these could not be used to buy land for other purposes. Adickes first presented a draft proposal to establish these powers in all Prussian cities in 1893. But it was only in 1901, on the sixth presentation of a bill, and after it had been considerably watered down, that the Prussian legislature passed the measure, and then did so on the condition that this Act, named 'Lex Adickes' should apply to the City of Frankfurt alone.

The results of the campaign for land reform were very unevenly distributed: Adickes's achievements in Frankfurt were exceptional. In Berlin the programme of land purchase and the development of a municipal *Bodenpolitik* was slow and unsure.[131] By 1900 the city owned 34.8 per cent of the area within its boundaries, and the

municipalities surrounding the city proper owned no more: Charlottenburg owned 32.8 per cent, Schöneberg 32.5 per cent, but most like
Neukölln, owned less than 20 per cent. More troubling for the development of a coherent land policy for the city as a whole, a number of
departments of state such as the army owned considerable areas of land
within the city and in the surrounding suburbs.[132] These departments
might pursue the development of areas like the Tempelhofer Feld, many
of them very large, in a way which would produce the largest short-term
profit but which would take no account of the larger planning and housing needs of the city. Indeed in large cities like Berlin, which necessarily
involved collaboration between different authorities, it was already clear
before 1914 that a coherent approach to land, transport and housing
could only be achieved by establishing planning powers that went
beyond those conferred on the individual cities by the *Fluchtliniengesetz*
in 1875.

While the land policies of a number of cities might be used to benefit
the non-profit sector, the Prussian cities were in a position to influence
through their planning powers not just the housing built by this sector,
but also the direction of housing development for the whole city.[133] As
the booming demand for land during the early 1890s and the early 1900s
showed, the structure of the city extension plans were critically important in shaping the form of new development. Through its planning
powers, and through the system of building bulk controls, particularly
the new 'stepped' building regulations, the city could, in principle,
though always subject in practice to the balance of local interests on the
council, prescribe alternative forms of housing to the *Mietskaserne*.

In Berlin the problem of coordinating planning for the city as a whole
was to become critical in the decade before the war. Within the Stadt
Berlin, Hobrecht's plan of 1862 still provided the overall framework of
control, although it had been modified by the introduction of new streets
in the areas lying between the major street system originally
proposed.[134] With growth in the 1870s and 1880s filling up the areas
planned by Hobrecht, the need for a larger framework of planning to
coordinate developments in suburban areas with those in the city became
more pressing during the 1890s.

At the turn of the century the planning authorities in the suburbs were
still the various *Gemeinden*, many of which were poorly equipped to
discharge the planning functions required of them by the *Fluchtliniengesetz* of 1875.[135] As the land companies started to buy up land in
the suburbs during the 1890s, the development plans in these areas
presented an oddly assorted appearance. Many were a product of designs
put forward by the land companies themselves. Carstenn and Quistorp
had laid out their developments in Lichterfelde in the late 1860s and
early 1870s as if they were the planning authority. In Schöneberg the
form of development was essentially a product of the collaboration
between the *Berliner Boden-Gesellschaft* and the *Gemeinde*, and here, in
the area around the Bayrisches Viertel, contemporaries applauded the
results. But in most other areas this system was less successful. The

results were frequently haphazard and uninspired: street patterns might be a product of original field boundaries cast, curiously but immutably, in the form of a plan backed with all the authority of the *Gemeinde*. In other areas development plans might simply be extended as occasion demanded in an opportunistic fashion with no view to the long-term needs of the community. Planning along these lines made it all too easy to forget the need for open space, schools, and other communal buildings which might simply be fitted into the plan at minimum cost with a fine disregard for the interests of the community.

Nor was the situation improved with the creation of the new municipalities like Schöneberg, Wilmersdorf and Neukölln around Berlin. The shifting balance of interests between the surrounding Vororte, Berlin and the Prussian state on issues such as incorporation were not stabilised by the creation of the new municipalities.[136] As the population of the Vororte expanded, conflict between the different municipalities increased in a variety of fields. Competition to attract growth, particularly middle-class developments with the tax income that they would bring to local coffers, naturally extended to competition to secure new lines of public transport and close links to the centre of the city. Given the rivalries between municipalities, boundary disputes between local authorities, such as that which arose over the development of the Tempelhofer Feld, could only be resolved by the Prussian state as the final authority. Overlaid across these local rivalries were also the planning and development decisions being taken by major state departments such as the War Office.[137] Often self-seeking and preoccupied with only short-term aims, these departments might be prepared to sell off major holdings of land, such as woodlands and forest, in order to balance their budgets, or to release funds for urgent projects elsewhere in the Reich with little thought for the needs of either the local community, or Berlin as a whole. To many planners, and housing, land and other reforming groups the increasingly difficult problems of rationally determining different land uses, such as open space, transport and housing could no longer be coherently resolved within the existing framework of planning. Some planning authority with metropolitan-wide powers was necessary, and just after the turn of the century a campaign to create such an authority began to gather momentum. The *Vereinigung Berliner Architekten* started pressing in 1905 for a general plan for the city and succeeded in 1910 in organising a competition for a structure plan for the whole city which attracted international attention.[138] Parallel to these initiatives there was also widespread support for city-wide planning through the popular campaign to preserve Berlin's forests and woodland. The campaign to develop a major system of forests surrounding the city on the pattern of Vienna's *Wald-und Wiesengürtel* had begun as early as 1892 and had led to strong popular support, evident in the forest and wood 'conservation days' held in 1908 and 1909. Bowing to pressure from these campaigns, the state finally agreed in 1911 to form a metropolitan-wide planning authority the *Zweckverband Grossberlin*, charged with responsibility for:[139] regulating public rail and tramways;

coordinating the drawing-up of development plans and the framing of any new building regulations within the metropolitan area; and acquiring and conserving areas of open space including forest, woodland and areas of open water. Despite the hopes that surrounded its creation, the *Zweckverband's* achievements before 1914 were disappointing. It achieved limited success in securing protection for some of the city's forest and woodland. But the larger tasks of rationalising the system of metropolitan transport, or the direction of new development, lay beyond its essentially consultative powers; only with the creation of *Gross-Berlin* in 1920 would a planning authority with sufficient power be established to undertake these tasks. Created without the planning powers of the individual authorities, the *Zweckverband* provides an illustration of the ambiguous attitude to planning of the Prussian state. It stands as a sad reflection of the desire to obtain the benefits of planning without a willingness to pay the political costs of doing so.

IV

The combination of the vested interests of property and government, which stood in the way of planning and the *Zweckverband* in Berlin, give some indication of the obstacles in the path of the campaign for housing reform before 1914. The difficulties faced by the reformers are well illustrated by the history of the campaign for Reich housing legislation, one of the central aims of the movement for housing reform from the turn of the century onwards. The first Reichstag debates on housing date from 1901, a time when the acute shortage of housing gave a certain urgency to the issue, but this first initiative was bought off by government's promise to prepare a separate housing bill for Prussia before proceeding further with national legislation. Published in 1904, the Bill attracted almost universal criticism: it fell far short of the reformers' aspirations on the one hand, and on the other, it went too far in limiting the freedom of property interests. With the shortage of housing largely forgotten by the mid 1900s, the need for legislation appeared less pressing and the Prussian government allowed the matter to lapse.

These delaying tactics appeared to pay off: there the issue rested until 1912 when the case for national legislation was again raised in the Reichstag. But again the rival interests of the Reich and Prussia served to frustrate this new initiative, and national legislation was called to a halt in order to allow the Prussian legislature to consider the matter first. By 1913 a new Prussian bill had been prepared, a watered-down version of the 1904 Bill. Predictably this was received with more, if still grudging, enthusiasm from property interests. For reformers it offered little comfort, most, like Jaeger, argued resignedly that it was better than nothing.[140] During the committee stages, the Bill was watered down still further; for Berger-Thimme the debates at this stage had little to do with questions of housing reform and were more a confrontation between representatives of the cities' interests and those of property.[141] Given the strength of property interests firmly entrenched behind the three-class voting system, it is small wonder that the balance of compromise should have leaned towards property. With the Reichstag's committee on housing legislation condemned to impotence by the Prussian initiative, progress on housing legislation for both the Reich and Prussia was negligible: the second reading of the Prussian Housing Bill was overtaken by the war.

The failure to secure national housing legislation exemplifies the difficulties and obstructions faced by reformers, but it should not distract attention from how much had been achieved by 1914: the non-profit sector had been greatly strengthened and expanded; provision had been made, through the WZS for example, to curb the profits made in land; the density of new housing was now subject to real control in a wide number of cities. These achievements depended on the initiatives taken by individual cities; in Frankfurt, in Ulm and a handful of other cities, an enormous amount had been achieved. But what of the vast majority of German cities? The example of Berlin suggests that on specific issues like the WZS, popular measures could be carried in the face of the opposition of the *Haus- und Grundbesitzer*. But without legislation to coerce the recalcitrant to action, the spur to a larger programme of reform was lacking, and the strength of property on city councils could further frustrate progress. The campaign for housing, or land reform had widespread support; even key members of government, Berlepsch, Possadowsky, Boetticher, Miquel, were sympathetic to the cause, but given the importance of Prussian within the Reich, and of property interests in Prussia, the hopes of a Reich housing law remained remote; not until after the revolution in 1918 would the reformers get their Housing Act.

Despite the achievements of the reformers, housing in cities like Berlin was to remain until the war, for the vast mass of the working class, as densely built, as heavily occupied, as poorly equipped and as expensive as it had been in the 1890s. Heinrich Zille's judgement of housing conditions in Berlin was as true in 1914 as it was twenty years before: 'You can kill a man with a tenement quite as easily as you can kill him with an axe'.

Notes

1. For a contemporary account of the housing market and the production of new housing in Berlin see E. Reich, *Der Wohnungsmarkt in Berlin von 1840–1910* (Munich and Leipzig, 1912); and V. Carthaus, *Zur Geschichte und Theorie der Grundstückskrisen im deutschen Grosstädten* (Jena, 1917).
2. For a discussion of the 'housing problem' and the various approaches to housing reform see N. Bullock and J.J. Read, *The Movement for Housing Reform in Germany and France: 1840–1914* (Cambridge, 1985); and D. Berger-Thimme, *Wohnungsfrage und Sozialstaat* (Frankfurt-am-Main, 1976).
3. W. Hegemann, *Das steinerne Berlin, die grösste Mietskasernenstadt der Welt* (Berlin, 1930).

4. The Verein für Sozialpolitik discussed the 'Wohnungsfrage' at length in both 1886 and again in 1900: the proceedings were published as *Der Verhandlungen der am 24 und 25 September 1886 am Frankfurt am Main abgehaltenen Generalversammlung des Vereins für Sozialpolitik*, in *Schriften des Vereins für Sozialpolitik*, Vol. 33 (Leipzig, 188-) 5–139; and *Neue Untersuchungen üeber die Wohnungsfrage in Deutschland und in Ausland*, Vols. 94–5, *Schriften des Vereins für Sozialpolitik* (Leipzig, 1901).

5. R. Eberstadt, *Handbuch des Wohnungswesens und der Wohnungsfrage*, (2nd ed., Jena, 1910).

6. Ibid. 70; the Grundbuch is a register of all charges on a property.

7. Hegemann, *Das steinerne Berlin*, see chapter XXII; A. Gut, *Das Berliner Wohnhaus des 17ten und 18ten Jahrhunderts* (2nd ed., Berlin, 1984).

8. Quoted in C. Bauer, *Modern Housing* (Boston and New York, 1934), 6.

9. This description by Beta is quoted in W. Strassmann and B. von Hasselberg, 'Anforderungen der öffentlichen Gesundheitspflege an die Baupolizei in Bezug auf die neue Stadtteile, Strassen und Häuser', *Vierteljahrschift für öffentliche Gesundheitspflege*, 7 (1875), 53.

10. For a discussion of the building regulations see D. Frick, 'Einfluss der Baugestze und Bauordnungen auf das Stadtbild', and F. Monke, 'Einflüsse der Baugeseze und Bauordnungen auf das Wohnhaus' in *Berlin und seine Bauten*, Part 4, Vol. A (Berlin, 1970), 41–57, 58–63.

11. For a discussion of the administrative structure of the Berlin Metropolitan area and its effect on development and its control see E. Escher, *Berlin und sein Umland*, Vol. 47 of the *Einzelveröffentlichungen der Historischen Kommission zu Berlin* (Berlin, 1985), especially chapter 4.

12. G. Assmann, *Grundrisse der städtischen Wohngebäuede mit Rücksicht auf die für Berlin geltende Bauordnungen* (Berlin, 1862).

13. Frick, 'Einfluss der Baugestze'; for a contemporary reaction see R. Baumeister, 'Die neue Berliner Baupolizeiordnungen', *Vierteljahrschrift für öffentliche Gesundhietspflege*, 19 (187-), 600–5.

14. See the tables in the annually published *Statistiches Handbuch der Stadt Berlin*; for a summary see J.F. Geist and K. Kürvers, *Das Berliner Mietshaus, 1862-1945* (Munich, 19-), 336–80.

15. For a discussion of the debate on the graduated building regulations see Bullock and Read, *Housing Reform*, 99–105.

16. Frick, 'Einfluss der Baugesetze', 46.

17. This difference is reflected in the rents charged for different dwellings see G. Müller, *Karte zur Berechnung des Grund- und Bodenwertes in Berlin* (Berlin, 1908), quoted in Geist and Kuervers, *Mietshaus*, 469.

18. See for example, T. Goecke, 'Das Arbeiter-Mietshaus, eine bautechnische-soziale Studie', *Deutsche Bauzeitung*, 14 (1890), 501–2, 508–10, 522–3.

19. Geist and Kuervers, *Mietshaus*, 272–81.

20. For a discussion of the provision of land for housing and the way in which this shaped the development of the city see P. Voigt, *Grundrente und Wohnungsfrage in Berlin und den Vororten* (Jena, 1901); for a contemporary account see, Escher, *Berlin*.

21. There is an extended contemporary literature on the land companies, for example: Carthaus, *Zur Geschichte*; Reich, *Der Wohnungsmarkt*; Voigt, *Grundrente*; however, much of the work of the land reformers is highly critical in tone: K. von Mangoldt, *Die städtische Bodenfrage, eine Untersuchung über Tatsachen, Ursachen und Abhilfe*, (Deutscher Verein für Wohnungsreform Heft 8, Göttingen, 1908); A. Damaschke, *Die*

Bodenreform, Grundsätzliches und Geschichtliches (Berlin, 1902).

22. G. Haberland, *Aus meinem Leben* (Berlin, 1931).
23. Voigt, *Grundrente*, 220–3.
24. Carthaus, *Zur Geschichte*, 172–3.
25. For example: S. Ascher, *Die Wohnungsmieten in Berlin von 1880–1910* (Berlin, 1914); L. Meinardus, *Die Technik des Terraingewerbes* (Berlin, 1913).
26. Carthaus, *Zur Geschichte*, 130–1.
27. Ibid., 108–24.
28. For example: Eberstadt, *Handbuch*, 110–11, 121–2.
29. Ibid., 107–20.
30. von Mangoldt, *Zur städtische Bodenfrage*; and Damaschke, *Bodenreform*.
31. This view is clearly reflected in Eberstadt's *Handbuch des Wohnungswesens*, a highly influential and, ostensibly, 'scientific' account of housing production, and even in the work of his students like Carthaus.
32. Haberland, *Aus meinem Leben*.
33. E. Wagon, *Die finanzielle Entwicklung der deutschen Aktiengesellschaft* (Jena, 1903).
34. Reich, *Der Wohnungsmarkt*, 16.
35. Carthaus, *Zur Geschichte*, 170–3.
36. A. Voigt, 'Bodenbesitzverhältnisse, das Bau- und Wohnungswesen in Berlin und seien Vororten', *Neue Untersuchungen*, Vol. 1, part 1, 339–64.
37. H. Höpker, *Denkschrift über die Verluste der Bauhandwerker und Bauliferanten bei Neubauten in Gross-Berlin in den Jahren 1901–1911* (Königliches Preusisches Statistisches Landesamt, Berlin, 1914), 87.
38. Ascher, *Wohnungsmieten*, 26–8.
39. G. Haberland, *Der Einfluss des Privatkapitals auf die bauliche Entwicklung Gross-Berlins* (Berlin, 1913), 41.
40. Eberstadt, *Handbuch*, 110–11, 121–2; Reich, *Der Wohnungsmarkt*, 19–29.
41. Ibid., pp. 21.
42. Eberstadt, *Handbuch*, 109–10, 120; Voigt, *Grundrente*, 145.
43. R. Goldschmidt, 'Wohnhäuser mit kleinen Wohnungen', *Deutsche Bauzeitung*, 25 (1891), 124.
44. Reich, *Der Wohnungsmarkt*, 24.
45. Goldschmidt, 'Wohnhaeuser', 125.
46. Ibid., 125.
47. Reich, *Der Wohnungsmarkt*, 26–7.
48. M. Ruşch, 'Die private Bautätigkeit', in C.J. Fuchs (ed.), *Die Wohnungs- und Siedlungsfrage nach dem Kriege* (Stuttgart, 1917).
49. Reich, *Der Wohnungsmarkt*, 24.
50. Ibid., 28; Ascher, *Wohnungsmieten*, 42–5, 49–51.
51. Carthaus, *Zur Geschichte*, 135.
52. Ascher, *Wohnungsmieten*, 42–5, Table 7.
53. See note 59.
54. Höpker, *Denkschrift*, 100–1.
55. Reich, *Der Wohnungsmarkt*, 30–1.
56. Ibid., 18.
57. Haberland, *Einfluss des Privatkapitals*, 4.
58. Ibid., 4–6.
59. The level of mortgaging of residential property was generally high: Voigt (*Bodenrente*, 207–13) found in the 1890s that it ranged from 88–92 per cent in Charlottenburg. Thus to remain profitable even small changes in the level

of interest rates had to be matched by correspondingly larger increases in rent.

60. Carthaus, *Zur Geschichte*, 85–9, 141–5, 231–3, Table XII; 228, Table VIII.
61. Ibid., 225, Table V.
62. There is an extended contemporary literature on the question of capital for the house-building industry. Reich lists nearly 50 titles on this subject alone: frequently cited are R. Eberstadt, *Der deutsche Kapitalmarkt* (Leipzig, 1901), and P. Voigt, *Hypothekenbanken und Beliehungsgrenzen* (Berlin, 1899). On the pathology of the capital market, see especially Carthaus, *Zur Geschichte*. For a contemporary summary see A.V. Desai, *Real Wages in Germany, 1870–1913* (Oxford, 1968).
63. Ibid., 74.
64. The rates for different areas and types of property in Berlin are discussed by Reich, *Der Wohnungsmarkt*, 47 and Ascher, *Wohnungsmieten*, 47–9.
65. Voigt, *Grundrente*, chapter 7, especially 205–13.
66. Carthaus, *Zur Geschichte*, 165–9, Reich, *Der Wohnungsmarket*, 109–18.
67. Ibid., 98–118.
68. A. Zimm, *Die Entwicklung des Industriestandortes Berlin: Tendenzen der geographischen Lokalisation bei den Berliner Industriezweigen von überörtlicher Bedeutung sowie die territoriale Stadtentwicklung bis 1945.* (Deutscher Verlag der Wissenschaft, Berlin (East), 1959); and F. Leyden, *Gross-Berlin, Geographie der Weltstadt* (Breslau, 1933).
69. Ibid., 84–92.
70. For a discussion of the development of the transport system and its impact on urban development see Voigt, *Grundrente*, 159–88; and D. Radicke, 'Die Entwicklung des öffentlichen Personnennahverkehrs in Berlin bis zur Gruendung der BVG' in K.K. Weber, P. Guettler, and D. Ahmadi (eds), *Anlagen und Bauten für den Verkehr (1) Städtischer Nahverkehr, Berlin und seine Bauten*, part 10, Vol. B (Berlin, 1979).
71. Zimm, *Entwicklung*, 61–8.
72. Escher, *Berlin*, 284–6.
73. Zimm, *Entwicklung*, 104–10; Voigt, *Grundrente*, 163–75.
74. Radicke, 'Personnennahverkehrs', 7–11.
75. Leyden, *Gross-Berlin*, 92–100.
76. The choice of city districts was based on census-data for 1910, 'Die verheirateten und die nicht verheirateten Selbsttätige nach Berufsgruppen, sozialer Stellung und Geschlecht in Standesamtsbezirken', *Statistisches Jahrbuch der Stadt Berlin*, Vol. 33 (Berlin, 1916), 32–47. The five districts chosen were those having over 40 per cent of the workforce described as 'Gesellen, Gehilfen, Lehrlinge und andere Hilfspersonen mit und ohne gewerbliche Ausbildung'.
77. The choice of suburban districts was based on the census data for 1900, 'Volkszählungs-Ergebnisse: Bevölkerung nach Beruf', *Statistisches Jahrbuch der Stadt Berlin*, Vol. 27, 38. Here the definition of 'Arbeiter' includes both those described as general labourer or 'Arbeiter ohne nähere Ausgabe' and 'Handel und Gewerbe, niedere Abhängige' or junior assistants in trade and crafts; the four districts were chosen as those with over 60 per cent of the workforce in these categories.
78. Eberstadt, *Handbuch*, 131–2.
79. Ibid., 131–8.
80. *Die Grundstücks-Aufnahme vom 15ten Oktober 1910 sowie die Wohnungs- und die Bevölkerungs- Aufnahme vom 1.12.1910 in der Stadt Berlin und*

44 Nachtbargemeiden, Berlin, 1913, Part 1, Heft 2, Table VI, 26–33.

81. The census for 1910 recorded the details of the availability of WCs, gas, electricity, central heating and even lifts for dwellings in each district: *Die Grundstücks-Aufnahme*, Part 1, Heft 1, Tables XI–XV.

82. This was clearly revealed in the 1925 census: 'Die Grundstücks- und Wohnungsaufnahme, sowie die Volks- Berufs- und Betriebszählung in Berlin im Jahre 1925', *Mitteilungen des statistischen Amts der Stadt Berlin* No. 5, Vol. 4, 1928.

83. A. Doerre, 'Entwicklung und Ergebnisse des sozialen Wohnungsbaues' in *Berlin und seine Bauten*, Vol. 4, Part A, 25.

84. I. Thienel, *Städtewachstum im Industrialisierungsprozess des 19ten Jahrhunderts, das Berliner Beispiel*, Vol. 39 of the *Veröffentlichungen der historischen Kommission zu Berlin* (Berlin, 1973), 212–15.

85. Lindemann, H. 'Wohnungstatistik' in Fuchs (ed.), *Neue Untersuchungen*, Vol. 1, Section 1, 353–60.

86. Thienel, *Städtewachstum*, 118–30; J. Ehmer, 'Wohnen ohne eigene Wohnung, zur sozialen Stellung von Untermietern und Bettgehern', in L. Niethammer (ed.), *Wohnen im Wandel, Beiträge zur Geschichte des Alltags in der bürgerlichen Gesellschaft* (Wuppertal, 1973), 132–50; F. Brüggemeier and L. Niethammer, 'Schlafgänger, Schnappskinos und schwerindustrielle Kolonie; Aspekte der Arbeiterwohnungsfrage im Ruhrgebiet vor dem ersten Weltkrieg', in J. Reulicke, J. and W. Weber (eds), *Fabrik, Familie, Feierabend; Beiträge zur Sozialgeschichte des Alltags im Industriezeitalter* (Wuppertal, 1978), 153–74.

87. There is a considerable volume of information on rents, but it exists in a variety of different forms which make comparisons between different data sets very difficult. Of most general use is the *Mietsteuerkataster* which gives an annual *Mietwert* per dwelling averaged over all dwellings for all districts; however disaggregated *Mietwert* values were occasionally published giving rents by districts, type and size of dwelling and the position of the dwelling within the block, see note 89. See also Reich, *Der Wohnungsmarkt*, 118–23, Table III; 126–8, Table IV; 132–3, Table XI; Ascher, *Wohnungsmieten*, 13–19, 118, Table XII.

88. *Statistiches Jahrbuch der Stadt Berlin*, Vol. 32 (Berlin, 1913), Section III, Table 9f, 302.

89. Voigt, 'Bodenbesitzverhältnisse', 222–3; Voigt, *Grundrente*, 201–5; and Eberstadt, *Handbuch*, 137; Müller, *Karto*, 469.

90. Reich, *Der Wohnungsmarkt*, 110–11, 117–18, 132, Table 11.

91. According to Schwabe's law, the lower the income, the higher the proportion paid in rent. The law was first formulated by Schwabe in 1868: H. Schwabe, *Berliner Gemeinde-Kalender und statistisches Jahrbuch* (Berlin, 1868).

92. An introduction to the surveys of income and expenditure carried out by the City's *Statistiches Amt* over a number of years is to be found in *Statistiches Jahrbuch der Stadt Berlin*, Vol. 27, 269; the results are summarised in *Stat J. Berlin*, Vol. 28, 200–4.

93. Ascher, *Wohnungsmieten*, 88–99; he also discusses very briefly similar studies in Cologne, Basel and Hanover.

94. R. Kuczynski, 'Miete und Einkommen', in *Wohnungsfrage nach dem Kriege*, 29–33.

95. Ibid., 33.

96. D. Englander, *Landlord and Tenant in Urban England, 1838–1918* (Oxford, 1983).

97. K. Flesch and Birndorfer, 'Das Mietrecht in Deutschland' in *Neue Unter-suchungen*, Vol. 1, Part 2, 271–33; and K. Flesch, 'Die Wohnungsfrage vom Standpunkt der Armenpflege', in *Schriften des deutschen Vereins für Armenpflege und Wohltätigkeit*, Vol. 6, 1888, 212–64.

98. A. Baron, *Der Haus- und Grundbesitzer in Preussens Städten, einst und jetzt* (Jena, 1911), 130–1.

99. M. Neefe, 'Hauptergebnisse der Wohnungsstatistik deutscher Grossstädte', in *Die Wohnungsnoth der ärmeren Klassen in deutschen Grossstädten und Vorschläge zu deren Abhülfe*, published as Vols. 30 and 31 of the *Schriften des Vereins für Sozialpolitik* (Leipzig, 1886), 194, Table XXXV.

100. Geist and Kuervers, *Berliner Mietshaus*, 416–33.

101. See the articles on *Mieterbewegung* and *Mieterrecht* in G. Albrecht, A. Gut, W. Luebbert, E. Weber, O. Wolz and B. Schwann (eds), *Handwörterbuch des Wohnungswesens* (Jena, 1930), 536–8.

102. For a discussion of the housing problem in Germany see Berger-Thimme, *Wohnungsfrage*; and Bullock and Read, *Housing Reform*.

103. Ibid., 52–70, 249–73.

104. E. Jaeger, *Die Wohnungsfrage* (Berlin, 1902), 269.

105. *Die Verbesserung der Wohnungen, Vorberichte, und Verhandlungen der Konferenz vom 25 und 26 April 1892*, published as Vol. 1 of *Schriften der Centralstelle für Arbeiter-Wohlfahrtseinrichtungen* (Berlin, 1892), 159–60.

106. M. Rusch, 'Die Förderung der Kleinwohnungsproduktion durch Riech, Staat und Gemeinden', in *Wohnungsfrage nach Kriege*, 313.

107. *Geschichte der gemeinnützigen Wohnungswirtschaft in Berlin* (Berlin, 1957).

108. Ibid., 50–7; for a detailed statement of the number of dwellings built by each organisation see the annual summary in the *Statistiches Jahrbuch der Stadt Berlin*.

109. 'Wohnungsfuersorge im Reiche und in den Bundesstaaten' in *Stenographische Berichte des deutschen Reichstages*, Session 1903/4, Appendices Vol. 4, No. 4; Rusch, 'Förderung der Kleinwohnungsproduk-tion', 312–19; D. Jacobi, *Die gemeinnützige Bautätigkeit in Deutschland: ihre kulturelle Bedeutung und die Grenzen ihrer Wirksamkeit*, published as Vol. 167 of G. Schmoller and M. Sering (eds), *Staats- und sozialwisseschaftliche Forschungen* (Munich and Leipzig, 1913), 47–52; 146–7, Table VII.

110. H. Albrecht, 'Die gemeinnützige Produktion', in *Wohnungsfrage nach dem Kriege*, 278–96.

111. See his almost dismissive treatment of the non-profit sector in *Handbuch*, 396–404.

112. Berger-Thimme, *Wohnungsfrage*, chapter V; Bullock and Read, *Housing Reform*, chapter 7.

113. Ibid., 98–105.

114. Damaschke, *Bodenreform*, 89.

115. The question of municipal finance was discussed at length by the Verein für Sozialpolitik, and its findings, *Gemeindefinanzen*, published as Vols. 126 and 127 of the *Scriften des Vereins für Sozialpolitik* (Leipzig, 1910). Of particular interest are E. Scholz, 'Das heutige Gemeindeabgabensystem in Preussen' in *Einzerlfragen der Finanzpolitik der Gemeinden* published as Vol. 1, Part 4, 281–318, of *Gemeindefinanzen*, and O. Landsberg, 'Die Entwicklung des Gemeindeabgabenwesens in den preussischen Städten unter der Herrschaft des Kommunalabgabengesetz mit besonderer

Berücksichtigung der östlichen Provinzen', in *Einzelfragen*, 1–42; for a convenient, if not very penetrating summary, see W.H. Dawson, *Municipal Life and Government in Germany* (London, 1912), 386–403.

116. Berger-Thimme, *Wohnungsfrage*, 101–7; A. Sutcliffe, *Towards the Planned City* (Oxford, 1981), 32, 35, 42.

117. Baron, *Der Haus- und Grundbesitzer*, 124; Dawson, *Municipal Life*, 425; however the level of rates on property in Berlin was just above the average for large Prussian cities.

118. W. Bangert, *Baupolitik und Stadtgestaltung in Frankfurt am Main: ein Beitrag zur Entwicklungs geschichte des deutschen Stadtebaues in den letzten 100 Jahren* (Würzburg, 1936), 59–60; Sutcliffe, *Planned City*, 37–8.

119. Dawson, *Municipal Life*, 394–402.

120. Bullock and Read, *Housing Reform*, 174–83; Berger-Thimme, *Wohnungsfrage*, 102–6.

121. Ibid., 101–2.

122. Dawson, *Municipal Life*, 392–99; Berger-Thimme, *Wohnungsfrage*, 101–7.

123. Ibid., pp. 429–34; much of Dawson's statistical information was drawn from the *Statistisches Jahrbuch deutscher Städte*, but for a general discussion of this subject see Landsberg, 'Entwicklung der Gemeindeabgabenwesens', especially 11–17.

124. Dawson, *Municipal Life*, 427.

125. Carthaus, *Zur Geschichte*, 81–3; Fischer, *Berlin*, 275–6.

126. Ibid., 311–13; Haberland's views are set out forcefully in a number of Haberland's polemical pamphlets, for example *Die Wertzuwachssteuer: Kritische Bermerkungen* (Berlin, 1910).

127. Baron, *Der Haus- und Grundbesitzer*, 137.

128. Dawson, *Municipal Life*, 123–40.

129. For a general discussion of Umlegung, see J. Stübben, *Der Städtebau* (published as the 9th half-volume of Durm (ed.), *Handbuch der Architektur*, 270–315); Berger-Thimme, *Wohnungsfrage*, 97–100; Bangert, *Baupolitik*, 55–8.

130. Ibid., 53–5.

131. Dawson, *Municipal Life*, 126.

132. Ibid., 292–308.

133. The relationship between the development of planning in Prussia and the construction of new housing is discussed in J. Rodriguez-Lorez and G. Fehl (eds), *Die Kleinwohnungsfrage: zu den Urspüngen des sozialen Wohnungsbaues in Europa* (Hamburg, 1988); for an English summary see Sutcliffe, *Towards the Planned City*, 19–35.

134. Geist and Kuervers, *Mietshaus*, 165–9.

135. Fischer, *Berlin*, 255–82.

136. Ibid., 276–82.

137. See particularly the example of the development of the Tempelhofer Feld by the Militaerfiskus, ibid. 301–5.

138. Ibid., 313–20; and *Geschichte der gemeinnützigen Wohnungswirtschaft*, 60–4.

139. Fischer, *Berlin*, 318.

140. E. Jaeger, 'Zur Beurteilung des preussischen Wohnungsgesetzentwurfs, *Zeitschrift für Wohnungswesen*, 11 (1912–3), 169–71.

141. Berger-Thimme, *Wohnungsfrage*, 239–42.

7 Rows and tenements: American cities, 1880—1914[1]

M.J. Daunton

Housing in American cities covered the whole range of European experience, from New York (which paralleled the *Mietskasernen* of Berlin or the tenements of Glasgow), to the single-family row houses of Baltimore or Philadelphia (which were similar to the terraces of London). Between the two extremes stood apartments in small blocks, akin to the Tyneside flats of the north-east of England, which were found in Chicago and Boston. There was no single American architectural idiom for working-class housing; and neither was there a single legal system or pattern of landlord–tenant relations. It is impossible to speak of American urban housing in a monolithic way, and the aim of this chapter is to provide some sense of the diversity which existed in the major cities.[2]

I

The divergence of architectural form may be observed in the census statistics showing the number of families who resided in buildings containing various numbers of families. In New York, 50.2 per cent of families were living in buildings which contained six or more families; in Philadelphia, the proportion was only 1.1 per cent. (See Table 7.1.)

There was a continuum of housing styles, with the 'row' houses of Philadelphia and Baltimore standing closest to the typical English house-style: the single-family, terraced house constructed from brick. (See Figures 7.1 and 7.2.) The most frequent type of working-class housing in Philadelphia had six rooms. The ground floor was usually divided into three rooms: a parlour which faced the street; a dining room in the middle of the house, with a corner window opening onto a passage formed by narrowing the kitchen; and a kitchen at the rear, which looked on to the passage and the garden. It was also common practice to erect a shed or summer kitchen at the back of the house, which would remove the need to cook in the house during hot weather. Upstairs there

Table 7.1 Percentage of families in properties containing various numbers of families, 1900

	Number of families per property				
	1	2	3–5	6–9	10+
New York	17.5	11.5	20.7	21.9	28.3
Chicago	29.0	28.6	32.7	7.5	2.2
Boston	32.2	26.5	34.0	5.0	2.3
St Louis	41.4	40.3	15.8	2.1	0.4
Pittsburg	64.3	24.6	9.8	1.0	0.2
Baltimore	72.6	20.0	6.7	0.5	0.2
Detroit	74.9	18.2	6.2	0.4	0.2
Philadelphia	84.6	9.6	4.8	0.9	0.2

Source: Twelfth Census of the United States, 1900, Volume II, Part II, Table 102

were three bedrooms over the ground floor rooms, usually with a bathroom and water-closet adjoining the front bedroom. A distinctive feature at the back of the house was the 'bay extension' on the upper floor: the building regulations permitted the construction of a bay window four feet deep, and this provided either an extension to the rear bedroom, or a small bathroom or bedroom in its own right. A cellar was also usually provided, with a storeroom for fuel and a heater that supplied warm air to the house.[3] A similar architectural form was found in Baltimore: a six-roomed house, with either three rooms on each of two storeys or two rooms on three storeys.[4]

A number of American cities had, by the early twentieth century, adopted flats in small blocks. At Boston, for example, the predominant working-class house form was the three-family or 'triple decker'. The type which was being built in the early years of the twentieth century was described by the Board of Trade:

Each dwelling is self contained, generally with a separate entrance from a public hall and stairway in front, and often with a similar entrance from a small staircase in the rear . . . [A] fairly representative dwelling with five rooms and a bathroom would contain a small private hallway, leading on the one side into the parlour, bedroom and dining room, the last with its window opening on to an open 'piazza' or balcony—one of the most desirable features of these houses; on the other side the private hall way leads into the second bedroom and the bathroom, and at the end is the door, leading to the kitchen, at the other side of which is the entrance from the back public stairway.[5]

Other cities adopted variants of this house form. In Pittsburgh, for example, the housing stock consisted of both single-family dwellings of four to six rooms, occupied by the better-paid workers of American or German descent, and two-family houses which were largely occupied by Italians and Eastern Europeans who were employed in the less skilled jobs in the steel works.[6] In St Louis, the two-family house was typical

Ground floor

alley

First floor

alley

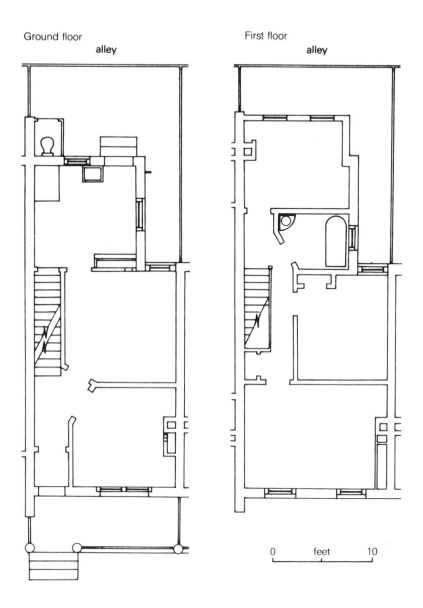

0   feet   10

Figure 7.1 Plan of Philadelphia mechanics' homes, from H.L. Parrish, *One Million People in Small Houses* (Philadelphia, 1911), 7.

of working-class accommodation: a three-roomed flat in a brick building with two floors.[7] In Chicago, flats of four rooms predominated, in detached buildings of two back-to-back houses on two or three floors (Figure 7.3). A block would contain between four and six apartments.

Figure 7.2 Baltimore, row houses on the 2600 block of Wilkens Avenue, photographed in 1952 (courtesy of the A. Aubrey Bodine Collection, The Peale Museum, Baltimore).

Figure 7.3 Rear view of tenements in Chicago, at Sibly and Taylor streets, photographed in 1934 (courtesy of Chicago Historical Society).

The bye-laws required that each unit should have a separate back and front entrance, which was achieved in the case of the back-to-back properties by one entrance in the middle of the side, which gave access to the front and rear flats; the second entrance was provided at the front to give access to the front property with external stairs at the back giving access to the rear flats. All the rooms within the flats opened into one another, and they could therefore be heated by one stove. The occupants shared an unpaved yard at the rear, and in the older properties a closet was used in common by two or three families. Flats with five or six rooms, which were occupied by skilled workers, were not usually built back-to-back, and were detached with side entrances and external stair-cases at the rear.[8]

At the other extreme from the row houses of Philadelphia and Baltimore was the tenement house, which dominated above all in New York City. The tenements in New York went through three stages. The first was the double-fronted dwelling, which had two sets of apartments on each floor, consisting of four rooms running from the street to the yard; since the building was constructed right up to the side lot line, the two rooms in the middle of the apartment had no direct light. At the rear of the plot, another block of tenements might be constructed, containing two sets of two rooms on each floor. The front and rear blocks might merge to form one continuous building, the so-called 'railroad tenements', which exacerbated the problems of light and ventilation. The next stage of tenement house design was to build on the full length of the plot, with a narrow shaft for air and light on both sides of the building. This shaft was an indentation about 28 inches wide running for 50 to 60 feet along the side of the block, producing the notorious 'dumb-bell' tenement, which the Board of Trade felt was 'probably one of the worst types of dwelling that has ever been designed and constructed on a large scale in modern urban communities'. The usual arrangement was to have four tenements on a floor, with two units of four rooms on the front and two units of three rooms at the rear. Bathrooms were not usually provided, and water closets were located in the hallway, and shared between two families.

The third form may be dated from the new regulations of 1901. These required separate sanitation to be provided within each apartment, with the intention of increasing the level of privacy within tenement blocks. The other main feature was the abolition of the air shaft, which was too narrow to be effective in providing fresh air and light, and which instead channelled smells and noise between apartments. The narrowness of the air shaft also failed to guarantee the privacy of families whose apartments opened on to it. This was a great concern of the housing reformers, and one aim of the regulations of 1901 was to create interior courts that could act as 'buffers' between separate units, so that space in the tenements could be 'privatised'. The tenement block was now to consist of six apartments grouped around a larger central court, and within the individual apartment no bedroom was to provide access to another room (See Figure 7.4). The outcome 'was to achieve "privatisation" of the

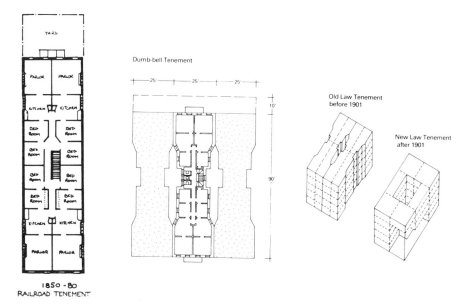

Figure 7.4 Plan of New York railroad tenement 1850–80, dumb-bell tenement 1879–1901, and new law tenement after 1901 (the second and third reproduced with permission from F.D. Case, 'Hidden social agendas and housing standards', *Housing and Society* VIII (1981).

dwelling unit, which protected not only the privacy of family from family but individual family member from individual family member'. The great disadvantage of tenement house life in comparison with self-contained houses was, according to contemporary critics, that it was not possible 'to obtain all necessary privacy for true home life and personal development'. The ambition was to bring tenements as nearly as possible in line with this domestic ideal.[9]

The conception of the middle-class house underwent change, and this influenced the ideals of the middle-class reformers towards the working-class housing problem, as well as establishing a pattern to which the better-paid workers could aspire. The form of the middle-class house in the postbellum era was modified in order to create a clear separation of public and private aspects of life. Women and children would have their separate spheres within the house, with each member of the family having a private room on the first floor; the family members would interact in the dining room, back parlour and on the porch; visitors would be confined to the front parlour. The family, starting in the middle class, became more private, 'characterised by relatively limited access and greater control over the observability of behavior'. This was true not only of the internal lay-out of the individual house, but also of the wider use of space within the city, for the middle-class house in the suburb may be seen as a retreat from the disorder of the inner city into the 'intimate, isolated family'. The middle-class home, argues Richard Sennett, had by the end of the nineteenth century 'become the focus for a new kind of intense family life'.[10]

These middle-class expectations and norms could collide with the practices of many working-class families in the cities who might still live in 'malleable households' which included non-family lodgers. The working-class family in the nineteenth century was 'an accommodating and flexible institution', and lodgers were a major way in which its 'biologically-defined limits were breached'. This strategy made economic sense, and was associated with the life-cycles both of the lodgers and of the families which took them into their households. It enabled the wife to earn income from work within the home; it stabilised the family income over periods of unemployment and sickness; it equalised income over the life cycle as lodgers were moved into rooms vacated by children; it gave widows and single women in middle and old age an opportunity to maintain their independent household; it provided accommodation for single men and women arriving in cities. But this was interpreted by many social reformers in a different way, for they saw lodgers as a threat, undermining privacy and the isolation of the family. Veiller referred to the 'lodger evil', and Aronovici deplored 'this widespread practice of exposing the private life of the heads of the family and that of the young girls to the presence of men in no way connected by blood relationships with the members of the household'. The practice seemed to preclude a true sense of home life and the virtues of the private family. In fact, lodgers were more likely to provide a means of *maintaining* the family against hardships, and 'reformers who bewailed the imminent breakup of the family had displaced their concern from the hardness of life inherent in the industrial system to an institution that not only was a sensible response to industrialization but, in cushioning the shock of urban life for newcomers, was decidedly humane'. This was realised by Robert Coit Chapin in his study of working-class families in New York: he concluded that a major incentive for taking in lodgers was to raise the family income in order to obtain better housing, in a way which allowed the wife and children to stay at home. There was agreement that the private family was the proper form to which society should conform: writers such as Coit were more confident that working-class families had such an aspiration, and were adopting a rational strategy towards its achievement.[11]

Certainly the pessimists and the optimists were agreed about the type of society they wanted, which they associated with a particular architectural form. This perception dominated the debate over the housing problem, which was essentially cast in terms of the avoidance of the tenement house which was considered to be physically inappropriate for the privatised family. The single-family houses of Philadelphia or Baltimore, with their high level of privacy and specialisation of function, were the ideal to which reformers hoped that American society would conform. It was the fear of the spread of tenements which was to dominate the American housing debate in the late nineteenth and early twentieth century, rather than the process of slum clearance which was a feature of the debate in British cities. Tenements were perceived as unAmerican, an alien European infection which should be controlled and contained. Lawrence Veiller, the prophet of tenement house regulation, was clear in 1910: 'the normal method of housing the working population in our cities is in small houses, each house occupied by a separate family, often with a small bit of land, with privacy for all, and with a secure sense of individuality and opportunity for real domestic life'.[12] 'The general effect of tenement-house life', argued T.J. Jones in 1904, 'is to retard the assimilation of immigrants to American ways . . . Crowded together into adjacent houses, the necessity and wisdom of learning the English language, and their rights as American citizens, dawn upon them very slowly'.[13] The report to the Tenement House Commission of Louisville in 1909 commented

The separateness, the sanctities, the privacies of home life can hardly be said to exist in the more crowded tenements . . . It is true that many cities in Germany, England, Scotland, and France show a large percentage of one-room apartments, but we do not want to Europeanize our American standards. We are going up, not down; forward to completer, sweeter living, not backward to a reproduction of the sordid squalor of swarming London slums.[14]

The answer seemed to be regulation: housing conditions were important determinants of efficiency, and should be preserved by stricter building codes, the enforcement of sanitary standards, and the 'socialisation' of rent collecting by introducing the techniques of Octavia Hill.[15]

This specification of the housing problem as the tenement problem meant that there was an emphasis upon a cultural explanation rather than a feeling that the private housing market had failed. The need, so it seemed, was to preserve what had been achieved. This did not entail the destruction of 'plague spots' as in London or Glasgow by slum clearance programmes. Rather, to vary the medical metaphor, the need was to inoculate society against the infection of the tenement, by encouraging the construction of owner-occupied single-family dwellings.

II

The ideal of housing reformers was not only that American cities should be dominated by single-family houses: they should also be owned by their occupiers. There was some connection between architectural form and the nature of ownership, for a fairly high correlation has been found between the proportion of tenancies in a city and the extent to which the number of families exceeded the number of dwellings. The main exceptions were cities in the south, where single family houses and tenancies were found together. Architectural form was not, however, the

Table 7.2 Percentage of private families renting and owning their residence, 1900

	Owner-occupied	Rented	Not known
New York	11.8	85.4	2.8
Boston	18.0	77.7	4.3
Philadelphia	21.1	74.5	4.3
St Louis	22.1	75.1	2.8
Chicago	24.4	73.0	2.5
Baltimore	25.9	67.0	7.1
Pittsburg	26.3	70.5	3.2
Detroit	37.7	58.8	3.5

Source: Twelfth Census of the United States, Volume II, Part II, Table 107

only factor: recent growth, the permanence of employment, and the proportion of young families were also significant. The tax system, it has also been argued, had an impact for there was some correlation between high property taxes and multi-family housing. A major part of local taxation was borne by real estate, falling disproportionately upon smaller houses. This, it was argued, discouraged owner-occupation. In the case of rental property, the incidence of taxes could be shifted to the tenant at least during downturns in the building cycle when the market was tight, so that it did not discourage investment ownership; the owner-occupier had to bear the burden of taxes and was less mobile. The argument might be exaggerated, for the level of property taxes and multi-family dwellings might both be related to other aspects of the socio-economic structure of the city, but it did allow housing reformers to argue that one way of encouraging home ownership was the correction of the bias within the property tax, and the greater use of a progressive income tax.[16] (See Table. 7.2.)

Reformers also focused their attention upon the methods by which occupiers might purchase their homes, so that the process might become easier for people with small means. In particular, they looked towards the building and loan associations. Tenements were perceived as the threat to American culture; building and loan associations were seen as the bastion of single-family homes, owned by their proud and self-reliant residents. When G.W.W. Hanger reported to the Bureau of Labor in 1904, he was clear about the origins of the BLAs: the first was started in Frankford, Pennsylvania, in 1831, 'doubtless due to the efforts of English workmen . . . who had brought with them a knowledge of building societies of the mother country'. Others argued for German origins, claiming that the first BLA was the Amerikanischer Darlehen und Bauverein, started in Philadelphia in 1846.[17] The precise date and the exact ethnic origin do not matter a great deal; what is clear is that the American BLAs diverged from the European pattern in a major way in the course of the nineteenth century.

The BLAs were, claimed Hanger, 'the most important and successful example of co-operation in the United States', and no other institution 'has contributed more largely than have building and loan associations to the material welfare of that portion of our citizens on a daily wage'.[18] A BLA, argued Edmund Wrigley, 'is perfectly democratic, admitting each individual corporator or member to a full, free and unrestricted voice in the creation and management of Associations . . ., and a constant over-sight of its operations and affairs'. He drew a contrast with savings banks which involved 'a mere mechanical act' of depositing money, and whose management had 'a tendency to aristocracy'.[19] Much the same might have been said of the English building societies, which were largely in the hands of the middle classes, and were non-participatory. There is an important distinction in the role of BLAs and building societies in the working-class economies of the two countries. The working class in England preferred contingency insurance, putting small sums into friendly societies which offered sick pay in the eventuality of ill-health. There was less inclination to save sums of money in order to provide security for the family, or to accumulate capital as a means of social mobility. The working-class institutions in America differed. The nearest equivalent to the friendly societies were the fraternal societies. Both were run by the members on principles of mutuality and ritual; yet the fraternal societies provided life insurance which gave a sizeable lump sum, rather than sick pay, as needed. The building societies, which offered the chance to accumulate capital, accorded less well with the ethic of the working class in English cities than did the building and loan associations in American cities.[20]

By the First World War, the BLAs fell into two main categories: the Pennsylvania or serial plan; and the permanent plan which was further refined as the Dayton or Ohio plan.[21] The serial plan was more obviously based on mutuality than the Dayton plan which was criticised by many within the BLAs for a tendency towards a bureaucratic and mechanical style of operation. The Pennsylvania plan formed the starting point for the movement in the United States. The number of shares in BLAs in Pennsylvania was limited to 500 until 1851, when it was increased to 2,500, with a further increase to 5,000 in 1874. Each share had a nominal value of $200, the member subscribing $1 a month. The money received by the BLA was put up to auction, and went to the member who was willing to offer the largest premium. Each share was entitled to a loan of $200, but a member might be willing to accept, say, $120 for the nominal loan of $200. The shareholder would continue to pay the monthly dues, and interest on the nominal amount of . $200 which had been borrowed. The loan was secured by house property which was inspected, although not built, by the BLA. The profits made were assigned to the shares, and when the profits and the monthly dues had reached the face-value of $200 per share, the series had come to maturity. The law in Pennsylvania allowed a BLA to obtain a perpetual charter, so that successive series of shares could be issued. Even if the existing series had not been fully subscribed, it made sense to issue a new series, for it was unlikely, once a series of shares had been offered for more than a few months, that any investor could afford to pay the back dues.[22]

The Pennsylvania system, so it was claimed, had advantages for working men:

The Association, being in receipt of part of the principal of its loans in advance in all cases, and having a proportion of it retuned to it every month, and receiving its interest monthly, can make its loans upon securities with a much narrower margin than is prudent for other classes of capitalist.[23]

Other commercial lenders would usually only make loans to the extent of 50 per cent of the value of a property, whereas BLAs would go almost to the full value. 'This *narrowness of margin*', it was claimed, 'is the peculiar advantage proffered by Building Associations to borrowers'.[24] The system of payment of interest and principal in small, fixed, monthly sums was also an advantage to working men, for commercial loans were not amortised. The interest was paid at long intervals and the principal was returned in a lump sum at the end of the loan, which meant that some arrangement had to be made to save the money required to repay the loan. This, it was pointed out, 'requires an ability for financiering and economizing not possessed by the million.'[25] The system of BLAs therefore fitted with the working-class economy, although many observers were quick to point to a disadvantage: interest rates were high.

Such middle-class complaints missed the point. Most working-class borrowers did not have the luxury of comparing rates, for they simply could not turn to the commercial loan market. The BLAs were making loans available which could not be obtained elsewhere.[26] It should be remembered, however, that many shareholders did not wish to obtain loans. A shareholder in a series which took nine years to reach maturity would pay $1 a month or a total of $108, for which he would obtain a sum of $200. This was a better rate than could be obtained from a savings bank.[27] There was, therefore, some justice in the criticism of the serial plan as it had developed in the late nineteenth century:

The early founders of the institutions reasoned that the bonuses which the borrowers paid on loans returned to them as dividends on their stock, and therefore they could suffer no prejudice by paying a bonus. This was true if all the members were borrowers, but true only in those circumstances. The error which had become fatal to the beneficent purpose of the institution was, that the principle was supposed to hold equally good in cases where a portion of the members of the institution were accumulators.[28]

However, it would appear that the members, whether borrowers or accumulators, were predominantly working class. A Department of Labor survey of 909 BLAs with 159,223 shareholders concluded that 70 per cent were working people.[29]

The permanent BLAs abandoned the system of separate series of shares, and simply admitted new members at any time, without back payment. The Dayton or Ohio plan was an extension of this: not only was membership possible at any time, but any sum could be paid whenever the members wished. This was a movement away from the basic feature of the BLA as it had developed in Pennsylvania—the payment of fixed sums at fixed intervals—and the result was to increase the amount of administration involved.[30] The proponents of the serial plan stressed the simplicity of book-keeping and the avoidance of heavy costs. The permanent plan, it was feared, would create a more bureaucratic organisation and 'would throw the enterprise on to the monopolist, the speculator and the place hunter . . . and deprive the scheme of the benefit of any co-operative or mutual feature'.[31] The permanent BLAs were, according to the supporters of the serial plan, becoming more like savings banks or commercial financial institutions. The US League of Local Building and Loan Associations was the bastion of the serial plan BLAs against the permanent plan. 'The Ohio Association', it was remarked, 'aims to become a financial institution rather than a neighbourhood club'.[32] This was considered to be dangerous. 'A building association can no more afford to drift away from the time-honored idea of restriction as to locality than it can afford to abandon the principles of equity, mutuality and conservatism'.[33] It was feared that as members ceased to play an active part in the administration of the permanent plan BLAs, they would be viewed simply as money-making institutions and would be taken over by professional financiers.

The US League sounded the alarm:

They must shake off all financiering schemes. They must return to the sound foundation of the past. They must be composed of a few friends and neighbors. They must be managed without expense. The members should reserve control. They should be limited by law to a small capital and to restricted neighborhoods.[34]

The motto of the US League was 'The American Home, the Safeguard of American Liberties', and membership of the serial plan building association was assumed to be linked with a particular set of social and political attitudes. One was the stress upon small-scale, local, personal relationships which, it was argued, were possible within the framework of the serial plan:

It tends to keep the work divided up and distributed among neighborhoods and small communities of the people, who avail themselves of the advantages it affords them . . . The capital accumulated is thus prevented from increasing to an amount that would be unmanageable and perhaps dangerous in the hands of even the most skilled financier.[35]

The local BLAs were welcomed as a counter to monopolies and syndicates; it was hoped that the BLAs 'will inevitably, more and more, draw the masses of population into co-operative organizations for purposes of self-defence and financial security and advancement'.[36]

Indeed, the local BLAs had similarities with the views of various categories of Progressive thought. The stress upon neighbourhood complemented the belief of Jane Addams or Frederic Howe that urban life should be redeemed through the creation of community. Other

Progressives expressed opposition to monopolies and finance capitalism; or were concerned for the reformation of local government. The BLAs could connect with these differing strands of Progressivism. The US League stressed that the BLAs were an antidote not only to radicalism but also to boss politics. 'Possibly its greatest mission is to reform taxation and to restore prudent and economic government'.[37] The purchase of a home through the agency of a BLA:

... localizes him and enlists him in the honest administration of public affairs, in the cause of industry, of law and order, in good citizenship, and in sound and conservative government. It adds to his pride of locality, endears him to his community and quickens his activities in all things that tend to the advancement and upbuilding of his neighbourhood.[38]

It was also claimed that the BLAs were associated with a socially desirable architectural form—self-contained family row houses rather than multi-occupied tenements in which 'privacy and self-respect are lost, decency often outraged and the poisonous influence of the worst inmates, adult or youthful, is intensified, and innocent lives are offered victims to its foul corruption'.[39] Together these points comprised a formidable ideological underpinning for the local BLAs, which were given a central role in the salvation of American society.

Their significance was in reality exaggerated. Many of the BLAs were utilised by builders. In Baltimore, for example, the German American Building Association was frequently used by the largest house-builders in order to finance their operations, and they were active as organisers and officers.[40] There was, indeed, no clear correlation between the percentage of families owning their houses in 1890, and the proportion of families borrowing from BLAs.[41] This may be explained by the existence of another and, at least in some cities, more significant route to home ownership: self-build. A study of Detroit has suggested that there were two housing markets. The first, formal, market was run by professionals in order to produce more expensive houses. Realtors sold vacant land and arranged mortgages through commercial channels. The few BLAs in the city were part of this formal market, linked to the banks and the property developers. The second, informal, market did not rely upon financing in the same way. There were no local BLAs on the model of Philadelphia to finance the purchase of a speculative row house. Rather, the pattern was to build new, detached houses on individual lots by using the labour of family and friends.[42]

The construction of a timber, balloon-frame house was a fairly simple exercise which did not need specialised skills. The balloon frame was largely prefabricated, and required nailing rather than complicated carpentry. The cost of timber components fell or remained stable in the later nineteenth century. The labour cost of making 50 pairs of pine sash windows, for example, fell from $60 in 1858–59 when they were made by hand, to $9 in 1896 when they were made by machine. Similarly, plastering was simplified by the replacement of laths by metal mesh in the 1890s. The construction cost index fell from 95.3 in 1870 to 69.8 in

Figure 7.5 Self-build house in Milwaukee, erected in 1892 by Batholomew Koperski, a railroad car inspector (from C.E. Clark, Jr, *The American Family Home, 1800–1960*, Copyright University of North Carolina Press, Chapel Hill, 1986. Reprinted by permission).

1895, from when it started to rise to 100.9 in 1915. The resulting pressure upon home ownership after 1900 perhaps helps to explain the concern about apartments and the desire to protect home ownership and the detached home.[43] However, the simplification of building and low costs in the late nineteenth century did mean that it was possible to invest the labour of family and friends to become a home-owner. John Kreft, a Polish day labourer who worked for the Detroit Brewery Co. was able to build a one-and-a-half storey frame house in 1887 at a cost of $340, parts of which he sub-let to other families. In 1896 63 per cent of employees of the street railways in Detroit who were home-owners did not have any outstanding debt, which indicates a high incidence of self-build. (See Figure 7.5.) The alternative was to contract with a builder, who would supply a loan, rather than to rely upon formal financial markets. Charles Manzelman, a German broom-maker, had a house built in 1892 by a German carpenter who lived in the neighbourhood. In 1896, 67 per cent of the street railway employees who did have a loan to buy a house were in debt to builders. The result was that owner-occupation in Detroit was as high amongst the unskilled working class as in white-collar occupations: in 1900, 34.0 per cent of adult heads of household in unskilled jobs were owner-occupiers, 34.9 per cent of skilled, 32.8 per cent of low status white-collar and 36.5 per cent of high-status white collar. The divergence was less by class or occupation than by ethnicity. In 1894, for example, 21.8 per cent of native workers on the railroads in Detroit were owner occupiers, compared with 64.5 per cent of those born in Germany.[44]

Whether owner-occupation was an avenue to social mobility or a dead end is doubtful. It has indeed been suggested that renters had greater prospects of social mobility, and that 'home ownership appears to have been of little help to either the occupational or total wealth mobility of owners or of their sons, and tended to tie up a large proportion of people's assets in an investment inferior to most'.[45] This claim might be true when a family incurred large loans which might entail pressure upon the household economy, and perhaps oblige children to leave school in order to enter the labour market. In the case of self-build, home ownership was less likely to have been a burden, for families could invest their own labour—what has been termed their 'sweat equity'—when the opportunity for any other kind of accumulation was remote. Kreft, for example, remained a day labourer but did have a capital asset which produced a cash income by sub-letting, making a significant contribution to the household economy.[46]

Despite the exaggeration of the contribution of the BLAs to working-class home ownership, they were important in establishing the basis for later housing policies designed to maintain the level of owner-occupation and the ascendancy of the self-contained home. In 1894, the principle of preferential tax treatment for BLAs was accepted when they were excluded from the 2 per cent tax on the net income of corporations. The BLAs' practice of offering amortised loans for a high proportion of the valuation of a house was to be a leading feature of housing reform:

[T]he relatively successful 100-year track record of the Philadelphia building and loan association in promoting homeownership served as a model for the creation of the Federal Home Loan Bank System and the FHA in the 1930s . . . By introducing the mutual mortgage insurance system, FHA revolutionized housing finance and brought the principles of long-term amortization of mortgage loans, and high loan-to-value ratios, both drawn from the building and loan associations, into the world of commercial banks, life insurance companies, mutual savings banks, and mortgage companies.[47]

These commercial mortgages were not amortised, that is the principal was not paid off over the term of the loan; it was usual for the loan to be repaid in a lump sum. This was, to many housing reformers, a severe drawback with the private mortgage market, and comparison was drawn with the BLAs which 'alone have pioneered the amortized, monthly payment mortgage which the history of home financing has proved to be more desirable than any other plan for the use and repayment of real estate mortgage credit'. The periodic repayment of the loan made for greater security and the ability to lend a higher proportion of the value of the house. Long-term amortised loans were perceived as a major encouragement to owner-occupation, avoiding the problem of the second mortgage which was seen to be a major hindrance. The BLAs did not necessarily welcome this emulation, for imitation is not only flattering; it is also a threat to survival.[48]

The debate over housing in American cities started from the position that the single family home was to be preserved and owner-occupation encouraged. There was not the sense, as there was in many European cities, that the private market had somehow failed; rather, it was believed that the market was working in a satisfactory manner if only certain 'unAmerican' incursions could be kept at bay. Where American cities differed from their British counterparts was in the absence of any obvious failure of the free market to supply housing before the First World War. The building industry was, as in Britain, highly cyclical; but there was in Britain a suggestion that by the early twentieth century there was a more permanent structural failure as well as a cyclical downturn. In North America, this was not a serious area of debate. Building costs had started to rise after about 1900, but not enough to suggest a collapse of profitability such as threatened the housing market in London, where the rising cost of building was compounded by a mounting burden of local taxation. Although there were problems in New York City which led to rent strikes, there was no sense that the private property market had failed. The building cycle nationally peaked around 1890, falling to a trough around 1900, and then moving to a peak from 1905 to 1909. In national terms, the threat to single-family dwellings was still slight enough to suggest that the development of tenements was a minor blemish to be regulated rather than the symptom of a basic malaise in the housing market. In 1900, single family dwellings accounted for 65.0 per cent of starts, two-family dwellings 16.3 per cent and dwellings for three or more families 18.6 per cent; in 1910, the proportions were 64.8, 14.8 and 20.3 per cent.[49] There was also confidence that owner-occupation was increasing its share of the housing stock in many cities, so that there was little sense of a deep-seated crisis in the housing market. The proportion of housing stock in owner-occupation rose from 22.8 per cent to 26.6 per cent in Philadelphia between 1890 and 1910, and from 20.5 to 25.0 per cent in St Louis. There was, it is true, a slight fall in some cities, such as Chicago and Boston, but the result was not to call the tenure into question so much as to generate support for home-ownership which seemed even more necessary to Americanise the urban population.[50] The housing problem was perceived as the challenge of tenements to the predominantly single-family housing of American cities, a threat which was defined in cultural rather than economic terms.

III

The concern so far has been to explain the development of the debate over policy, which took a different path in Europe. The emphasis has been upon the cultural values associated with tenements versus single-family houses, and with tenancies versus home ownership. It is important, however, not to lose sight of the realities which lay below these ideals. What was the nature of the development process which led to the single-family homes of Philadelphia or Baltimore, and the tenements of New York? It should also be remembered that, although owner-occupation was idealised, the majority of the population were tenants rather than owners. The social relationships which arose from the ownership and management of house property could play a significant role in the life of cities.

A commonplace in the debate on the housing problem in Britain was to lay the blame for bad housing conditions upon the landowner. The land market, it was claimed by radical critics, was imperfect because of the high level of concentration of ownership which was blamed upon the operation of primogeniture and entail. The result, they believed, was that the large, aristocratic or institutional landowners could 'hoard' land, holding it off the market in order to obtain high prices; they might also be able to force the adoption of short leases which allowed them to repossess at the end of the term both the land and the property erected upon it, without compensation. In this debate, a comparison was drawn with the United States where—so it was claimed—the abolition of primogeniture and entail meant that a free land market existed. American land, S.B. Warner has remarked, was

> . . . free to reflect the economic market and to respond to the social and political barometer of contemporary events. No hindrance has been imposed by the existence of giant tracts of land left tied up in enduring legal restrictions . . . Land could be leased, bought, sold and bequeathed with great simplicity . . . Thus the nation emerged from the Revolution and the formation of the Union with the freest land system anywhere in the world.[51]

How valid is this broad contrast between Britain and the United States, and how far may the nature of the land market explain the pattern of housing?

Historians have tended to the view that the extent to which freehold or leasehold tenure influenced the nature of the housing in English cities has been exaggerated: it is possible to point to bad conditions in freehold towns such as in the north-east of England, and to good conditions in leasehold towns such as Cardiff. Neither is it clear that large owners had a vested interest in holding land off the market: they were just as likely to attempt to sell ahead of demand, leaving them with large tracts on their hands.[52] Is this to say that the nature of the land market did not matter? The example of Scotland might suggest that it did have some relevance for the feu has been seen as one major factor in the explanation of tenements in Scottish cities in contrast to their absence in England.[53] However, other European cities had tenements without the peculiar Scottish system of land tenure, as is clear from other chapters in this collection of essays. Tenure and land law perhaps did not matter as much as has been thought in determining architectural form. Nevertheless, the land market should not be dismissed, for it did affect the development process by influencing the precise methods of finance and the relationship between the various interests which were involved in the construction of cities. The nature of the land market cannot be excluded from the discussion of the determinants of the urban form, even if it is accepted that some writers have been too ready to adopt the crudely simplified views of contemporary political propaganda which emphasised the particular issue of leases versus freeholds. This obscured more significant features of the land market which should not be reduced to the abstractions of neo-classical economic theory: there were complex institutional and social factors involved in the provision of land for builders.[54]

There were major differences between American cities in the method of land development. At one extreme stood New York, in part because the constraints of a site bounded by water forced the population into a small area. It was also the outcome of changes in the land market in New York in the early nineteenth century. In the eighteenth century, ownership of land within the built-up area was widely diffused. Land on the periphery was, however, in the hands of a relatively small number of wealthy families who were seeking a secure investment for the profits of trade. The ownership of land became increasingly concentrated, and prices rose rapidly as the population grew and development was pushed on to land held by substantial owners, including families such as the Astors and Goelets. Such owners, it has been argued, could control the market, introducing short leases of 21 years, forcing up prices, and requiring the construction of costly buildings by inserting restrictive covenants in the leases. The result was to attract a different sort of lessee in place of small artisans who had built for their own use. Instead, lessees emerged 'who saw leaseholds as marketable interests in land'. The process of development changed in the early years of the nineteenth century, establishing the main lines which persisted in the late nineteenth and early twentieth centuries. Land in New York was expensive, and a high proportion of total costs of a tenement. By 1870, the cost of a lot of 25 by 100 feet in New York was $5,000 and the cost of the tenement $9,000, so that land accounted for 36 per cent of the cost. By the early twentieth century, Veiller put the cost of a 25 by 100 foot lot on the Lower East Side at $18,000 to $20,000 and the cost of the tenement at the same figure, so that land was 50 per cent of the total.[55]

The construction of costly tenements on expensive land created a particular set of responses within the New York property market: a division between the building loan operator, the builder, and investor. The operator would buy land and resell to a builder at a premium: two lots for which he paid $36,000 might be sold to a builder for $40,000. A speculative builder generally had little capital and, since tenements were usually erected in groups of three to twelve at a time, he was normally obliged to borrow money. The operator would, at the time of sale, agree to provide a mortgage for the land and also lend money to cover about half of the cost of constructing the tenement, which would be paid in stages up to its final completion. The operator might therefore lend

$40,000 for the land and a further $25,000 for building expenses at 5.5 to 6 per cent: he had made a profit from the sale of the land and from the interest charges. The builder might have enough capital to supply the remainder of the funds needed for construction, or he might raise it from other sources. Once the building was erected, the builder would obtain a loan from a trust or insurance company and pay off the building loan operator; he could then sell the tenement to an investor who would take over the loan from the trust or insurance company. The investor or land-lord might in turn let the tenement to a sub-landlord, who would then collect the rents from the individual tenants. The conclusion which Veiller drew was that the ultimate purchaser of the tenement paid about $11,000 more for the property than was necessary, for the operator took a profit of about $6,000 and the builder $5,000.[56] However, this attempt to pin the blame for tenements upon the operator is not altogether valid. Once tenement construction became the norm, some such system became necessary if builders were to erect buildings requiring large amounts of capital. A vicious circle was created. Tenements were expensive to build, which led to the need to raise funds to finance the process, the result being the creation of additional charges that forced up rents. Once tenements became established as the normal building form, their ability to bear high land prices in itself justified their continuation.

The belief that freehold tenure dominated American cities was not correct, as the example of New York suggests. However, leases could just as easily be associated with self-contained houses. In Baltimore, which stood at the opposite pole from New York in terms of architectural form, the tenurial pattern was based upon a system of annual charges or ground rents which, at first sight, appears to be akin to the leasehold system followed in many English towns. The usual term of the lease was 99 years, as in England. There was, however, a major difference: there was no reversionary interest in the property, for the 99-year leases were renewable forever. The leaseholder could, at any time within the term of the lease, renew it on the same terms with effect from its expiry, and in 1886 this was deemed to happen automatically if a lessee retained posses-sion after the expiry of a lease. The leases were, in effect, perpetual or 'chief rents' such as existed in some English cities (for example Manchester and Sunderland), with the difference that these were perpetual by virtue of the original lease rather than through covenants for renewal. Until 1884, leases in Baltimore did not give the leaseholder a right to purchase the freehold. Thereafter, irredeemable ground rents could no longer be created and all new ground rents could be converted to freehold by capitalising them at 6 per cent at any time after they had been in existence for 15 years; the term was reduced successively in 1888 and 1900 to 10 and 5 years. Thus a $90 ground rent could be redeemed for $1,500. This was entirely optional, and most house-owners did not exercise the right to become freeholders. However, the law of 1884 meant that the lessor could no longer be certain of having a long-term investment, while the lessee had the knowledge that he had the oppor-tunity to purchase the freehold.

Builders claimed that the system had advantages for prospective house-owners:

The man earning moderate wages or a moderate salary as a rule cannot afford to pay cash for a home. He must 'buy on time', or else not buy at all. The purchase must accordingly be financed. The modern ground rent . . . represents virtually a first mortgage on land and improvements. But from the purchaser's point of view the redeemable ground rent possesses this great advantage over the first mortgage—it never becomes due. He can redeem it, purchase it, if he so elects; but it is optional with him. He is never compelled to liquidate the ground rent as he does the mortgage. The ground rent accordingly takes care of that portion of the financing which would otherwise devolve upon the first mortgage . . . The remainder of the financing is taken care of by the building and loan associations, which, to a bona fide homebuyer, are willing to lend within a few hundred dollars—and in some cases reduce even this margin—of the purchase price of the house. Thus the purchaser is enabled to buy his house with only a small outlay of cash. His building association loan is paid off gradually and he may redeem the ground rent or not, just as he sees fit and his circumstances permit.[57]

The redeemable ground rent was akin to a mortgage without a due date, which could be paid off at a fixed capitalisation, entirely at the discretion of the lessee. This had certain advantages for the builder, for it was argued that it was easier to sell a leasehold property subject to a redeemable ground rent than a freehold property subject to a first mortgage. This was because the buyer would know that he would not be forced to repay the principal, whereas on a mortgage, he either had to amortise the loan and pay it off gradually, or be faced with a lump sum payment at its termination. It was also easier to borrow further on the security of the leasehold than to take a second mortgage on a freehold, because it was known that the lessor (unlike a normal mortgagee) could not demand repayment of the principal. The lessor was confident that, with such a large stake in the property, the lessee would not fail to pay the ground rent. The BLAs were more wiling to lend on property burdened by a ground rent than on a property burdened by a mortgage.[58]

The ground rent system has therefore been seen as the basis for high levels of owner-occupation in Baltimore. It has also been seen as the explanation of the row house. Ground rents offered an attractive investment with safe and steady returns, for which there was a ready market. The builders of row houses in Baltimore could utilise the ground rent system in order to make a profit. They would purchase a plot of land, subdivide it and create ground rents which could then either be sold in order to raise capital, or retained as a source of income. Their profit could come from ground rents, rather than the sale of the house which could, so it was claimed, be sold at cost. 'Advance' or 'bonus' building was another feature of the property market in Baltimore, by which the landowner made advances to the builder as each storey was completed. The arrangements varied a great deal, which gave more or less chance of profit to the builder. In some cases, such as the agreements made by

George Vickers, the original landowner retained the freehold, and the builder was exempted from paying ground rent during construction. The builder had no opportunity to profit from ground rents, but it did mean that he did not have to carry land costs. The agreement made by the builder Joseph Cone with the landowner Frederick Rice in 1889 was a variant of this practice. Cone leased plots at ground rents of $70 to $120 a year, which he surrendered to Rice in return for new leases at 1 cent; then, when the houses were completed and sold, Cone reverted to the original ground rents. He had the use of the land during the process of development for a nominal charge. The builders' profit in these cases came entirely from the sale of the houses, and not from the development of the land: the concern was to reduce land costs and not to create ground rents. The example of the builder Edward J. Gallagher suggests a variant. In 1893, Gallagher bought half a block from the Patterson estate on which he was to erect 59 houses; he paid a price based on the capitalisation of the ground rents at 6 per cent on part of the land, and received the freehold of the remainder. By these various procedures, the system of ground rents was believed to facilitate the process of development by reducing the burden of land costs upon the builder and helping to finance the process of construction.[59]

Here, it was believed, was the explanation of the high level of home ownership and the development of the row house at low prices. The institutional and legal system clearly had some significance, but it must be remembered that the row house was found elsewhere in the absence of the ground rent, and 'Baltimore would seemingly have had its red brick houses without its ground rents'. Further, the level of owner-occupation in Baltimore was not unique (see Table 7.2). In any case, it could be argued that the ground rent allowed a *high* price to be obtained for land, for a plot capitalised at 6 per cent was a high rate of return for a safe investment. 'A man might pay more money for a leasehold property subject to a ground-rent, when the capitalized value of the ground rent is added in, that he would for the fee simple title to the property'.[60] Tenure and the land law led to particular responses within the development process, but did not alone determine the architectural form of housing and the pattern of ownership. The encouragement of small-scale ownership was equally possible in the case of freehold developments. Tenure was less significant than other features of the land market.

Real estate, as S.B. Warner has commented, 'provided an open, readily accessible market in which capital could be invested in moderate quantities'. The mortgage market consisted of 'thousands of private investors . . . [who] lent money to homeowners and builders in small quantities for terms of six months to ten years'.[61] This mortgage market was divided into two groups, one conservative and the other more speculative: the first mortgage, for around half of the value of the property, which had priority in the settlement of debts; and a second mortgage for 10 to 15 per cent of the value of the property, which received a higher rate of interest as compensation for the greater risk. This 'system of divided agency and successive mortgages had the advantage of gathering ever new sources of money'. There was a plethora of interests: the subdivider and his mortgagee, the builder and his two mortgagees, and then the purchaser of the house and his mortgagees. The process tended to be highly fragmented and competitive, based upon a very free land market, and 'Because of the nature of the mortgage market and the divided tenure of suburban land the building of the metropolis went forward with thousands of small-scale operations'.[62] The trend after the First World War was towards a more consolidated system of subdivision, in which a single developer handled the whole process of laying out the plots and building the houses, often with finance from large institutions.[63]

One consequence of the 'divided agency' was that the process of subdivision was highly speculative. The concern of subdividers was to sell lots on the promise of large appreciations in capital values; they were less interested in when they would come into use. There was accordingly no clear connection between the number of lots provided and the growth of the population of a city, with the result that periods of intense speculative activity were followed by prolonged and deep depression. In Cleveland, for example, the number of new lots slumped from a peak of 9,178 in 1873 to a trough of 55 in 1878. This was an unusually intense cycle: more typical was the fall from 6,903 lots in 1891 to 1,717 in 1897. Purchasers of lots might therefore make large gains on a rising market, but it was equally possible to make losses. Critics of the system complained that speculation rather than use was the driving force behind subdivision, leading to an extreme amplitude in the cycle.

The concern which was expressed after the First World War was that speculative subdivision checked the natural—and socially desirable— ambition of owner-occupation. Home ownership would be encouraged, it was argued, by creating a greater stability of values in order to protect the investment of the home-owner and mortgagee, which would be achieved by holding back activity in periods of inflation. The means of achieving such an outcome, so it was believed, was the provision of better information about the relationship between subdividing and the need for lots, which would frustrate the speculative process. 'The basic evil in bad housing is land overcrowding. The basic reason for land over-crowding has been speculation in land prices.' In part, this reflected the fact that builders, who were major purchasers of vacant lots, were themselves engaged in a highly speculative industry, in which over-building was followed by periods of low activity as population growth reduced the level of vacant houses. There was also a demand for vacant lots from small investors amongst the skilled and white-collar workers who were attracted to this outlet for their capital. Real estate had a sense of familiarity and safety in comparison with investment in stocks or bonds which were, in any case, often not available in small denominations.[64] The conclusion to draw is, in fact, the opposite of the interwar critics of the subdividers: land was in fact cheap relative to wage rates and more readily available to a larger number of people than in most countries. Rather than frustrating home ownership and creating poor housing conditions, the highly competitive land market allowed for the easy acquisition of sites.[65]

The participation of these small investors was encouraged by the development of an instalment system of purchase in place of a down-payment with a mortgage for the balance, which 'permits those who cannot accumulate sizeable sums easily to acquire a home site and pay for it out of savings. To this extent it contributes to the promotion of home ownership on a wider scale'. The burden of acquiring a building site could be eased in freehold as well as leasehold areas. The instalment system might make BLAs irrelevant, providing an alternative means for small purchasers to acquire property, both for home ownership and investment. In Chicago, for example, 'The building of houses for sale is done almost entirely by private speculation, building societies of a philanthropic or co-operative character being almost non-existent'. The instalment system was encouraged by land companies and builders. The purchaser would make a down-payment which might amount to 10 to 20 per cent of the purchase price, and the balance would be paid off in monthly instalments of around $10, at an interest rate which was usually 6 per cent. In some areas, the balance was divided into two equal parts. One part was paid off in monthly instalments along with the accrued interest; the other part remained as a mortgage which would be paid off in a lump sum, with interest charged half-yearly. The system might be associated with a life insurance policy which would pay off the balance in the event of death. The period allowed for repayment varied: in some cases, the term was as long as 10 to 12 years to purchase both the site and building, in other cases 5 years or less. The system might be used to sell merely the site. In 1868, for example, William A. Butters and Co. offered 368 residential lots for sale in Chicago on 'The "old time terms" of one quarter down, balance in one, two or three years with interest at 6 per cent'. The developer might, however, also make loans to purchasers who wished to build. The great attraction of buying lots was speculative, the expectation that land could be obtained ahead of increases in prices. S.E. Gross and Co. encouraged purchasers: 'Rents will be higher, and also prices of lots. BUY A LOT NOW, and make your lot and home YOUR SAVINGS BANK'. (See Figure 7.6.) Gross also offered sites with brick cottages for $1,500 or $1,600, for 'very small cash payments' and the balance at $15 per month. The title of the property did not usually pass to the purchaser until the final payment was made, so that the developer had the security to accept a small down-payment. Of course, the developer needed substantial sums of money at the outset, and he might be able to raise funds by selling the contracts to a financial agency at a discount. The house became the centre of a complex web of financial connections.[66]

The precise tenurial system did not matter greatly in determining architectural form and housing standards. What does stand out in both the leasehold developments of Baltimore and the freehold developments of Chicago is the emergence of institutional arrangements designed to

Figure 7.6 Advertisement by S.E. Gross for lots and cottages for sale on easy terms, 1883 (courtesy of Chicago Historical Society).

Table 7.3 Wages and rents in American cities, 1909

	Wages*	Rent	Ratio wages:rent
New York	100	100	1.0
Boston	91	82	1.1
Philadelphia	86	79	1.1
Detroit	81	57	1.4
Chicago	110	70	1.6
Baltimore	87	54	1.6

* Wages of skilled builders.
Source: Board of Trade, USA, lxxx

permit small-scale investments in real estate. The system in New York might be seen as a *consequence* of the existence of tenements which created particular demands to finance large blocks, rather than as the prime cause. The exact explanation of the variation in housing form remains elusive. The Board of Trade inquiry found that the relationship between rent and wages varied between cities. It was, if the wages of skilled building-workers are taken as a guide, most unfavourable in New York where the influx of immigrants held down wage rates and put pressure upon the limited supply of land on Manhattan. The figures in Table 7.3 are in fact likely to underestimate the gap between New York and other cities, for they do not indicate the proportion of the population in the skilled categories. This was likely to be lower in New York, with its casual labour and sweatshops, than in Philadelphia with its manufacturing industry. There is, however, not the obvious connection which was found in English cities between self-contained property and favourable wage:rent ratios. The ratio between skilled wages in building and rents was identical in Baltimore and Chicago, although Chicago had a high proportion of apartments and Baltimore a preponderance of self-contained houses. Furthermore, Philadelphia had a less favourable ratio than Baltimore, despite the common architectural form. Clearly, the figures have important consequences for the household economies of working-class families in American cities which merit further investigation, but they do not fully explain the variation in house form. This might be because two variables are being confused: house form and housing standards or size. In Britain, the census allows these variables to be separated, for the number of rooms per dwelling and the level of overcrowding were recorded. The American census reflects the concern about the incidence of the tenement, recording the number of dwellings per building rather than the number of rooms per dwelling or the level of overcrowding, which might well show a closer connection with the ratio of rents and wages. Housing standards should not be confused with housing form, which would be to accept the contemporary perception that the self-contained house was by definition superior to the apartment. It might in fact be the case that the apartments of Chicago or Boston had a lower level of overcrowding than the row houses of other cities.

Economic determinism does not work in any simple way to explain the divergences in the patterns of home ownership and house form. Indeed, it might be better to think in terms of variations in the local property *culture* rather than in the local property *markets* which implies that the economics of housing was paramount. This has been suggested by the most detailed research which has been undertaken on patterns of owner-ship in North American cities: the attempt to explain the differences between the Canadian cities of Toronto and Montreal. The levels of home ownership drew apart in the two cities over the late nineteenth and early twentieth centuries. In 1862, the proportion of residential units which were owner-occupied stood at 18.3 per cent in Toronto and 18.0 per cent in Montreal; in 1901 the figures were respectively 27.0 per cent and 11.1 per cent. The architectural form also differed, with a higher proportion of single-family dwellings in Toronto and of apartments in Montreal. The explanation was not a simple matter of economics, for although incomes were lower in Montreal, so were house prices. Architectural form was not the main factor behind the difference in the level of home ownership, for the lower proportion of owner-occupation in Montreal persisted when dwelling type was held constant. There was a higher level of self-build in Toronto than in Montreal, which clearly had some significance. Even so, this cannot provide a complete explana-tion for the divergence in home ownership was also found amongst middle-class families who did not rely upon self-build. The answer which has been suggested, perhaps as an act of desperation, is that the 'culture of property' differed between the cities. This was the combination of social attitudes and institutions which favoured owner-occupation in one city and not the other. Builders and landowners developed institutions which made it possible to sell to landlords or to occupiers: building regulations took a particular form of housing for granted; the inhabitants of the city became accustomed to renting or to buying, and to living in a particular type of property. The initial institutional pattern might rise from fortuitous factors for which it is difficult to find a systematic explanation. Even if there was an original economic explanation, the institutions and culture which were created took on lives of their own and were not easy to shift. Perhaps the historian should concentrate upon explaining how the local property culture functioned, and with what consequences for social relationships within the city, rather than pursuing the chimera of why they diverged in the first place.[67]

IV

Although the level of owner-occupation in American cities was generally higher than in Europe, the majority of the population was made up of tenants. It would be wrong to allow the contemporary concern for home ownership to obscure this fact.[68] The relationship between landlord and tenant might, at its most extreme, become a serious source of social and political tension. The historian should not, however, be concerned only with conflict: the nature of the relationship between the owners and occupiers of housing had an influence upon urban society even when it was harmonious. Did the tenant have security of tenure, or the owner a right to speedy eviction? Were lets long or short, rigid or flexible? Was rent collected regularly or infrequently? Was management left to professionals and middlemen, or was it direct and personal? The answers to these questions had consequences for the household economy of working-class families.

The American law of landlord and tenant had its origins in the English common law of distress.[69] In England, the trend in the course of the later nineteenth century was to impose tighter restrictions upon the use of the law of distress, and in any case the owner of a working-class house was more interested in securing repossession than the dubious prospect of securing repayment of arrears. The law until 1838 was even-handed between landlord and tenant, and repossession was given only after the owner had proved his title before a jury. The balance did not really shift to the landlord until 1838, when the Small Tenements Recovery Act gave the owner of working-class properties the right to apply to the nearest magistrate for repossession. It was simply necessary to show that the tenancy had been terminated, so that the magistrate was 'a mere cipher'. Yet the process was still time-consuming. A tenant might be in arrears for two or three weeks' rent; a week's notice would then be given; if this did not produce action, the landlord gave notice that he would apply for a warrant of ejectment; and when this was granted, twenty-one days were allowed for repossession. The landlords, not surprisingly, campaigned for a speedier means of securing their property.[70] How did the system develop in the United States?

The pattern with respect to distress varied. In New York State, for example, it was abolished in 1846 as an invidious distinction in favour of one class of creditors, so that the owners of working-class tenements in New York City could not use the law of distress. Similarly, in Baltimore distraint could not be used against working-class tenants, and 'the only method of procedure open to the landlord is to give the tenant five days' notice to leave; if this notice is not complied with, he may place the furniture upon the street'. In the case of Philadelphia, the right to levy distress had not been abolished as it had in New York, but it was severely limited in 1849 when goods up to the value of $300 were exempted, which meant that it was of little use against the poorest tenants who were the most likely to default. In Massachusetts, legal opinion was divided as to whether or not the use of distress was permitted, which would suggest that, in practice, it had fallen into disuse. In Chicago, the law of distress remained in force, with the proviso that goods of other residents of the premises were not to be seized.[71]

In effect, however, most American landlords were, like their English counterparts, more concerned with the repossession of property from defaulters. Although most states took as their starting point the English statute law of the eighteenth century as it existed prior to the passing of the Small Tenements Recovery Act, in the course of the nineteenth century divergences were to appear. There was no single American development from the English legal inheritance. In the case of Philadelphia, for example, the redress of landlords against defaulting tenants was highly constrained and the process of eviction very slow. Under an Act of 1830, landlords were obliged to give notice to tenants who were in arrears and whose goods would not cover the value of the rent due. This notice was for a period of fifteen days between April 1 and August 31, and thirty days for the rest of the year. Only then, if the tenant did not leave or pay the arrears, could the landlord make a complaint to two justices who would summon the tenant to appear within three to eight days. If the case was proved, they would issue a writ giving possession after five days. The landlord had to prove failure to pay, the insufficiency of goods to answer the levy of distress, the service of notice to quit, and the subsequent failure to pay or remove. This meant that, even after the tenant had fallen into arrears, the landlord might have to wait up to 43 days to secure repossession, during which time the tenant would presumably not pay any rent. The process was costly, and placed all the obligations upon the landlord to prove the case, unlike the English law of 1838. The landlord who tried to circumvent the procedure by securing possession by re-entry was effectively prevented from doing this in 1860, when the use of force was prohibited. The landlord in Philadelphia was in a weak legal position *vis à vis* the tenant.[72] This was not, however, the case in all large cities.

The legal system might be more or less favourable to the tenant; in practice, however, the high level of mobility meant that the usual response of a tenant facing arrears was to leave. More important, perhaps, in determining the character of the relationships between landlord and tenant was the nature of the tenancy agreement. Was it flexible or rigid? Did it offer some security to the tenants? The term of tenancies tended to be longer than in England, yet gave the tenant some flexibility which struck a balance between security and ability to move. Rent was usually paid monthly in advance. In Philadelphia, written agreements were the rule, usually with three months' notice on either side. The tenancies fell into two categories, either 'implied' by tacit consent or 'express' with the terms explicitly stated. Implied tenancies ran from year to year from the date of the tenancy, unless the landlord gave three months' notice before the end of the year. Express tenancies could be for any term: when they were for a year, three months' notice was required; and when they were monthly, a month's notice was needed. Whichever was the case, only the landlord was required to give notice, for the tenant had the right to leave at once. The tenant therefore had considerable security, yet without any constraint upon mobility. In New York, written agreements were the exception. When the period of a tenancy was not explicitly stated, it was held to be 1 May, but in practice this did not lead to inflexibilities such as were apparent in Glasgow. When rent was paid monthly in advance the tenancy was held to run from month to month, and this was the usual system. The tenancy was renewed monthly, the payment and acceptance of rent being held to constitute renewal. The landlord could terminate the tenancy by giving five days' notice, except when it expired on 1 May. The tenants could simply continue or 'holdover' at the end of the term for an equivalent period.[73] Where 1 May did have significance was that this was normally when rent increases were announced. The relationship between landlord and tenant was not simply—or even mainly—a matter of the legal system. There were two other important influences: the state of the market, which would give more or less power to the landlord depending upon the level of vacancies; and architectural form. Both of these considerations were to lead to particular problems in New York City.

The tenement block of New York imposed one imperative need which was not found in the single-family 'row' houses of Philadelphia or Baltimore: strict control over the collective space within the property. The owner was obliged to clean the building, and to whitewash shafts and courts. The tenement house law of 1901 insisted that 'whenever there shall be more than eight families living in any tenement house, in which the owner thereof does not reside, there shall be a janitor, housekeeper or some other responsible person who shall reside in said house and have charge of the same'. This was to give force of law to what had long been standard practice. The janitor was, remarked the Board of Trade, a distinctive figure in New York. He was responsible for small repairs, cleaning the block, controlling the steam-heat system. Usually, he was not responsible for the collection of rent, but he did act as the letting agent. Although the janitor was often the representative of the owner, it was not unusual for the owner to live on the premises. The Board of Trade reported that small owners were numerous, particularly in the Jewish and Italian communities.[74]

The scale of tenement blocks created problems of controlling the public spaces; it also created greater problems of management than in small, single family property. One outcome in the case of New York was a system of management based upon a class of sub-landlords, which introduced a speculative element and a search for high returns. Many of the owners, claimed James Ford, 'acquired slum property before their own standards of living and of housing had been raised to what would be considered American levels'. A frequent practice in New York was for the owner to let the whole block to a sub-landlord who would then let to individual tenants. The sub-landlord aimed to maximise the differential between his payment to the landlord and his receipts from the tenants. The owner had a secure return and no trouble of supervision; the sub-landlord, often an immigrant, introduced a highly speculative element in search of high returns. The result, it was claimed, was to force rents up by between 12 and 25 per cent.[75]

The landlord–tenant relations in New York became a matter for dispute with the outbreak of rent strikes in 1904 and 1907–8.[76] This was not the result of the nature of tenancies or the legal system, which were not a matter of contention in the strikes. The timing of the rent strikes of 1904 was determined by the announcement of increases of 20 to 30 per cent on 1 May. The underlying issue was the upward drift of rent, rather than the legal structure of long, inflexible tenancies which was the major focus of conflict in Glasgow. The dispute arose essentially from the economics of the property market: a tightening of the housing market as the level of vacancies fell, which imposed particular pressures upon the sub-landlords.

The strikes were largely a product of the specific problems of the Lower East Side, where there was a crisis in the housing market. This arose from a combination of clearances for construction of bridges and parks, the heavy Jewish immigration to the area, and the location of the garment trades which employed a large number of people who needed to be near their place of work. At the same time, the new regulations of the tenement house law of 1901 imposed a temporary check on building, which was intensified by the labour troubles of 1903. The problem of housing shortages was essentially one of the Lower East Side rather than a general phenomenon. 'It is intense', remarked the *Real Estate Record and Builders' Guide*, 'wherever the East Side Jews are spreading; but it is by no means intense elsewhere'. In addition, the existence of sub-landlords exacerbated the problem. 'Many houses are leased by men who in turn lease to the actual tenants, and these lessees are almost invariably strict in collecting what is due them.' In some cases, the sub-landlord had leased the block ten or fifteen years earlier, so that their payments to the landlord were relatively modest, and most of the benefits of higher rents went to them. There was, however, also a numerous group of sub-landlords who rented blocks from landlords who had purchased at speculative prices in the previous two or three years. These sub-landlords were under much greater pressure to increase rents in order to secure a return after paying the landlords. Many of them lived in the property, relying upon the rents for their income. They were very exposed to a concerted refusal to pay rent, for a failure on their part to pay the landlord risked the loss of the security they had deposited. It would seem that there was a large speculative element in the rent increase, and the *Real Estate Record* claimed that the 'constant exchange of equities in tenement house properties . . . placed the status and ownership of that class of property in a condition different from that which it has ever before obtained'.[77] The architectural form of tenements could therefore contribute to the onset of social unrest, both because of the need to control the public spaces and because of the economics of ownership and management.

V

The variation in housing between American cities went far beyond the architectural form. There were also marked divergences in the level of home ownership, with a high incidence arising from self-build in some areas and building and loan associations in others. The process by which land was made available to developers was not uniform, and the methods of finance varied. This created different relationships between social groups within American cities. The nature of the housing market or property culture within American cities is of interest in its own right, but it also connected with other aspects of urban society. Rents varied independently of incomes, which obviously affected the standard of living. The level of home ownership, and the means by which it was achieved, affected the nature of the household economy of working-class families. Rental, self-build and borrowing helped to shape the life-time flow of income. Investment in rental property, or the provision of mortgages, was an important element in the strategies of middle-class families. The nature of the law of landlord and tenant might create social tension, particularly when it intensified the problems of management and control of multi-occupied buildings. And the precise architectural layout of property had implications for the social relationships within families, allowing more or less separation between and within families. Housing should be integrated with other aspects of the social history of American cities.

The variation between the property cultures of American cities started to give way to a greater uniformity after the First World War. This was in part because of the incursion of the federal government into housing finance in the 1930s, and also because of changes in the development process. Development became a much more integrated and large-scale process, so that the range of strategies which existed before the First World War gradually disappeared.[78] Until these changes took place, it is not possible to talk of a single North American housing market, but rather of distinctive and complex local patterns in Baltimore or New York or Detroit or Chicago.

Notes

1. This chapter incorporates material from two earlier papers: 'Cities of homes and cities of tenements: British and American comparisons, 1870–1914', *Journal of Urban History* 14 (1988) and 'Home loans versus council houses: the formation of British and American housing policy, 1900–20', *Housing Studies* 3 (1988). Research in the United States was financed by the Nuffield Foundation and the British Academy, to which I wish to express my gratitude.
2. The literature on American housing is still scarce in comparison with the work on Britain. The situation has not changed to a great extent since the publication of J. Tygiel, 'Housing in late nineteenth-century American cities: suggestions for research', *Historical Methods* 12 (1979). There are several general accounts of American housing: G. Wright, *Building the Dream: A Social History of Housing in America* (New York, 1981); C.E. Clark Jr, *The American Family Home, 1800–1960* (Chapel Hill, 1986); D.P. Handlin, *The American Home: Architecture and Society, 1815–1915* (Boston, 1970). They concentrate upon architecture and domesticity, especially in the middle class.
3. PP 1911, LXXXVIII, *Report of an Enquiry by the Board of Trade into Working-Class Rents, Housing and Retail Prices, together with the rates of wages in certain occupations in the principal industrial towns of the USA*, 329.

4. Ibid., 80-1; M.E. Hayward, 'Urban vernacular architecture in nineteenth-century Baltimore', *Winterthur Portfolio*, 16 (1981), 45-6, 57-63.
5. *Board of Trade Enquiry, USA*, 112.
6. Ibid., 345-50; see also M.F. Byington, *Homestead: The Households of a Milltown* (New York, 1910), chapter IV.
7. *Board of Trade Enquiry, USA*, 376-7.
8. Ibid., 145.
9. *Board of Trade Enquiry, USA*, 26-8; R.W. DeForest and L. Veiller, 'The tenement house problem', in DeForest and Veiller (eds), *The Tenement House Problem* (New York, 1903), I, 7-10; E.E. Wood, *Slums and Blighted Areas in the United States* (Federal Emergency Administration of Public Works. Housing Division Bulletin 1, Washington DC, 1935), 25-7; F.D. Case, 'Hidden social agendas and housing standards: the New York Tenement House Code of 1901', *Housing and Society* 8 (1981), 3-17; Handlin, *American Home*, 199-231; J. Ford, 'Fundamentals of housing reform', *Annual Report of the Board of Regents of the Smithsonian Institution, 1913* (1914), 747.
10. R. Sennett, *Families Against the City: Middle-Class Homes of Industrial Chicago, 1872-90* (Cambridge, Mass., 1970); B. Laslett, 'The family as a public and private institution: an historical perspective', *Journal of Marriage and the Family* 35 (1973); G. Wright, *Moralism and the Model Home: Domestic Architecture and Cultural Conflict in Chicago, 1873-1913* (1980) and *Building the Dream*, chapter 6; C.E. Clark Jr, 'Domestic architecture as an index to social history: the romantic revival and the cult of domesticity in America, 1840-70', *Journal of Interdisciplinary History* 7 (1976); J. Modell, 'Suburbanization and change in the American family', *Journal of Interdisciplinary History* 9 (1979); K.T. Jackson, *Crabgrass Frontier: The Suburbanization of the United States* (New York, 1985), chapter 3.
11. Handlin, *American Home*, 371-7; J. Modell and T.K. Haraven, 'Urbanization and the malleable household: an examination of boarding and lodging in American families', *Journal of Marriage and the Family* 35 (1973); R.C. Chapin, *The Standard of Living among Workingmen's Families in New York City* (New York, 1909; Byington, *Homestead,* 42, 55-6.
12. L. Veiller, *Housing Reform: A Hand-Book for Practical Use in American Cities* (New York, 1910), quoted by R. Lubove, *The Urban Community: Housing and Planning in the Progressive Era* (Englewood Cliffs, NJ, 1967), 58.
13. T.J. Jones, *The Sociology of a New York City Block* (New York, 1904), 122-3.
14. J.E. Kemp, *Report of the Tenement House Commission of Louisville under the Ordinance of Feb. 16, 1909* (Louisville?, 1909); see also *The Housing Problem in Minneapolis: A Preliminary Investigation made for the Committee on Housing of the Minneapolis Civic and Commerce Association* (Minneapolis, 1914?), 92, 108-9.
15. See, for example, C. Aronovici, *Housing Conditions in Fall River: Report Prepared for the Associated Charities Commission* (Fall River, 1912?); *Housing Conditions in the City of St Paul: Report Presented to the Housing Commission of the St Paul Association* (St Paul, 1917).
16. G. Harley, 'Multi-family housing units and urban tenancy', *Journal of Land and Public Utility Economics* 1 (1925); C. Woodbury, 'Taxation and the trend in multi-family housing', *Journal of Land and Public Utility Economics* 7 (1931); E.M. Fisher, *Principles of Real Estate Practice* (New

York, 1923), 238; President's Conference on Home Building and Home Ownership, *Home Finance and Taxation: Reports of the Committees on Finance and Taxation, edited by J.M. Gries and J. Ford* (Washington, DC, 1932), 103–7.

17. G.W.W. Hanger, 'Building and loan associations in the United States', *Bulletin of the Bureau of Labor* ix (1904), 1491–2; H.S. Rosenthal, *Manual for Building and Loan Associations* (2nd ed., Cincinnati, 1891), 25.
18. Hanger, 'Building and loan associations', 1491.
19. E. Wrigley, *The Workingman's Way to Wealth: A Practical Treatise on Building Associations: What They Are and How to Use Them* (5th ed., Philadelphia, 1872), 3, 5–6.
20. On the nature of working-class thrift in Britain, see P. Johnson, *Saving and Spending: The Working-Class Economy in Britain, 1870–1939* (Oxford, 1985).
21. R. Riegel and J.R. Doubman, *The Building and Loan Association* (New York, 1927), 5–7.
22. Riegel and Doubman, *Building and Loan Association*, 5–7; Hanger, 'Building and loan associations', 1500–28; E. Wrigley, *How to Manage Building Associations: A Director's Guide and Secretary's Assistant* (Philadelphia, 1880), 14–25; Wrigley, *Workingman's Way*, 28–40; A Solicitor of a Philadelphia Building Association, *The Building Association Manual* (Philadelphia, 1854), 3–10.
23. A Solicitor, *Building Association Manual*, 16.
24. Ibid., 16.
25. Ibid., 16; H.F. Clark and F.A. Chase, *Elements of the Modern Building and Loan Association* (New York, 1925), 14–7.
26. W.F. Willoughby, *Building and Loan Associations* (Boston, 1900), 21.
27. Wrigley, *Workingman's Way*, 41–4; A Solicitor, *Building Association Manual*, 21.
28. W. Franklin, *The Building Associations of Connecticut and Other States Examined* (New Haven, Conn., 1856), 4.
29. Hanger, 'Building and loan associations', 1571.
30. Riegel and Doubman, *The Building and Loan Association*, 5–7.
31. Wrigley, *Workingman's Way*, 26.
32. United States League of Local Building and Loan Associations Proceedings, 1903, 80.
33. Ibid., 87.
34. US League of Local BLAs, Proceedings, 1898, 125–6.
35. Wrigley, *How to Manage Building Associations*, 26.
36. H.S. Rosenthal, *Manual for Building and Loan Associations* (2nd ed., Cincinnati, 1891), 33.
37. US League of Local BLAs, Proceedings, 1898, 126.
38. C.E. Clark, *The Local Building Association: A Cornerstone of the Commonweal* (Covington, Kentucky, 1908?), 8–9.
39. R.T. Paine, *Co-operative Banks* (Boston, 1880), 9.
40. M.J. Vill, 'Building enterprise in late nineteenth-century Baltimore', *Journal of Historical Geography* 12 (1986), 175–6.
41. R.G. Barrows, 'Beyond the tenement: patterns of American urban housing, 1870–1939', *Journal of Urban History* 9 (1983), 417.
42. O. Zunz, *The Changing Face of Inequality: Urbanization, Industrial Development, and Immigrants in Detroit, 1880–1920* (Chicago, 1982), chapter 6.

43. M.J. Doucet and J.C. Weaver, 'Material culture and the north American home: the era of the common man, 1870-1920', *Journal of American History* 72 (1985), 560-87; Jackson, *Crabgrass Frontier*, 124-8.

44. Zunz, *The Changing Face of Inequality*, 152-76; also R.D. Simon, 'The city-building process: housing and services in new Milwaukee neighbourhoods, 1880-1910', *Transactions of the American Philosophical Society* 68 (1978), 3-64.

45. D.D. Luria, 'Wealth, capital and power: the social meaning of home owner-ship', *Journal of Interdisciplinary History* 7 (1976-7), 278, 282; see also S. Thernstrom, *Poverty and Progress: Social Mobility in a Nineteenth Century City* (Cambridge, Mass. 1964), 201.

46. Zunz, *The Changing Face of Inequality*, 173. The role of self-build in Toronto has been shown by R. Harris: see 'The growth of home ownership in Toronto, 1899-1914', Research Paper 163, Centre for Urban and Community Studies, University of Toronto, 1987. He argues that the crucial difference between Britain and America was not in the existence of suburbs, but rather in the availability of suburbia in America to the working class: R. Harris, 'American suburbs: sketch of a new interpretation', *Journal of Urban History* 15 (1988); and R. Harris and C. Hamnett, 'The myth of the promised land: the social diffusion of home ownership in Britain and North America', *Annals of the Association of American Geographers* 77 (1987).

47. Handlin, *American Home*, 238-9; M.A. Weiss, 'Richard T. Ely and the contribution of economic research to national housing policy, 1920-40, unpublished paper, Lincoln Institute of Land Policy, 1987, 8, 13. I would like to thank Dr Weiss for his comments on an earlier version presented to the Social Science History conference and for providing references.

48. E.M. Fisher, *Principles of Real Estate Practice* (New York, 1923), 154-69; H.M. Bodfish and A.D. Theobald, *Savings and Loan Principles* (New York, 1938), 2; H.M. Bodfish, *Money Lending Practices of Building and Loan Associations in Ohio* (Columbus, 1927); President's Conference on Home Building and Home Ownership, *Home Finance and Taxation: Reports of the Committees on Finance and Taxation, edited by J.M. Gries and J. Ford* (Washington, DC, 1932), 6-9; see also W.N. Loucks, *The Philadelphia Plan of Home Financing: A Study of the Second Mortgage Lending of Phila-delphia Building and Loan Associations* (Chicago, 1929).

49. L. Grebler, D.M. Blank and L. Winnick, *Capital Formation in Residential Real Estate: Trends and Prospects* (Princeton, 1956), 332-3. On the problems of the London property market, see A. Offer, *Property and Politics, 1870-1914: Landownership, Law, Ideology and Urban Develop-ment in England* (Cambridge, 1981).

50. Barrows, 'Beyond the tenement', 403, 415-6; Harris and Hamnett, 'The myth of the promised land'.

51. S.B. Warner Jr, *The Urban Wilderness: A History of the American City* (1972), 17-18.

52. M.J. Daunton, *House and Home in the Victorian City: Working-Class Hous-ing, 1850-1914* (1983), chapter 4.

53. See Introduction, pp. 4-7.

54. See D. Cannadine, 'Urban development in England and America in the nine-teenth century: some comparisons and contrasts', *Economic History Review* 2nd ser. xxxviii (1980).

55. J. Ford, *Slums and Housing with Special Reference to New York City* (Cambridge, Mass., 1936), 908; L. Veiller, 'The speculative building of

tenement houses' in DeForest and Veiller (eds), *Tenement House Problem* I, 370; New York State, *Report of the Tenement House Committee* (Albany, 1895), 8; B. Blackmar, 'Rewalking the "walking city": housing and property relations in New York City, 1780–1840, *Radical History Review* 21 (1979), 136–9; Cannadine, 'Urban development'; G. Myers, *History of the Great American Fortunes* (2nd ed., New York, 1936), Part II, chapter 1.

56. Veiller, 'Speculative building', in DeForest and Veiller (eds), *Tenement House Problem*, I, 370–6; Handlin, *American Home*, 266–7; on sub-landlords, see below pp. 278–9.

57. Report on building operations in Baltimore, prepared by the Builders' Exchange in 1916. I owe this reference to Mary Ellen Hayward of the Maryland Historical Society.

58. F.A. Kaufman, 'The Maryland ground rent system: mysterious but beneficial', *Maryland Law Review* 5 (1940).

59. *Board of Trade, USA*, 82; Hayward, 'Urban vernacular architecture'; Vill, 'Building enterprise'; Kaufman, 'Maryland ground rent'; exhibition on the ground rent system at the Peale Museum, Baltimore.

60. Kaufman, 'Maryland ground rent', 2, 62.

61. S.B. Warner Jr, *Streetcar Suburbs: The Process of Growth in Boston, 1870–1900* (Cambridge, Mass. 1962), 118.

62. Warner, *Streetcar Suburbs*, chapter 6.

63. A.D. Theobald, *Financial Aspects of Subdivision Development* (Chicago and New York, 1930), 1–2.

64. E.M. Fisher, *Real Estate Subdividing Activity and Population Growth in Nine Urban Areas* (Ann Arbor, 1928); W.N. Loucks, 'Increments in land values in Philadelphia', *Journal of Land and Pubic Utility Economics* 1 (1925); H.L. Shannon and H.M. Bodfish, 'Increments in subdivided land values in twenty Chicago properties', *Journal of Land and Public Utility Economics* 5 (1929); H.C. Monchow, 'Population and subdividing activity in the region of Chicago, 1871–1930', *Journal of Land and Public Utility Economics* 9 (1933); H.C. Monchow, *Seventy Years of Real Estate Subdividing in the Region of Chicago* (Evanston and Chicago, 1939); Theobald, *Financial Aspects*; President's Conference on Home Building and Home Ownership, *Home Ownership, Incomes and Types of Dwellings. Reports of the Committees on Home Ownership and Leasing, Relationship of Income and the Home, and Types of Dwellings, edited by J.M. Gries and J.S. Taylor* (Washington DC), 1–4, 169 and *Home Finance and Taxation*, 45; Weiss, 'Richard T. Ely', 9–11.

65. Jackson, *Crabgrass Frontier*, 128–30.

66. *Board of Trade, USA*, 144, 182, 192, 278, 378; Chicago Historical Society, Broadsheets, real estate—Chicago; Monchow, *Seventy Years*, 142–8.

67. The research of Canadian cities is still at an early stage. I wish to thank Dr R. Dennis and Dr R. Harris for information on the project. See R. Harris, 'The unnoticed homeownership boom in Toronto', *Histoire Sociale/Social History* 18 (1985); R. Harris, 'Working-class home ownership and housing affordability across Canada in 1931', *Histoire Sociale/Social History* 19 (1986); R. Harris, 'Home ownership and class in modern Canada', *International Journal of Urban and Regional Research* 10 (1986); Harris, 'The growth of home ownership in Toronto'; M. Choko, 'The characteristics of housing tenure in Montreal', Research Paper 164, Centre for Urban and Community Studies, University of Toronto, 1987; R. Harris and M. Choko, 'The evolution of housing tenure in Montreal and Toronto since the

mid-nineteenth century', Research Paper 166, Centre for Urban and Community Studies, University of Toronto, 1988; Harris and Hamnett, 'The myth of the promised land', *Annals of the Association of American Geographers* 77 (1987); R. Harris and M. Choko, 'The local culture of property: a comparative history of housing tenure in Toronto and Montreal since 1862'.

68. The only attempt to analyse investment ownership in North America is for Toronto: R. Dennis, 'Landlords and rented housing in Toronto, 1885–1914', Research Paper 162, Centre for Urban and Community Studies, University of Toronto, 1987. The changing structure of ownership and profitability is a subject which merits study in the cites of the United States.

69. See Introduction, p. 20.

70. D. Englander, *Landlord and Tenant in Urban Britain, 1838–1918* (Oxford, 1983), 22–7; Daunton, *House and Home*, 148–52.

71. J.N. Taylor, *The American Law of Landlord and Tenant*, II, (9th ed., revised by H.F. Buswell, Boston, 1904), 187–91; C.G. Delgano, *Outline of the Law of Landlord and Tenant in Massachusetts* (Boston, 1884), 27; W.A. Schonfeld, *The Law of Landlord and Tenant with References* (Chicago, 1901), 206; A.E. Whitney, *Landlord and Tenant* (Chicago, 1890), 11–12; *Board of Trade, USA*, 39, 82, 332; A. Guillou, *House Renting and Room Renting . . .: A Manual for Landlords and Tenants* (Philadelphia, 1887), chapters 7, 8, 18, 19; R.J. Williams, *The Law of Landlord and Tenant in Philadelphia* (2nd ed., Philadelphia, 1901), 34–9, 43–59, 82–7; C.W. Sloane, *A Treatise on the Law of Landlord and Tenant with Special Reference to the State of New York* (New York, 1884), 53–4, 72–84, 100–7, 146; *Walker's Landlords' and Tenants' Guide for New York . . .* (New York, 1885), 18, 21–8, 46–7; S. Chaplin, *A Treatise on the Law of Landlord and Tenant in the State of New York* (New York, 1889), 98, 140, 253; E.W. Dinwiddie, *The Tenants' Manual . . .* (New York, 1903), 28–9.

72. *Board of Trade Enquiry, USA*, 332; Guillou, *House Renting and Room Renting*, chapters 7,8, 18, 19; R.J. Williams, *The Law of Landlord and Tenant in Pennsylvania* (2nd ed., Philadelphia, 1901), 34–9, 43–59, 82–7.

73. *Board of Trade Enquiry, USA*, 39; C.W. Sloane, *A Treatise on the Law of Landlord and Tenant with Special Reference to the State of New York* (New York, 1884), 53–4, 72–84, 100–7, 146; *Walker's Landlords' and Tenants' Guide for New York . . .* (New York, 1885), 18, 21–8, 46–7; S. Chaplin, *A Treatise on the Law of Landlord and Tenant in the State of New York* (New York, 1899), 98, 140, 253; Dinwiddie, *The Tenants' Manual*, 28–9.

74. *Board of Trade Enquiry, USA*, 39–40; Case, 'Hidden social agendas'; W.J. Fryer, *The Tenement House Law and the Lodging House Law of the City of New York* (New York, 1902), 50.

75. K.H. Cleghorn, 'Foreign immigration and the tenement house in New York City', in DeForest and Veiller (eds), *Tenement House Problem*, II, 71–2; Ford, *Slums and Housing*, 449–50; see E.R.L. Gould, 'Financial aspects of recent tenement house operations in New York', in DeForest and Veiller (eds), *Tenement House Problems*, I, 357–9.

76. R. Lawson, 'The rent strike in New York City, 1904–80: the evolution of a social movement strategy', *Journal of Urban History* 10 (1984), 235–58; M. Lipsky, *Protest in City Politics: Rent Strikes, Housing and the Power of the Poor* (Chicago, 1970).

77. W. Mailly, 'The New York rent strike', *The Independent* 64 (1908), 148–52;

Real Estate Record and Builders' Guide, 6 February 1904, 9 April 1904, 21 May 1904, 14 January 1905.

78. See M. Weiss, *The Rise of the Community Builders: The American Real Estate Industry and Urban Land Planning* (New York, 1987).

Index